A History of International Oil Politics
Theoretical Perspectives and Case Studies

Murad Gassanly

A History of International Oil Politics
Theoretical Perspectives and Case Studies

Murad Gassanly

St. James's Studies in World Affairs

Academica Press
London-Washington

Library of Congress Cataloging-in-Publication Data

Names: Gassanly, Murad, author.
Title: A history of international oil politics : theoretical perspectives and case studies / Murad Gassanly.
Description: London ; Washington : Academica Press, [2020] | Series: St. James's studies in world affairs | Includes bibliographical references and index. | Summary: "A History of International Oil Politics is both an argument for multi-theoretical pluralism and a proposal for a theory-synergetic approach in international relations. Murad Gassanly, a distinguished international relations scholar and rising British politician, explores how international relations paradigms could be utilized in approaching the vital field of international oil politics, specifically historical issues of international energy politics and comparative case studies of energy transmission networks – the Baku-Tbilisi-Ceyhan Pipeline and the Southern Gas Corridor. This highly original study explores the historical timeline of global energy to demonstrate how a theory-synergetic analysis might offer a deeper and more holistic understanding. As an academic discipline, international relations now offers a maelstrom of competing epistemological, ontological, and normative contestations. Gassanly, however, argues that theoretical diversity has knowledge-producing and maximizing potential and that pluralism does not impede academic progress. Applying different theoretical models to oil politics reveals different realities, but the synergetic whole is greater than the sum of its constituent paradigmatic parts. Empirical convergences between theoretical accounts provides a broad analytical framework for active theoretical synergy"-- Provided by publisher.
Identifiers: LCCN 2020018358 | ISBN 9781680532319 (hardcover) | ISBN 9781680539448 (paperback)
Subjects: LCSH: International relations--Philosophy. | International relations--Case studies. | International economic relations--Case studies. | Petroleum industry and trade--Political aspects--Case studies. | Energy policy--International cooperation--Case studies. | Pipelines--Political aspects--Case studies.
Classification: LCC JZ1305 .G38 2020 | DDC 327.101--dc23
LC record available at https://lccn.loc.gov/2020018358

Dedication

To my parents, Asif and Fira, to whom I owe everything.

Preface

This book is both an argument for multi-theoretical pluralism and a proposal for a theory-synergetic approach in international relations. It explores the ways in which IR paradigms could be utilized in research of a substantive problem-field – international oil politics.

The entire historical timeline of global energy is explored here in order to demonstrate how a theory-synergetic analysis might be applied to attain a deeper, more holistic understanding of a given puzzle than would be possible within a single-paradigm research mode.

International relations may be as a discipline characterized by ongoing theoretical debates, a maelstrom of competing epistemological, ontological and normative contestations. However, it is argued here that theoretical diversity has knowledge-producing and maximising potential and pluralism does not impede academic progress.

Applying different theoretical models upon the same substantive problem-field reveals different realities of that same problem field; yet the resultant synergetic whole is greater than the sum of its constituent paradigmatic parts. Focus on empirical convergences between theoretical accounts normally posited separately provides a broad analytical framework for active theoretical synergy.

By bringing these insights to bear upon historic issues of international energy politics and a comparative case-study of energy transmission networks – the Baku-Tbilisi-Ceyhan Pipeline and the Southern Gas Corridor – it is demonstrated that synergetic analysis allows for more complex, multidimensional and multi-layered understanding of the problem-field than single-paradigm research.

Contents

Introduction

Has international relations[1] (IR) failed as an intellectual project? That was the question posited by Barry Buzan and Richard Little in their seminal paper in the *Millennium - Journal of International Studies* (30 (1) 2001). Is IR theory at an end? What is IR? Can it even still be described as an academic discipline? Should it try to be one? These and similar questions are increasingly being repeated in the wake of the major upheavals of the latest, Fourth, great debate (Lapid, 1989, Darby, 2008; Wæver, 2013; see also the special issue of *The European Journal of International Relations* (Wight et al, 2013).

This may seem strange given that IR remains an attractive subject for an ever growing number of students and scholars, with expanding research and teaching programmes (and budgets) at universities worldwide, not just in the U.S. and Europe. There has been a marked growth in academic literature on IR, specialist publications, and research centers devoted to its study. By some accounts international relations has made major advances in methodology, scope of enquiry, adding new themes and dimensions to the discipline which, "now straddles the globe and provides a common language with which to analyze world politics" (Darby, 2008, p. 94).

Yet those concerned with the apparent decline and stagnation in international relations point to the discipline's peculiar insularity from other Social Sciences. As Buzan and Little argue this insularity "allows ideas from other disciplines to filter into IR, but seems to block substantial traffic in the other direction" (Buzan and Little, 2001, p. 19). International relations borrows heavily from other disciplines – from philosophy and economics to anthropology and psychology. Yet one would be at a great

---

[1] Capitalized form of IR is used to refer to the academic discipline and the general term "international relations" to refer to the processes and practices.

difficulty identifying any substantial intellectual impact or influence of IR upon wider social sciences.

Even on the issue of theoretical development and the endless quest for a Grand Theory of International Relations is at a disadvantage. As Brown argues IR has been a consumer not a producer of Grand Theory, borrowing extensively from other social science disciplines, such as Philosophy of Science, and making little by way of own contribution (2013, p.485). He goes further in identifying the effect of this uneven exchange and suggests that this disciplinary insularity had obstructed IR from having a wider impact, beyond academia (Ibid, p.484).

While IR had arguably always been multi-disciplinary it appears this multi-disciplinarily simply masks "dependency on other disciplines" (Buzan and Little, 2001, p. 21). Meanwhile these other disciplines maintain a self-conscious distance from IR and for many international relations is an intellectual minefield best avoided. Or as historian John Lewis Gaddis put it, IR theory is "a field that has troubles enough of its own without my adding to them" (2007, ix).

Moreover, debates and discussions within IR had not captured public imagination in the way history and economics, for example, had. IR's big names, the stars of the discipline such as Kenneth Waltz, are hardly known in the wider political science and even less in the world beyond. Some prominent IR figures, such as Zbigniew Brezinski and Henry Kissinger did gain a higher public profile, but this was due largely to political posts they held rather than their scholarship (Buzan and Little, 2001, p. 21).

Furthermore, Brezinski and Kissinger are exceptions that appear to prove the rule. In an article in *The Washington Post* Joseph Nye (2009) pointed out that the *Teaching, Research and International Policy (TRIP)* poll by the Institute for Theory and Practice in international relations revealed that only three of the twenty-five scholars rated as producing the most interesting scholarship during the preceding five years had ever held policy positions (one at the United Nations and two in the U.S. Government) (Jordan et al, 2009).

For Nye (2009) the responsibility for this lies not with governments but with the academic community, which has neglected policy-relevant research in favor of "mathematical models, new methodologies or theories expressed in jargon that is unintelligible to policymakers." This lack of relevance to "real world" policy-making and the neglect of the practice of international relations marginalize IR and reduce its social impact. A growing concern over this gap between theory and policy and a desire to make the discipline more relevant are the driving forces behind the recent turn towards pragmatism and pluralism in IR (see below) (Sil and Katzenstein, 2010).

If disciplinary insularity, lack of wider public impact and marginalization from the practice of international relations are the symptoms of the apparent malaise afflicting IR, then theoretical fragmentation is often seen as its cause (Buzan and Little, 2001, p. 31). There are clear delimitations within the theoretical framework of IR that shape both ontological and epistemological foundations of all research in the field, making it in practice "a discipline of theoretical disagreements" (Burchill, 1996, p.3).

Buzan and Little (2001, pp. 22-28) identify and locate the a-historicism, even anti-historicism, of IR's tradition in what they call "IR's Westphalian Straightjacket" – a Eurocentric focus on the state and its role in international relations. The straightjacket did not hold for long. The reflectivist critique threw a major challenge to mainstream theoretical orthodoxy, undermining dominance of positivism and ending its, "role as the only legitimate epistemology within the discipline" (Langlois, 1997, p 155). The anti-positivist turn is seen by many as marking a fundamental shift in meta-theoretical discourses in IR (Lapid, 1989).

The so-called "great debates," often characterized by "frenzied emotionalism," have collectively shaped and structured the discipline of IR, leaving it "divided, directionless and disputatious" (Buzan and Little, 2001, p. 32). The three "great debates" (or four, if one accepts Ole Wæver's inclusion of the inter-paradigm debate (Wæver, 1996)) have often been used as the conceptual matrix through which to view the discipline.

This produced a narrative according to which scholars in IR assumed positions within sets of warring "isms" (realism, liberalism, constructivism and so on) and engaged in an ultimately fruitless battle to establish their preferred model as the dominant universal theory of International Relations, or at least, have it acknowledged as a superior one to others. Paradigm-specific research and teaching continue to dominate the discipline (Jordan, et al. 2009, p.18).

As David Lake argues, IR is organized into "academic 'sects' that engage in self-affirming research and then wage theological debates between academic religions" (David Lake, 2011, p. 465). Whatever the stated objectives of various theoretical approaches in IR may be, the end result is to drive focus away from the substance of international politics to an endless, self-reflective insular debate about inherent superiority of this or that assumption – a sort of an ongoing game of intellectual one-upmanship. Presently, at the tail end of the most recent, fourth "great debate," IR community appears no closer to any concrete resolution, with most scholars either explicitly or implicitly accepting this ambiguous status quo.

The much heralded end of IR theory is subject of intense debate and discussion. For example, a special issue of *European Journal of International Relations* entitled "The End of International Relations Theory?" (Wight et al (Eds.), September 2013; 19 (3)) was complimented with a novel online symposium dedicated to the issue of the future of IR in the "post-Grand Theory" era (Nexon, 09.05.2013).

Meanwhile, a quarter of the century since the publication of Yoseph Lapid's seminal paper "The Third Debate: On the Prospects of International Theory in a Post-Positivist Era" (1989) International Studies Quarterly also hosted an online symposium to mark the anniversary, assess the state of the discipline and examine if IR is at an end of its "great debates" (Jackson, 20.03.2014).[2]

---

[2] Lapid himself is quick to recognize that his approach to sequencing and defining issues and milestones in IR theoretical evolution introduced "unnecessary confusion into the "great debates" story" (20.03.14). There is now a clear recognition that Weaver's clarification of the issues is not only accurate but essential to understanding the current state of affairs in IR (1996). Without re-treading a familiar narrative, it is sufficient here to accept the designation of the Third Debate as the inter-paradigm debate of the 1970s and 1980s leading to a kind of rationalist synthesis between neorealism and neoliberalism. Whereas the reflectivist critique of rationalist IR - presenting as it does a foundational challenge to positivism - constitutes the Fourth Debate. Summarising Weaver's argument, Schmidt (02.02.2014) defines this fourth

As Lake (2013) argues elsewhere, "[if] grand theory was king, it was an evil tyrant" (p.568). This move away from grand-theoretical development and contestation is exemplified, especially in American IR, by a growing interest in pragmatist, multi-theoretical models and a new-found focus on mid-level theories grounded in practical, substantive discourses in international relations.

An example of this approach is the analytical eclecticism advocated by Rudra Sil and Peter Katzenstein (Katzenstein and Sil, 2008; Sil and Katzenstein, 2010). Their pragmatist vision of the kind of knowledge that IR can and should produce has rapidly become part of mainstream discussions within the discipline, although it is also being seriously examined, assessed and critiqued (Reus-Smit, 2013, p.591).

It will be argued in this book that pessimistic readings of the state of the discipline are misplaced. First, it is not necessary to discard the heritage of the Great Debates – in fact they may be viewed as essential elements in the genealogy of the discipline (Smith, 1995, pp.1-37; Schmidt, 2013, pp. 3-28; Waever, 2011, p.98).

Second, it will be argued that the Fourth Debate had reconstituted international relations as an academic discipline and recast it as a meta-social science. It massively expanded the ontological scope of IR and widened its epistemological reach far beyond the narrow confines of positivism. It opened up IR from below and from outside, inviting in voices that had not ordinarily been heard in the past. And this all has profound implications for the kind of empirical output IR research has the potential to produce.

IR today, it will be argued, is a multi-theoretical, supra-disciplinary, intellectual enterprise, animated by normative commitments. While its "geography" is still dominated by a Euro-Atlantic pivot, it is a far more global science today than twenty or thirty years ago. It is an increasingly self-reflective discipline, more aware of its history of privileging certain culturally determined social scientific approach, and of

---

great debate as being "characterized by a schism between reflectivist approaches, which includes critical theory, post-structuralism, postmodernism and specific versions of constructivism and feminism, that fall under the post-positivism label, and rationalist approaches that define the mainstream theories of neorealism and neoliberalism."

its relationship to power. As historicism and recognition of *the historical* in international relations takes center stage there is a growing awareness of the relationship between the material and the ideational, structure and agency.

In 2001 Buzan and Little set out an ambitious vision of what IR could be – "a kind of meta-discipline, systematically linking together the macro-sides of the social-sciences and history: If IR has an obvious role in the intellectual and academic division of labor, it is precisely to build bridges and establish a common ground in ways that transcend disciplinary boundaries. Its comparative advantage lies in its potential as a holistic theoretical framework, which should be able to speak equally well to political scientists, economists, lawyers, sociologists, anthropologists, and historians" (p. 22).

In the post-Fourth Debate IR this ambitious vision may be a reasonable proposition. The problem is how to systematize or at least make sense of IR theoretical pluralism. First, it is important to state outright that the task is not to discipline knowledge-production. It is doubtful that theoretical synthesis is possible and those dismissing the incommensurability dilemma outright are clearly not sufficiently mindful of important epistemological and foundational claims in IR.

Mid-range theorizing and eclectic approaches, on the other hand, are limited in their pluralist applications by their restricted ontologies and underlying metatheoretical assumptions. Meanwhile, continued theoretical disengagement is also not an option – it leads to fears of fragmentation and claims that IR theory, or even international relations as a discipline, is at an end.

The solution might be in reconceptualising the identity of the discipline. What is needed is a common language through which to communicate across the breadth of IR spectrum and with the world beyond; a language to express theoretical pluralism and the expanded ontology of international relations; a language that would reflect theoretical diversity through establishment of a kind of scholarly culture of IR. This language needs to be expansive and its vocabulary rich enough to accommodate the sheer breadth of knowledge created over the past century.

Bracketing this knowledge is counterproductive – IR is empirical and theoretical scholarship; concerned with both the material and the ideational, with a normative mission at its heart. As the 1919 anniversary passed, the "One Hundred Years of Solitude" and introspection can surely now come to an end and the redemptive foundational ethos of International Relations – "a global vision, forged in the fires of war, aimed at repairing the shattered family of nations"-- be re-imagined and renewed.[3]

IR scholarship should be relevant to the practice of world politics. However, in determining the contours of theoretical pluralism issues of theory selection cannot be reduced to questions of "usefulness" or limited by arbitrary notions of "suitability." The full spectrum of IR theoretical power should be utilized, harnessed and brought to bear upon substantive matters in international politics. Developing an approach that would achieve the above requires adopting a particularly expanded notion of pluralism of IR and a specific scientific research model to accommodate it.

This is not a question of a grand-methodology – methodological pluralism is itself a major achievement of the Fourth Debate. Rather it is a matter of *science as method*, as articulated by Karl Pearson over a century ago: "The field of science is unlimited; its solid contents are endless, every group of natural phenomena, every phase of social life, every stage of past or present development is material for science. The unity of science consists alone in its method, not its material" (1892, p.15).

What is required in order to harness the inherent power of IR's theoretical pluralism is a common methodological culture – a language, an analytical toolkit - by means of which scholars could utilize and apply different theories to the limitless substantive field of the science of international relations. A metaphor for IR theories as lenses through which to see different aspects of the same material reality has sometimes been employed (Smith, 2014).

Borrowing from J.R.R. Tolkien, a different metaphor would be to see the world of International Relations as a picture tapestry and each theory as a particular thread in that picture. The incommensurability problem arises only if the attempt is made to synthesize the threads or have

---

[3] From the University of Aberystwyth, Department of International Politics website.

them work within the picture together but separately. Instead it is possible to envisage them operating in *synergy*,[4] to constitute a picture greater than the sum of the individual threads that make it up: "It is indeed easier to unravel a single thread — an incident, a name, a motive — than to trace the history of any picture defined by many threads. For with the picture in the tapestry a new element has come in: the picture is greater than, and not explained by, the sum of the component threads. Therein lies the inherent weakness of the analytic (or 'scientific') method: it finds out much about things that occur in stories, but little or nothing about their effect in any given story." (J.R.R. Tolkien, (1947, 1964), 1983. p. 121).

The idea that stories in IR can be told simultaneously in real time and in the resulting narrative produce a whole greater than the constituent theoretical parts that make it up is the defining feature of the theory-synergetic approach, or TSA. But it is an idea that is grounded in IR foundational problems and is characterized by the implications of the Fourth Debate. These issues are addressed and the state of IR, post-Fourth Debate is assessed in chapter I.

In chapter II a proposal for TSA is advanced in the context of a wider discussion of its place in IR foundational and theoretical debates and how it can contribute to advancing the discipline's empirical priorities. Key elements of synergetic theorizing, TSA analytical tools and processes of sequencing are also explained. While this book is an argument for a synergetic approach to theoretical pluralism, it is essential to demonstrate how such synergetic theorizing might work in practice when applied to concrete substantive problems in international relations.

Chapter II is, therefore, an introduction to the rich and expansive problem-field of international oil politics. Case-studies of Baku-Tbilisi-Ceyhan (BTC) and Southern Gas Corridor (SGC) pipelines are particularly interesting subjects for synergetic theorizing and are set out as the proposed empirical testing ground for TSA. The aim here is to show how using theoretical tools synergetically can be useful in understanding substantive problems around these complex energy projects.

In chapter III the empirical field of international oil politics is expanded and examined in greater detail; its properties as a substantive

---

[4] From Greek *synergia*, from *synergos*,(συνεργός), meaning "working together."

case-study for exploring theory-synergetic approach are characterized and investigated. Single-paradigmatic models of international oil politics are then set out in chapters IV and V - Rationalist and Reflectivist respectively.

By focusing on various events, issues, debates in the history of oil politics it will be shown how different paradigms tackle different aspects of the same substantive matter, treading the same empirical ground of Baku oil, but together comprising a whole picture of world oil (and gas) politics, which is ontologically greater than the sum of its rationalist or reflectivist parts.

This theory-synergetic approach to international oil politics is explored in chapter VI. Building on the single-paradigm models of BTC and SGC pipeline projects set out in preceding chapters, synergetic readings of the problem-field are developed to demonstrate how harnessing IR multi-theoretical potential properly can amplify empirical accuracy of research outputs; and how excluding different strands of knowledge or theoretical claims based on a priori assumptions or foundational commitments can have empirical costs, undermining explanatory and predictive qualities of scholarship.

In chapter VI these claims are explored by focusing on examples of thematic commonalities and convergences around common empirical material. TSA is operationalized on specific ontological overlaps identified between single-paradigm models of energy politics. It will be shown how using these analytical techniques can help produce empirical outcomes which better correspond to the reality of world energy politics than single-paradigm and eclectic approaches, amplifying both explanatory and predictive qualities of theoretical claims and scholarship on complex international phenomena such as BTC and SGC pipelines.

I
Foundational and Theoretical Debates in International Relations

Introduction

The story of the Great Debates shapes the structure and the self-image of International Relations and in large part forms the core of traditional chronicling of IR history (see, for example, Smith, 1995 in Booth and Smith (eds.); pp. 1-37; Schmidt, 2013 in Carlsnaes et al (eds.) pp. 3-28). Any proposal for pluralist, multi-theoretical engagement in IR requires at least an implicit acknowledgement of their integral role in development of intellectual and social structures of the discipline (Waever, 2011, p. 98).

However, the contentious and unresolved nature of these theoretical debates in IR is further compounded by distinct foundational philosophical disputes, which run in parallel and overlap with the paradigmatic ones (Monteiro and Ruby, 2009, p. 19). At the core of these "science" debates are questions about IR's position as an intellectual enterprise. As such, this is philosophical debate and it is essential here to recognize the role of another discipline, Philosophy of Science (PoS), in shaping foundational disputes in International Relations (Ibid.).

Whether or not IR is a science, what counts as science in IR and other foundational questions are ostensibly posited in order to establish criteria for validity; to serve internal disciplinary structures (academia, journals, etc.); to attain disciplinary credibility in the eyes of the practitioners and policymakers (Ibid. p. 16). In practice these questions carry significant implications for theoretical debates and the state of the discipline more generally. They go to the heart of epistemological and ontological contests as well as issues of methodology and politically important matter of what counts as valid, "acceptable" knowledge.

Perhaps it is useful, therefore, to begin with an explicit acknowledgement of the symbiotic relationship and mutually reinforcing dynamic of foundational-philosophical and theoretical/paradigmatic debates in IR. Indeed, the proposal for theory-synergetic approach, as set out in chapter II, is informed by problems and challenges thrown up by the latest of these debates. Questions of epistemology and ontology are central to understanding prospects for a pluralist international relations.

This chapter, therefore, begins with a comprehensive overview of the four theoretical Great Debates and the two Foundational debates, set out in a common chronological timeline. Implications of the latest of these debates are then examined with the aim of assessing current state of the discipline and its prospects for theoretical and scientific development. It will be argued that rather than heralding the end of international relations theory, the latest scientific and theoretical debates have opened the discipline up to a possibility of greater intellectual pluralism and created opportunities for innovative multi-paradigmatic engagement with substantive issues in the field of global politics.

The chapter concludes with a brief review of some of these efforts to move away from meta-theoretical concerns and grand-theory construction. Yet such efforts at inter-paradigmatic synthesis, mid-range theorizing and multi-methodological research models are fraught with their own difficulties and shortcomings. The overall aim here, therefore, is to examine conditions necessary for emergence of credible multi-theoretical approaches in international relations in the context of theoretical and foundational challenges thrown up by the latest of the Great Debates.

Epistemology, Ontology, and Philosophy of Science (PoS)

Epistemology is the philosophy concerned with establishing the scope and nature of knowledge, the means by which it can be acquired, and the extent to which it can be justified. It is about how and what we know. Ontology is the philosophical study of reality and existence. It deals with what the world is made of in the literal sense of being, and which entities, and categories of entities, can be determined to actually exist. Epistemological and ontological commitments (what is to be studied and how) form the basis of philosophical foundations of scientific knowledge and define its scope (Reus-Smit, 2013, p.592; Monteiro and Ruby, 2009, p.25).

Foundational knowledge is by definition *a priori* knowledge, which does not require its truth-status to be proven or upheld. Commitment to such foundational knowledge means there are no further or other commitments by which standards of knowledge might be determined or justified. What makes a foundational philosophical position foundational is that it has pretensions of infallibility, and irrefutability. If this is really true then such a position cannot be complimented or made compatible with other foundational positions (Monteiro and Ruby, 2009, p.25-26).

As noted above the academic discipline of International Relations has been especially prone to existential debates concerning foundational issues of epistemology and ontology, which informed much of the quest for a grand meta-theory of IR (Kurki and Wight, 2013, p. 14). Foundational debates are at the forefront of IR disciplinary divisions, with majority of scholars in the TRIP survey, for example, clearly identifying with either positivist, anti-positivist or post-positivist positions (Jordan et al, 2009, pp.10-11).

Uneasy about its philosophical foundations IR turned for reference to another academic discourse in order to reinforce its status as a social science. Contemporary Philosophy of Science[5] (PoS) – the branch of philosophy concerned with foundations of science – emerged as a distinct analytical field in the mid-Twentieth Century; its rise to prominence is associated with the works of Karl Popper (1959) and Thomas Kuhn (1962). PoS essentially deals with *a priori* foundational sets of questions – how science should be conducted? How science is conducted? What is the purpose of science?

In "IR and the False Promise of Philosophical Foundations" – their critique of PoS influence on International Relations - Monteiro and Ruby (2009) identify this first set of foundational questions as granting the PoS "the status of a special discourse – a normative discourse capable of evaluating science and legislating its boundaries and practices" (p.24).

---

[5] For a review of the field see Rosenberg, 2012.

Although Kurki and Wight (2013, p.16) argue that IR has not taken PoS seriously, it is evident that at least from the behavioralist turn in the 1960s-1970s onwards, PoS provided IR with its key foundational positions.

Further, it can be argued that as the discipline evolved and sought to ground itself ever more firmly within wider scientific enterprise, it sought (either explicitly or implicitly) ever greater validation and legitimisation through self-conscious adoption of established foundational philosophical positions within PoS (Monteiro and Ruby, 2009).

Monteiro and Ruby point out a continuous chronological overlap in the development of IR paradigmatic matrix and the rise and fall in prominence of various philosophical traditions in PoS (Ibid, pp.19-20; see Table 1). Their analysis does gloss over myriad philosophical differences as they tag competing paradigmatic camps in IR by their corresponding philosophical positions in the Philosophy of Science; and they acknowledge that their "simplifications are often ruthless" (Ibid. p.26). Yet their approach provides a useful framework through which to analyse the relationship between International Relations and PoS, and is followed here in broad terms.

Table 1. International Relations and the PoS

International Relations Debates	Philosophy of Science Positions
Behaviorism versus Traditionalism (Second IR/First Foundational)	Logical Positivism
Neo-realism versus Neo-Liberalism (Third IR/Neo-Neo Synthesis)	Instrumentalism
Reflectivism versus Rationalism (Fourth IR/Second Foundational)	Social Constructivism Scientific (Critical) Realism

The four Great and the two Foundational Debates

The first Great (theoretical) Debate between Idealists and Realists in the 1920s and 1930s was the first time foundational questions about IR were posed but it was not a foundational debate in strictly PoS terms. The so-called Idealists envisioned the discipline as an academic tool for furtherance of peace, abolition of war and conflict between states, and creation of institutions of global governance and international law, such as the League of Nations.

Realists subsequently dismissed such liberal idealism as naïve and lacking objective, scientific criteria by which its claims could be assessed. Europe's slide to World War II gave credence to realist critique of apparent utopianism of early IR and led E. H. Carr to herald Realism as the starting point in the scientific development of the discipline: "The course of events after 1931 clearly revealed the inadequacy of pure aspiration as the basis for a science of international politics, and made it possible for the first time to embark on serious critical and analytical thought about international problems." (Carr, 2001 (1981;1939), p9).

Traditional or Classical Realists may have called for a more rigorous, analytical methodology in International Relations, yet they sought to explain world politics in terms of "objective laws that have their roots in human nature" (Morgenthau, 1985, p.4). Indeed, Morgenthau's "six laws" of political realism rely not so much on observable data or other verifiable evidence as on arguably untested assumptions about what constitutes power and interests. As influential as it subsequently proved to be and for all its scientific claims, classical Realism was not a foundational argument, certainly not in PoS terms.

If anything, in terms of IR disciplinary development, it is the Idealists who had performed the most important, literally foundational, function – in the aftermath of the horrors of World War I they had established the discipline of International Relations. Although they had no clear conception what kind of science would constitute this discipline they had set its normative course towards the aim of abolition of war through pursuit of knowledge about human affairs (Kurki and White, 2013, pp.16-17).

It was the behavioralist turn in the 1950s and 1960s – the second Great (theoretical) Debate – that marked the first time a philosophical position from PoS was explicitly adopted as a foundational discourse in IR. Behavioralists sought to apply methodologies of natural sciences to social scientific scholarship and in the first instance adopted Logical Positivism in their attempt to provide International Relations with a firmly grounded scientific status.

This marks the first time that PoS becomes "central to field's self-definition as science" (Monteiro and Ruby, 2009 p.20). Logical

Positivism was the dominant philosophy of science in the early and mid-twentieth century and was defined by its commitment to empiricism. As a theory of knowledge Logical Positivism holds that the truth-status of knowledge claims can only be ascertained through logical or empirical verification.

This emphasis on verifiability of scientific statements is reinforced by a rejection of mind-independent reality. According to Logical Positivism scientific method must exclude all talk of unobservable (therefore unverifiable) aspects of nature. Instead scientific enterprise is envisaged as a systematic search for natural laws through rigorous empiricism with an emphasis on mathematical and attendant logical processes; theory-production and explanation are thus subordinate to theory-testing and analysis (for a review of Logical Positivism see Friedman, 1999).

It was in the Second Great Debate that issues of what constitutes science in IR were first explicitly and systematically addressed. The behavioralist ascendancy had made Logical Positivist epistemology, ontology and methodology, the foundational orthodoxy in International Relations for a generation, with traditional historical analytical methods being abandoned in favour of hard empiricist methodology. This First Foundational Debate in IR accounts for the wider historical preponderance of positivism in the field. Importantly, it also ensured that PoS would continue to shape and influence foundational debates in IR to this day (Monteiro and Ruby, 2009, p.29).

By the time of the neo-realist/neo-liberal inter-paradigm debate in the 1970s - 1980s (the Third Great Debate), Logical Positivism had come under sustained critique in the Philosophy of Science and new positivist PoS positions, in particular Instrumentalism, emerged to challenge its dominance. Instrumentalism is an expressly non-realist philosophy of science. It shifts the focus of evaluation of knowledge claims away from ontological realism (descriptive explanation), towards analysis of the predictive qualities of a given explanation.

Instrumentalism emphasizes empirical epistemology over preoccupation with ontology; its empiricism is more refined and attenuated than that of classical Logical Positivism. Predictive success of a scientific endeavour to explain an observed reality is considered more important than strictly truthful, verified description. Theories are thus evaluated on the basis of their empirical reliability in predicting observed phenomena – "useful instruments in proving our understanding of the observable world – thus the name 'Instrumentalism'" (Monteiro and Ruby, 2009, p.27).

Instrumentalists recognize that assumptions and causal mechanisms underpinning scientific theories ordinarily cannot be observed (e.g. in quantum physics or astronomy) and treat them "as if" they are true (Ibid). This approach has made Instrumentalism in social sciences particularly popular in economics, where scholars postulate about fictional actors and processes in an abstracted fashion, "as if" they were true, and make predictions accordingly.

As Milton Friedman, a key proponent of Instrumentalism in economics, argued in his essay "The Methodology of Positive Economics" (1966), "the only relevant test of the validity of a hypothesis is comparison of its predictions with experience:" "Viewed as a body of substantive hypotheses, theory is to be judged by its predictive power for the class of phenomena which it is intended to 'explain.' Only factual evidence can show whether it is 'right' or 'wrong' or, better, tentatively "accepted" as valid or 'rejected.'" (pp.8-9).

This emphasis on instrumentality of theory is the defining feature of Instrumentalism as a philosophy of knowledge. In International Relations a quintessential example of Instrumentalism is Kenneth Waltz's seminal 1979 classic "Theory of International Politics." Waltz clearly delineates between observable reality – laws, and theories as instruments that explain these laws: "Because a law does not say why a particular association holds, it cannot tell us whether we can exercise control and how we might go about doing so. For the latter purposes we need a theory" (p.6).

In his pursuit of a parsimonious, structural, non-reductionist theory of international politics Waltz treats unobservable entities "as if" they exist, and uses them to explain and predict observable phenomena in international politics (Monteiro and Ruby, 2009, pp.27-28). It is this instrumentalist approach (and its attendant methodology borrowed heavily from economics) that made neo-realism and its synthesis with neoliberal institutionalism possible.

In the course of the third Great Debate, Neo-Liberal Institutionalists such as Robert Keohane fully accepted rationalist scientific project and Instrumentalist positivist epistemology of the Neo-Realists (Keohane and Nye, 1977, pp.42-46). Nevertheless, they argued that structural theory overlooks and underestimates the role of transnational actors and processes and called for "something in- between: systemic theories that retain some of the parsimony of Structural Realism, but are able to deal better with differences between issue-areas, with institutions, and with change" (Keohane, 1986, p. 197).

Rationalist consensus emerged directly as the result of universal adoption of Instrumentalist philosophy of science and its dominance of IR. Regardless of whether or not the neo-realist/neoliberal inter-paradigm debate was a "debate" at all, it was certainly not a foundational debate – the foundations of IR as science were hardly debated and a considerable degree of convergence around a positivist center-core took place within the discipline (Kurki and Wight, 2013, p. 19).

As Stein (2008) argues: "The use of game-theory and the demonstration that institutionalized cooperation could be explained from a starting point of the power and interest of independent actors made possible not only a rapprochement between realists and neoliberal institutionalists but even an intellectual union in a perspective some dubbed as rationalism" (p.205). Yet despite this high degree of foundational convergence in the mainstream rationalist IR there remained a set of problems relating to theory choice, especially that of alleged incommensurability of different paradigmatic approaches.

The concept of paradigms in IR is also borrowed from the Philosophy of Science. It was introduced in the early 1960s by Thomas Kuhn who defined paradigms as problem-solving achievements "that some particular scientific community acknowledges for a time as supplying the foundation for its further practice" (1962, p. 10). In his seminal work "The Structure of Scientific Revolutions" Kuhn (1962) identifies scientific progress proceeding in two phases – normal science and scientific revolution.

In the first instance knowledge production progresses within a commonly accepted theoretical framework, a dominant paradigm generally accepted and adopted by a scholarly community. In the second phase theoretical innovation occurs as the dominant paradigm faces growing number of anomalies and either attempts to address them or faces a challenge from an alternative paradigm, which claims to address those anomalies.

As the alterative paradigm gathers greater support and acceptance it becomes the new dominant paradigm. Different competing paradigms just as, for example, different political ideologies or systems, are incommensurable, claim to solve different problems and employ their own distinctive properties which makes it impossible to evaluate truth claims (Ibid. p.93).

Instrumentalists embrace Kuhn's emphasis on problem-solving as key component of scientific practice as the most important determinant in theory-choice. For Waltz, for example, the search for a parsimonious structural theory of international politics was informed in part by a pressing need to avoid the pitfalls of reductionist approaches with their inherent incommensurability problems. For instrumentalists there is a need for IR to adopt a single paradigmatic model around which research could converge, and this may help explain the discipline's perennial search for Grand Theory.

Yet it is clear from Kuhn's own analysis that empiricism on its own is not sufficient to account for the dominance of this or that paradigm at any given time and the "issue of paradigm choice can never be unequivocally settled by logic and experiment alone..." (1962, p. 93). Kuhn argues: "As in political revolutions, so in paradigm choice—there is no standard higher than the assent of the relevant community" (Ibid).

It is a growing acceptance of a particular theoretical position within a particular policy community or scholarly circle that determines its paradigmatic dominance and Kuhn goes to great length to provide a historical overview of an ever-changing pattern of dominant paradigmatic positions.

It follows from the above observation that scientific-claims are conditioned not by some universal standards of objectivity and truth but by the social practices and discourses of a scientific community. Subsequent challenges to Kuhn's framing of theories as paradigms are also, to a lesser or greater extent, ambiguous in their judgement of what constitutes scientific progress.

Lakatos re-characterized theories as "research programmes" but agreed that core foundational assumptions of these research programmes cannot be easily falsified or even subjected to empirical testing (Lakatos, 1970). Laudan's looser concept of "research traditions" as an alternative to paradigms and research programmes seeks to move away from the idea of science as competing centralized theoretical clusters (1977). As such it is even more vague and relativistic on the issues of theoretical progress and theory choice (Bennett. 2013, p.464).

Scientific truth is not discovered but is invented and established by social acceptance, rather than the world *per se*. While different conceptualisations of theories as paradigms, research programmes or research traditions may differ in their assessment of what constitutes scientific progress, they all acknowledge its social condition. This focus on social construction of knowledge-claims is at the heart of the third key Philosophy of Science to make a major impact on International Relations - Social Constructivism.[6]

For PoS social constructivists all knowledge is constituted by linguistic discourse and social practices, with language as the central determinant of meaning in the world. The distinction between epistemology and ontology is less prominent in social constructivism because these are seen as deeply enmeshed, mediated as they are through language and social context. Therefore, possibility of objective knowledge of reality is dismissed. For social constructivists the purpose of scientific inquiry is not the search for truth as such but the process of unmasking how such truth-claims are themselves product of power-relations in a socially-produced consensus.

For example, Nelson (1994) employs Constructivist Counterfactual Argument to point out that what are considered to be

---

[6] Social Constructivism in PoS is not to be confused with social constructivist theory in International Relations, which takes up Scientific Realist philosophy of science as its foundational basis.

scientific facts are not simply contestable but that this contestability is due to scientists making certain choices and not others, and that other choices could have been made: "If scientists had chosen to confer facthood otherwise than they actually did, then subsequent history would reflect this in world-view consistent with the choice they counterfactually made. Therefore, the 'facts' are determined by scientists' choices, not by 'objective reality'" (p.541 in Kukla, 2000, p. 3).

In international relations the Social Constructivist philosophy of science is taken up by critical theory, post-structuralism, feminism and pragmatic approaches, and forms the cornerstone of the fourth Great Debate. These reflectivist approaches reject positivist dominance of IR and emphasize "reflexivity and non-neutral nature of political and social explanation" (Kurki and Wight, 2013, p.24). Poststructuralists and other anti-positivists may well reject any notion that they are engaging in foundational debates but the very fact of their explicit commitment to social construction of knowledge makes them Social Constructivist in the PoS sense.

Critical theory's starting point is the Marxian dictum that the purpose of science is not only to understand but to change the world – a commitment to an idea of practical philosophy (Shapcott, 2008, p.327). At the core there is a normative commitment to a scientific emancipatory project, which firmly ties critical theory to a practical discourse on possibilities and conditions of human freedom. It may be an anti-positivist paradigm but is nevertheless laden with far-reaching foundational commitments.

The latter are rooted in the Social Constructivist PoS. For example, the Frankfurt School theorists' emphasis on the dialectical imagination as the driving force of the emancipatory project is rooted in the idea that "it is the imaginational that allows one to connect the social purpose of ideas and creative faculties with the radical desire for social change" (Roach, 2013, p.183). Thus critical theory harvests Social Constructivist PoS exploration of the dynamism between linguistic expression and material action.

Critical theory rejects neutrality of knowledge and emphasizes its social and political dimensions – "Theory is always for someone and for some purpose" (Cox, 1986, p.207). Simultaneously its proponents explicitly assume a highly normative, foundational purpose for the science of IR. As Cox argues: "The study of international relations should focus first on the key issues affecting the biological survival of the human race; and then on the pursuit of justice in the condition of peoples, which is essential to maintaining their support for a survivable world order" (2008, p.87). This far-reaching philosophical framework of IR as envisaged by critical theory is in itself a metanarrative of emancipation – science as a practical, normative project.

Similarly, feminism and poststructuralism represent a set of foundational projects, grounded in the Social Constructivist PoS. Postmodern or poststructuralist strand of critical theory represents a self-consciously combative effort to challenge dominant practices and conceptualisations in IR. The aim and motivating force behind this challenge are explicitly normative – to uncover, unmask, debunk modern institutions, structures, events and show them as historically contingent products of human action, language and thought (Burke, 2008, p. 359). Existence of a mind-independent reality or Objective Truth is thunderously rejected.

Poststructuralism is explicit in its anti-foundationalism but as such it constitutes a meta-theoretical critique of positivist IR. As Campbell defines it, poststructuralism is "a critical attitude, approach, or ethos that calls attention to the importance of representation, the relationship of power and knowledge, and the politics of identity in an understanding of global affairs" (2013, p.225). This is simultaneously a critique of the discipline of International Relations and an expose of the practice of international relations, and a critical exploration of the relationship between the two.

The strong influence of the linguistic turn - a philosophical tradition focusing on the relationship between philosophy and language – and the works of Michel Foucault, places language at the center of poststructuralist analysis; and this binds poststructuralism firmly to the epistemological and ontological foundational commitments of the Social Constructivist philosophy of science.

As Burke argues, when it comes to the ethics of poststructuralism, its critique of positivism and rationalist IR aims to "unmask the operations of power in the 'knowledge' of global politics, and to uncover its formal and rhetorical structures, so as to open up suppressed choices in policy-making and bring out the voices of the marginalized and the oppressed" (2008, p. 354). Poststructuralism, therefore, constitutes not just a foundational metatheory but a fully developed normative political mission. Campbell (2013) is only too right when he demands that critiques of poststructuralism "need to engage it on its own terms" (p.244) - because that is what one does with metatheoretical, foundational arguments.

Feminist international relations theory is similarly explicitly a normative project (True, 2008). Determinations of masculinity and femininity in international relations matter because they determine forms of exclusion and inclusion in decision-making and distribution of power (Enloe, 2007). Furthermore, feminists insist that simply acknowledging gender is not enough. When traditional IR is not ignoring gender the discipline engages with the concept in a highly depoliticized fashion, which "removes from it any examination of the ways in which relations of power sustain (or sometime challenge) prevailing assumptions about men and women and masculinity and femininity" (Whitworth, 2008, p. 392).

By placing gender as a social construct at the heart of their international political analysis, feminists are making a foundational truth claim – that gender is a key, central factor in the ideational, material, historical, and institutional configurations of power (Ibid, p.400; Tickner and Sjoberg, 2013, p. 205). From a metatheoretical viewpoint, feminist IR theory shares common reflectivist scepticism about possibility of objective knowledge and scientific truths. With its emphasis on politics of identity, feminist IR is an example of Social Constructivist PoS analytical framework.

The pragmatic turn in IR is also circumscribed by foundational claims rooted in Social Constructivist PoS (Monteiro and Ruby, 2009, p.29). It is counterintuitive to assume so if one takes IR pragmatism's expressed prioritization of the practical and its pluralist, anti-foundational claims at face value. However, pragmatism too is bound by empirical-theoretical commitments which establish it as fully-fledged metatheoretical framework.

Pragmatist philosophical epistemology has wide-ranging implications for Philosophy as a whole and the Philosophy of Science specifically. Yet this influence is highly heterogeneous and intellectually diverse, reflecting perhaps pragmatism's epistemological agnosticism. Pragmatism is a twentieth century American philosophical tradition, commonly associated with the works of John Dewey, William James, Charles Pierce;[7] it is based on the principle that science is to be practical, useful and judged upon predictive quality of its inquiry, rather than representative, descriptive accuracy.

In the Philosophy of Science, a broader pragmatist influence was brought to bear on Instrumentalism and Logical Positivism, as well as Social Constructivism and Scientific Realism. Yet in IR, the pragmatic turn came from an expressly Social Constructivist PoS standpoint. It is characterized by a deep scepticism over possibility of any meaningful resolution to epistemological and ontological debates (Sil, 2000, p.354).

For IR pragmatists there is no way to settle arguments of what constitutes truth or about validity of moral claims. Epistemological disputes are thus seen as excluding possibility of other rationales and purposes for social enquiry, for example the search for solutions to real-world problems and addressing immediate concerns of policy-makers and other practitioners.

For Monteiro and Ruby (2009, p.29) the pragmatist turn in IR is bound by a foundational commitment to the practicality of knowledge – "inquiry is inextricable from intervention in the world, in effect ascribing common normative goals to the discipline as a whole." This sets pragmatic approaches in IR, such as Sil's and Katzenstein's *Analytic Eclecticism* (2010), within a clearly structured metatheoretical framework – "a distinctive kind of social-scientific

---

[7] For a review of classical and contemporary pragmatist philosophy see Goodman, R. (ed.), 2005. Pragmatism: Critical Concepts in Philosophy, London: Routledge; Haack, S. (ed.), 2006. *Pragmatism, Old and New* Amherst NY: Prometheus; Talisse, R. and S. Aikin (eds.), 2011, *The Pragmatism Reader: From Peirce through the Present*, Princeton: Princeton University Press

project, one with particular boundaries and particular content" (Reus-Smit, 2013, p.596).

What all reflectivist theories of IR founded upon Social Constructivist philosophy of science share is a deep scepticism on the possibility of objective knowledge and agnosticism about (and often denial of) reality that exists "out there," independently of human mind. Above all they represent a critical discourse on the practices of IR as a discipline itself.

These practices influence and shape the world IR scholars claim merely to be observing. From this follows that when it comes to science, interpretation and critiques are the best that can be done. Thus the anti-positivist discourse of the Social Constructivist PoS had had a profound impact on the course of the Fourth Debate in IR, challenging the very notion of what constitutes science of international politics. This marks it as the second Foundational Debate.

Scientific Realism and IR

By contrast Scientific (Critical) Realist[8] philosophy of science is "committed to (indeed founded upon) the possibility of scientific progress" (Monteiro and Ruby, 2009, p. 31). As a philosophy of science Scientific Realism holds that the world is knowable in principle, especially since science had already produced considerable progress.

Knowledge about the world corresponds to the truth of how the world really is. This truth is accessible to scientists and there should be no limitations on the pursuit of the scientific enterprise. As Leplin argues: "What realists do share in common are the convictions that scientific change is, on balance, progressive and that science makes possible knowledge of the world beyond its accessible, empirical manifestations" (1984, p.2).

Scientific Realism challenges epistemic scepticism of other PoS positions. Observable and unobservable elements of scientific theories must actually be true and correspond to the reality of the world out there. Otherwise, there would be no accounting for the technological successes

---

[8] See Archer et al (Eds.), 2007, Critical Realism: Essential Readings, London and New York: Routledge

of modern science without recourse to miracles – the so called "no miracles" argument (Monteiro and Ruby, 2009, p. 30; Putnam, 1984, p.141). At the heart of Scientific Realism is a foundational commitment to a "correspondence theory of truth" (Ibid, p. 140).

Table 2. Fourth IR/Second Foundational Debate

International Relations Theories	PoS Positions
Critical Theory Poststructuralism Feminism Eclecticism	SOCIAL CONSTRUCTIVISM
Social Constructivism	SCIENTIFIC (CRITICAL) REALISM

This ontological realism is coupled with epistemological relativism and methodological pluralism. Scientific realists posit that there should be no *a priori* limitations on what and how can be known about the world. This epistemological relativism does not, however, prevent possibility, in principle, of choosing between different competing theories or explanations - what Patomaki and Wight call "judgemental rationalism" (2000, p. 224).

There is a degree of confusion and conflation when it comes to determining between Scientific and Critical Realism.[9] For Monteiro and Ruby there is no distinction between the two versions, as "the boundaries between Critical and Scientific Realism are fuzzy" (2009, p.31). Indeed, the terms are often used interchangeably and both share common philosophical foundations and commitments. What distinguishes Critical Realism as a more nuanced and attenuated upgrade on the original is a critical stance towards truth claims and the attendant notion of *deep ontology* (Patomaki and Wight, 2000, p. 225).

Critical Realists build on the work of the philosopher Roy Bhaskar (1975) to argue that social outcomes are produced by the dynamics of both ideational and material factors: "According to critical realists, the question

---

[9] For a review of Critical Realism see Archer, M., *et al.* 1998, *Critical Realism: Essential Readings*. London: Routledge. For a review of Scientific Realism see Leplin, J. (ed.) 1984. *Scientific Realism*. London, Berkeley and Los Angeles: University of California Press.

of whether material factors or ideational issues are the most important in determining outcomes is an empirical matter that can be decided only on the basis of research that examines the relationship and interplay of both" (Kurki and Wight, 2013, p.26).

It follows, therefore, that the social reality is more than its experiential qualities and intersubjective elements. The concept of deep ontology emerges from an understanding that this social reality consists of more than can be experienced and is not exhausted by intersubjective meanings. In fact, "the surface appearance of inter-subjectivity, although possessing causal power, is typically distinct from its underlying - and potentially hidden, reified, or mystified – essential relations" (Patomaki and Wight, 2000, p.225).

Critical Realism is thus an ontological endeavor, committed to the notion of perpetual science where "no claim is ever immune from challenge" (Ibid. p.218), and which "rather than being committed to a dogmatic insistence on the certainty of its claims, rests on a commitment to constant critique" (Murki and Wight, 2013, p.25).

Critical and Scientific Realism form a single PoS super-structure that consists of a) prioritization of ontological realism; b) general epistemological relativism; and c) judgemental rationalism – the view that despite epistemological relativism it is still possible to establish justifiable criteria for theory/explanation choice (Ibid. p.31). Distinctions emerge where Scientific Realism focuses its broad attention on the correspondence theory of truth, calling on science to adhere to strict ontological discipline and to get at the way the world *really* works (Leplin (ed.), 1984; Wight, 2006; 2007).

Meanwhile Critical Realism adopts a vision of science as a perpetual and open-ended endeavor to test and challenge truth claims about the world constructed of the interplay between the material and ideational elements (Bhaskar, 1975). Whether treated as a single analytical framework or via its component perspectives, realist philosophy of science stands out within PoS by its central and contentious claim that science provides a roadmap to mind-independent reality (Monteiro and Roby, 2009, p.32).

Scientific and Critical Realism have been enthusiastically endorsed in International Relations, predominantly by proponents of social constructivism (Wendt, 1999; Patomaki and Wight, 2000; Chernoff, 2002; Wight, 2007; Joseph and Wight, 2010; Kurki and Wight, 2013). By prioritising ontology, epistemic relativism and methodological pluralism Scientific Realism is seen as carrying a post-positivist potential to bridge IR's foundational divisions. Alexander Wendt, a key proponent of Scientific Realism, argued in "Social Theory of International Politics" that Scientific Realism "captures what IR scholars of all stripes already do" (1999, p.67).

Patomaki and Wight dismiss IR inter-paradigmatic debates as an arbitrary "epistemological speculation in an ontological vacuum" and endorse Critical Realism as "a broader, non-reductive perspective, capable of incorporating the strengths of all" (2000, p. 227). Critical Realism is seen as a philosophical foundation upon which a multi-theoretical, multi-methodological IR framework can be built, thus providing the discipline with the elusive post-positivist consensus.

As Monteiro and Ruby define it, Critical Realism comprises "...relativism at the epistemological level (making for pluralism by allowing all sorts of approaches, theories, paradigms, research traditions, etc., to operate side-by-side within a discipline) and realism at the ontological level (continuing to view scientific knowledge as getting at the way the world really works, independent from our efforts to know it" (2009, p.31).

Implications of the fourth Great Debate

International Relations today may be seen as an intellectual maelstrom of competing philosophical frameworks and normative and theoretical visions, with little internal coherence or external relevance. Janice B. Mattern describes it as "an (un)discipline" - "less of a discipline than a collection of insular research communities" (2008, p.692). She proposes return to metatheoretical discussion and a search for a singular theoretical framework, albeit more permissive of internal pluralism (Ibid. pp.696-697).

Yet today even realists like Randall Shweller are sceptical of the very possibility of IR theory and question its potential as scientific enterprise. In "Maxwell's Demon and the Golden Apple: Global Discord in the New Millennium" (2014) Shweller argues that contemporary international relations are increasingly characterized by growing entropy – unpredictability, randomness and inexorable chaos, on macro and micro-levels, which over time reduce IR's explanatory power as it becomes ever impossible to predict and explain world events.

If Positivist dominance is at an end, then the last Great Debate cannot be considered as having been completely inconclusive. Its outcomes and implications are complex and it is difficult to characterize the Fourth Debate in terms of conventional IR historiography (Schmidt, 2013, p.19). And few would actually agree that IR theory has come to an end in its wake. It is therefore important to examine future directions of theoretical development and how these could contribute to meeting the challenges facing the discipline of International Relations.

Indeed, the editors of the special issue of *European Journal of International Relations* dedicated to the question – "The End of International Relations Theory?" cautiously concluded that the Fourth Debate does not mean "theoretical peace" or a return to a paradigmatic "war of all against all." Instead they argue that "...one of IR's comparative advantages over other disciplines might just be its strong sense of being a theory-led and theory-concerned field" (Dunne et al, 2013, p. 420).

Other contributors similarly argue that the state of IR theory is in much better shape that is generally thought (Jackson and Nexon, 2013, p. 544). Charlotte Epstein (2013) goes further to argue that the last Great Debate was a reformative process which greatly expanded the "world" of IR and the scope of the discipline. Rather than decline or diminution of theory the process instead is one of theoretical consolidation, as IR acquires a stronger grasp of its enlarged subject matter and seeks to deepen understanding of its workings (p. 500). There is no sense here that theoretical pluralism is detrimental to the intellectual enterprise of IR.

Elsewhere, Ole Wæver underlines this implicit connection between theoretical inquiry and knowledge of real world – the ideal of "relevance through theory" (2013, p.324). Development of theoretical debate within IR is indeed a formative function for the structure of the discipline: "The debates serve to focus the discipline and to define both a hierarchy of forms of work and to give a meaningful role to larger parts of what goes on" (Ibid. p.317). Casting the discipline in terms of "great debates" should not therefore be seen as having a disabling effect on IR, as is often argued. Instead, as Wæver points out, the Debates are a framework for intellectual continuum – a process of knowledge production in IR, with new theories emerging from and of a pre-existing IR setting (2013, p. 318).

Abandoning this framework and adopting a narrow empiricist approach to theory risks reducing the discipline to "IR for IR's sake" (Ibid. p. 323). Treating the discipline as an end in itself is erroneous in the case of IR because of the importance of its subject matter – a view of International Relations as a scientific enterprise "ultimately justified by the severity of its issues" (Ibid, p. 324).

Implicit in Wæver's argument is recognition of the symbiotic relationship between theoretical and practical and the inherently complimentary nature of epistemological and ontological inquiries in IR: "In a diverse discipline like IR, the challenge is not to achieve knowledge, but how to understand multiplicity of it, and this is only possible when we understand both the world and the processes through which our understanding of it came about. By knowing how we know, we know more about what we know" (Ibid. p. 324).

Thus one area of consensus in the post-Fourth Debate IR may be a general recognition that theory should and does remain at the heart of IR and animates its intellectual vigor – there is a "shared commitment to the importance of theory in understanding the world" across IR paradigmatic matrix (Smith, 2013, p. 8; Guzzini, 2013: Mearsheimer and Walt, 2013). As Reus-Smit and Snidal argue, "theoretical assumptions (and debates surrounding them) determine the contours of the field and inform even the most empirical research" (2008, p.5). Similarly, theory shapes the discipline's relevance to the real world – "In practice, theory is unavoidable" (Nye, 2008, p.648).

What is being energetically contested, therefore, is not whether there *is* theory or that it is at an end but rather *what* constitutes theory in

International Relations? Indeed, what emerges from the overall reading of the special issue of the *European Journal of International Relations* on the end of IR theory is that approaches to the issue are largely determined by different conceptions of theory (Berenskoetter, 2013). When David Lake, for example, declares theory dead he expressly means "grand theory," not all theory (2013, pp. 567-568). His conception of theory reflects a wider turn in IR towards mid-range theorizing, focused on producing practice-relevant real -world knowledge, and placed outside grand-theoretical debates (Ibid., pp. 571-572).

Mid-level or eclectic theorizing of the type proposed by Sil and Katzenstein (2010) and championed by David Lake (2013), is called upon to provide a way out of paradigmatic wars of the "isms" and to offer a multi-theoretical analytical framework capable of illuminating "substantive relationships and revealing hidden connections among elements of seemingly incommensurable paradigm-bound theories, with an eye to generating novel insights that bear on policy debates and practical dilemmas" (Sil and Katzenstein, 2010, p.2).

Other mid-level theoretical models similarly focus on explanation via study of causal mechanisms in international relations, but take a more structured approach (Bennett, 2013). What they have in common is explicit disavowal of Grand Theory – David Lake's "evil tyrant" (2013, p.568) – and prioritization of practice-orientated academic work, free from dogmatic constraints of inter-paradigmatic contestation.

Yet as Reus-Smit persuasively argues, metatheoretical assumptions cannot be avoided no matter how much they are bracketed (2013, p.590). Even the most explicitly pragmatic and self-reflectively eclectic approaches are structured by implicit epistemological assumptions which constitute metatheoretical constraints, undermining their very goal of producing practically-relevant knowledge (Ibid, p.602). The kind of knowledge required to address key questions in global politics cannot be produced by a purely empirical inquiry. Such knowledge by definition demands normative analysis and awareness (Ibid. p.606).

New prominence of norms and ethics in international relations is therefore another characteristic feature of the post-Fourth Debate IR theoretical pluralism. As Robert Keohane put it, "We do not study international relations for aesthetic reasons, since world politics is not beautiful" (2008, p.708). For all the theoretical diversity a characteristic feature of contemporary IR is the serious attention increasingly being paid to normative questions and issues of morality and ethics in world politics (Erskine, 2008; 2013).

Normative IR theory can be viewed as a distinct body of scholarship focused on international ethics (Nardin, 2008). But, as Smith argues, in contemporary post-Fourth Debate IR, all theoretical approaches should be seen as having normative commitments (2008, p. 727). When, for example, Brown cautions against abandoning the aspiration to produce "Grand Theory," he qualifies it with a need to make such theory "action-guiding as well as world-revealing," concerned with "critical problem solving" and addressing the challenges facing disempowered communities – rationalist IR as a normative theoretical pursuit (2013, p. 494).

Multi-theoretical, pluralist and self-reflective – contemporary IR is an expanding field and this is reflected in growing attention being paid not only to different conceptions of theory and its functions, but its normative properties and practice-relevant implications. The image of IR as an un-discipline, facing demise and plagued by disagreement and fragmentation is only valid if we are to accept that it is necessary to have agreement on aims, objects and definitions in a discipline. As Wæver points out – "history of science is full of disciplines that didn't agree at all on their self-definition, subject-matter, or methodology, and continued nevertheless" (2013, p. 309).

Implications of the second Foundational Debate

Ironically one such discipline with unresolved foundational issues is Philosophy of Science (PoS), which, as noted above, continues to have a profound impact on the "science debate" in IR. As was shown above, PoS provides vocabulary and analytical frameworks for foundational disputes in IR, with various theoretical paradigms seeking scientific validation and legitimacy through association with corresponding PoS positions. The fourth Great Debate was explicitly the Second "Foundational debate" in IR, concerned with what the discipline should study and how (Kurki and Wight, 2013, p.16).

However, Monteiro and Ruby are sceptical of PoS general influence on IR. They point out that each philosophical approach when applied as foundational basis for science in IR falters, because each demands "at least one leap of faith" (2009, p. 32). For example, instrumentalism limits knowledge to what can be observed, yet the notion of "observability" itself is not scientifically knowable. In other words, there is no scientific basis for determining where the distinction between observable and unobservable lies, making the boundary fuzzy and arbitrary.

Social constructivist leap of faith is that "despite the social nature of knowledge, claims about social construction of knowledge are themselves not socially constructed" (Ibid p.34). But it is Scientific Realism that requires the deepest faith, according to Monteiro and Ruby. The correspondence theory of truth that underpins the approach is "plagued by a problem of logical circularity" (2009, p.34). The observation that science is successful and therefore must be "right" or "correct" is an example of inference to the best explanation and that in turn has no solid logical foundation, rather a great leap of faith.

None of the foundational positions in PoS can fulfil the promise of philosophical foundations for IR and Monteiro and Ruby argue for "an attitude of foundational prudence in IR" (Ibid, p.35) – a move away from taking a foundational position, in favor of simply having an attitude towards the foundational debate – a kind of agnosticism that acknowledges philosophical diversity but does not seek to impose one or another foundation upon the discipline. They rightly point out that it is highly problematic when. "..IR scholars deploy foundational arguments to show how their scholarship is 'scientifically' superior to that of others" (Ibid., p.36).

Instead, they argue that IR pluralism, both theoretical and methodological, can be better served by rejecting *a priori* criteria and various forms of essentialism and instead determining theory and method choice on the basis of their contribution towards substantive understanding of international politics. Hence, arguments in IR should be judged on their substantive merits, not foundational claims and, therefore, scientific standards should not come from outside the discipline. Monteiro and Ruby argue that standards generated outside the discipline, specifically foundational PoS standards, "allow for no gains compared to the standards generated by our own discipline – and make for important losses" (Ibid., p.37).

Yet the authors do not extrapolate on what internal IR scientific standards are or could be. Their foundational prudence is agnostic on the questions of scientific progress and objectivity – it is defined more by its opposition to attempts to apply foundational commitments "as the basis for determining the scope of scientific IR" (Ibid. p.40). They conclude that the Great Debates should "be about substantive questions, not about inevitably shaky meta-theoretical positions" (Ibid. p.44).

As we have seen, however, attempts to bracket foundational commitments in any case are unlikely to succeed and foundational prudence advocated by Monteiro and Ruby is in the end yet another attempt to bracket metatheoretical issues in IR. And it is premised upon nothing less than a leap of faith of its own – that International Relations has empirical foundations as an independent academic discipline that require no metatheoretical philosophies to underpin them.

Monteiro and Ruby actually call for scholars "to trust IR's ability to stand on its own, without recourse to philosophical foundations" (Ibid., p. 37). For some critics of Monteiro and Ruby these problems with their notion of "foundational prudence" stem from the authors' unintended misunderstanding and mischaracterisations of PoS positions, leading towards a hyper-empiricist, neo-behavioralist vision of IR (Jackson, 2009).

But even on its own terms the notion of foundational prudence is problematic. What are the empirical standards inherent or internal to IR, for example, is never defined or elucidated – there is a quality of arbitrariness to the argument. Its stated purpose ("a truly pluralistic IR" (Monteiro and Ruby, 2009, p.41)) – is never developed or explained. It claims to be scientific but post-foundational, and that "bad science" "can be debunked on theoretical, methodological or empirical bases" (Ibid. p.43).

But what are the foundations of those theoretical, methodological and empirical bases? What should constitute as criteria for theory choice;

for choosing one methodology over another? And how does one build an empirical body of scholarship when philosophical questions about what constitutes the ontology of International Relations are at the very heart of post-Fourth Debate disciplinary diversity?

Philosophy of Science may itself be a contested field, divided on questions of epistemological and ontological commitments, and what constitutes "scientific" inquiry (Monteiro and Ruby, 2009, pp. 24-25). But for PoS these are substantive issues which do not impede theory development and dialogue amongst scholars. There is no reason why they should do so in IR. Given the correspondence in the relationship between evolving PoS positions and foundational debates in IR, it is not difficult to view the rise of anti- and post-positivist PoS schools of thought in parallel with the ending of rationalist dominance of IR. Cast in this light, "science debate" in International Relations is not deadlocked. Instead, it should be seen as having re-founded International Relations as a massively expanded field of social inquiry.

It can be argued furthermore, that the Fourth Debate was informed and shaped by growing awareness of philosophies of science which are more enabling of theoretical and methodological pluralism. Thus theoretical diversity in IR is a reflection of growing foundational confidence across the discipline and a more refined and nuanced understanding of epistemological dynamics. More importantly it potentially points to a (re)discovery of an expanded ontology of International Relations – a distinct social realm not studied by other, older disciplines.

One outcome of the Second Foundational Debate could be that "IR has finally found its world" (Epstein, 2013, p.500). This is now potentially a meta-social science, constituting the study of the totality of human interactions across the globe and a normative intellectual enterprise animated by an ongoing emancipatory interest rooted in the foundation of the discipline in the aftermath of the horrors of World War I.

And this may help explain a peculiar phenomenon in IR foundational debates – scholars "IR-theoretical allegiances do not always (or even often) match or correspond to PoS-foundational positions either explicitly or implicitly endorsed by them. Thus, for example, some IR social constructivists and realists endorse Scientific Realism, which is a post-positivist philosophy of science" (Wendt, 1999, p.67; Mearsheimer and Walt, 2013, pp.432-434).

Meanwhile other realists take Instrumentalism as their positivist PoS position of choice, including Kenneth Waltz (1979 pp. 1-13; p.124). Poststructuralists and critical theorists (mostly implicitly) embrace PoS Social Constructivism – expressly anti-positivist philosophy (Cox, 1981); those rejecting paradigmatic discourse and seeking to do practice-oriented IR often root their middle-range causal accounts in the Pragmatist PoS tradition (Sil and Katzenstein, 2010).

This philosophical diversity, with sometimes counterintuitive matches between IR theories and PoS traditions underpinning them, suggests that IR scholars engage with foundational ("science") questions through the prism of their own discipline and on its own terms. The fact that today post-positivist philosophies of science, such as Pragmatism and Critical Realism are being increasingly accepted by IR scholars from across theoretical backgrounds and are then employed to facilitate IR theoretical pluralism, simply means that this is useful for contemporary, post-Fourth Debate IR.

Problems of Pluralism in International Relations

On foundational level, therefore, the discipline is characterized by philosophical pluralism, marking the end of positivism as the only science of IR, and (re)establishing and considerably expanding its ontological realm. On theoretical and methodological levels, a picture of dynamic diversity emerges, as the discipline adapts to multiplicity of knowledge and ways of producing it.

On one level, this is reflected in the changing structures of IR academia – renewed focus on university teaching and research, growth in the number of journals and periodicals, and in transformation in the way IR knowledge is presented in traditional text books (see, for example, Booth and Smith (Eds.), 1995 (1997); Reus-Smit and Snidal (Eds). 2008; Dunne et al (eds). 2013; Carlsnaes et al (Eds.), 2012; Edkins and Zehfuss (eds), 2009).

But IR is also being opened up from below, with proliferation of online blogs and social media resources, which have not only provided platform to voices that would not ordinarily be heard, but also massively expanded the reach of the discipline, e.g. *E-International Relations* blog has an average of 200,000 unique visitors a month (*E-IR*, 2014; see also *The Duck of Minerva*). Unaffiliated to any academic institutions but often endorsed by the scholarly community (*E-IR*, 2015), ran not-for-profit by enthusiastic volunteers and hugely popular amongst students, academics, practioners and wider general public, these new IR platforms simultaneously shape and respond to disciplinary diversity and facilitate flows of interdisciplinary exchange.

This is not to suggest that the discipline had reached some lofty peak of its development. But in his contribution to *International Studies Quarterly* symposium "The Third Debate" 25 Years Later (Jackson (ed.) 20.03.2014) Yosef Lapid tellingly references Randall Jarrell's remarkable refrain that the "people who live in a golden age usually go around complaining how yellow everything looks" (1958, p.290).

Lapid acknowledges the decentring of metatheoretical enterprise in IR but enthusiastically endorses its growing reflexivity and makes the following observation: "If the discipline is in reasonable theoretical health, why do we witness all this talk about 'the end of theory' with or without a question mark? The answer to this question is, of course, very complex, but my hunch is that a secret urge to become a 'normal' science is still deeply rooted in the disciplinary psyche... Strong and sustained therapy is needed to successfully address this insatiable urge" (2014).

That is certainly a legitimate position to take but it does not address some of the fundamental questions facing IR. Diversity is established and normalized yet the extent to which it is being contested is equally undeniable. What may appear as a blooming if unruly garden to some, is "an ivory-tower effete debate about very little of consequence" to others (Ferguson and Mansbach, 2014).

There is no agreement on what constitutes proper theory in IR and different conceptions or types of theory are utilized across disciplinary landscape. Pluralism appears to have also put an end to metatheoretical engagement as the primary focus of theoretical development. Moreover, different paradigms prioritize different ontologies of international relations – what should constitute a proper empirical focus or unit of study is also being robustly contested. In post-Fourth Debate IR pluralism is not limited to epistemological and ontological issues – methodology can be argued to be very much at the heart of the contested diversity.

Pluralism raises a whole range of wider disciplinary issues – what is the relationship between IR scholarship and the practical world of international relations? What is the effect of the emergence of a growing set of autonomous subfields on the International Relations? What impact pluralism is having on the academic and administrative structures of the discipline? But the issue of theoretical diversity is the one that animates debates around pluralism in IR, not least because reaffirmation of theory as its intellectual center of gravity is the single most important outcome of the Fourth Debate.

Perhaps, it is anxiety over these kinds of questions, rather than some psychological urge for a "normal science" that provokes a profound angst about whether "IR theory is dead." As Dunne, Hansen and Wight point out in the special issue of European Journal of International Relations nobody "is arguing against pluralism per se: in fact, everyone agrees that it is a desirable position (albeit under certain conditions, such as 'relevance' or 'science'). This leads us to consider the question: what kind of pluralism can, and should, IR embrace?" (2013, p. 415).

If pluralism to be welcomed unconditionally, it means envisaging IR as a social scientific enterprise animated by an ever expanding, critical and reflective theoretical diversity. It means embracing the fact that there is no possibility of ever settling theoretical disputes in International Relations and allowing for an open-ended and unrestricted proliferation of theoretical positions. Commitment to pluralism as an end in itself would characterize such an approach. After all, since there are no common epistemological standards by which to assess competing knowledge claims why not accept all perspectives and just get on with it?

Yet, in reality post-Fourth Debate IR is characterized by a pluralism of a different kind – a "disengaged pluralism" (Ibid, p.416). If all claims are valid in their own right there is little incentive for theorists to engage with different viewpoints. Theory-development thus proceeds in separate, independent islands of knowledge-production, with "no attempt to specify the relationships between theories" (Ibid).

However, for proponents of theoretical diversity, relativism is not a real constraint on inter-paradigmatic engagement. Some go as far as to dismiss the "incommensurability" problem altogether: "The notorious 'specter' of relativism is rarely invoked and the once formidable obstacle to cross-paradigmatic communication known as Kuhnian 'incommensurability' has been so utterly demolished that one finds herself secretly hoping for partial restoration" (Lapid, 2014).

Whether or not this assessment is over-optimistic depends on what is meant by cross-paradigmatic communication. Could it be taken as far as a genuine theoretical synthesis? Such a synthesis would require combining of different elements, in this case abstract entities of International Relations theories, to form a new unified, coherent and complete theoretical whole. This, in turn, would require constituent theoretical components to shed their constitutive epistemological and ontological properties and then arrive at a new common set of core foundational assumptions to form a theoretical synthesis - another grand-theory, a supra-theory in fact.

An alternative to such metatheoretical solutions to the challenges of disciplinary pluralism is increasingly sought amongst mid-level or eclectic theoretical approaches to global politics. These broadly positivist approaches eschew paradigmatic pretensions and holistic accounts of international relations, focusing instead on various parts of the political process, rather than the whole; examining individual variables and how they determine policy choices and outcomes.

Mid-level theorizing is methodologically pluralist and places great emphasis on historical contingency, while also looking to broader patterns in world politics: "Bridging and in many cases simply violating boundaries between the levels of analysis, this strain of theorizing about international politics was self-consciously eclectic" (David Lake, 2013, p. 571).

The argument for such an approach is not necessarily a new one and it has been argued that many of the classical theoreticians of international relations have indeed been either proponents of eclectic endeavor in IR or at the very least recognized a need for multiplicity of approaches, especially when it came to practical issues in foreign affairs. As Kenneth Waltz argued: "The prescriptions directly derived from a single image [of international relations] are incomplete because they are based upon partial analyses. The partial quality of each image sets up a tension that drives one towards inclusion of the others... One is led to search for the inclusive nexus of causes" (1959, pp.229-230).

Admittedly Waltz's search ultimately led him to parsimonious structural vision of international relations. What is undeniable, however, is that eclecticism does have a strong historical foundation in IR, especially in the United States. It is no surprise, therefore, that its most prominent and coherent articulation had emerged there with the publication of Rudra Sil and Peter Katzenstein's influential "Beyond Paradigms. Analytic Eclecticism in the Study of World Politics" (2010).

Sil and Katzenstein's approach is based on a key argument that various features of theoretical analyses, which are initially embedded in separate paradigms or research traditions can be separated on foundational level, reinterpreted in a coherent way and then "recombined as part of an original permutation of concepts, methods, analytics, and empirics" (2008, p. 111).

What sets analytic eclecticism apart is an explicit commitment to production of practically relevant knowledge. By integrating empirical observations and causal stories from different paradigmatic traditions it seeks to identify important substantive issues that have relevance to real world problems and have practical value beyond abstract academic debate. As an intellectual project it seeks first and foremost to address normative and policy debates in which real-life actors in international relations find themselves in real-time.

This concern over practicality of theoretical endeavor is rooted in the Pragmatist Philosophy of Science. In fact, Katzenstein and Sil go to great length to provide strong foundational underpinnings to their approach, arguing that Pragmatism offers the most solid philosophical basis for analytic eclecticism because of its "aversion to excessively abstract ontologies and rigid analytic principles in favor of useful interpretations that can be deployed to cope with concrete problems" (Ibid., p.113).

Analytic eclecticism is thus driven by an urge for relevant and practical knowledge about international politics, and therefore constitutes an explicit rejection of grand theoretical meta-projects in IR: "The making of practically relevant knowledge cannot wait for the emergence of a definitive consensus on methodological procedures or axiomatic principles that may reveal 'final' truths'" (Ibid).

Sil and Katzenstein go to great length to promote a vision of pluralist International Relations rooted in the Pragmatist Philosophy of Science and committed to production of practical, useful knowledge about world politics. However, it will be shown in the next chapter that for all its ambition analytical eclecticism remains limited in its pluralism - limited by its curtailed ontology and by its implicit, if unacknowledged, metatheoretical commitments. Both these limitations stem from a specific and highly delineated choice of pluralism – rooted as it is in dominant IR theoretical traditions and practices.

Conclusion

This chapter offered an overview of theoretical and foundational debates in IR with the aim of setting the context for theory-synergetic approach. It is not clear whether the latest, Fourth Great Debate and the Second Foundational debate running alongside it are yet at an end. But it is beyond doubt that they have already profoundly impacted the study of international politics and greatly advanced and expanded the field.

The end of the rationalist consensus and opening up of the IR to multiplicity of knowledge and ways of producing it, create both opportunities and problems for the development of the discipline. Whether International Relations can fulfil its potential as a multi-disciplinary, pluralistic social science, confident of its normative mission and foundational status, depends on whether intellectual output of the latest debates translates into further fragmentation of the field or results in fruitful cross-paradigmatic dialogue and scholarship.

It is not enough to overcome incommensurability problems across a limited range of paradigmatic positions characterized by common foundational commitments. Nor is it sufficient to employ combinatorial techniques or offer open-ended multi-theoretical critiques of problems and puzzles in international politics. It is argued here that any multi-theoretical engagement in IR must proceed from foundational beginnings – how epistemological and ontological divergences between different paradigms are to be reconciled is a fundamental question.

In the next chapter it will be shown that when assessed present efforts at theoretical synthesis and mid-range theorizing are characterized by major shortcomings and flaws, severely limiting their potential as a way forward for a truly pluralistic IR research agenda. Theory-synergetic approach is then advanced as a means of achieving this and responding to foundational and theoretical challenges of the latest debates in International Relations.

II
Theory-Synergetic Approach

Introduction

Foundational challenge posed by the Fourth Debate goes to the very heart of International Relations as a scientific enterprise. What constitutes science in the discipline is a philosophical question and at the core of the theory synergetic approach (TSA) is a clear recognition of this foundational and defining condition - no attempt is made here to avoid meta-theoretical debates or the scientific ones.

The overall aims of this chapter are to establish these foundational claims, to explain TSA and how it might work in practice, as well as to demonstrate how it differs and may be superior to other contemporary multi-theoretical approaches. The chapter opens with an exploratory definition of TSA and introduces international energy (oil and gas) politics as the proposed empirical field to serve as case study in this book, to demonstrate how the approach is to be operationalized.

Issues of epistemology and ontology are very much at the forefront of the analytical framework characterising theory-synergetic approach. The latter is not a proposal for a new paradigm or a specific methodology – it is a pitch for a wider, more general conception of a disciplinary *method*, a common way of doing things or to approach substantive issues. TSA makes use of existing theoretical and methodological diversity. As such it makes no sense to attempt an escape from the discipline's history and structure. TSA is an explicitly IR approach; it proposes no abandonments or new starts, merely restructuring and reformulation of existing thinking.

TSA, therefore, is not an attempt at meta-theory, nor a paradigm, nor a research programme in a Lakostian sense. Neither is it a specific methodology. It is a technique or a systematic approach, which seeks to chart a roadmap for fully utilising knowledge-producing potential of the post-Fourth Debate IR. It is posited that TSA is a systematic way of thinking about substantive issues in international politics and approaching empirical research tasks – which allows for full application of the discipline's theoretical and methodological pluralism.

Theory-synergetic approach is epistemologically pluralist in the widest sense and is called upon to address the challenges posed by the changed intellectual environment of IR - its deep ontology. TSA calls for a greater focus on real-world issues, normative commitments and reflective qualities in IR scholarship. But this self-conscious epistemological relativism is not arbitrary. TSA holds that IR theories can be viewed as *research tools* and proposes to study and reveal international political reality through a systematic application of these tools to specific substantive issues and empirical puzzles, such as the case studies in this thesis: international energy politics in general and specific oil and gas pipeline projects.

Theoretical matrix of IR is held to be comparable to the periodic table in chemistry – the importance is attached not only to individual theories but to reactions and interplay between them, as they come into the empirical mix of TSA. It is a proposed framework for organising epistemological and ontological properties of contemporary IR and as such, it is founded and rooted in Critical Realist Philosophy of Science. This chapter explores foundational claims that underpin the argument for theoretical synergy and demonstrates how applying Critical Realist concept of *deep ontology* helps unlock the inherent knowledge-maximising potential of multi-theoretical IR.

This chapter also details general principles, mechanisms and workings of TSA and demonstrates how they are to be operationalized through empirical modelling, using case-studies of energy politics. This will be achieved by showing that TSA represents a superior method of harnessing IR pluralism, especially compared to attempts at inter-paradigmatic synthesis. It will be argued that such efforts are unlikely to succeed at tackling incommensurability problems without highly abstracted disaggregation of epistemological and ontological elements and properties of various constituent theories. Instead of synthesis the concept of theoretical synergy is proposed as a means of engaging with epistemological and ontological divergences across the IR-theory matrix.

Similarly, it will be demonstrated that mid-level theoretical approaches such as analytic eclecticism are characterized by distinct epistemological commitments that limit their theoretical pluralism. Attempting to avoid meta-theory and refocus IR as a practice-led project ends up arbitrarily constraining theory-choice and results in a highly delineated, curtailed ontological field. Theory-synergetic approach shares analytic eclecticism's concern with real-world problems and its emphasis on ontology. However, it proposes to tackle substantive issues in IR without seeking to bracket theoretical diversity or by sacrificing normative concerns. TSA holds that theory-choice should be determined by specific problems of a given empirical puzzle, not be restricted by a priori assumptions about what constitutes valid knowledge or how the puzzle fits within parameters of an "acceptable" eclectic-theoretical combination.

Theoretical synergy

Theory-synergetic approach is called to realize the inherent meta-disciplinary power of IR and to reveal a deeper ontology of international relations. As such it is a proposed mechanism for systematic application of IR epistemological matrix to complex ontological problems, puzzles and challenges that encompass the widest possible range of global social incidence.

That IR theories are lenses through which to view the reality is a common analogy (Smith, 2014). What TSA does is to translate that analogy into a practical and systematic approach. If the discipline of International Relations is to take seriously its commitment to a deeper (expanded) social ontology, then a common standard for a multi-paradigmatic approach is needed.

That is not to suggest an attempt to impose uniformity or to "discipline the discipline." Rather, TSA is an attempt at a minimal IR epistemological reconciliation. Epistemological relativism implicit in the synergetic approach may suggest that anything goes. Ultimately, however, there are always good reasons for choosing this or that particular lens through which to examine a particular puzzle – what Patomaki and Wight call epistemological opportunism (2000, p. 227).

However, the rationale for judging which theories are most suitable for addressing a given puzzle should be grounded in the ontological priorities of that specific research, rather than grand theory dogmas. And, as will be shown, ontological problem field of international politics of energy allows for a wide range of IR theoretical applications, with each epistemic lens revealing a particular set of questions and issues, which all overlap in a synergetic way upon the same empirical question or puzzle.

Epistemological incommensurability thesis posits that since different theories have different epistemological criteria there is simply no way to compare them. TSA directs attention to the question of ontological overlap between theories. If incommensurability thesis declares that theories clash then there must be something to clash over: "Put simply, if there is no ontological overlap then there is little point in trying to compare theories, or bemoan the fact that we can't" (Patomaki and Wight, 2000, p. 227). Theory synergetic approach is essentially a technique for in depth theoretical analysis of such ontological overlaps.

For example, a neo-realist analysis of oil pipeline politics in the Caspian-Mediterranean region in the period following collapse of the USSR, might focus on the relationship between the Russian Federation and the United States, Turkey and Iran, and/or the implications of additional volumes of hydrocarbons on the balance of power in the region and beyond.

Green Theory, by contrast, would seek to establish the additional amount of CO_2 that would be produced when that additional volume of hydrocarbons is burnt, its implications for global warming and the politics which prioritize fossil fuels over renewable energy. Critical theory would seek to expose the interests driving the building of particular pipelines (and not others) and how these serve hegemonic tendencies, and so on.

All levels of theoretical applications would have something valid and useful to reveal about the ontological problem at hand – international politics of energy. The picture that emerges at the end is far richer, textured, detailed and complete than if this given ontology was subjected to a single grand theoretical level of analysis. But the real value of TSA is the *synergy* that emerges through such intensive multi-paradigmatic application. This theoretical synergy pivots upon ontological overlaps.

It is immediately clear, for example, that all theories when applied to international politics of energy will address to greater or lesser extent the issue of environment. But the angle at which the problem will be viewed will depend on the paradigmatic properties of a given theory. The coloring of the lens will determine what aspect of reality is revealed. It is in the way different lenses interact and interplay with each other within a single research framework − theoretical synergy as a kaleidoscope made up of multi-colored lenses − that makes TSA what it is.

Politics of oil (and gas)

Politics of oil and gas provide for a particularly dynamic empirical field upon which TSA might be applied (see chapter III). The emergence of petroleum as a key strategic resource in the aftermath of World War I overlapped with the timeline of the first Great Debate between Idealists and Realists.

Prominence accorded by Realists to oil as a strategic factor in world politics is not accidental. Realists pointed to the value of oil in its material impact on relative and absolute power of states and as subject of international competition. As Wheeler and Whited put it in their seminal account of the oil industry: "The name of the game is power − power to mobilize transportation, industry, and mechanical hardware; power to heat and cool; power to influence foreign affairs and domestic policies; power to conduct the most expensive and uncertain gamble on earth; and power to win or lose world conflicts" (1971, p.1).

Possession and control of natural resources generally and oil specifically are thus a central component of national power (Morgenthau, 1985, pp.131-135; Waltz, 1979, p.131). Hence the relative value of oil - its implications for power politics. E.H. Carr identified economic strength as instrument of political power through its relationship with military strength (Carr, 2002 (1981; 1939), p. 105).

Pursuit of economic self-sufficiency or autarchy, especially in raw materials, is the first measure by which states utilize economic power in the service of national policy (Ibid. p.110). Carr viewed economic independence as. "...primarily a form of preparedness for war" (Ibid, P.111). Morgenthau is even more emphatic about "the power of oil" (1985, p.133). He too recognized the historical relationship between raw materials, economic power and military strength (ibid, p.131).

These brief observations serve to underline how theoretical debates do not take place in a vacuum and have always been informed and structured by substantive issues and real-world concerns, and contemporary questions in international affairs. Moving from realism onwards through Great Debates, IR theoretical matrix offers a unique prism through which to analyse evolution in international energy politics.

The latter in turn provides for a particularly advantageous empirical problem-field for studying how different IR theories tackle real-life puzzles, from inter-state war to global climate change. As such it is precisely the type of ontological overlap referred to by Patomaki and Wight, over which theories clash and may be compared (2002, p. 227). TSA, however, goes further in arguing that they can be synergized. Specific case-studies of Baku-Tbilisi-Ceyhan (BTC) oil pipeline and the Southern Gas Corridor (SGC) pipeline project, will be used to demonstrate how this can be done in practice and to operationalize the workings and mechanisms of theory-synergetic approach.

BTC is an international commercial oil pipeline, operated by BP, spanning three countries, from the Caspian Sea to the Mediterranean coast and has been in operation since 2005 (BP Operations and Projects 1, 2017). The Southern Gas Corridor is a proposed EU-backed, multilateral international energy project, comprising a series of natural gas pipelines, running from Azerbaijan to Italy (BP Operations and Projects 2, 2017; European Commission 1, 2017).

The advantage of using synergetic, as opposed to single-paradigm or eclectic approaches, is that it unlocks a deeper ontological realm of any given problem field. Applying TSA to study international projects, such as BTC and SCG pipelines will necessitate understanding of the underlying material and ideational factors, social forces and historical processes that constitute those projects and determine their real location in the deeper ontological realm of energy politics.

There are no *a priori* limitations or brackets on what constitutes that realm – the wider the epistemically-defined scope of applied theoretical synergy on a given problem, the more can be revealed about its material constitution, normative claims and debates surrounding it, historical contingencies and conditions that gave rise to it, in other words - its place in the "world out there." Ontology, therefore, precedes epistemology - theory-synergetic approach begins with a recognition that the first purpose of IR here is to study politics of oil and gas by all means available; the choice of the means being determined by empirical concerns alone.

Synthesis vs synergy

There are, of course, other multi-theoretical pluralistic approaches, briefly discussed in the previous chapter, that are animated by the same sense of ontological focus, the drive to produce practically-relevant knowledge and by the same commitment to epistemological flexibility as TSA.

At this stage. it is worth examining these analytical frameworks, not least because TSA proceeds from the same starting positions as synthesis and eclectic approaches in identifying the need for pluralist theoretical engagement as the necessary direction for IR to pursue in the aftermath of the Fourth Debate. There is agreement that complexity of modern international phenomena precludes mono-causal explanations and requires more comprehensive elucidation, even at the cost of diminished theoretical parsimony (Moravcsik, 2003, p.131).

However, there are fundamental problems with synthesis and eclectic approaches which raise doubts over their potential to fulfil the task of building multi-theoretical IR. First, as previously stated, synergy is not synthesis. It is highly debateable that a truly cross-paradigmatic theoretical synthesis in IR is possible at all, whatever its proponents might claim. It is true that for them incommensurability is not considered an obstacle because, as Moravcsik argues: "... the elements of a synthesis, though necessarily coherent at some fundamental level, need not share a full range of basic ontological assumptions. Although the overarching assumptions embedded in a given model must be minimally coherent and justify the relative position of the elements within a multi-theoretical synthesis, there is no need for each sub-theory of the synthesis to make identical assumptions about fundamental ontological matters" (Ibid., p. 132).

For Moravcsik IR theoretical synthesis can and should be theoretically diverse – its only test comes from the necessity for proposed syntheses to be empirically established. Epistemological status of any given synthesis is thus no different to that of its component individual theories: "in both cases, our confidence is a function of plausibly objective empirical support" (Ibid). However, methodological problems associated with testing of complex theoretical syntheses are likely to be considerably more significant than those of a single theory. Moravcsik proposes to overcome or rather bypass this hurdle by disaggregating or breaking down elements of the synthesis and testing those separately using specific methods (Ibid, p.133).

The main reason Moravcsik believes this is possible and that theoretical synthesis is easier than one might think is because he proceeds under a particular conception of synthesis: "Most syntheses comprise a set of discrete theories, linked by a set of overarching assumptions." (Ibid, p.132). However, in reality genuine synthesis means that component elements are subsumed by a synthetic new entity and cease to function as independent variables. Their material or abstract integrity is deconstructed and then reconstructed as part of a new whole.

Therefore, disaggregating component elements of theoretical synthesis and empirically testing each one and the assumptions underpinning them separately will not tell us anything about how they operate within synthetic theoretical model. Since they do not function as distinct entities within a synthesis their foundational properties and underpinning epistemological and ontological assumptions would by definition have been subsumed and incorporated into a new unified theoretical model. They would have effects within the synthesis but not of the causal kind that can be discerned through disaggregation – to be a genuine IR theoretical synthesis its causal claim must have intellectual integrity independent of its constituent parts.

Moravcsik, by contrast sees synthesis as characterized by a set of overarching assumptions; his argument proceeds from there and his choice of examples to illustrate workable synthesis models is telling: "The overarching assumptions take various forms, each embedding subtly different formal and substantive assumptions: multivariate regression equations, game theoretical models, explicit models of interactions, decision trees, lexicographical orderings, narrative accounts, multistage sequences..." (Ibid). But is it really that simple?

We know that theoretical synthesis is possible in IR but only when its component elements are founded on common ontological and epistemological assumptions. Common subject matter is not sufficient to provide a basis for a credible synthesis. For example, a neo-realist, a Marxist, a social constructivist and a feminist might all study armed conflicts in the South Caucasus but the conflicts they will see will differ markedly given different foundational claims underpinning their respective paradigms. Proponents of the synthesis approach have not yet provided a compelling illustration of how this degree of incommensurability might be overcome on substantive level.

Setting the above aside and, for the sake of the argument, accepting disaggregation as a way around the problem of theoretical incommensurability would still not provide a workable synthesis model, because "different methods of theory testing are predicated on different epistemological assumptions..." (Sil and Katzenstein, 2010, p.17). Without a common and agreed unity of method the standards by which component theories would be empirically tested will be internal only to those theories and not the synthetic whole. While a degree of synthesis may well be possible between theoretical positions which share common epistemologies, any wider inter-paradigmatic synthesis is not therefore a credible model for IR theoretical pluralism.

Analytic eclecticism vs synergetic analysis

Turning now to analytic eclecticism it is important to first acknowledge that TSA shares some of its concerns with prioritization of real-life problems and its eschewal of excessive simplifications, often employed to fit within paradigmatic boundaries – what Sil and Katzenstein call the "no extrageneous factors" rule (2010, p.10). They set out their eclectic theoretical model as a means to explore "how diverse mechanisms posited in competing paradigm-bound theories might interact with each other, and how, under certain conditions, they can combine to affect outcomes" (Ibid).

Yet there again is the spectre of incommensurability and Sil and Katzenstein do acknowledge difficulties it poses, especially when it comes to the old problem of establishing objective criteria for evaluating theoretical claims drawn from different paradigms (Ibid., p.15). However, unlike the disaggregation approach offered by proponents of theoretical synthesis, analytic eclecticism posits the way out of incommensurability problem based expressly upon its substantive focus.

Analytic eclecticism prioritizes ontology over epistemology and therefore questions of theory-selection and testing are to be determined and operationalized by empirical referents, embedded within specific substantive matters and concepts. Analytic eclecticism overcomes the incommensurability thesis not through abstract theoretical evaluations but through systematic empirical analysis of research-specific substantive indicators: "It is possible to ensure that concepts and analytic principles are properly understood in their original conceptual frameworks, and to adjust or translate these terms by considering how they are operationalized in the relevant empirical contexts by proponents of various paradigms" (Ibid).

Sil and Katzenstein go to great length to stress that analytic eclecticism is not a metatheoretical approach and nor is it an attempt "to hedge the bets to cope with uncertainty" (Ibid., p.16). They are explicit in their insistence that it is not theoretical synthesis and that does not imply that "anything goes." What marks eclectic scholarship out are a set of key features (Ibid, p. 19):

- open-needed, non-paradigm-bound problem formulation;
- middle range causal accounts of international political phenomena drawn from more than one paradigm;
- research outcomes which pragmatically engage both academic and practical dimensions and address the needs of policy makers and practioners.

This combinational approach employing middle range theories is "specifically constructed to shed light on specific sets of empirical phenomena" but is not a juxtaposition or substitution for paradigm-based research (Ibid., p22-23). Analytic eclecticism is concerned with pragmatic engagement with social reality with the aim of identifying those knowledge clusters "that can enrich policy debates and normative discussions beyond the academe" (Ibid.): "Even when it is not offering explicit policy prescriptions, eclectic scholarship should have some clear implications for some set of policy debates or salient normative concerns that enmesh leaders, public intellectuals, and other actors in a given political setting" (Ibid).

A consistent commitment to production of practically-useful knowledge is informed in part by a sense that historic privileging of grand contests over epistemology has made IR less relevant to the world of practioners. As Ferguson and Mansbach argue contemporary IR should seek to use its pluralist theoretical framework in a "practical fashion" to address issues of importance in world politics. Analytic eclecticism certainly responds to their call to enhance the use of traditional paradigmatic perspectives in order "to bring more than one of them to bear on particular problems—different theories illuminate different aspects of 'reality'" (2014).

Yet this systematic commitment to practical scholarship is not without problems of its own. Sil and Katzenstein briefly acknowledge the risk of loss of critical thinking "in relation to existing policy agendas" (2010, p.13). They also refer to Anne Norton's paper "Political Science as a Vocation" warning, as she does, that "problem-orientated scholarship can end up enlisting scholars in the unreflective service of those exercising power" (2004, p.68). But they quickly move on to warn of the danger of over-preoccupation with purely academic debates "that are hermetically blocked off from public discourse and policy debates about important issues of interest to both scholars and practioners" (2010, p.13).

Yet, perhaps, it would have been useful to pay more attention to Norton's warnings about the ethical implications of the relationship between knowledge and power. All science is a priori political and is conducted in languages which both constitute and reflect "contemporary preferences, prejudices, norms, standards, and assumptions" (2004, p. 74): "Science comprises institutions and discourses. We have studied institutions. We have learned that institutions call identities and interests into being. The presence of funding for particular projects, the absence of funding for others, will ensure that in some (if not in many) cases, individuals will undertake research projects not because they think these are the most important, but because these are the projects that can be accomplished, or even because these are the projects that bring the greatest rewards. The power of the state is evident here but that of private funding is no less to be deprecated" (Ibid., p.73).

The above is not a mere abstract warning. For example, Joseph Nye's article "Scholars on the Sidelines" in *The Washington Post* (13.04.2009) is often cited (including by Sil and Katzenstein (2010, p.1)) to argue in favor of academics and researchers becoming directly involved in the world political practice. But that is the world of power and politicians, some of whom are tyrants. Joseph Nye's own experience with the now defeated regime of Colonel Gaddafi of Libya should serve as a cautionary tale (Silverstein, 2014, p.9).

As Norton argues problem-orientated scholarship "is bad for politics and bad for science:" "It encourages arrogance; persuading the young and the uneducated (and occasionally the old and the erudite) that they can solve problems beyond their reach; that they can answer questions they do not fully understand... Quick conclusions are encouraged; study, consideration, refection, and debate are not. Science is not advanced in this economy. Politics is harmed by it" (2004, p.73).

It is not necessary to subscribe to Norton's view in its entirety. But it is important to acknowledge that practical, real-world problem-orientated scholarship must be rooted in a reflective and critical understanding of world politics. It is essential to spell out what is meant by useful knowledge and this is where the problem with Sil and Katzenstein's approach stems from.

Theirs is an unapologetically an empirical enterprise and its theoretical focus is circumscribed by clearly delineated material categories – structural factors, causal mechanisms, various social processes. These are drawn from existing mainstream paradigmatic traditions in IR. As

Reus-Smit contends, this makes analytic eclecticism "epistemologically an empirical-theoretical project" (2013, p. 591). Normative reflection is absent from it with IR remaining an explanatory enterprise, interested in only empirical problems.

And there is a reason for this. Sil and Katzenstein self-consciously seek to bracket metatheory and prioritize ontology by locating analytical eclecticism in the wider framework of the pragmatic turn in American social science. Geographic location matters because Sil and Katzenstein refer to the TRIP surveys (Maliniak et al, 2007; Jordan et al, 2009) to argue that paradigmatic research continues to dominate the discipline (2010, p. 24). They then point out that almost two thirds of all IR scholarship comes from the triad of realism, liberalism and constructivism (Jordan et al, 2009, p. 18).

And it is on that basis that Sil and Katzenstein proceed to locate their eclectic vision of international relations scholarship in the context of realist/liberal/constructivist matrix – the Triad. They do concede that "other paradigms have acquired significance, at times for long periods, in various countries" (2010, p. 25). However, they refer to TRIP studies to indicate that the Triad remains the most viable contender for paradigmatic dominance in IR and argue that "it is in the context of debates between realists, liberals and constructivists that we find it most useful to elaborate on the significance of analytical eclecticism for the study of world politics" (Ibid). The reason they find it "most useful" is because "these are the most prevalent approaches in the United States and worldwide" (Ibid, p.36).

Limiting the approach to a three-dimensional paradigmatic framework provides both its distinct ontology and the epistemological foundation of analytical eclecticism. The examples of eclectic scholarship Sil and Katzenstein presented in *Beyond Paradigms* (2010) are chosen specifically to highlight convergences and overlaps within the Realist/Liberal/Constructivist paradigms (which could be tagged as Neo-Neo-Con). Interestingly, constructivism here appears as consequentially logical addition to a dominant paradigmatic pairing – its addition is useful, almost utilitarian, adding value to analytical eclecticism, which Sil and Katzenstein explicitly posit as a practical empirical-theoretical approach, aimed at providing useful knowledge for policy-makers. One is tempted to recall Walt's prescription from two decades ago: "The 'complete diplomat' of the future should remain cognizant of realism's emphasis on the inescapable role of power, keep liberalism's awareness of domestic forces in mind, and occasionally reflect on constructivism's vision of change" (1998, p.35).

Furthermore, as Reus-Smit argues, bracketing metatheory "does not free one's work of metatheoretical constraints" (2013, p. 605). In Sil and Katzenstein's analytical eclecticism these constraints are structured by "a grund epistemological assumption that admits only empirical-theoretic forms of inquiry and knowledge" (Ibid). He examines the concept of practical knowledge from Aristotelian and Kantian perspectives, and revisits E.H.Carr's supposed ultra-realism, concluding that for all these thinkers, "practical knowledge is the kind of knowledge that can address questions of how I, we, or they should act" (Ibid, p.602). Such knowledge requires "the integration of empirical and normative insights, yet the latter are epistemologically outside the scope of analytical eclecticism" (Ibid., pp. 605-606).

Even without committing to production of practical knowledge it is clear that these criticisms are valid - for all its pluralist claims analytic eclecticism remains bound by restrictive ontological and epistemological constraints. To demonstrate how theory-synergetic approach can overcome these problems it is first necessary to explain fundamental philosophical differences between the two approaches. Unlike eclecticism, which is founded in the pragmatist tradition, TSA is rooted in critical realist philosophy of science.

Critical Realism and TSA

The rationale for placing theory-synergetic approach within the realist PoS springs from a starting foundational proposition, a thesis that holds that in the course of the Fourth Debate an ontological realm has been revealed and established, comprising an international reality – a global political subject matter, consisting of both material and ideational properties and qualities. This ontological realm is specific and particular to the discipline of IR and is not studied by other, older social sciences - IR has found the world of its own (Epstein, 2013, p.500).

Moreover, this international realm comprises *deep ontology* of IR – a complex reality consisting of multiple layers and dimensions. It exists as a historical fact and process in its material and ideational condition, regardless of whether it is observed or spoken of. In fact, its existence is a condition of possibility of it being observed or spoken about – it is a mind-independent reality.

For example, as Wendt argued, in mainstream and critical IR scholarship states and states systems are treated as real structures and are referred to even if they are physically unobservable (1999, p.47). As such, theory-synergetic method is designed and called for to provide a model for studying and revealing the deep ontology of IR, one puzzle and one layer at a time.

Yet to take this stance requires accepting a proposition that international realm exists independently and that it comprises a real, although often unobservable structure that can be revealed through science, in this case IR. Ontology precedes epistemology. Although Wendt argues that "most IR scholars are at least tacit realists" (Ibid), these claims need to be further justified, as they are highly contested and disputed, both in PoS and in IR.

For example, the correspondence theory of truth that underpins critical realism may be viewed as simply inference to best explanation – the idea that that something that has been proven to be true must have always been true because it has now been proven true – and, therefore, lacks solid logical foundation (Monteiro and Ruby, 2009, p. 33-35).

Can ontology really be defined simultaneously as both a fallible interpretation of reality and as a definitive definition of a reality beyond our knowledge-claims? Critical realism is charged with confusing and conflating these meanings in attempt to justify the claim that critical realist ontology ought to supply the terms of reference for the scientific project (Cruickshank, 2004).

Instead, critics argue, ontological theories in social sciences ought to be revised and replaced in the course of an on-going critical dialogue about reality (material and ideational) and should be defined in terms of fallible, empirically-testable interpretations of social reality (Ibid, p. 582). Social reality is just too complex to be assessed within one fixed ontology supplying universal terms of reference for the sciences. In fact, reality is such that "it is not possible to describe and explain it theoretically using the forms in which it immediately appears to us, without irresolvable problems and contradictions arising" (Magill, 1994, p. 131).

That means even if one acknowledges applicability of ideational, unobservable, illusionary concepts, it is not necessary to accept any overarching philosophical ontology in social science to apply them in research (Ibid, p.121). Critical realism is just too vague and general to provide any real guidance or clear implications for resolving specific ontological problems with social sciences, such as IR (Ibid). This echoes Monteiro and Ruby's call for foundational prudence and abandonment of ontological philosophies (2009, p.35).

The problem with these criticisms is that in challenging Critical Realism they offer no clear alternative criteria by which ontological claims could be evaluated and no roadmaps of their own for resolving foundational problems in the social sciences, save for a call for renewed empirical focus. Some critics drew on a contrast with ontological arguments in the natural sciences to claim that critical realist concept of deep ontology lacks legitimacy.

In the natural sciences, ontological claims can be given some justification, but only when they are derived from research that is widely held to be empirically successful, whereas realist ontological claims in the social sciences do not have this basis and alternative critical realist mode of justification for these claims is simply unconvincing (Kemp, 2005).

However, arguing that social scientific research should be conducted without philosophical legislation takes us back to narrow empiricist ontologies which posit that the fundamental characteristics of the social realm can only be established *ex post facto* to the production of empirically successful research in that realm. That, in turn takes us back to unresolved debates in IR. Drawing analogies with the natural sciences to borrow their ontological standards poses no special problems for materialists who hold there are no fundamental differences between natural and social realities but would not be acceptable for post-structuralists or social-constructivists (Wendt, 1999, p.49).

TSA's justification in seeking an epistemologically relativist, ontologically-centered foundational rooting is in seeking to resolve these problems and contradictions. Nevertheless, reliance on critical scientific analytical concepts, such as deep ontology, mind-independent reality, the no-miracles argument, requires further elaboration and validation.

Critical realism holds that both positivist and anti-positivist philosophical approaches are inherently anti-realist. Empiricists are agnostic about "the world out there" that exists independently of scholars studying it, but posit that it can only be made *real* though observation and experience. Anti-positivists are categorical in denying the existence of "the world out there," claiming that reality is socio-linguistically constructed. Thus positivists embrace anti-realism in their attempt to purge science of any traces of subjectivity, while anti-positivists become anti-realist through their emphasis on human agency in the process of creating or constructing reality (Wendt, 1999, p.47).

It is a common metaphysical structure – "anthropocentric reality" – a shared belief that reality can be real only if it is experienced (positivists) or spoken (anti-positivists) (Patomaki and Wight, 2000, p.216-217). Yet to exist must surely mean more than to be "experienced" or "spoken:" there must be a reality that gives rise to that experience and language in the first place - "A world prior to the emergence of humanity is a condition of possibility for that emergence" (Ibid.).

The workings and techniques of TSA are explored in this book using the case-study of international oil and gas pipelines. Yet the grund-ontology – the deep reality – of this case-study is neither "international politics," nor "energy," nor "production and transmission," but hydrocarbons.

Oil and gas are hydrogen combined with carbon (hydrocarbons), deposited underground in liquid and vapour forms respectively. Hydrocarbon deposits are the buried remnants of ancient algae, plankton and vegetation – they have a biogenic historical origin. Through various industrial processes, such as blending, distillation and refining, hydrocarbons can be transformed into a multitude of products for a whole range of uses, generation of power emerging as the most important since in the course of the twentieth century.

Before hydrocarbons can be burnt in internal combustion engines of our world they must be extracted and transported from the few locations on the planet where they are found. The geography of oil and its chemistry, the engineering and industrial processes that go into production of energy are all deeply ingrained and enmeshed in the social, economic, cultural and political fabric of the hydrocarbon reality of modern human civilisation.

And yet oil has a much longer human history, having been used by generations since deep antiquity, for a variety of purposes, from medicine to illumination, from lubrication to religious ceremonies. Most significantly, however, it predates the emergence of humanity and is of itself a state of metamorphosis of biological matter – an ongoing historical process. The few thousand years of human experience and discourse of oil are but a blip in the timeline of many millions of years. Oil, therefore, exists in a "world out there" – a mind-independent reality, which shapes the deep ontology of this TSA case-study.

Thus, for example, Zoroastrian fire worshippers on the western coast of the Caspian Sea around 600BC had no conception of the origins and the chemical composition of the gases that fed the naturally occurring flames at their temples, or the complex geology that created the seemingly eternal fires breaking out of rocks. The social construction of oil began before its scientific discovery and empirical observation. But the prior existence of oil constitutes a condition of possibility for both.

And the discovery of oil involved no miracles. Scientific advances over the course of centuries have revealed chemical composition of hydrocarbons and technologies were developed to apply oil and gas to multiple uses. The latter process itself was incremental. In the early stages of industrialisation oil was used almost exclusively for illumination because technology available for refining at the time allowed for creation of only one product – kerosene. As science progressed technologies were developed creating thousands of uses for oil products (Montgomery, 2010, pp.14-29).

Perhaps, the "no miracles" argument for the success of science is not necessarily "better off" argument. Science can be used for good and ill and technologies can have positive and negative consequences. The "no miracles" claim "is merely that because of science we can manipulate the environment in ways we could not before, even when we wanted to. By that limited criterion scientific knowledge is progressive" (Wendt. 1999, p.64). As Wendt argues the "no miracles" claim shows how science has been successful by gradually bringing our theoretical understanding of the world "into conformity with the deep structure of the world out there" (Ibid., p.64-65).

The brief discussion above illuminates the fallacy, even arrogance, of anthropocentric philosophical approaches and anti-philosophical critiques of realism. Hydrocarbons do not stop "being" if not measured or made subject of a discourse. Their existence is not conditional upon human agency and given that humans are themselves a carbon-based life form, a degree of humility would not be out of place. Critical realism is informed by this sense of humility on the wider scale of scientific endeavor. It holds there are no miracles in the process of knowledge discovery and is premised upon the argument that "the world is real and science is dependent upon the making of existential hypothesis" (Patomaki and Wight, 2000, p.218).

There is, therefore, complexity to the critical realist conception of the world – it is not limited to discourses, impressions, experiences and so on, but is also of deeper underlying structures; there are different levels of reality, with the latter making the former possible. This is what is meant by deep ontology and the reason why critical realism is sometimes referred to as Depth Realism. Critical realism therefore is an ontological enterprise – a perpetual scientific enquiry: "Science is seen to proceed through a constant spiral of discovery and understanding, further discovery and revision, and hopefully ore adequate understanding" (Ibid, p.224).

But there is also an implicit recognition that knowledge is not arbitrary – it is a social product which is dependent on antecedent social products and comes into being in non-spontaneous manner (Bhaskar, 2007, p.18). Not only different disciplines but different theories within a discipline can interpret the same ontological reality in radically different ways. This means that there are grounds for choosing one approach over another and justifiable reasons for preferring one theory to another (Patomaki and Wight, 2000, p.224).

Theory-synergetic method pivots on the idea that Critical Realism, with its commitment to perpetual scientific enquiry, ontological foundationalism, epistemological relativism, and "judgemental rationalism" (grounds for choosing between theories (Ibid)), can be applied to the social world. And that is a major challenge - can "social kinds" exist independently of human mind? And can the "no miracles" argument really be applied in the case of social science, such as International Relations, where there is less compelling evidence of scientific success (Wendt, 1999, p.67-68)?

Roy Bhaskar had set out three key differences between social and natural kinds ((1979) 1998), p. 42). Firstly, the existence of social structures is dependent on the activities that govern them. That is to say the social kinds are more space-time specific than natural kinds. Oil has been found at various times in various locations – it is a general natural phenomenon. Meanwhile the eighteenth century Scottish Enlightenment is defined and constituted by its spatial and temporal context.

Secondly, the existence of social kinds is dependent on the conceptions, beliefs and theories held by actors or agents participating in the activities that make-up the social structures. For example, the emergence in the late nineteenth/early twentieth century of a particular category of the oil trader created a certain set of shared ideas about that category, which are not reducible to the actual act of trading oil. Before the emergence of these shared ideas the category did not exist.

Thirdly, social kinds are ultimately dependent on human practices and "may be only relatively enduring" (Bhaskar, 1998, p. 42). As Wendt argues, social kinds, are "a function of belief and action" (1999, p.71). Again, this raises question whether social kinds can be independent of the human agency and discourse.

Critical realists have responded to these problems with various counterarguments. For starters, the social world may well depend on the concepts agents acting within it possess, "but it cannot be the case that any given social phenomenon requires the existence of a social scientist to conceptualise it before it comes into being" (Patomaki and Wight, 2000, p.225).

Critical realism envisages a deep ontology of the social world that cannot be reduced to the simple fact of its experience or to its intersubjective elements. The sense that when it comes to social kinds intersubjective meanings have causal power may well obscure their deeper, previously hidden, essential relations.

Furthermore, the role of material forces in forming and shaping the social kinds cannot be overstated. Ultimately human beings are natural kinds of themselves. As Wendt puts it: "In the last analysis a theory of social kinds must refer to natural kinds, including human bodies and their physical behaviour, which are amenable to a causal theory of reference. Constructivism without nature goes too far" (1999, p.72). But for Wendt excessive materialism is unhelpful and he brings forward a further argument – the self-organization hypothesis. This is a claim that the social world is self-organising in the same way as the natural world.

For example, the human descriptions of animals in no way make the animals what they are. The self-organising quality of natural kinds determines our understandings and theories about them. Similarly, social kinds of various types can also be self-organising. For example, Wendt focuses on the distinction between the empirical and the juridical sovereignty of states to argue that when it comes to states as self-organising social kinds, the "process of boundary-drawing receives much of its impetus from forces 'inside' the space around which the boundary will be drawn" (Ibid, p.74).

It is not simply a question of whether social kinds can be self-organising, or whether they are underpinned by material foundations greater than the force of intersubjective meanings attached and brought to life by them. Neither is it enough to simply emphasize the role of material forces in constituting and forming social kinds. Critical realism as applied through theory-synergetic approach seeks to demonstrate that natural and social kinds can exist in a mutually referential relationship, as one and the same, simultaneously.

The example here is again oil. Crude oil is a most natural kind – unrefined hydrocarbon straight from the pressure cooker of Nature where it has accumulated over millions of years. A barrel of oil contains 159 litres of crude. It is extracted in one place, sold in another and then physically transported to a power plant elsewhere to be burnt to produce electricity. Or it might be transported to a refinery where it can be turned into petroleum for cars, diesel or jet fuel. The various by-products of refining can then be utilized to produce anything from plastics to Vaseline. While all these production and transportation processes, and arguably their outcomes, are social endeavors and structures their relation to oil (the natural kind) is ultimately determined and limited by material factors – its molecular structure that allows for an X number of uses and transformations.

But a barrel of oil can also exist as a product of agents' imagination and nothing else. A paper barrel exists in the virtual international realm of futures commodities trading even when the physical barrel does not. It can be bought and sold but will never change hands. It is not a source of energy or anything material at all but an investment opportunity for a hedge fund or a local government authority somewhere in the world.

Futures markets emerged in nineteenth century America primarily for agricultural products – a way for farmers to manage long-term risks of expanding production. Basic human needs give rise to complex social structures. The role of oil futures markets, such as NYMEX (New York Mercantile Exchange, formerly Butter, Cheese and Egg Exchange), is discussed in chapter VII. Here it suffices to say that what first emerged as a risk management tool for people who used and those who produced oil – "hedgers" – has now become something else entirely.

It is a social structure of its own kind, where traders – "speculators" – who have no interest in taking delivery of the physical commodity, operate with a single purpose of making profit by anticipating and acting on constant changes in price. These "speculators" could be institutional investors representing, perhaps, a major European pension fund or independent traders in South East Asia in search of greater returns on their personal wealth funds. Most of them have never seen crude oil in their lives. Millions of paper barrels can be sold and bought around the world without being extracted, delivered, burnt into energy or refined into other products. It does not mean they do not exist.

A barrel of crude and a paper barrel of oil, a natural kind and a social kind, exist as one and the same but separately and simultaneously. The former has no causal relationship with the latter; the latter is underpinned by materialist assumptions but is entirely self-organising, possessing social qualities and properties which add specific value distinct and different from the former. It is possible, for example, to do with paper barrels what is physically impossible to do with actual crude oil barrels e.g. buy them two years in the future while someone else hedges their retirement pension to your purchase, in the future, and all of that takes place virtually on a computer screen.

This suggests that trans-historical claims can be made about social kinds. While the Scottish Enlightenment is specific to its temporal/spatial context, insofar as enlightenment refers to a broader social kind of outpouring of intellectual and cultural achievements, it is not limited by time and place. Similarly, futures trading in eggs in nineteenth century United States is space/time specific, while general futures trading in commodities, be these paper barrels of oil or other goods, are trans-historical phenomena and are not defined or limited by the spatial/temporal context in which these activities take place.

Furthermore, as argued above, the emergence and existence of social kinds may be dependent on interlocking concepts, beliefs and theories held by agents as well as the human practices that carry them from location to location over time. A critical realist account of the world, however, identifies a deeper multi-layered ecological, biological and social reality and a more causally interactive relationship between social and natural kinds.

A paper barrel – a social kind – may come into existence as a product of human imagination and agency, rooted in the material assumptions associated with the value of a natural kind (crude oil). However, once it is operational it acquires self-organising quality and real-life value of its own, independent of the intersubjective meanings attached to it by actors. And what can be said about mind-independent quality of social kinds when we consider that such activities as emissions trading in pollution or commodity futures trading in oil often take place virtually with almost no input from humans – complex risk assessment and price adjustment operations are carried out by computers, acting on advanced algorithms.

Importantly these social kind/natural kind transactions and interactions have profound real-life economic, political and social impacts. For example, international financialisation of oil has been one of the driving factors in the rise of global oil prices from mid 2000s onwards. The rise in the price of oil and other commodity prices in turn led to new political dynamics in relations between energy producing and consuming states, and so on. Implicit and explicit historicism of critical realism unlocks analytical mechanisms for identification of trans-historical characteristics of international political phenomena.

If, for example, we take systemic theories of IR such as structural realism and ask whether its insights can be generalized through time and space, a philosophical answer would be yes, "provided the essential features of the relevant kinds are preserved" (Wendt, 1999, p.70). States interacting under conditions of anarchy are the relevant kinds in this case and while the cultural characteristics of "states" and "anarchy" are variable ("anarchy is what states make of it" (Ibid)), the formative defining characteristics that make them "social kinds" are not historically variable: "The culture of international politics in ancient Greece may have been different than the culture of international politics today, but this does not mean there are no commonalities between the two worlds which distinguish them jointly from bowling leagues" (Ibid).

Theory synergetic approach seeks to adapt critical realist historicism with the aim of identifying these trans-historical commonalities within given pieces of research. This is possible to achieve without dismissing the complexity of culturally-contingent social phenomena. For example, strategic value of oil retains its essential features as a trans-historical relevant social kind regardless of the time-specific analytical framework, e.g. World War I and the Russian Civil War, or Germany's Caucasus Campaign in World War II.

It follows, therefore, that trans-historical claims can be made about, for example, pipeline politics as all pipeline projects share certain trans-historical commonalities. This trans-historical-interplay between natural and social elements constitutes, defines and influences the multi-layered reality revealed by critical realist analysis – the multiplicity of global political, economic, social, cultural, demographic and other aspects of human condition.

These can be studied separately within particular disciplinary sub-fields of social science designed to tackle particular sets of questions – economics, (international) finance, (international) law, political theory, demography, anthropology, history, sociology, strategic studies and so on. However, IR comes with a disciplinary superstructure that possesses the necessary intellectual toolkit (from theoretical diversity to methodological pluralism) that could allow for a holistic analysis of complex global phenomena, one that is multi-layered and is made up of the dynamic interplay between natural and social realities of human condition and experience.

Through application of critical realist reasoning theory-synergetic approach is capable of demonstrating complex trans-historical dynamics between the material and the ideational in international relations. Critical realism is a sound philosophical grounding for TSA, an ontology-centered, epistemologically-relativist theoretical IR approach.

Operationalising theoretical synergy

In summary, theory-synergetic approach is primarily an ontological enterprise that envisages international realm to be a real entity, comprising material and ideational structures and processes, and the discipline of IR is the science dedicated to studying it. TSA is an epistemologically-relativist multi-theoretical method of enquiry that rests on a hypothesis that IR paradigms are analytical tools that shed light on specific aspects of international political phenomena and that applying them systematically in a synergetic fashion can considerably enhance and amplify holistic understanding of a given empirical problem (Table 3 sets out broad outlines of TSA).

Table 3. Theory Synergetic Approach and International Relations

- TSA holds that there is a deeper ontology of IR and that it exists "out there," independently of the scholars who study it;
- TSA is epistemologically and methodologically relativist and committed to the widest possible multi-theoretical enterprise;
- TSA is judgementally rationalist, holding to the view that theory selection should be determined in terms of ontological relevance in a given empirical problem and not upon *a priori* theoretical bracketing;
- TSA seeks to reveal a deeper social reality and answer important substantive questions about international politics by generating theoretical synergy through a systematic application of IR multi-theoretical matrix to substantive empirical puzzles.

To avoid the disaggregation problem identified with the synthesis multi-theoretical model, it is proposed instead to use the principle of paradigmatic dynamism. Broadly, it could mean an idea that scholars should internalize disciplinary-theoretical discourse as an integral language of IR, permeating all aspects of research.

Multi-theoretical matrix of IR should be viewed as a kind of a periodic table, with each theory representing elements with corresponding epistemic and ontological properties and methodological characteristics, capable of producing specific types of knowledge about the international realm. Paradigmatic dynamism requires engaging with IR research outputs, regardless of methodology, in the context of a roadmap. Data sets, secondary sources, historical accounts, questionnaires, interviews etc. can all be analysed and assessed in a paradigm-dynamic fashion, even if produced within confines of specific single-paradigm models.

In effect, theoretical matrix of IR is a sieve through which substantive issues can be passed through to produce multidimensional vision of international reality. Each theory, as mentioned, is a potential research tool. There is always more than one way of reading a particular set of results and the real interesting and revealing quality of any piece of research is identifying the ways in which these different dimensions of the same ontological framework interact and clash with each other.

This relates to the second element of the theory synergetic method. Once the logic of paradigmatic dynamism permeates research and is applied to concrete substantive puzzles and problems, the prospect of theoretical modelling arises. The different visions of international reality that emerge can be systematically sorted into specific theoretical models. Over the next chapters this approach is systematically applied to the case-studies of international energy pipelines and politics of oil and gas production, transmission and consumption.

Briefly, it is being argued here that substantive subject matter of the case studies, set in a deeper ontology of global energy politics, can be modelled in accordance to epistemic values associated with various paradigmatic traditions of IR theoretical matrix. For example, a classical realist model of energy politics might center on the role of great powers, drawing on the historical ebb and flow of strategic interests; a Marxist one might examine the dynamics of oil politics through analysis of class interests; a neo-realist model might in turn focus on how variables such as production and transmission of oil impact on distribution of power amongst states under conditions of anarchy; and so on.

The principal idea here is that multi-theoretical analysis of the same ontological problem can produce widely different accounts and that these accounts can be systematically organized into epistemologically integral models. This is not an attempt to merely avoid the incommensurability problem. In fact, much of the incommensurability arises from methodological differences and significant divergence in the data (research outputs) produced by these different methods.

For example, a liberal institutionalist analysis of politics of Caspian oil is likely to focus on the activities of multi-national energy corporations, with emphasis on trade volumes, business geography, technologies, the role of financial institutions and banks, and a plethora of other commercial factors. Meanwhile, a critical model will inevitably seek to expose underlying power relations of Caspian energy politics and identify how the choices informing them came to be configured at specific points in time.

It is unlikely that a synthesis of these two models can be produced in an epistemologically integral format and disaggregation on empirical level negates the very purpose and aims of a multi-theoretical research approach. Instead, theory synergetic method insists on preserving epistemological integrity of individual theoretical models built around the same subject matter, puzzle, or substantive problem.

Theoretical synergy is built through such dynamic interactions between these epistemologically integral theoretical models, overlapping around specific ontological core. This is possible because it quickly becomes apparent that rather than unbridgeable incommensurability ontologically-focused multi-theoretical modelling is in fact characterized by a multitude of conceptual overlaps and thematic commonalities.

These stem from directions of substantive research which cut across paradigmatic divides because their essence is not epistemological. Different theories may be addressing different aspects of international reality but because the substantive problem is the same it is inevitable that these different narratives will produce specific convergences, to greater or lesser extent.

Thus, for example, as will be shown, *all* theoretical models of international politics of oil and gas address the issues of environment and climate change. The diversity of theoretical knowledge addressing this complex issue produces a kaleidoscopic panorama, ranging from neo-liberal preoccupation with environmental transaction costs and resulting regulatory regimes to environmentalist critique of increased CO_2 emissions and the politics leading to them. Such thematic commonalities, conceptual overlaps and various substantive convergences is the stuff that synergies are made of.

They are, however, messy and do not fit neat patterns – instead they cut across paradigmatic lines. Different research sources and pieces of analysis (even, for example, the way quantitative data is created and read) can produce widely different conclusions and may contain elements of more than one paradigmatic analytical framework. The challenge for a theory-synergetic IR scholar, therefore, is to be able to identify thematic commonalities and other convergences by consistently retaining ontological focus while exercising and applying the wealth of the discipline's theoretical knowledge.

Systematic identification of substantive convergences (thematic commonalities and conceptual overlaps) between different theoretical models of the same ontological puzzle or problem is a crucial part of the theory synergetic method. However, the key objective of TSA research is to build a holistic theory-synergetic model of a given subject matter. That requires bringing theoretical synergies into operation within a single analytical framework. There needs to be a format for organising synergetic knowledge in a coherent and credible way.

The active part of theoretical synergy arises when substantive convergences between different theoretical models are identified and operationalized within a holistic narrative – the way they interact in a particular analytical framework and the mechanism by which they do so are referred to in TSA as inter-paradigmatic pivots. These are the pins or shafts upon which the whole analysis rotates.

The task is to establish how different paradigmatic analytic frameworks of the same ontological phenomena interact with each other. Specific points of that interaction within wider areas of theoretical convergence constitute inter-paradigmatic pivots upon which the whole synergetic narrative revolves. The purpose of TSA is that theoretical pluralism is brought to life, activated within a specific substantive problem-field and is animated in an intensive and live-action, continuously expanding body of analysis of that problem-field. The more inter-paradigmatic pivots in a research the richer, more diverse and amplified theoretical synergy will be.

Constructing inter-paradigmatic pivots

The process of engaging paradigmatic dynamism, developing theoretical models, identifying ontological convergences, conceptual overlaps and thematic commonalities between single-paradigm models and constructing inter-paradigmatic pivots to generate synergetic analytical insights is explored systematically over the next chapters using empirical case-studies of BTC and SGC oil and gas pipeline systems. At this stage it is necessary to introduce this process and set it out sequentially to illustrate operations of TSA mechanisms in principle.

Take, for example, a substantive issue - the Southern Gas Corridor project (SGC) (BP Magazine, 12.10.2017). Theory-synergetic approach proceeds by first recognising that the empirical depth of SGC as a subject of investigation cannot be predetermined. One way to proceed is to envisage SGC as a substantive issue or puzzle, set within wider empirical field of oil and gas politics, which in turn is established within the grund-ontology of international politics of energy. That is to say that that while the subject matter is SGC, a project comprised of series of existing and proposed gas pipelines, the ontology of this study is not bracketed by *a priori* assumptions about what constitutes the reality of the project - complex material/ideational structure that might be revealed through synergetic theorizing.

The latter similarly begins with broad assumption that all IR paradigms will reveal something important about some aspects of SGC, even if each theory might be more useful at explaining or exposing certain elements, features, facets and characteristics of the project than others. No *a priori* assumptions are made on theory selection and the logic of paradigmatic dynamism dictates that such judgements should be made after empirical test is applied to theoretical assumptions about SGC. Single-paradigm models of SGC serve as the building blocks of multi-theoretical construction, as well as the basis for judging whether a particular theory is an appropriate analytical tool in a given research.

Rationalist models of SGC focus on the role of states, international financial institutions, multilateral lenders, regulatory bodies and regimes, strategic issues of energy security, cooperation and competition (see chapter IV). Meanwhile, reflectivist models constitute both intellectual and praxeological critique of the project, aiming not only to expose its normative implications but to prevent the project from happening at all (see Chapter V).

A synthesis of rationalist approaches is centered on the strategic and institutional dimensions of the project (see chapter IV). Neo-realist modes of analysis of Southern Gas Corridor might address such issues as EU/Russia energy cooperation/rivalry (Shiriyev, 19.07.2017), EU energy strategy of gas supply diversification and relations with countries-suppliers (Karagöl and Kaya, 2014). Neo-liberal institutionalist model might focus on the role of EU bodies, such as the Commission (Van Aartsen, 2009) and actions of multilateral financial institutions (Gurbanov, 09.03.2017).

Analytic-eclecticism approach builds on the rationalist synthesis by drawing on social constructivist insights to explore how politics of SGC are shaped by competing normative-regulatory frameworks and policy agendas of various participants, state and non-state (Siddi, 2017; Verda, 2016). Meanwhile, critical post-structuralist theories submit SGC to sustained normative and political critique, seeking to expose its negative consequences for the environment (Counter Balance, Platform and Re:Common, 08.03.2016), and to demonstrate how the project contributes to human rights abuses (ARTICLE 19, Banktrack & Others, 12.09.2017).

Reflectivist critique of SGC is coupled with a praxeological element - an international political campaign by counter-hegemonic agents (NGOS, activists, civil society groups) aimed at stopping the SGC project (see chapter V). Critical-poststructuralist alternative to the rationalist consensus around the politics of Southern Gas Corridor involves plethora of activity, from direct action on local grassroots level in countries traversed by SGC pipelines to empirical-normative research, aimed at challenging dominant narratives about SGC (Gotev, 29.03.2017; Stone, 30.11.2017; Bacheva-McGrath, 2015).

Construction of these single-paradigm models of SGC, as set out in the next chapters, requires IR scholar to employ different epistemologies and ontologies of the subject matter, engaging with different theories on their own terms and paying attention to multiplicity of understandings and claims about the project. In essence, this is IR experimentation – the same subject is consistently submitted to the same empirical test but with different variables.

The outcomes will differ and result will illuminate a particular property of the subject matter. It is clear that for all this epistemological diversity, SGC project comprises a common ontological intersection on which different single-paradigm models pivot. All theories will address common themes and issues, e.g. the role of EU and its member-states, and all theories will overlap over concepts such as, for example, environmental and social impacts of the pipelines (see chapter VI).

Constructing synergetic inter-paradigmatic pivots means more than simply extricating theoretical concepts, logics, mechanisms from these single-paradigm or synthesis models of SGC and then attempting to translate and selectively integrate them into a new holistic analytic framework. Synergetic theorizing must go further and requires looking at causal dynamics and reactive relationships between these analytic elements in real time and identifying how these are manifested in real world situations and in political outcomes.

Theory-synergetic approach engages with specific empirical puzzles but enables operationalisation of complex multi-causal questions which shed light on the deeper ontology of international relations. For example, operationalising the issue of SGC financing as an inter-paradigmatic pivot can help illuminate co-constitutive relationship between socio-normative change and political decision-making of major states and institutions (see chapter VI).

For example, how do post-modernist critiques and civic-popular opposition to SGC stimulate state behavior and institutional responses of international actors involved in the project? Do normative changes in state and institutional environmental identities and socio-economic interests influence multilateral financial organizations when it comes to funding decisions on SGC, BTC and other fossil-fuels projects? How do counter-hegemonic networks – coalitions of environmentalist NGOs, climate change campaigners, civil society groups, marginalized communities, human rights activists and others – employ international regulatory systems and institutional normative standards, to challenge prevailing social order in global energy politics and to set out possible alternatives? How do competing national identities and strategic interests of energy-producing and consuming states determine political outcomes in the wider global energy order and are we at a point of fundamental transition in this order?

Conclusion

In this chapter TSA is grounded in the Critical Realist philosophy of science. It is argued that international relations constitute a distinct ontological sphere, which exists independently of attempts to study it but one that can be revealed through a systematic scientific enterprise. This science is the discipline of International Relations and its language and intellectual properties are contained in its theoretical diversity and methodological pluralism. It is a mega if not a meta-social science.

If we are to accept that unity of science consists alone in its method then what IR requires is a common language – a cross-disciplinary discourse and a general technique to utilize, apply and coherently communicate IR disciplinary diversity. This approach, with all its normative priorities and theoretical pluralism, should aim towards resolution of concrete substantive puzzles and problems in international politics. Theory synergetic approach is proposed as this common ontology-prioritizing technology for maximising the value potential of intellectual properties and vigor of IR theoretical pluralism.

It is worth repeating that TSA is not a methodology in itself and is not an attempt to impose any universalising conditions on the multi-theoretical progress. It is, however, an argument for a more self-confident disciplinary approach and one that recognizes the full empirical potential inherent in IR's multi-disciplinary and theoretically heterogeneous knowledge pool.

It is also a proposal for a disciplinary way of thinking – the method in TSA consists of internalising theoretical diversity, until it becomes part of IR architecture and is treated as a matter of fact. No theory or combination thereof should be accorded a higher status in any given research, until and unless ontological conditions demand prioritization of particular set of explanations. Anything goes as long and as much as it is practically useful.

TSA can therefore be seen as a proposal for an applied science of IR. Theoretical models are to be utilized as tools for experimentation. The latter is posited to consist of specially constructed synergies – a mechanism for pivoting into motion IR theoretical pluralism and bringing it to bear upon concrete empirical questions. The reward for mobilising synergetic thinking is a deeper, multidimensional and hyper-active real-time panorama of the subject manner, not limited by any a-priory paradigmatic assumptions, and unshackled from any dogmatic grand-theory commitments. The king of IR is the subject matter of international relations and theories are the interactive tools of the synergetic method, called to reveal them.

In disciplinary terms, therefore, TSA may be said to be responding to the challenges of the Fourth Debate and addressing its many implications. It is a way to challenge the chaos and entropy. It is intended as a way to reconcile IR's disciplinary diversity; to bridge cross-paradigmatic divide; to find a solution to the incommensurability problem; to develop a common discourse; to make IR more practical and relevant to real-life challenges of international politics; to effectively integrate the normative/ideational content into an accentuated empirical enterprise; to provide a degree of ontological cohesion to a highly diverse and eclectic theoretical field. In the following chapters theory-synergetic approach is demonstrated through its application to the study of international politics of oil.

III
IR and Politics of Oil (and Gas)

Introduction

Oil. Power. World. Security. Glory. Quest. Scramble. Earth. Struggle. Prize. Blood. These are the words most commonly featured in the titles of some of the most famous and prominent histories, textbooks and critiques of oil politics. There are few topics that capture imagination the way oil does. It is a subject that crosses disciplinary boundaries and concerns the broadest spectrum of human activity. Directly and indirectly oil shapes the modern world, impacting on everything from physical condition to popular culture. There is drama, romance and adventure in the story of oil, which underline its essential quality.

Our relationship with oil and the world it created, our fascination and ambivalence towards it, and all the paradoxes therein are borne out by that very essentialism – we live in the hydrocarbon age. Over one hundred and fifty years after Edwin "Colonel" Drake first struck oil at Titusville, Pennsylvania we still have "oil on the brain."[10] That is not to say that the

---

[10] "Oil on the brain" refers to the title of a popular Joseph Eastburn song (1865, Lee & Walker, Philadelphia, USA), which captured the frenzy of the first ever oil boom that hit Western Pennsylvania in the aftermath of 'Colonel' Drake's discovery and successful commercial drilling of oil at Titusville in 1859:

"The Yankees boast that they make clocks
    Which "just beat all creation:"
They never made one could keep time
    With our great speculation.
Our stocks, like clocks, go with a spring,
    Wind up, run down again;
But all our strikes are sure to cause
    "Oil on the brain."
Stock's par, stock's up, Then on the wane;
Ev'rybody's trouble with Oil on the brain."

story of oil begins at the point of its modern "discovery" and industrial application. Indeed, the question of what *is* oil in terms of its ideational (social) *and* material (physical) kinds – the deep ontology – lies at heart of its own subject matter. It is so expansive a subject that few have attempted to provide a universal account of oil (although Daniel Yergin (1991) is often credited as having done just that – see below).

Therefore, the choice of oil and natural gas projects as case-studies for TSA is by no means arbitrary. Oil provides a broad empirical field upon which theories of IR can be systematically applied and tested in a synergetic method. The task is not to determine which theory gets it "right" about the deeper reality of oil; it is to find out which aspects of that reality, or rather what different realities different theories of IR reveal. What should emerge at the end of this enterprise is an expanded and complex ontologies of these substantive puzzles, which will remain subject to further challenge and open to greater clarification and explanation. There are no legitimate *a priori* limits or brackets that can be placed upon what *can be* potentially known about the material and social realities of oil and gas projects studied here.

The task is somewhat aided by the fact that there is a broad chronological overlap between the story of petroleum and the history of IR, with debates about oil developing roughly along the same timeline as the evolution of IR theory through the Great Debates. Case-studies of BTC and SGC pipelines are not random events or stand-alone subjects – they are located in the wider historical timeline of human energy production and debates around it. This makes energy politics a particularly well-suited subject matter for the application of a multi-theoretical analytical framework.

This chapter explores this wider empirical field of international oil and gas politics, and sets out the case-studies of BTC and SGC pipelines that are examined in this book. It opens with a historical review of IR engagement with oil politics and examines how different theoretical traditions shaped contemporary political and academic discourses. The overall aim of this chapter is to set out a theoretical rationale for choosing energy politics and the case-studies of oil and gas pipelines as the empirical testing ground for applied theory-synergetic approach.

Theories of international oil and gas politics

Oil emerges as a distinct international political theme in the second decade of the twentieth century, and studies of oil often begin with examination of the role it played in imperial politics of the late nineteenth century, leading up to and through World War I. Indeed, Daniel Yergin opens *The Prize* (1991), his much lauded history of oil, with Winston Churchill's fateful decision to convert the Royal Navy from coal to oil in the aftermath of the 1911 Agadir crisis and the ratcheting up of the Anglo-German arms race: "He decided that Britain would have to base its 'naval supremacy upon oil' and, thereupon, committed himself, with all his driving energy and enthusiasm, to achieving that objective ... There was no choice – in Churchill's words, 'Mastery itself was the prize of the venture.'" (1991, xiv).

Churchill's use of the term "mastery" goes to the heart of the political subject of oil and introduces its most potent theme. It is no surprise therefore that the classical Realists of the interwar and post-World War II period focused their attention on the role of oil as both constitutive of state power and as its instrument. Classical Realist assumptions about strategic value of oil are evident in this excerpt from Edmond J. W. Slade's lecture entitled "The Influence of Oil on International Politics," delivered at Chatham House, in 1923: "The lack of money has never stopped a nation from fighting, but the lack of the means of producing mechanical power brings everything to a standstill... It is therefore evident that since, under existing conditions, petroleum is indispensable, the country which can control the supply of petroleum to the rest of the world is in a position to enforce its will so long as its sources of supply are not open to attack" (p. 254).

E.H. Carr clearly identified this central relationship between economic and military power in "The Twenty Years' Crisis," published in 1939. In his examination of autarchy as political instrument Carr argued that pursuit of economic self-sufficiency and independence are issues of military significance and are "primarily a form of preparedness for war" (Carr, 2001 (1981), p.111).

A clear relationship between oil and power, especially military power is for the first time located as a causal factor in policy making. This theme is echoed, then defined and expanded upon, by Hans Morgenthau in *Politics Among Nations*, first published in 1948: "The absolute and relative importance of natural resources in the form of raw materials have for the power of a nation depends necessarily upon the technology of the warfare practiced in a particular period of history" (1985, p. 131).

Referring to "the power of oil" Morgenthau is first to identify its critical quality – in the post- World War II world oil was no longer one of many natural resources that go into making up the power of a nation-state but "a material factor whose very possession threatens to overturn centuries-old patterns of international politics" (Ibid, p.133). Thereafter realist analysis of oil focuses almost exclusively on its function in power relations between states, in particular its role in war and military affairs.

This approach was further reinforced and refined by neo-realists, who showed little interest in the workings of the global oil industry or wider issues, dismissing such concerns as reductionist and posing their questions about oil solely within the framework of a parsimonious structural theory of international relations. Oil was interesting only in so far as it could help explain differentials in power capabilities of states.

The 1973 oil crisis ("the first oil shock") served to further consolidate this structural approach and to bring center stage issues of resource dependency and national strategies for withstanding embargoes. Kenneth Waltz, writing in his "Theory of International Politics" (1979) (published at the time of the 'second oil shock' caused by the Islamic revolution in Iran), discussed the impact of the OPEC embargo in precisely in those terms, asking whether the crisis showed "that the unequal capabilities of states continue to explain their fates and to shape international political outcomes" (p.152).

For Waltz and other neo-realists oil was not "special" and did not constitute a factor in its own right. States are not ranked on the basis of excelling in one or another sphere, and their economic, military and other capabilities cannot be disaggregated and assessed separately. The status of nations depends on how they score across a broad spectrum of items, resource endowment being just one of these (Ibid., p.131).

What interested neo-realists is how possession of oil or lack thereof impacted on behavior of states in a self-help, anarchic system. As

Waltz argued: "Countries that are highly dependent, countries that get much of what they badly need from a few possibly unreliable suppliers, must do all they can to increase the chances that they will keep getting it" (1979, p. 153).

Yet ideas about politics of oil then continued to develop broadly in parallel with the evolving themes of IR theory and debates about oil continued to correspond roughly with the intellectual schisms of the Great Debates in IR. So much so that by 1991, as the Soviet Union collapsed and the world was shaken by the Gulf War, Daniel Yergin identified three great themes which underlie the story of oil: the rise of capitalism and modern business; oil as a strategic commodity central to global politics, national strategies and power; and what he called the "anthropological argument" – the rise of the "hydrocarbon society" and the "Hydrocarbon Man" (*The Prize*, pp.13-15).

It is not surprising that Yergin chose to rank the business of oil above its politics. While realists were preoccupied with the power-maximising capability of oil as a strategic resource, the impact and consequences of the 1973 and 1979 oil crises prompted a growing attention to the oil industry itself - "the world's biggest and most pervasive business" (Ibid., p. 13). From the late nineteenth century onwards the scale of the energy enterprise began to draw together the worlds of engineering, commodities trading, banking, international financial institutions, commercial and property law, marketing, to name but a few. Driven by the global geography and geology of oil and by the constant need to discover new sources the industry rapidly expanded across the world, and the force behind this expansion was the power and the capital of the oil companies – the first truly multinational corporations.[11]

Writing about these giants of industry in his seminal 1975 study "The Seven Sisters," Anthony Sampson observed: "For decades the Companies (with a capital C) seemed possessed of a special mystique, both to the producing and the consuming countries. Their supranational expertise was beyond the ability of national governments. Their incomes

---

[11] Sampson remarks that Exxon 1973 Annual report referred to the company as having been a multinational corporation "at least fifty years before the term was commonly used" (1975, p.24).

were greater than those of most countries where they operated, their fleets of tankers had more tonnage than any navy, they owned and administered whole cities in the desert." (p. 24).

For Yergin the business of oil is full of the drama and the adventure reminiscent of the golden age of exploration: "No other business so starkly and extremely defines the meaning of risk and reward – and the profound impact of chance and fate" (1991, p. 13). Yet the story of corporate oil is one of continuous transformation, shrinkage and growth again. As governments, independent producers, global, national and local regulators sought to curb the growth and power of the oil companies and to develop a rules-based system to keep "Big Oil" in check, there developed complex relationships, bodies and organizations, all possessing their own institutional dynamics and cultures, which became a focus of a new, neo-liberal turn in energy studies. The role of markets and institutions came to the fore of the field.

The politics and the business of oil, two of Yergin's themes in combination constitute the mainstream core of oil studies. It can also be argued that the epistemology of this combination corresponds roughly to the "neo-neo synthesis" in IR. For neo-realists, oil was a strategic commodity that goes into making up national state power. Therefore, states, acting in a self-help system, will behave in ways designed to maximize access to reliable supplies of this precious commodity while seeking to lessen their dependence on other countries.

For neo-liberal institutionalists, who built upon the insights of earlier, classical liberals, oil was first and foremost a major enterprise of complex legal and institutional design, involving trans-national actors and processes and driven primarily by market forces and regulatory pressures. For example, some economists at the time of the 1973 crisis argued that the rapid rise in prices was caused exclusively by market forces (Gilpin, 2001, p. 59).

Focusing on the power of international oil corporations and their ability to mobilize technology, capital and human resources on monumental scale some neoliberals point to the fact that these forces are often more powerful than nation-states. Additionally, neoliberals are more likely to pay attention to the role of personalities and individuals (leaders and innovators) as active actors in shaping outcomes.

The synthesis of these two approaches provides the framework of much of the discussions around oil today. Yet Yergin (1991, pp. 14-15) identifies a further theme – what he terms as the anthropological argument - that oil forms the basis of modern civilisation, fuelling both its late industrial and the post-industrial phases. The invention of kerosene and later of the internal combustion engine marked the end of the dominance of coal, which came to be displaced by oil as the fuel of modernity. An entire culture had arisen as the result – the "Hydrocarbon Society:" "Today, we are so dependent on oil, and oil is so embedded in our daily doings, that we hardly stop to comprehend its pervasive significance" (Ibid., p.15).

Meanwhile, what started out in the 1960s and 70s as a set of broad concerns over ecological implications of industrial society, was by early 1990s a fully-fledged movement, led by international civic organizations and campaigning groups such as Greenpeace. It was informed by a growing awareness of the risks of pollution, wider environmental impact of the use of fossil fuels and the emerging debate about human-made climate change.

Ethical concerns were not limited to this newly political environmentalism. The latter was further reinforced by a growing distrust and criticism of the oil industry and of the very politics of oil. Decolonisation and anti-imperialism of the post-war period saw nationalisation of oil assets around the world, cancellation of concessions and often violent resistance to exploitation of natural resources from indigenous groups (see for example, Betancourt, 1978).

The wider post-structuralist, critical turn in social science was beginning to influence debates around oil. Yergin, whose epistemological and normative commitments fall within the broad "neo-neo synthesis" framework, is forced to acknowledge that the oil industry was being "increasingly scrutinized, criticized and opposed" and that the growth of ethical concerns "challenges the basic tenets of industrial society" (1991, p.15). But he goes on to argue that the appetite for oil remains unabated, the demand is growing, driven by the developing world and population growth, as more and more countries join the ranks of industrialized countries and exercise their "right to consume" (Ibid).

Looking ahead, Yergin then identifies the terms of the key normative debate at heart of *The Prize:* "In the meantime, the stage has been set for one of the great and intractable clashes of the 1990s between, on the one hand, the powerful and increasing support for greater environmental protection and, on the other, a commitment to economic growth and the benefits of the Hydrocarbon Society, and apprehensions about energy security" (Ibid). The very nature of industrial modernity is at stake.

At this stage it is important to acknowledge the full significance of *The Prize* - Yergin's encyclopaedic work in the field of oil and wider energy studies. Daniel Yergin is a figure not only of considerable academic but also political authority, serving in senior advisory roles to U.S. government and the private sector; he is a founder of IHS Cambridge Energy Research Associates – a major political and business consultancy firm (Yergin, 2016).

Few texts have had as much impact across such a wide disciplinary spectrum as Yergin's *The Prize,* which won the Pulitzer Prize for General Nonfiction (1992). As the result Daniel Yergin had established what Dwight Garner described in *The New York Times* as "a virtual monopoly on the subject of energy and geopolitics. Such is his influence that one half expects his competitors to file antitrust litigation against him" (20.09.2011); for a contemporary review see Vietor, 1991). However, it can also be argued that *The Prize* represents an apogee of mainstream rationalist approaches to oil politics. At its core is a solidly positivist analytical framework that could be seen as prioritizing modernist interpretations of social phenomena.

All of this has interesting implications for this study, part of which is concerned with charting the ways in which theoretical debates are translated on empirical level, and how such scholarship relates to political practice. For that purpose, *The Prize* takes a prominent position in the bibliography of this study, not only as a source of empirical data but also as an example of a possibly hegemonic academic discourse.

In the decades that followed publication of *The Prize* the world of oil had undergone further dramatic transformations and cataclysmic crises, developing into one of the most fiercely contested fields in public policy and wider debates. Environmental concerns have been elevated from isolated direct action campaigns of eco-groups of the 1970s to the top of the international political agenda. By the time of the historic 2015 UN Climate Change Conference in Paris the link between fossil fuels and rising global temperatures has been widely accepted and the task of cutting human-made CO_2 and other greenhouse gas emissions has been identified as the key challenge facing the world (*The Paris Agreement,* 12 December 2015).

The impact of the post-structuralist turn on the development of oil studies and associated debates around the issue can hardly be overstated. If oil is the fuel of modernity, then by definition any post-modern critique of social reality is, at least implicitly if not explicitly, about oil. For much of the history the world of oil was dominated by politicians and lawyers, engineers, oil company executives, bankers, traders and speculators. Therefore, discussions around oil were bracketed by clearly defined parameters of what can arguably called a "problem-solving" conceptual framework (Cox, 1983).

Questions about oil were confined solely to issues of supply and demand, distribution of political power and competition between oil-producing and consuming states, strategic control over prices and production, transportation and refinement and so on. Oil remained a dominant topic, whose "doings and controversies are to be found regularly not only on the business page but also on the front page" (Yergin, 1991, p.13).

But by early 1990s a critique began to emerge seeking to expose power relations in the world of oil and to illuminate the social and material costs of a civilisation built upon consumption of fossil fuels. This critique was strong enough so that mainstream positivist scholars, such as Daniel Yergin, were forced to acknowledge its impact. In initial stages it sought to raise awareness of environmental concerns, to challenge the power of international energy companies and the conduct of governments engaging in oil politics, with the Middle East in particular focus. A whole range of issues, from post-colonialism to human rights, began to bear upon the debates about oil.

But the post-modern critique went further and with the new century it came to question the very foundations of the "Hydrocarbon Society," the basis of modernity. It asks whether there is really no alternative to the reality of industrial and economic growth, consumerism and global free trade fuelled by the burning of oil and other fossil fuels. Technological, economic and cultural change in the decades that followed the end of the Cold War, sped up and amplified by rapid advances in computing and the exponential growth of the Internet, reinforced the intellectual and social impact of post-modernism on discussions about oil.

Thus, the rise of renewable sources of energy came to represent not merely a replacement for oil but a force for a total transformation of society, heralding possibility of a different kind of living (see, for example, Armaroli & Balzani, 2010). Oil is no longer seen as a monolithic, perennial and inescapable reality. Post-structuralist insights brought not only a renewed historicism to the critique of the modern oil industry, but brought a critical edge to mainstream thinking about energy, reconceptualising the terms in which it is understood. Climate change, for example, is no longer an "environmentalist" issue but a major economic challenge (Stern, 2007) and potentially catastrophic security threat (Schwartz and Randall, 2003).

Therefore, given the fact that humanity had been using sustainable energy sources for its entire history up to the industrial age, might it not mean that, as Aitken argues, "the world will necessarily again have to turn to sustainable resources before the present century is over?" "The fossil fuel period is therefore an 'era,' not an age, and highly limited in time in comparison with the evolution, past and future, of civilizations and societies. Accordingly, it is critical for governments to view what remains of the fossil fuel era as a transition" (2003, p.3).

For positivists, such as Yergin, this may only be possible if the problems associated with renewable energy are solved (by government policies and market forces). The question for him is: "What kind of energy mix will meet the world's energy needs without crisis and confrontation?" (2012, p. 5). But the fact that *The Quest: Energy, Security, and the Remaking of the Modern World* (2012), Yergin's follow up to *The Prize*

(1991), is not about oil per se but is about energy, is indicative of the extent of the transformation in the thinking about the subject.

Synergetic readings of oil and gas politics

The brief overview of the evolution of debates around oil and energy issues is presented here, in broad brush-strokes, in conjunction with the corresponding set of developments in the epistemological and ontological evolution of IR theory, as told through the history of the Great Debates, culminating with the reflectivist turn of the Fourth Debate.

The two strands intertwine continuously, presenting a broad common timeline from World War I to present day; the implications of the post-structuralist challenge may mean that the timeline should be in fact moved back to earlier human interaction with oil and forward – towards possible alternatives to fossil-fuel dominated energy order. A scientific realist might well argue from a philosophical standpoint that there should not be any arbitrary limits placed on the ontological space-time framework at all.

Ontological turn in IR provides the rationale for the theory synergetic approach. It is no longer feasible, in the aftermath of the Fourth Debate, to bracket the greatly expanded ontology of IR in either exclusively positivist or anti-positivist frameworks. To take ontology seriously is to posit that the discipline of IR encompasses the study of the totality of organized human relations across the globe - from affairs of states to institutions and processes; the normative expanse - international ethics, justice and law, the interests of marginalized groups; the "problem-solving" agenda and the "emancipatory project" – the entirety of IR knowledge capital – "all that we've learnt."

This does not mean an end to paradigm-driven research, but rather a reconceptualization of what paradigms represent in IR. Prioritizing ontology does not mean dismissal of theoretical questions or blind adherence to epistemological relativism. It means, for example, that if the empirical task at hand is an investigation into politics of oil, then issues of epistemology are to be subordinated to the demands of that task. The questions are not what is the right way to study politics of oil or what should be studied and how. The question here is which part of the empirical puzzle of oil is revealed by what theory and how these different elements come together in the grand ontology of oil politics?

Within the empirical framework of theory synergetic research individual theories and schools of thought are valuable tools for revealing different aspects or layers of reality (if not altogether different realities) of and about the same phenomena. Taking such view may suggest that in terms of the IR disciplinary structure, paradigmatic research constitutes specialisation – scholars focusing on particular set of questions, requiring different methodologies and research skills, but all striving towards the same goal of "getting at the way things really are."

But the disadvantage of paradigmatic research is that it can only reveal a partial, epistemologically-specific and ontologically-bounded element of the grander reality under study. This in turn will have normative implications. There is ever only so much that can be discovered through theoretically limited research. Synergetic research, by contrast, offers a way for harnessing specific paradigmatic insights in a holistic analytical framework systematically applied to grand-ontology of a given problem field. This grand-ontological approach applies equally to issue-specific, mid-range empirical puzzles and to wider, more comprehensive investigations of various socio-political phenomena.

To take an example of another major pipeline project, a theory-synergetic study of the Turkmenistan-Afghanistan-Pakistan-India Pipeline (TAPI) (Asian Development Bank, 2016) would aim to reveal the grand ontology of its subject matter, comprising a diverse and complex mix of social, economic, cultural and political forces, actors and processes, all operating across a wide historical span. The scope of such an enquiry could include but not be limited to issues and themes, such as:

- inter-state relations in Central Asia;
- 9/11 and the U.S. power in the region;
- the heritage and local dynamics of political Islam;
- the role of Pakistani and Afghan Taliban;
- the interests of ethnic minorities in the regions traversed by the proposed pipeline;

- the impact of the TAPI project on women, tribal and clan groups and other marginalized communities in the affected territories traversed by the pipeline;
- the role of China in the regional energy market;
- the role of Russia in Central Asia;
- religious demography of the regions traversed by the proposed pipeline;
- the role of international energy corporations and international financial institutions, such as the Asian Development Bank;
- environmental impact assessments of the TAPI project, locally and globally;
- energy market implications of the project;
- comparative historical analysis of the Great Silk Route and the TAPI pipeline;
- political and civic opposition movements and domestic politics of states participating in the TAPI project;
- wider legal and normative debates about the project.

This is by no means an exhaustive list and may in fact underestimate the complexity of the empirical challenge. The starting point is recognition of the material foundation of the social discourse of the proposed pipeline. The TAPI pipeline project is an engineering challenge of considerable magnitude – a 1,420 millimetres (56 in) in diameter pipeline, of over 1800 kilometres in length, running from Galkynysh gas field in southern Turkmenistan, traversing complex topography of Afghanistan and Pakistan through Herat to Multan, and culminating at the city of Fazilka, in north-western India.

When operational it will carry 33 billion cubic metres of natural gas per year, supplying 5 billion cubic metres to Afghanistan and 14 billion cubic metres to Pakistan and India respectively. Six compressor stations would be constructed along the pipeline, which will run alongside Kandahar-Herat Highway in western Afghanistan. The cost of the project, being led by the Turkmenistan's state energy giant Turkmengaz, is expected to rise to $12 billion (*Alexander's Gas & Oil Connections*, 21.11.06; Graeber. D.J., 03.12.14; Abdurasulov, A. 16.07.15; Tanchum. M. 3.12.15; Gurt & Auvezov, 13.12.15).

The immense scale of the physical reality of the TAPI pipeline endows it with a historical and imaginational history, before it is even constructed. This history goes back beyond the mid-1990s when the project was first envisaged, all the way back to the ancient Silk Route, the geographical route of which is relatively closely matched by the proposed pipeline. The sheer range of stories, narratives, ideas – the full spectrum of imaginative potential - is implicit in such an analytical framework. This material, physical reality, therefore, exists as a condition of possibility of any kind of social discourse around the TAPI pipeline project.

As such there is no reasonable justification for a priori assumptions about what constitutes legitimate scholarship about the TAPI project, or for limiting or circumscribing the ontological scope of the study. The set of hypothetical questions listed above, modest as it is, indicates the breadth of knowledge that is possible about this subject matter and might be revealed through scholarship.

Any attempt to exclude one or other question would necessarily be a product of political decision, and not of some arbitrary standard of scientific or scholarly objectivity or judgement. For it would determine which parts of the grand-ontology of the TAPI pipeline project are to remain obscured, unrevealed and unexamined, and this would inevitably have normative implications. The same is true for the case-studies examined in this thesis – BTC and SGC pipelines represent a complex social-material reality not subject to reduction.

By contrast, theory-synergetic analysis seeks to systematically expand the scope of scholarship, striving for an ever growing, open-ended epistemological engagement with various ontological challenges presented by a given empirical problem-field. The key here is not simply identifying specific paradigmatic insights but determining how these different theoretical models of the same subject matter interact with and relate to each other within a single, holistic research framework.

Therefore, a theory-synergetic analysis of a major pipeline project would include a model of inter-state relations, a normative enquiry, a critical examination of its social order, a study of institutions, processes and identities from global market forces to local tribal traditions and so on, set within an expansive timeline and exploring complex ideas and concepts about changing relations between East and West, emergence of the Eurasian sphere, modernity and tradition, religion and nationalism and more. The resulting theory-synergetic multidimensional map of a vibrant, epistemologically pluralist, deep(-*er*) grand-ontology of a given project contrasts markedly with what appears from a theory-specific, single paradigm research perspective as a straightforward, clearly-defined and reducible empirical puzzle, e.g. a regional gas pipeline.

The same approach can be taken to a more expansive subject matter of global politics of energy by envisaging a greatly enhanced social and material ontology of "oil international." A synergetic study of international oil and gas politics would comprise a holistic examination of the totality of paradigmatic models. Thus, for example, a positivist analysis, what Robert Cox (1986) termed "problem solving theory," might take "the prevailing social and power relationships and the institutions in which they are organized, as the given framework for action" (p. 208) when it comes to oil politics e.g. what to do to stabilize oil prices? how a merger between two international energy corporations affects the oil market? what might a state do to reduce its dependency for oil on another country? what impact will the development of alternative energy sources, both fossil fuels and renewables, have on energy markets of tomorrow and on relations between energy-producing and consuming states? etc.

A reflectivist critique, by contrast, "does not take institutions and social and power relations for granted but calls them into question by concerning itself with their origins and how and whether they might be in the process of changing." In doing so it "allows for a normative choice in favor of a social and political order different from the prevailing order" (Ibid.) e.g. who and how sets the oil prices? who benefits and who loses out from the operations of international energy corporations? how sustainable is the existing energy order? what alternative energy sources might be used and who benefits from maintaining the fossil fuel status quo? etc.

What is interesting from theory-synergetic perspective is how these two levels of analysis interplay as they converge on specific empirical questions. If, for example, the empirical puzzle under investigation relates to political regulation of a major international oil project (an off shore deep-water development or exploration in an environmentally and socially sensitive area) it is important to ascertain the role of international financial institutions and their environmental and social impact assessment apparatus and mechanisms, the role of states and how they compete and cooperate on these projects and for what purpose (how do they seek to maximize their power and interests by promoting this or that option?); as well as to investigate whether there is an alternative to the world envisaged by these projects and to expose existing power relations, underlying the dynamics driving these projects to completion.

To continue with this hypothetical empirical example - what is ultimately of interest here for an IR scholar is the international relations of a major international oil project, and not the debate about what constitutes legitimate scholarship about a major international oil project and so on indefinitely and without final determination. In order to gain as full an understanding of how things really are – complex knowledge – it is essential to pursue explanatory and prescriptive research agendas, systematically applying and deploying the full spectrum of epistemological and methodological tools available in the IR toolkit.

All approaches are taken as potentially valid models of a same given empirical problem, coexisting simultaneously but independently. This does require taking each paradigmatic model on its own terms. The synergetic value is generated through construction of inter-paradigmatic models of the same subject matter. It is in these substantive intersections of various autonomous paradigmatic models that theoretical synergy can be operationalized.

One reason why this may be possible is because theory-synergetic method is located and grounded within the disciplinary pluralism of IR. As noted above, IR is the only social science with the necessary structures and properties - a sufficiently extensive international ontology, encompassing both material and ideational/social kinds; an epistemological heritage of considerable diversity, making it an ideal platform for complex, multidisciplinary social-scientific enterprise. But this is only possible if we engage with IR as a discipline that prioritizes and expands our conception of what constitutes ontology and allows for true epistemological pluralism.

The social and the material in oil and gas

Alexander Wendt is right to argue that, "Epistemology generally will take care of itself in the hurly-burly of scientific debate" (2010 [1999], p.373). But the theory-synergetic approach departs from Wendt in two important ways – it differs considerably to his conception of an exclusively "social" and "constructionist" ontology of international life and employs a more nuanced understanding of epistemological relativism. It is worth briefly commenting on this.

Wendt prioritizes ideational factors over material, taking distribution of ideas and culture as the starting point of theorizing about international politics, with material forces coming in later (Ibid, p.371). He draws upon realist philosophy of science to support his view of a constructivist ontology of international relations (Ibid., p. 372). Finally, Wendt argues that, "it is through ideas that states ultimately relate to one another" and these ideas "help define who and what states are" (Ibid).

Positivists remain sceptical about constructivist emphasis on ideational factors as key units of analysis. Robert Gilpin (2001) argues that any international theory must "seek to integrate both ideas and material forces," because ideas are important but, "the world is composed of many economic, technological, and other powerful constraints that limit the wisdom and practicality of certain ideas and social constructions" (p.20).

What echoes in Gilpin's observations is a positivist notion of ontology of international relations that is on final account a materialist one. And this materialism is ultimately defined in terms of power: "While I agree that ideas are very important, they are important politically only insofar as they are supported by the interests and power of important actors such as states or domestic political coalitions" (Ibid., p.86n).

Wendt's critique of materialist ontology in IR (and hence his justification for replacing it with a socially constructed one) is limited to this narrow conception of material forces "defined as power and interest" (2010 [1999], p. 371). However, the theory-synergetic approach is premised on a deeper conception of international ontology. As discussed above, theory-synergetic approach employs scientific realist philosophy of science to posit an unlimited international ontology, composed of material and ideational forces. This ontology is "unlimited" in the sense that there are no a priori limits on what constitutes legitimate ways of generating knowledge about it.

For it exists independently of the mind, as a condition of possibility of it being discovered and have ideas formed about it. As, for example, mentioned before, the ontology of oil predates human agency i.e. just because humans were not capable of refining kerosene until late nineteenth century does not mean that oil did not have the potential of being refined until then. Of course, oil does represent power and interests of powerful actors but only because of its energy-generating chemistry.

The process of scientific discovery suggests a complex relationship between material and social forces which should not, therefore, be viewed exclusively through the prism of causality and agent/structure modes of analysis. The symbiotic interactions between the two present a far more interesting focus for scholarship. The fact that material forces can give rise to ideas that then shape identities and determine types of political behavior is evidenced by the historical experience of oil producing societies and states. Therefore, when it comes to ontology, scientific inquiry should seek to pose causal *and* constitutive questions.

It is difficult, therefore, to agree with Wendt's argument that "relatively little of international life is a function of material forces as such without us ascribing implicit ideational content to power and interest explanations" (Ibid.). Geography, environment, topography, natural resource endowment, even terrain type can have a determining impact on both material and social development of states, societies and community identities. Natural catastrophes, pandemics and climate change can have as material an impact on international relations as war or genocide, while simultaneously giving rise to ideas and social constructions capable of generating social change.

Therefore, a theory-synergetic conception of the materialist component of its ontology of international life is not bracketed but is defined in broadest terms, from planetary conditions and physical and environmental forces to power and interest of powerful actors, and not only between states but all international human communities (for example, from multinational corporations to global digital social movements).

Implicit here is a recognition that material (physical) kinds can give rise to construction of social (ideational, imaginational) forms. And in turn ideas and culture often constitute the content and meaning of material forces, as Wendt argues (Ibid, p.371).

The social component of theory-synergetic international ontology is taken to be similarly expanded, possessing causal and identity-constitutive potential in international politics. Social kinds do not form in vacuum and are shaped by interplay with material kinds. Certain ideas may give rise to particular identities, which in turn provide impetus for social change; or they may in turn be products of material forces impacting on imaginational, social constructionist dynamic of international life.

In sum, theory-synergetic ontology of international politics of oil and gas is social-materialist, in the sense that it is through a continuous, flowing and mutually-constitutive interplay between ideas and material forces (defined in broadest possible terms) that international life occurs and proceeds. It therefore makes more sense to begin our theorizing about international politics with the dynamic interplay between ideas (identities, culture and so on) and material forces (physical environment, power, wealth and so on).

Coupled with this enhanced and fluid ontology is a nuanced understanding of epistemological relativism. Wendt draws on a realist philosophy of science to argue that there is "nothing in the intellectual activity required to explain processes of social construction that is epistemologically different than the intellectual activity engaged in by natural scientists" (Ibid., p. 372).

He acknowledges that different social and material kinds of objects of study may require different methodologies of scientific inquiry, but "methods are not epistemologies" (p.373). Wendt then asserts that what constitutes "epistemic authority of any scientific study" is the applicability of the falsifiability criteria on empirical level – something that post-positivists acknowledge (Ibid.).

There is, however, nothing incompatible between commitment to epistemological relativism and recognising significant differences where they exist. Methods of inquiry are not epistemologies but they do differ in significant ways between sciences and amongst paradigmatic traditions on intra-disciplinary level. Different objects of scientific enquiry requiring different methodologies involve different disciplinary structures, contents, cultures and ultimately different procedural standards for applying falsifiability criteria.

It is therefore important to recognize in different paradigmatic traditions their specific natures as forms of various specialisations in International Relations, requiring their own specific standards of epistemic authority. Retaining epistemological integrity of individual paradigmatic models of the empirical puzzle under research is an essential part of TSA.

These models can then be examined and falsified by those specialising in those particular theoretical traditions. Epistemic authority of theory-synergetic research as a whole, however, is determined not by deconstruction of its synergetic parts but on its holistic merit, i.e. that on empirical level it constitutes a unit of publicly available evidence and its results (the synergetic model of a research subject matter) can be falsified.

Epistemological relativism does not require us to abandon all sense of theoretical integrity, which could lead to what is likely to be fruitless attempt at theoretical synthesising. The intellectual value of paradigm-bound research within a synergetic empirical programme stems from a unique set of knowledge-generating properties specific to that particular paradigm. It is therefore counterproductive to seek to gloss over these real differences because to do so would be to undermine the very purpose of the synergetic intellectual enterprise.

Because, as noted above, synergy is a simultaneous operation of different, fully autonomous, self-contained parts. Through this operation a new whole emerges which is necessarily greater than the sum of its constituent parts. Therefore, an IR theory-synergetic method relies upon a systematic application of different, epistemologically-integral modes of paradigm-bound analysis upon the same empirical puzzle.

The synergetic model of that puzzle that emerges through this process constitutes something more than simply agglomeration of theoretical perspectives. Thus, it will be shown that the synergetic model of international oil politics (Chapter VI) is necessarily greater, deeper and more substantial than the sum of its individual constituent parts - realist, critical, liberal, social constructivist, Marxist, post-structuralist and other paradigmatic analytical models (chapters IV and V).

This relates to an earlier statement that TSA first and foremost aspires to serve as a pan-disciplinary culture – a formalized acknowledgement and acceptance of multiplicity of knowledge in International Relations and a way for IR scholars to communicate across theoretical boundaries, and collaborate on empirical level in meaningful and potentially more fruitful ways. Turning to the empirical question at hand – theory-synergetic analysis of international politics of oil and gas – the task is to demonstrate how such a professional cross-theoretical discourse can be established and operationalized in practice.

Case-studies: BTC and SGC projects

Over the past fifteen years Baku-Tbilisi-Ceyhan pipeline proved central to unlocking Caspian hydrocarbon reserves. It provided Azerbaijan, Kazakhstan and Turkmenistan - oil and gas producing states in the region - with a critical infrastructure link to global energy markets (Starr, 2005, pp. 8-9). The pipeline runs from the Azeri-Chirag-Gunashli (ACG) off-shore field across Azerbaijan, Georgia and Turkey, and links Sangachal terminal on the shores of the Caspian Sea to Ceyhan deep-water marine terminal on the Turkish Mediterranean coast (see map 1). The 1,768km pipeline became operational in 2006 and has since carried around about 2.8 billion barrels of crude oil to world markets (BP 3, BTC co. Shareholders, 2017).

Yet, the BTC pipeline represents far more than an energy conduit. It is a multifaceted international project, involving a wide range of actors and comprising a complex mix of multi-level politics. Multinational corporations (MNCs), international financial institutions (IFIs), global advocacy groups and NGOs participated in the project alongside states, in a drawn out process that was marked by much friction and controversy (Carroll, 2010, p.2). As such, it was characterized by "the close correspondence that existed at all stages of the pipeline's development between politicians, businessmen, and economists who defined the project's ends and the engineers and builders who devised the means by which those ends could be achieved" (Starr, 2005, p.8).

Furthermore, BTC and related projects are underpinned by an impressive legal architecture made up of national constitutions, international agreements and commercial contracts between MNCs, host governments and IFIs, and an array of additional legal instruments. In total it comprises a hierarchal legal structure that governs the operation of the project and determines relations between its participants. Provisions of this international legal framework supersede domestic laws of the countries hosting the pipeline (Blatchford, 2005, p.120; Kandiyoti, 2012, pp.167-169).

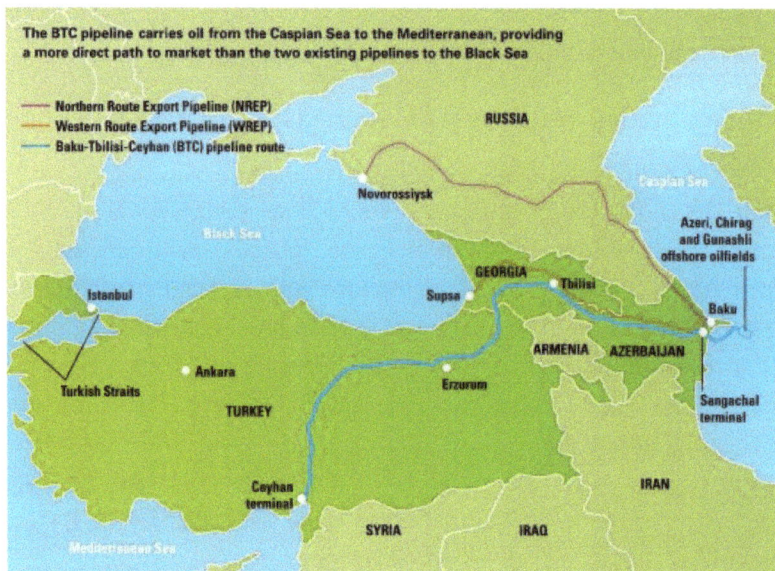

Map 1. BTC pipeline (Source: Oxford Engineering Alumni, 2008)

BTC project had also had considerable normative implications, with concerns raised over human, social and environmental impact of the pipeline. These concerns are at the heart of the debate around BTC, both within participating states and internationally. This is reflected in the sustained criticism of the project before and since its operation commenced (Muttitt and Marriott, 2002; Carroll, 2010; Marriott and Minio-Paluello, 2013).

It is also reflected in the widespread integration of social, environmental, human rights and developmental considerations in the workings of the project Starr, 2005, pp. 11-13). Therefore,

BTC project and political debates around it in the late 1990s and early 2000s should be understood in their wider historical context, as part of an evolving story of energy exploration and development in the region.

Running alongside BTC for much of its route is its natural gas sibling the South-Caucasus Pipeline (SCP). The 700km pipeline transports gas from Azerbaijan's Shah Deniz off-shore gas field, running across Azerbaijan, Georgia and Turkey, where it is currently connected to the local distribution network, although it has been considerably expanded over the past few years (BP, SCP, 2017). It is intended as the first link in an interlocking chain of pipelines which, when completed, will form the Southern Gas Corridor (SGC) – SCP, Trans-Anatolian Pipeline (TANAP) and Trans-Adriatic Pipeline (TAP) (BP Magazine, 12.10.2017).

Just as BTC proved central to unlocking Caspian oil reserves, SGC is seen as a major energy project of global significance: "Seven countries, 11 companies, as many gas sales agreements, more than $40 billion of investment and upwards of 30,000 people employed during its busiest phase of activity: the Southern Gas Corridor is one of the global oil and gas industry's most significant – and ambitious – undertakings yet. It is also one of the largest projects in BP's portfolio – and of strategic importance in the business's shift towards gas" (BP Magazine, 12.10.2017).

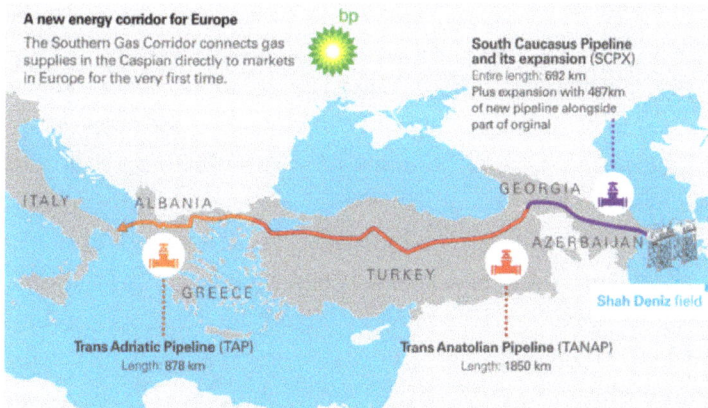

Map 2. BP Visual Guide to SGC (Source: BP Magazine, 12.10.2017)

It is clear, therefore, that while SGC and BTC represent different points in evolution of energy politics they form part of a common empirical framework when it comes to adopting the theory-synergetic approach. Like BTC, Southern Gas Corridor is a multifaceted international project, characterized by a set of complex multi-agency interactions and informed by highly polarized normative debates.

The project is of crucial importance for states, companies and institutions involved in its development but for environmentalists and others who oppose it, SGC is "an emblematic project likely to lock in a fossil fuel model instead of promoting a de-carbonised future" (CounterBalance, Platform and Re:Common, 08.03.2016). BTC and SGC projects are not merely pieces of industrial infrastructure for energy transmission – they symbolize normative choices about energy, environment, and the kinds of possible social orders these choices determine.

In this chapter international politics of oil and gas is introduced as the broad ontological field of this study and is placed within historical framework of IR theoretical debates. The next two chapters set out rationalist and reflectivist/post-positivist models of BTC and SGC case-studies. Perhaps the most important observation to be drawn at this point is that oil serves as a single, common but complex empirical field, upon which different theoretical models (from Classical Liberalism, Realism and Marxism, through to the "neo-neo synthesis," to the reflectivist critique and then on to positivist response and so on), operate independently but simultaneously, in synergy.

Again, the objective is not to ascertain which theory gets it right about oil but to accurately determine which part of the deep ontology of oil is being revealed by the insights of a specific theoretical model or paradigm, and how that particular framework relates to others in forming the empirical problem-field of international oil and gas politics.

Thus feminism may not be useful in explaining the crude oil prices collapse of 2015, but it is invaluable in identifying the effects of the Niger Delta oil crisis on marginalized groups (Ihayere et al, 2014). Marxism may not be the best theoretical tool to address the question of the environmental impact of Chinese state energy policy in Africa in 2000s, but it does, for example, provide a sharp analytical framework for understanding the rise of anti-imperialist and socialist movements in oil producing regions of the Russian Caucasus in the 1900s (Suny, 1972).

Positivist approaches might focus on the power of oil (physical, material and political) (Montgomery, 2010); critical theories - on exposing the costs and vagaries of its industry (and who benefits from it globally) (e.g. Silverstein, 2014); post-modernist analysis - on deconstructing the narrative of oil consumption (e.g. Margonelli, 2008); constructivist paradigm - on the development and outcomes of social processes in the business and politics of oil (e.g. Bower, 2010) and so on.

These different paradigmatic approaches are telling the same story, or rather different threads of the same story, occurring simultaneously or at different times in history but cumulatively constituting an epic, Tolkienesque tapestry of knowledge about oil, into which a new element has come in: the resultant picture is greater than, and not explained by, the sum of the component threads. It is explained and animated by the knowledge-maximising effect of theoretical synergy. A commitment to synergetic analysis, with its implicit historicism, requires constant recognition of a deeper ontology of any given subject matter or empirical puzzle – a mystified, obscured reality which can be revealed through an open-ended scientific engagement. This commitment is not an ideological standpoint or an arbitrary aspiration.

It is beyond debate that the grand, deep ontology of oil suggested in this cursory analysis is expansive, multi-layered, complex, multidimensional, and one that encompasses a wide array of concepts, actors and processes of both social and material kind. As a complex ontological field its geographical scope is truly global in terms of the physical, geological occurrence of oil in different locales around the world, and international in terms of the historical process of its distribution and movement across the planet. As Francisco Parra observes: "Most of the oil consumed in the world today has moved from one country to another" (2013, p.1).

Conclusion

As an empirical research problem hydrocarbons pose an implicitly interdisciplinary challenge. The natural science of oil and gas comprises a multidisciplinary combination, bringing together geology, chemistry, seismology, engineering; it is highly-technology dependent and is driven by a continuous process of innovation and discovery. As will be shown technology emerges as one of the key factors determining the course and nature of relations between oil producing and consuming states, societies and multinational energy companies.

As a social scientific enterprise oil studies represents an even broader range of disciplinary approaches, ranging from history and sociology to game theory modelling and international finance and economics, domestic and international law, anthropology, business management and administration. This is before wider arts and humanities are considered – the drama, even romance of oil has a potential to capture imagination few other phenomena possess. It has had a profound cultural and social impact, inspiring works of art, literature and cinema.

This ontological complexity has profound empirical implications, for it transmits and permeates the entire subject matter, on macro and micro-levels, on grand- and mid-range theoretical scale. For example, a pipeline carrying 700,000 barrels of oil per day is not merely a product of an intergovernmental agreement, cannot be reduced to the terms of the corporate contract underpinning it and does not represent a purely technological enterprise. It encompasses all three and many other elements, social, political, cultural, even imaginational.

An oil pipeline can be a symbol, representing simultaneously a triumph of corporate endeavor, a standard of great technological achievement, a threat to national security, a solution to the problem of regional energy diversification, an environmental threat to local natural habitat, a hope for national progress and prosperity, additional CO_2 in the atmosphere, a reminder of past historical accomplishment, challenge to national pride e.g. as a reminder of loss of territorial or imperial control, and many other different things to different actors.

Therefore, any attempt at construction of a parsimonious model of oil politics is bound to be unsuccessful. Seeking to ascribe systemic, structural qualities to a complex, multidimensional ontological field (one that is constantly evolving and changing in response to external stimuli and internal dynamics, and is hyper-sensitive to ideational and material shifts) is a futile enterprise.

Similarly, the belief that this ontology can be reduced solely to the sum of its social construction, e.g. forms of linguistic expressions through which it is constituted or its underlying, hidden power-structures, is unfounded. Ontological complexity is universal and remains true at all levels of analysis and for this reason no forms of knowledge can be excluded on a priori grounds.

Given the task of tackling such a challenge a social scientific project of meta-disciplinary proportions is required. The extent of theoretical, methodological and wider analytical properties of this meta-discipline must match the challenges presented in empirical problems, on all levels of analysis. It needs to possess a particular disciplinary culture and a common language to effectively communicate across disciplinary and epistemological boundaries.

As has been argued already IR has the potential to fulfil this function. Post-Fourth Debate IR is a discipline bursting with epistemological diversity. It is increasingly interdisciplinary, reflective, intellectually responsive to real world developments. And the wealth of its intellectual capital, accumulated through nearly a century of Great Debates, provides for the right analytical toolkit with which to tackle the ontological complexity of oil. The next chapter takes the story of petroleum through the first three IR debates and sets out the rationalist models of international oil politics.

IV
Rationalist Models

Introduction

This chapter explores rationalist approaches to oil and gas politics and sets out rationalist models of the BTC and SGC pipelines. Neo-realism/neo-liberal institutionalism together form the core of mainstream international energy studies and formed the dominant discourse for over a century. This chapter examines evolution of the field through the prism of the first three Great Debates, charting the history of the oil industry from its early beginnings in the nineteenth century through to present day, with a particular focus on developments in the Caspian-Black Sea-Mediterranean region.

BTC and SGC pipeline systems take their place in the structure of oil politics set in its expansive timeline but key themes and issues that characterize rationalist paradigm as shaped by the neorealist/neo-liberal discourse recur continuously throughout the three debates. The chapter opens with overviews of classical realist/liberal and neo-realist/neo-liberal institutionalist examinations of oil politics. It then charts historical evolution of BTC and SGC pipelines through the three great debates and concludes with integrated rationalist models of the two projects.

Classical Realist and Liberal Approaches

Classical realist analysis of international politics of oil begins with examination of *power*, and in particular military power. As E.H. Car puts it, "… the ultima ratio of power in international relations is war" (1939 (1981), p. 102). Given this fact, military power becomes not only an instrument of state policy but an end in itself. Acquisition of military power is closely linked with the economic strength and capabilities of a state, especially in relation to other states.

There is a strong association, therefore, between economic and political power (Ibid., pp.104-106). This point is emphasized by H.J. Morgenthau: "Control over [oil deposits] has been an important factor in the distribution of power, in the sense that whoever is able to add them to his other sources of raw materials adds that much strength to his own resources and deprives his competitors proportionately" (1985, p. 133)

Carr is dismissive of neo-classical economists' insistence on theoretical separation of the economic from the political, symbolized by the *laissez-faire* approach of the nineteenth century. He criticizeds what he calls "the illusion of a divorce between politics and economics" (ibid., p.107). From a realist standpoint economic forces do not constitute an independent factor in international relations and, along with military strength of nations, are integral to the political dynamics of inter-state competition and balance of power. As Carr argues economic power "…cannot be separated from military power, nor military from economic. They are both integral parts of political power; and in the long run one is helpless without the other" (Ibid., p. 120).

Not surprisingly, access to and control of natural resources, such as oil, are prioritized as fundamental functions of economic and therefore political military power. Carr identifies autarky as one of the means by which "economic power is pressed into the service of national policy"– (Ibid., p.110). Autarky or pursuit of self-sufficiency can refer to state policy aimed at total economic independence or a narrower focus on self-sufficiency in key raw resources, such as oil, food-stuffs, water.

Possession of natural resources such as oil is instrumental to a state's ability to exercise military force and is therefore essential. As Carr wryly observes: "Where home supplies were not available, the unfettered control of overseas supplies became a primary objective. The desire to control adequate supplies of oil inspire an active British policy in more than one oil-producing country" (Ibid., p. 113).

Autarky, therefore, as realists define it is above all "a form of preparedness for war" (Ibid., p.111). Morgenthau paid particular attention to this relationship between military strength and economic power in the form of raw materials. He considered that their relative and absolute importance for the power of a state depended "necessarily upon

technology of the warfare practiced in a particular period of history"
(1985, p. 131). Hence, from a realist standpoint the importance of oil in
international politics over the past century and a half is determined chiefly
by the central role it plays in the efficacy of various dominant military
technologies.

Military technology/strength – autarky – power: this schematic
symbolizes the crude material value of oil as translated into power politics.
It also provides for a starting point in the classical realist analysis of
international oil politics, with oil emerging as the instrumental raw
material of war in the early twentieth century. In the 1890s Germany,
recently unified and vying for a great power status, embraced *Weltpolitik*
– a global policy driven by an assertive diplomacy, acquisition of overseas
colonies and crucially development of a modern, industrial navy second
only to Britain's Royal Navy (see von Bülow, 1932).

As Germany demanded its "place in the sun" it sought a decisive
technological advantage over its rivals to give itself a critical military edge
(see, for example, Kelly, 2011; Sondhaus, 1997). Growth of German
power in late nineteenth century was stimulated in large part by its
consistent pursuit of a decisive technological advantage over its rivals to
give itself a critical military edge (see, for example, von Bülow, 1932;
Kelly, 2011; Sondhaus, 1997). This aggressive arms build-up, especially
construction of oil-powered, ocean-going gunboats, was to have a
decisive consequence (1991, p.152). The Royal Navy, including its
dreadnought-class warships, still ran on coal and German military
technological innovation – switching their navy to oil - threatened the
balance of power.

Winston Churchill was appointed the First Lord of Admiralty in
1911, just as German gunboats began to carry out exercises in the
Mediterranean.[12] Although initially sceptical, he quickly realized that
converting the Royal Navy from coal to oil was a strategic priority. It
would allow higher speeds, greater rapidity, increased operational scope

---

[12] The Agadir Crisis of July 1911 came as a particular shock to France and Britain.
German battleship *Panther* sailed into Moroccan port of Agadir under a pretext of
protecting German residents, thus demonstrating Germany's growing naval power
(Hiro, 2007, p.75).

and required less man-power (Ibid., p. 155). The decision was made in April 1912 and, as Yergin states, the great shipbuilding programmes of 1912, 1913 and 1914 "constituted the greatest addition – in terms of sheer power and cost – in the history of the Royal Navy up to that time. All the ships of those three programs were based on oil – not a coal ship among them" (Ibid., p.156).

Yet the question of where the oil to power these ships was to be found remained. Britain required a reliable and independent source of oil to ensure its military security was not compromised. In the first decade of the twentieth century there were two oil companies representing private British interest – the Royal Dutch/Shell and smaller Anglo-Persian Oil Company (APOC), operating a concession in Iran. It became clear from the outset that the British government was particularly concerned about APOC,[13] fearing its concession might pass under control of a foreign syndicate (Ibid., p. 159).

For their part, APOC's management consistently emphasized "that Anglo-Persian was a natural adjunct to British strategy and policy and was a significant national asset – and that all the company's directors saw it just that way" (Ibid.). By contrast, Royal Dutch/Shell by virtue of being a joint international concern, symbolized by its Dutch chairman Henri Deterding, could potentially be susceptible to German pressure. By May 1914 the British Government acquired 51% stake of APOC and a 25-year contract with the Admiralty to supply Royal Navy with cheap fuel oil (Ibid, p.160).

Thus, in line with Carr's observations, Britain lacking domestic supplies of oil, sought unfettered control of overseas supplies, which in turn inspired an active British policy in Iran and wider Gulf region. In fact, in "The Twenty Years' Crisis" Carr mentions British government's purchase of Anglo-Persian Oil Company as an example of political objectives being attained by direct government economic investment (1939 (1981), p. 114). Indeed, many in Whitehall wondered about the purpose of Anglo-Persian – was it to simply supply the Royal Navy with fuel or was it "to help create an integrated, state-owned oil company, a

---

[13] Anglo Persian Oil Company was renamed Anglo-Iranian Oil Company in 1935 and British Petroleum Company in 1954. It is one of antecedents of the modern BP.

national champion, and then to assist that company in expanding its commercial interests worldwide?" (Yergin, 1991, p.175).

And in line with Morgenthau's dictum, Britain's decision to switch the Royal Navy to oil "was driven by the technological imperatives of the Anglo-German naval race. Even as Germans sought equality, the British Navy was committed to maintaining naval supremacy, and oil offered a vital edge in terms of speed and flexibility" (Yergin, 1991, p. 163). But the strategic impact of oil was not limited to naval power as was demonstrated by mass application of the internal combustion engine to military uses.

The invention of the tank and its first successful deployment by the British in the Battle of Cambrai in late 1917 proved decisive: "When the German High Command declared in October 1918 that victory was no longer possible, the first reason it gave was the introduction of the tank" (Ibid., p. 171). Furthermore, motorisation of military transportation, nascent use of air power and general rapid technological transformations in warfare all served to underline the critical value of oil, now an essential element of military power (Hiro, 2007, p.37). As Yergin observes: "Oil for the first time, but certainly not the last, had become an instrument of national policy, a strategic commodity second to none" (Ibid, p.163).

Meanwhile, a classical liberal analysis of international oil politics begins with an explicit recognition that "virtually from the very beginning, petroleum was an international business" (Ibid. p.56). For classical liberals, or idealists, unlike the realists, the focus of enquiry is not limited to aspects of state power but is directed towards identifying opportunities for international cooperation. Liberal internationalism, underpinned by Kantian ethics, holds "democratic government, economic interdependence, and international law and organizations as means to overcome the security dilemma of the international system" (Russett, 2013, p.95).

The story of oil, therefore, begins with the establishment and growth of the global oil industry in the second half of the nineteenth century. Particular attention is, therefore, paid to the prominent role of international oil companies, banks, various regulatory frameworks under international law, especially international commercial law, and the relationships between various actors participating in global oil trade.

By liberal account, this is first and foremost the story of international oil companies and their leaders, whose names have become synonymous with the very idea of capitalism – John, D. Rockefeller and his Standard Oil empire, the Nobels, the Rothschilds, Marcus Samuel and his Shell/Royal Dutch amongst others. This is the story of free trade and enterprise, of global banking and financial forces, of international organizations and firms, led by irrepressible characters, committed to promoting the causes of commercial industrialism and scientific and technological advancement.

This is also a story of how the interests of states and governments are subsumed and shaped by the interests of private commercial enterprise. By late nineteenth century oil was already a valuable commodity, traded around the world in the form of finished products, namely kerosene (Yergin, 1991, p.56). The business of oil preceded the politics of it. By 1900 oil was already a global industry, dominated by the Standard Oil Company in the United States and the Nobels, the Rothschilds and Marcus Samuel's Shell Transport and Trading Company in Iran and the Russian Transcaucasus (Azerbaijan and Georgia) (Hiro, 2007, pp.10-12).

There were also many other smaller, independent producers and traders around the world, and along with the oil giants, they were brought together in a complex web of commercial competition, technological innovation, financial expansion, geographical race for new sources and an evolving regulatory legal framework to govern it all. It is inconceivable from an idealist perspective to reduce this complexity to mere power politics and inter-state military competition. Classical liberal thinkers emphasized how economic integration and open commercial relations between countries have made war both costly and futile. Realist concepts such as autarky belied the reality of free trade and the potential for international cooperation, and were in fact ruinous.

This latter point was made forcefully by Alfred Zimmern in his 1918 pamphlet "The Economic Weapon in the War Against Germany." Zimmern argued that rather than reinforce a country's preparedness for war autarky is in reality the very opposite and is virtually impossible to achieve. By embarking on a war of conquest Germany came undone by an unprecedented global economic blockade, which deprived her from access to markets and natural resources: "The Central Powers are being besieged by practically the entire world and they have no means at their disposal for bringing the siege to an end" (p.2). Zimmern goes on to quote a leading German industrialist describing his country in December 1915 as a "besieged fortress:" "Closed in by land and sea, it was thrown upon its own resources, and a prospect of war opened out before us boundless in time and expense, in danger and sacrifice" (p.3).

Unlike realists, classical liberals such as Alfred Zimmern treat economic forces as independent factors, separate from military and political power, and more important: "It is enough to emphasize the fact that the economic weapon is the most powerful in the varied armoury of the Allies" (Ibid. p.20). German military success and territorial gains counted for nothing: "Germany has conquered Belgium, Poland, Serbia, Lithuania, Courland and Friuli. But the Allies have conquered cotton, wool, jute, leather, copper, and feeding-stuffs" (Ibid). In the age of commerce and industry, global trade and economic interdependence, rapid scientific progress and technological innovation, autarky was impossible, territorial expansion - self-defeating.

This theme runs consistently through the idealist accounts of international politics. In *The Great Illusion* Norman Angell (1913) explicitly rejects a proto-realist world-view and argues that: "…it belongs to a stage of development out of which we have passed; that the commerce and industry of a people no longer depend upon the expansion of its political frontiers…" (p. x-xi). Instead, he states, the wealth of nations is based upon development of credit and commercial law, with trade and industry becoming so interdependent and integrated into the system of international finance, "that if conquest is not to be self-injurious it must respect the enemy's property, in which case it becomes economically futile" (Ibid).

The story of the Turkish Petroleum Company (TPC) serves to illustrate the point and provides an opportunity to engage in a wider liberal analysis of oil politics. By 1914 German commercial interests had already established a considerable presence in the race for new sources of oil in present-day Iraq, securing a 25% stake in a joint venture with the Royal Dutch/Shell (25%) and the Turkish National Bank (50%), a British financial syndicate dominated by the trader and financier Calouste Gulbenkian (Yergin, 1991, p. 185). Gulbenkian was nicknamed "Mr. Five Percent," having acquired five percent of TPC in negotiations over its restructuring, with the Anglo-Persian Oil Company (APOC) replacing the Turkish National Bank as the primary British concern, just before the outbreak of World War I.

Known as the Turkish Petroleum Company (TPC) the consortium of Anglo-Persian, Royal Dutch/Shell and Deutsche Bank represented conglomeration of British, Dutch and German business interests, all committing that "none would be involved in oil production anywhere in the Ottoman Empire" unless through TPC (Ibid., p.187). The outbreak of the war brought the Germans and Ottomans into conflict with the British across the Mesopotamian region. It ended in 1918 when the British forces captured Mosul.

Germany may have been pursuing imperial ambitions in the Middle East but her defeat in World War I meant the loss of the 25% stake in the Turkish Petroleum Company –Deutsche Bank shares were transferred to Compagnie Française des Pétroles (CFP), the French Petroleum Company (known today as Total) (Ibid., p.190). A similar fate befell other Deutsche Bank oil enterprises and subsidiaries, such as British Petroleum – a large European distribution and marketing network that served as an outlet for German-produced Romanian oil before the war; it was later acquired by the Anglo-Persian Oil and adopted as the official corporate name by which it is known to this day (Ibid., 174).

As the Paris Peace Conference opened at Versailles, British troops were in control of Mosul but under the Sykes-Picot Agreement the city was assigned as a French area of influence. The region was crucial to both France and Britain and the compromise reached between the two countries in April 1920 – as part of the San Remo Agreement - adhered to traditional, pre- World War I principles of imperial "great power" politics – France abandoned her claim to Mosul, which would pass under British control though a League of Nations mandate; in return France would get the

German shares in the Turkish Petroleum Company as part of the reparations settlement (Parra, 2013, p.8; Sampson, 1975, p.83).

The deal caused an international uproar and was denounced as old-fashioned imperialist carve-up. The Agreement ran counter to both the letter and the spirit of President Woodrow Wilson's "Fourteen Points" speech and the broader tide towards national self-determination and collective security, as exemplified by the establishment of the League of Nations. The Ottoman Empire was no more (Wilson's point XII) and TPC was now negotiating with the sovereign government in Baghdad, the capital of independent kingdom of Iraq. TPC did not secure a concession from Baghdad to explore for oil until March 1925 (Yergin, 1991, p.201).

Furthermore, Franco-British attempt to close access to Iraq's oil resources to other countries ran counter of U.S.-championed "Open Door" principles, aimed at securing access for American capital and business. U.S. firms were excluded from participation in the Turkish Petroleum Company and this was not acceptable to Washington. Daniel Yergin is sceptical of Wilsonian liberalism and its professed norms and values – "high-minded vagueness" (Ibid., p. 189). As a realist he views Wilson's championing of U.S. oil companies against the San Remo Agreement as an example of state policy driving commercial priorities of private business: "Cynical observers were struck by the degree to which the Wilson Administration, the embodiment of progressivism, now gave support in its final phase to the companies" (Ibid., p. 195).

Yet for idealists there is no ethical contradiction. Wilson's point III clearly states: "The removal, so far as possible, of all economic barriers and the establishment of an equality of trade conditions among all the nations consenting to the peace and associating themselves for its maintenance" (1918). Acrimony gave way to serious negotiations and what emerged eventually in 1928 as the Red Line Agreement was a new multinational deal involving British, American, Dutch and French oil companies entering into contract with the Iraqi government to explore and develop oil fields in Iraq, and other former Ottoman territories (with some important exceptions).

In the liberal account the dynamics of international oil politics are driven by the economic and technological forces, by free trade and international finance, and by the global reach of international oil companies, which exercise considerable influence over national policy. For example, the decision by the British government to lift the prohibition on tanker traffic through the Suez Canal in 1890 was dictated in large part by Shell's expansion into cross-ocean oil trade and the need to give a British-owned private company a competitive edge against the dominance of the American Standard Oil (Yergin, 1991, p. 67).

Liberal international politics of oil are conceptualized normatively as rule-governed behavior of multiplicity of actors, from states to international organizations, driven by the progressive global agenda of industrial progress, open economic competition, prosperity and democratic peace. This is translated on empirical level as a construction of an ontological model which includes the study of institutions and processes of the international oil industry.

Epistemologically such study would rely on logical positivist philosophy of science, and historical and sociological methodologies. This ontological and epistemological model can be applied to the entire cycle of oil history up to the present. For the purposes of this study, however, it is sufficient to place the idealist analysis within its actual historical timeline in relation to the developments of the Great Debates in IR (see Appendix 1).

IR scholars today should remember that the First Debate was a very acrimonious affair. E.H. Carr was dismissive of liberalism's proclaimed ethical aspirations, in particular Woodrow Wilson's "high-sounding moral rhetoric," which he regarded as "little more than an idealistic fig-leaf masking America's ambition of extending its own influence at the expense of others" (Cox, *Introduction* in Carr, 2001 [1939], xvi). Liberal scholars in turn were aghast by what they saw as "moral vacuum" at the heart of Carr's vision of international relations (Arnold Toynbee quoted in Ibid., xxix).

Alfred Zimmern "was disturbed by Carr's lack of moral compass" and Norman Angell was even more scathing in his criticism of "The Twenty Years' Crisis," and what he saw as the book's ethical shortcomings and ambiguities, unforgivable at a time of rising fascism and totalitarian communism: "Ultimately, all that Carr had done, and presumably done quite consciously, was to provide 'aid and comfort about equal degree' to the followers of Karl Marx and Adolf Hitler'" (Ibid., p. xxx).

Classical realists, and E.H. Carr in particular, were in turn scathing of liberal assessments of world politics. First, they argued that economic power is merely an instrument of national policy and second, that the economic weapon is "pre-eminently the weapon of strong Powers" (Carr, 1981 (1939), p. 119). Thus, importantly, they challenged the legitimacy of the normative framework advanced by idealists. For example, Carr asserted that powerful states can achieve political objectives by utilising the economic weapon while weaker states are more likely to use force but that the objectives for both were morally equal: "The substitution of the economic weapon for the military weapon – what Marx calls the replacement of cannon by capital – is a symptom not as much of superior morality as of superior strength" (Ibid., p. 117).

What distinguishes classical realist analysis of oil politics is the central role it accords to power (see Appendix 2). Instrumentality of oil as a source and conduit of economic, military and political strength of states is prioritized. The normative framework of such analysis is far from absent but it is bracketed by the terms of core power relations amongst national states. This is well illustrated by E.H. Carr's treatment of economic factors in international politics. Having characterized economic power as an instrument of policy, he sets out two means by which it is deployed – the export of capital and control of foreign markets (1981 [1939], p. 113).

In the former case, British government's direct purchase of shares in the Suez Canal and Anglo-Iranian (formerly Anglo-Persian) Oil Company are amongst the examples of direct government ownership as means of projecting and accumulating state power (Ibid., p.114). The role of private companies and individual entrepreneurs, celebrated by idealists, is downplayed as subordinate to the priorities of states: "More often, government used their power to stimulate investments by banks and private individuals in the interests of national policy. Political interests were furthered by private investors enjoying, like the chartered companies of the nineteenth century, government patronage or, more commonly, diplomatic support" (Ibid.).

By this account, international oil companies in the first decades of the twentieth century were extensions of state policy, rather than autonomous economic actors, pursuing independent objectives. The liberal narrative of progressive advance of industrial capitalism and international systems of legal governance is rejected in favor of analysis of inter-state competition in an anarchic system. Therefore, processes such as the internationalisation of trade, commerce and industry are seen as a product of the struggle between states for control of foreign markets.

And to paraphrase Carr, it is not clear whether political power is being used to acquire control over oil resources in far flung corners of the world for the sake of their economic value or whether oil resources are being sought in order to establish and strengthen political power: "...powerful countries found their 'natural' markets in areas where their political interests lay and where their political interests could be most readily asserted" (Ibid., p. 116). For example, Carr brings up the example of Britain's Export Credit Guarantee Department, set up by the government to apply its purchasing power as an international political asset, by issuing guarantees for overseas private projects considered to be "in the national interest" (Ibid, p. 116).

Invariably, the arc of the realist narrative returns to issues of power and war. The expansion of U.S. presence in the Middle East in the 1930s and 1940s (at the expense of the British), for example, had little to do with Wilsonian principles and everything to do with the rise of the American hegemony and the urgent need to secure reliable extraterritorial supplies of oil – a strategic resource needed to fuel modern industrial economies and armies; this point was argued forcefully at the time by the then U.S. Secretary for Interior and Petroleum Administrator for War, Harold L. Ickes (1943a; 1943b).

Neorealist/Neo-Liberal Institutionalist Approaches

World War II was a turning point in the history of global energy. It marked the pivotal shift from coal to oil as the primary fuel of industrial and economic growth, ushering in a new world petroleum order. Oil production and consumption in the West and in the USSR increased rapidly, fuelling the reconstruction effort and the post-war economic boom (Yergin, 1991, p. 409-410).

Oil proved to be the strategic commodity in war – powering tanks, ships and planes, but also trucks and other internal combustion engine vehicles. And the post-war period heralded a golden age of the automobile – by 1950 there were forty million cars in operation in the United States alone, leading to an explosion in demand for petroleum (Ibid.). By 1960 worldwide consumption of oil rose to 21 million barrels per day (from just 6 million barrels in 1945) (Roberts, 2005, p.40). What began as a cottage industry in the nineteenth century had become the life-force of the Modern Age.

Coal remains to this day an important fossil fuel, especially in power generation, but as Roberts observes, it does not have "oil's political and economic importance or its star status as the world's first geopolitical commodity" (Ibid.). This is first and foremost due to the fact that oil is a highly versatile material, with an almost inexhaustible range of applications. Boosted by the post-war boom, the oil industry expanded rapidly, developing new uses and applications for oil, such as rubber and plastics, and employing new technologies to find, produce and market it.

There were now more operating fields and the attendant infrastructures, from pipeline networks, ocean-going tankers and deep-water sea ports and oil terminals, to storage complexes and petrol stations. The rapid enlargement of the global oil industry was driven by no less rapid advances in geology, chemistry and other natural sciences, which enabled more effective methods of exploration and development of oil fields, better drilling technologies, new refining techniques, and therefore a greater range of fuels and other oil products (see Downey, 2009; Montgomery, 2010).

The Soviet oil industry, for example, marked an important milestone in 1949 with a first successful off-shore development at Oily Rocks, near Baku, Azerbaijan. By mid-1960s some five thousand oil workers lived in a sprawling off-shore platform city out in the Caspian Sea, complete with its own cinema and hotels (Igorev, 2010).

Meanwhile, the discovery of the giant Ghawar field in Saudi Arabia in 1948 proved a decisive and formative experience for the Arabian

- American Oil Company (ARAMCO), cementing the United States as a preeminent oil power: "By 1950, the estimate of the reserves of this mammoth field – more than eighty-five billion barrels – had surpassed the wildest dreams of oilmen" (Hiro, 2007, p. 90). Several more such fields would be found throughout the Middle East in the 1950s.

Oil was now a colossal international enterprise comprising a myriad political, economic, social and technological processes and interactions on a truly global scale, bringing together geologists and engineers, lawyers, traders and corporate executives, politicians and civil servants, in pursuit and competition for the world's critical commodity: "to be a world power a nation needed either oil or the money to buy it" (Ibid.).

Moreover, the post-war scientific turn in the oil industry was complemented by development of increasingly specialized theories about the economics of oil. The sheer volumes now being traded on the open markets and the growing complexity of the international political economy of oil and energy more generally, required holistic understanding of a wide array of issues, from supply and demand dynamics, to prices and corporate governance, to marketing and trade, to international contract and commercial law (for a definitive rationalist overview of oil politics in World War II and the post-war petroleum order see Yergin, 1991, pp. 289-370; pp. 371-431)

These themes were all playing out against a backdrop of escalating Cold War tensions. Indeed, one of the first crises in the conflict was the Soviet occupation of northern Iran. Soviet troops were ordered out of the country in May 1946 but this did little to assuage Western fears over possible Soviet advance in the Gulf. As Daniel Yergin argued, while oil was not the prime motivation for Soviet actions in Iran, Stalin was nevertheless interested in Iranian oil, and historically Russia had consistently sought to expand its influence in that country– "a traditional objective of Russian foreign policy, one that was almost a century and a half old" (1991, p. 403).

U.S. policy makers were worried about the security of oil supplies and the threat of Soviet expansionism in the region; this being at least partly the motivation behind the launch of the Truman Doctrine in 1947:

"Ostensibly aimed at Greece, Iran and Turkey, its true target was the oil-rich area of Western Asia" (Hiro, 2007, p. 90). As Daniel Yergin summarized: "Oil provided the point at which foreign policy, international economic considerations, national security, and corporate interests would all converge. The Middle East would be the focus" (1991, p. 410).

It should not come as a surprise, therefore, that the post-war behavioralist turn in the social sciences had had a profound impact on the contemporary scholarship of international politics of oil. Behavioralism heralded the Second (theoretical) Debate in IR but also the First Foundational (philosophical) Debate, broadly pitting traditionalists of the logical positivist PoS school against proponents of instrumentalism. As the "behavioralist revolution" proceeded it gradually transformed the empirical landscape of IR in general, and international oil politics in particular. But by the 1960s a degree of epistemological and ontological convergence emerged between what Eulau described at the time as "behavioralists" and "institutionalists."

"The issue of behavioralism versus institutionalism has largely disappeared. Both institutionalists and behavioralists have discovered their common commitment to the empirical investigation of political phenomena... Political behaviorists have come to realize that in attempting to explain the varieties of political behavior, institutions provide their own methodological advantages" (Ibid., p.5).

On an empirical level, this convergence contributed to the development of a more attenuated forms of realist and liberal analyses of oil politics. Access to stable and secure supplies of petroleum emerged as a key issue. Heavily influenced by economics, scholars working in the field of oil and energy politics produced complex quantitative studies focusing on issues of available oil reserves, security of supplies and the behavior of actors in the global energy market in the context of evolving dynamics of the Cold War.

This scholarship was not limited to raw data analysis, but also involved a systematic examination of key topics and themes in oil studies – strategic value of oil, interplay between government and business, the impact of various regulatory frameworks, interstate competition for control of the supplies, the role and increasingly power of oil-producing states, and the influence of international institutions and legal frameworks. For example, Stocking and Watkins (1948), "Cartels or competition: the economics of international controls by business and government" is an example of the contemporary political studies of the economics of international regulatory frameworks in the oil industry.

Schwartz's "Russia's Soviet Economy" (1950) is a classic example of early "Sovietology," with a characteristic comparative focus on the Soviet economic performance, including but not limited to the crucial post-war Five Year Plans and the oil industry. Shwardon's "The Middle East, Oil, and the Great Powers" (1974 [1955]) – one of the first examinations of the growing importance of the Middle East as a strategic, oil-producing region and a Cold War arena (see also Stocking (1970) "Middle East oil: a study in political and economic controversy;" and Shwardon, (1977)).

Hartshorn's "Oil Companies & Governments: An Account" (1962) is an early and quite characteristic response to the emergence of OPEC and the growing pressure on international oil companies; as such it constitutes an emphatic defence of the role of IOCs. Reviewing the book in *The Spectator* in May 1962 Alfred Sherman argued that it "shows how utterly irrelevant are the traditional Leninist theses on economic imperialism to the oil industry, which represents by far the greatest Western investment in most underdeveloped countries."

In "A Financial Analysis of Middle Eastern Oil Concessions: 1901-65," Mikdashi (1966) offers a retrospective historical analysis of the economics of the concessionary system, while Nash (1968), "United States Oil Policy, 1890-1964: Business and Government in Twentieth Century America" and Nordhauser (1979), "The quest for stability: domestic oil regulation, 1917-1935," both similarly provide overviews of the historical evolution of U.S. governmental oil policy and its international implications. The stand-out text on the oil industry in this period is Morris Adelman's "The World Petroleum Market" (1972) – a classic study of economics and politics of oil, with a specific focus on the operations of emerging global commodities markets.

The above overview is intended as an illustration of the scope and range of scholarship on international oil politics that emerged in the

Second Debate. It can be argued, looking at the literature of the period, that this was a formative stage in the development of the mainstream, rationalist approach to energy studies. The key themes of the positivist model – security of supply being the paramount one – were set out in the scholarly and political debates of the post-war period, not least by the policy-makers themselves.

For example, below is an an extract from the U.S. Joint Chiefs of Staff memo to the U.S. State Department in September 1946, on the issue of Soviet activities in northern Iran and their implications for U.S. interests in the Middle East:

From U.S. Joint Chiefs of Staff memo to the U.S. State Department, September 1946 (Foreign Relations of the United States, 1946, Vol. II. Doc. 396):

> The Joint Chiefs of Staff consider that United States strategic interest in Iran is closely related to United States strategic interest in the Near and Middle East area as a whole as follows:
>
> Our best estimates indicate that the USSR does not now derive sufficient oil from sources within her borders to support a major war. The objective of the fourth Soviet five-year plan is 35,000,000 metric tons' production annually. Again, our best estimates indicate this tonnage is only sufficient to meet the total Russian peacetime needs upon the expiration of this fourth five-year plan. The USSR and Iran have formed a joint Russian-Iranian oil company to develop oil resources in northern Iran, an area geologists consider an improbable source of large oil production, a fact which must be well known to the Russians. Hence, her motives in forming this Russian-Iranian oil company are subject to suspicion." Loss of the Iraq and Saudi Arabia sources to the United States and her allies would mean that in case of war they would fight an oil-starved war. Conversely, denial of these sources to the USSR would force her to fight an oil-starved war. However, due to Russia's geographic position, great land mass, and superior manpower potential, any lack of oil limiting air action by the United States and her allies or hampering their transportation ability or their war production would be of great advantage to the USSR. It is therefore to the strategic interest of the United States to keep Soviet influence and Soviet armed forces removed as far as possible from oil resources in Iran, Iraq, and the Near and Middle East..."

Key rationalist concepts of international oil politics can be clearly discerned in the observations and recommendations contained in the U.S. Joint Chiefs of Staff memo – oil is a strategic commodity, central to a war effort; because of its oil reserves the Middle East is a geographical area of strategic importance to the United States; USSR poses a strategic threat that must be contained and the Soviets physically kept away from the region. Yet these concepts are not coached in vague generalisations; they are quantified and instrumentalized – balance of oil power is measured (in metric tons) and its application (in specific terms e.g. air power) extrapolated, as are the intentions behind the behavior of actors.

For example, why would the USSR form an oil company with Iran when there is no oil in the northern region (which was recently under Soviet control), if not to gain a footbridge for grander expansion plans in the wider Middle East? This in turn would represent an unacceptable security threat to the United States, threatening the loss of Middle Eastern resources. Meanwhile, denying Moscow control of these resources would undermine Soviet military capability. That is where the strategic interests of the United States therefore lay.

The Cold War structured international oil politics in the late 1940s and through the 1950s, setting out key elements of the international political economy of oil. Fears of Soviet expansion in the Middle East and concerns over security of supplies informed Western understanding of oil politics, in the academia and among policy-makers. For example, U.S. Secretary of the Interior Harold Ickes, who oversaw American oil policy during World War II, wrote in his (at the time highly influential) essay "We're Running Out of Oil!" (1943) that "if there should be World War III it would have to be fought with someone else's petroleum, because the United States wouldn't have it... American crown, symbolizing supremacy as the oil empire of the world is sliding down over one eye."

Such concerns remained at the forefront of U.S. policy-making and drove responses to various crises through the late 1950s, including the CIA-backed overthrow of Prime Minister Mossadegh in Iran in 1952-53 and the Suez Crisis in 1956. They also helped prioritize Middle East, and Saudi Arabia in particular, as a new center of gravity in the post-war world (Yergin, 1991, p.393).

These themes and modes of analysis dominated both scholarly and policy debates throughout the 1950s. It can be argued that the Second Debate had the effect of transforming the study of international oil politics from a historical-sociological intellectual enterprise into a highly specialized, data-focused subfield of strategic studies. Behaviorist-institutionalist convergence translated on empirical level into a systematic analysis of Cold War politics and inter-state balancing in competition for control of oil resources, and measurement of behavior of states and international oil companies in a global competitive oil market (for example, volumes of oil traded, proven and recoverable reserves estimations, impact of regulatory frameworks and price controls, cartels and "price-fixing" agreements, a whole array of corporate and other institutional dynamics).

It should not be all that surprising that the study of energy politics should lend itself so easily to economics-influenced, quantitative methodology-driven scholarship. Oil is a commercially-traded commodity, control of which translates into political (military) power. As such it is power that can be quantified and measured. For example, it is possible to calculate how much oil Soviet Union can produce to meet peace-time demand as opposed to war-time demand, just as it is possible to statistically compare proven reserves held by each of the major oil companies, the Seven Sisters, and the impact this or that production cut or increase might have on global oil prices.

With the rise of OPEC, academic (and public) attention shifted to relations between producing and consuming countries, but the core characteristics of the rationalist oil paradigm remained in place – quantitative methodologies, game-theory applications, states and their relation to private and national oil companies as key units of analysis. The Middle East crises and wars of 1960s and 1970s only served to bring oil to the very top of political, academic agenda and, importantly, to the attention of the general public. The issue of Western dependence on Middle Eastern oil came to the fore in the debates about energy and petroleum.

Kenneth Waltz's seminal *Theory of International Politics* was published just months before the second major oil shock, brought about by the Islamic Revolution in Iran in 1979. Applying his economics model to set out a structural theory of international politics, Waltz argued that, like a market, the international system "is made by the actions and interactions of its units, and the theory is based on assumptions about their behavior" (Waltz, 1979, p. 118).

His discussion of oil politics therefore, proceeds within the framework of this parsimonious structural theory, where states competing in a self-help system, do all they can to ensure secure supply of strategic resources: "Countries that are highly dependent, countries that get much of what they badly need from a few possibly unreliable suppliers, must do all they can to increase the chances that they will keep getting it" (Ibid., p. 153).

The OPEC embargo of 1973, the fall of Shah's regime in Iran in 1979 and the consequent spikes in oil prices (and shortages) shook Western confidence and raised fears of permanent dependence on the Middle Eastern oil. Writing in the later editions of *Politics Among Nations*, Hans Morgenthau observed that in the past the consumers controlled prices "through colonial and semi colonial arrangements," but now it is the producers who were organized to raise prices considerably by means of their independent, collective control of oil production.

Morgenthau advocated energy conservation, stockpiling of reserves, developing alternative energy sources and interestingly, limiting and curtailing importation of oil – classical realist strategy of self-sufficiency and autarky: "While there is no way of destroying this stranglehold short of war, there is a way of mitigating its results. It lies in weakening the monopolistic or quasi-monopolistic position of the oil producing nations by strengthening the position of the oil-consuming ones" (1985, p. 135).

By contrast Waltz advocated increasing imports in the short to medium term and conserving domestic resources: "Having imposed quotas on foreign oil for decades to make sure, in the name of resource development, that we would use our own oil first, it makes sense now to rely more on imports" (1979, p. 155). Perhaps on this issue there emerge early distinctions between offensive and defensive realisms, but in other respects Waltz's policy prescriptions on oil matched that of Morgenthau, other experts and indeed the U.S. Government – energy conservation and building up of reserves to withstand embargos. Establishment of the U.S. Strategic Petroleum Reserve in 1975 echoes Waltz's suggestion of a "petroleum stockpile sufficient for riding through, say, a six-month embargo" (Ibid., p.156).

Neo-realism did not completely subsume more traditional forms of realist thinking on oil – many scholars continued to produce historical comparative analysis, emphasising themes of change in the international energy system and inter-state oil politics, as well as the role of non-state actors (see, for example, Stoff, 1982). Yet given the overall impact of neo-realism on IR it is not surprising that international oil politics, as an academic sub-field (as well as wider policy community), came to be heavily influenced by neo-realist thinking.

Analysis of oil politics now took place in the context of a structural international political theory. Natural resources such as oil did not constitute independent units of analysis and were not especially important by themselves; their significance was tied to their contribution to the composition of national power, resource endowment being one of the key elements that determines a nation's power-ranking (Watz, 1979, p. 131).

The experiences of the 1960s and especially the oil shocks of the 1970s served to underline the salience of neo-realist insights – anarchy and war (and how anarchical conditions lead to war) and the power balance in a bi-polar international system. "Behavioralist revolution" and neo-realism introduced systematic use of economics as the dominant instrumentalist positivist analytical framework in the study of oil politics, and indeed for international relations in general (Guzzini, 1998, p. 129). This was in no small part due to the impact of oil crises as "the accrued influence of economic weapons moved economic issues to the level of high politics, i.e. to questions of diplomacy and war" (Ibid., p. 142).

This shift is perhaps best illustrated by comments made by President Jimmy Carter in his now famous "Crisis of Confidence" speech on 15 July 1979:

> In little more than two decades we've gone from a position of energy independence to one in which almost half the oil we use comes from foreign countries, at prices that are going through the roof. Our excessive dependence on OPEC has already taken a tremendous toll on our economy and our people. This is the direct cause of the long lines which have made millions of you spend

aggravating hours waiting for gasoline. It's a cause of the increased inflation and unemployment that we now face. This intolerable dependence on foreign oil threatens our economic independence and the very security of our Nation.

Revolution in Iran was soon followed in by the outbreak of Iran-Iraq war and the Soviet invasion of Afghanistan. U.S. response, in the form of the Carter Doctrine, formally placed the Middle East at the heart of U.S. sphere of strategic interests. Comparing Jimmy Carter's 1980 State of the Union Address (below) and the U.S. Joint Chiefs of Staff 1946 memo to the State Department (above), one is struck by the consistency of the principles underlying the rationale for international oil politics and the role of United States as the world's preeminent oil superpower:

President J. Carter. Extracts from the he State of the Union Address Delivered Before a Joint Session of the Congress. January 23, 1980

"The region which is now threatened by Soviet troops in Afghanistan is of great strategic importance: It contains more than two-thirds of the world's exportable oil. The Soviet effort to dominate Afghanistan has brought Soviet military forces to within 300 miles of the Indian Ocean and close to the Straits of Hormuz, a waterway through which most of the world's oil must flow. The Soviet Union is now attempting to consolidate a strategic position, therefore, that poses a grave threat to the free movement of Middle East oil. This situation demands careful thought, steady nerves, and resolute action, not only for this year but for many years to come. It demands collective efforts to meet this new threat to security in the Persian Gulf and in Southwest Asia. It demands the participation of all those who rely on oil from the Middle East and who are concerned with global peace and stability. And it demands consultation and close cooperation with countries in the area which might be threatened. Meeting this challenge will take national will, diplomatic and political wisdom, economic sacrifice, and, of course, military capability. We must call on the best that is in us to preserve the security of this crucial region. Let our position be absolutely clear: An attempt by any outside force to gain control of the Persian Gulf region will be regarded as an assault on the vital interests of the United States of America, and such an assault will be repelled by any means necessary, including military force."

Carter's two defining moments – the 1979 "Crisis of Confidence" speech and the 1980 State of the Union Address, setting out the "Carter Doctrine" – illustrate a convergence of strategic and economic thinking, which was not reflected by the neo-realist structuralist analysis of international oil politics. To engage seriously with issues of global oil trade, finance and markets, oil companies and different types of nationalized oil industries, corporate vs. state political and legal dynamics, international organizations and institutions would be to succumb to reductionism and therefore not constitutive of proper theory-construction.

Instead the structural quality of economic power was emphasized. For example, a state possessed an ideal structural base for exercising economic power if "(1) it exported things in urgent demand abroad while importing things regarding which its own demand was highly elastic, and (2) it held monopoly control over the supply of things demanded by foreign importing countries..." (Knorr, 1973, p. 86). For neo-realists OPEC and European Economic Community (EEC) were merely examples of states extending control over "resources and markets by forming monopolist or monoposnist arrangements with other states," e.g. by creating regional blocs and protectionist cartels (Ibid, p. 89).

Yet such approach undoubtedly obscured the complexity of international oil politics. Specifically, neo-realist accounts failed to incorporate within their analytical framework the growing role of trans-national, intergovernmental and non-governmental actors and economic and social processes, whose dynamic interactions had direct and often decisive impact on political outcomes. This shortcoming was clearly demonstrated by the oil crises of the 1970s – the market, the companies, the oil traders and speculators, even domestic consumers had all played critical parts in the unfolding drama of rising prices, petroleum shortages and economic recession.

Academic discourse between behavioralists and institutionalists in the Second Debate was played out in the background of more important epistemological and ontological disputes. In the Third IR Debate it was about to take center stage. As the oil crisis of the early 1970s unfolded some scholars, notably Robert Keohane and Joseph Nye, were already tentatively beginning to seek to "to establish the political significance of international organizations in certain issue areas – as arenas and members of trans-governmental coalitions, and as potential points of intervention in transnational systems" (1974a, p. 61; see also, Ibid., 1972).

Keohane and Nye (1974b) focused on the role of non-state actors, such as multinational corporations pursuing profit in a global marketplace, and emphasized significance of trans-national processes in world politics and their implications for national states: "Trans-national economic relations, for instance as symbolized by multinational enterprise acting as investor, trader, employer in several countries and monetary speculator, create important and frequently novel problems for governments" (1973, p. 158). Indeed, relations between states and oil companies has been a major theme in international oil politics ever since the dissolution of Standard Oil Company in 1911.

As this renewed interest in international institutionalism gathered momentum new theoretical insights into world politics began to be developed, in particular the concept of complex interdependence (Keohane and Nye, 1977). The scope of analysis of what came to be neo-liberal institutionalism expanded to include rule-based behavior in international relations and a focus on possibility of international cooperation, because "unlike realism, neoliberalism is a variant of IR liberalism and it is premised on basic liberal assumption about the possibility of cumulative progress in human affairs" (Sterling-Folker, 2013, p. 114; see also Stein, 2008).

Without rehashing the history of the Third Debate here, it suffices to say that by the early 1980s a broad rationalist consensus developed in IR theory, through convergence of neo-realist and neo-liberal institutionalist paradigmatic programmes – a "neo-neo synthesis." It constituted a "modified structural research programme," founded upon a common rationalist epistemology and an enhanced and expanded ontology, one that retained states as primary units of analysis in international politics, but also placed greater emphasis on non-state actors and trans-national relations and processes (Keohane, 1986, p.193) It also severely qualified the underlying realist assumption that state interests are based solely on pursuit of power: "Under different systemic conditions states will define their self-interests differently" (Ibid., p.194).

From the beginning, institutions, international legal frameworks and trans-national relations among state and non-state actors have been at the heart of the subject-matter of the sub-field of oil studies. The impact of the new IR rationalist paradigm – a theoretical synthesis combining structuralism and institutionalism – served not only to reinvigorate the social science of oil in general, but also make it a subject of political as opposed to purely economic or historicist analysis.

It is possible to view this as a dual development: 1) the addition and growth of rationalist modes of political analysis within the sub-field of Energy Studies, and 2) the emergence in the 1970s and 1980s of a distinct issue-area or problem-field relating specifically to international oil and wider energy politics, e.g. proliferation of field-specific academic programmes and research centers, such as the Oxford Institute for Energy Studies, set up in 1982 (OIES, 1982-2019).

Within the sub-field of oil/energy studies there was a new emphasis on issues of political economy. Today, specialist scholarship on the science, technology and business of oil, routinely includes chapters on political geography, inter-state relations and non-state institutions, and history of the global oil industry. For example, Morgan Downey's *Oil 101* (2009) is an exhaustive examination of the science and business of oil – a highly technical, data-heavy piece of scholarship, covering a wide array of subject matter, from chemistry and geology to futures markets and price-setting dynamics. And Scott L. Montgomery's *The Powers That Be* (2010) is a less technical but no less demanding study of the global energy in the twenty-first century.

Neither book is of IR scholarship – Morgan Downey is a commodities trader and Scott L. Montgomery is a consulting geologist. Yet both texts share a de facto underlying rationalist international political analytical framework as applied to the oil industry; even if this is at times treated as an exogenous factor to the scientific, technical project of oil extraction, production, refining, marketing, financing and so on. Both texts share a characteristically common modernist ontological and epistemological position:

- energy matters are critically important because they are "fundamental to our way of life" (Montgomery, 2010, p.4);
- energy has a material basis – entailing specific natural resources, whether fossil fuels, enriched uranium or flowing water etc. ("We don't import or trade 'energy,' after all" (Ibid., p.6)); oil is the

dominant fuel today and for the foreseeable future (Ibid, p. 9; Downey, 2009, pp. 25-29).

- Ultimately (at some unspecified point in the future when markets and technology make it possible or when resource depletion forces us) it will become necessary to switch to another, "as yet untamed, source of energy:" "One way or the other, in the 22nd century there will be transportation energy. It may be much more expensive, perhaps not. It is almost certain that the source of that energy will not be conventional petroleum" (Downey, 2009, p. 29).

- For now, however, natural energy resources are scarce/non-renewable/possibly-running-out and access to them determines distribution of economic wealth and political power: "It is the simplest of truths, yet the most challenging of realities: energy relations are geopolitics by other means" (Montgomery, 2010, p. 213).

What is especially important here, is that the "neo-realist - neoliberal institutionalist" assumptions about global energy politics are treated as a given, an unchanging structural politico-economic reality that is a "matter of fact:" "Nations will continue to pursue their own self-concerned agendas about energy security – the U.S. and foreign oil; China and imports; the EU and its umbilical natural gas ties to Russia; OPEC and the global demand for petroleum. But all are integrated deeply, irreversibly, and more than ever before into a global web of markets and relationships" (Montgomery, 2010, p.2).

Meanwhile, mainstream IR scholars began to pay increasing empirical attention to politics of oil and the structural, strategic role it plays in determining global political and economic outcomes. For example, Joseph Nye's essay "Energy Nightmares" (1980) sets out a characteristic combinational neo-realist/neoliberal institutionalist analysis of the energy security problem-field – one that applies neo-realist concepts of balance of power, inter-state competition and threat of war alongside analysis of institutional actors (such as the International Energy Agency (IEA)), non-state units and transnational processes (such as the oil majors, market forces, systemic price volatility).

Yet it also examines possibility of a U.S.-led international cooperation regime as a means of resolving or managing systemic flaws causing the energy crises e.g. overdependence on Middle East oil or the threat of supply disruption. While Nye was sceptical about possibility of "an equitable international regime for international energy issues," arguing that "the world is now a long way from the structure of power and control of energy issues" that would make such a regime possible, he nevertheless contended that "there is a long-run common interest, and ideally collective energy security is a worthy goal" (1980, p. 154).

Much of the IR scholarship on oil politics in the early 1980s was U.S.- and Eurocentric, Cold War-grounded and focused on key questions of military security, the balance of power, the role of markets and various transnational phenomena, such as international oil companies; but energy security remained the dominant issue amongst these.

Major differences between neo-realist and neoliberal institutionalist components of the rationalist consensus were limited to a) disagreements over a possibility and the degree of international cooperation, which offered ample opportunities for applying various game-theory scenarios to international oil politics; and b) the extent to which transnational factors can be said to impinge on the primacy of states as key units in the international system.[14]

Additionally, through the 1980s there emerged a growing body of literature on the pivotal role of the United States, both as a producer and consumer of petroleum, and the world's energy superpower. For example, David Painter's classic work *Oil and the American Century* (1986), studiously analysed close collaboration between U.S. public policy makers and international oil companies' executives, in formulating a comprehensive U.S. foreign oil policy, aimed at securing access to foreign petroleum, protecting independent domestic producers (and conserving reserves), and ensuring defence needs (for similar analysis, see Ickenberry, 1988).

Arguably Painter's remained the authoritative text on international oil politics until publication of Yergin's *The Prize* in 1991. Indeed, David Painter made a considerable contribution to the

---

[14] For example, on the role of energy, especially petroleum industry in national defence and security, see Bucknell III (1981) and Ebinger (1982); on possibility of international cooperation in the world energy regime, see Hoffman and Johnson (1981); on oil crisis management strategies, such as resource stockpiling, see Krapels (1980); on energy independence strategies, see Ross and Williams (1981).

development of rationalist scholarship on international oil politics in the 1980s and early 1990s. By that stage a substantial body of empirical work on the subject had already emerged (within the realm of IR and beyond), charting the course of oil's ascent as the world's premium geopolitical fuel, driving U.S. foreign policy and determining the shape of post-war economic order (see, for example, Painter's *Oil and the Marshal Plan* (1984)). His scholarship in the 1990s continued to focus on key concepts central to the rationalist paradigm of oil politics – national security of states and their military and economic power (see, for example, *International Oil and National Security* (1991); *Oil and World Power* (1993)).

Another important component of the rationalist research programme of international oil politics centered on the study of non-state corporate institutions that dominated production and trade in oil – the international oil companies (IOCs). Ever since publication of Anthony Sampson's definitive "The Seven Sisters" (1975), which to this day remains the benchmark text on corporate history of oil, academic scholars consistently sought to incorporate international oil companies as units, or at the very least sub-units, in the architecture of international political oil regimes.[15]

The extent to which international organizations, such as the IEA and non-state actors, such as IOCs, influenced political outcomes remained a strongly contested issue in the realm of international oil politics throughout the Third Debate. For state-centric rationalists the role of multinational corporations and arguments about growing global economic interdependence remain overstated. As Hedley Bull argued in *The Anarchical Society* (1995): nation-states "have displayed a considerable ability to stand up to multinational corporations," by denying them access and restricting their activities: "Certainly, the agreements in which states enter with multinational corporations may be viewed as an exercise of their sovereignty and not as an impairment of it" (pp.-261-263).

---

[15] On one level, this took form of comprehensive histories of various oil companies; for an example of a rationalist corporate institutional political analysis, see Ferrier (1982) – a detailed history of British Petroleum (BP); or on the politics of corporate consolidation in the inter-war and post-war periods, see Gary Liebcap's "The Political Economy of Crude Oil Cartelization in the United States, 1933–1972" (1989).

The dynamics of relations between producing and consuming states on one hand, and international oil companies on the other, represents another level of complexity. In 1945 U.S. Navy Secretary James Forrestal stated that he did not "care which American company or companies developed the Arabian resources, as long as they were American" (quoted in Yergin, 1991, p. 412).

IOCs are certainly trans-national in their operations, which are determined by the facts of geology above all, but their headquarters and shareholder base remains in their countries of origins. Meanwhile, the 1960s and 1970s saw proliferation of publicly-owned national oil companies (NOCs) emerging to take their place alongside the majors – a process driven by decolonisation and independence movements across the developing world, as oil producing nations increasingly assumed control over their own resources, leading to the decline of the old concessionary system.

Therein lies the paradox – Western oil majors have historically been viewed as national champions, promoting state interests, often with direct state involvement (for example Anglo-Iranian/BP (Sampson, 1973, pp. 70-74)); yet they also had had a complicated, often fractious relationship with national governments in Europe and especially in the United States, beginning with the dissolution of Standard Oil in 1911 and the ongoing anti-trust battles between oil companies and the federal government (for an example of contemporary "trust-busting" in academic literature, see Blair, 1978).

From the outset these competing dynamics produced what Yergin described as two "contradictory, even schizophrenic, strands of public policy towards the major oil companies" in the U.S.: "On occasion, Washington would champion the companies and their expansion in order to promote America's political and economic interests, protect its strategic objectives, and enhance the nation's well-being. At other times, these same companies were subjected to populist assaults against 'big oil' for their allegedly greedy, monopolistic ways and indeed for being arrogant and secretive" (1991, p. 472).

For example, Francisco Parra described as the "crowning irony" the situation after World War II, when American oil companies were being encouraged by the U.S. Government to develop Saudi Arabian petroleum reserves, just as they were being subjected to prosecution under anti-trust legislation by the U.S. Federal Trade Commission (FTC) in 1952, "for doing precisely what Ickes (the U.S. Secretary of the Interior) had wanted them to do – one of the first of many instances when the United States was to pursue simultaneously two diametrically opposed policies in the Middle East" (2013, p.11; see also Sampson 1973, pp. 134-140).

These debates were not taking place in a vacuum – the 1980s was a decade of growing global, especially financial, markets and, in the West, government deregulation and privatisation of public enterprises. Oil was first introduced in the futures markets at the New York Mercantile Exchange (NYMEX) in 1983. And in 1985 Margaret Thatcher abolished British National Oil Company (BNOC) and then, two years later, "reversed Winston Churchill's historic decision of 1914" and sold off the government's 51% stake in British Petroleum (BP) (Yergin, 1991, pp. 746, 767). Such developments were seen as victories for the market – could it be that oil was becoming just another commodity (Ibid., pp-743-744)?

These themes – the declining role of the state in the oil industry, growing power of international oil companies, gradual marketization of oil pricing mechanisms, growth in global commodities and financial markets, the weakening of OPEC and of other producers (including Soviet Union), growing regulatory authority of international organizations, and gradual decrease in oil prices – provided the backdrop to discussions about oil in the 1980s. Yet there was another emerging theme that began to impinge on the mainstream rationalist thinking about oil politics – environmentalism.

Specifically, towards the end of the decade, there developed a consistent strand of scientific argument that the use of fossil fuels is having an impact on global climate, coupled with a growing public awareness of the issue; thereafter, "when people wrote about heat waves and droughts, it was not only about their severity and the disruptions and distress they caused, but also about links to carbon dioxide and climate change, and as alarm bells for global warming" (Yergin, 2012, p. 463).

Establishment of the Intergovernmental Panel on Climate Change (IPCC) in 1988 marked the beginning of the political evolution of international environmental and climate change agenda – from the Earth Summit in Rio de Janeiro in June 1992 to the Paris Agreement (to cut carbon emissions) in December 2015 (UNFCC, 12.12.15). But it was the *Exxon Valdez* tanker disaster on 24 March 1989 which came to symbolize and mobilize public concern over the oil industry, strengthening "the reborn environmental consciousness and the willingness on the part of many people to trade off energy production in favor of environmental protection" (Yergin, 1991, p. 778).

Two years later Daniel Yergin's *The Prize* was published and as mentioned above, it remains, perhaps, the most important and influential book on oil within the mainstream rationalist framework. What Yergin calls the "anthropological argument" forms the third key theme of this monumental study (business and politics of oil being the other two) (Ibid., p.14). This is the argument that oil is the basis of modernity, underpinning the very foundations of daily life – the rise of "Hydrocarbon Society" (Ibid.).

While Yergin hardly addresses substantive environmental issues in any real detail (in the first editions of the book), it is notable that *The Prize* opens with questions about environment that are pertinent to a rationalist understanding of the problem: "In the meantime, the stage has been set for one of the great and intractable clashes of the 1990s between, on the one hand, the powerful and increasing support for greater environmental protection and, on the other, a commitment to economic growth and the benefits of Hydrocarbon Society, and apprehensions about energy security" (Ibid., p. 15). And the book concludes with Yergin envisaging possibility of "the almost incomprehensible costs and disruption… that could result if there's a major climate change" (Ibid., p. 779). It is striking that this first mention of the issue comes in the penultimate pages of the Epilogue.

There are, therefore, two strands of thought emerging here: 1) that environmental issues represent a policy problem to be managed on balance with other considerations or as Yergin describes it: "a competition of two great themes – energy and security, and energy and the environment" (Ibid, p. 779); and 2) that the climate change is a foundational threat to the very notion of modernity: "Indeed, with the fate of the planet itself seeming to be in question, the hydrocarbon civilization that oil built could be shaken to foundations" (Ibid., p. 780).

These two approaches were to increasingly dominate mainstream rationalist debates around politics of oil in the 1990s and beyond. In the meantime, Iraq's invasion of Kuwait and the collapse of the Soviet Union (and of the Soviet oil industry) in 1991 served to remind Western publics and governments of the political importance of oil and the threat of war in the Middle East. As Yergin vividly concludes in *The Prize:* "The fierce and sometimes violent quest for oil – and for the riches and power it conveys – will surely continue so long as oil holds a central place. For ours is a century in which every facet of our civilization has been transformed by the modern and mesmerising alchemy of petroleum. Ours truly remains the age of oil" (Ibid., p.781).

Yet in the 1990s the rationalist paradigm of international oil politics had to contend not only with the environmentalist challenge but also increasingly with a wider critique of its positivist assumptions. For the Fourth Debate in IR went further than simply questioning this or that aspect of the workings of the global oil industry or a Western foreign policy – it challenged the very foundations of modernist claims about possibility of limitless progress and economic growth, just as Yergin predicted (see chapter V).

One way that mainstream observers of oil politics responded to these challenges was to ignore them and continue business as usual. The immediate effect of the Gulf War helped to reprioritize geostrategic factors and served to underline again the pivotal importance of the Middle East oil reserves. Saddam Hussein's occupation of Kuwait was widely seen as being motivated by desire to control Kuwaiti oil as a stepping stone to wider expansion.

As Yergin put it, Saddam's aim was "...to dominate the Arab world, to gain hegemony over the Persian Gulf, to make Iraq into the predominant oil power – and ultimately to turn Greater Iraq into a global military power" (1991, p. 771). The war also stimulated research on the political economy of Arab states and emerging internal political trends in the Middle East (see, for example, Alnasrawi, 1991). But its immediate effect was to realign an old analytical connection between oil, power and war.

Joseph Nye's essay "Why the Gulf War Served the National Interest" in *The Atlantic* in July 1991 is a good example of such realignment, baring the hallmarks of a neo-realist/neoliberal aggregated rationalist analysis, encompassing such concepts and themes as the military-strategic significance of oil; the relationship between physical control of petroleum production and the power of price-setting in the market; the critical importance of Saudi Arabia as the swing producer; the role of the United States as a guarantor of regional security, and the implications of the weakening of Soviet power.

Had Hussein succeeded, Nye contends, "he would have been able to cow Saudi Arabia and the smaller states into cutting their oil production and jacking up the world price by the ten dollars a barrel or more...." And the U.S. could not allow such a challenge against "Saudi monopoly as OPEC's swing producer" to succeed (Hiro, 2007, p.128).

However, Nye rejects the notion that the United States intervened against Iraq simply because of oil (1991). The answer as to why the Gulf War was in the U.S. national interest must also involve other aspects, such as "'a new world order' collective security, interdependence, prevention of regional hegemony, and reversal of American decline." This is because "the national interest is broader than protection against geopolitical threats. The strategic interest is part of, but not necessarily identical to, the national interest."

Nye then lists a range of factors contributing to national interest in motivating U.S. policy in the Gulf War - from U.S. support for Israel, to domestic political factors, to the potential impact of the impending U.S. victory in the Cold War, and that "most intangible of the American interests," the "new world order:" "In a world of interdependence Americans cannot afford to define the national interest in domestic or international terms alone."

Nye's analysis of the international oil politics in the Gulf War combines several subjects that were to become characteristic of scholarship in the field and wider thinking on oil and energy in the 1990s. Throughout the decade there was a steady empirical stream of traditional, economics-centered rationalist analysis of the oil industry, focused on conventional themes of security and market forces (see, for example, Shojai, 1995; Bohi et al, 1996); the politics of oil trade (Hartshorn, 1993); and the dynamics in the relationship between states and international oil companies (Van der Linde, 1999).

The latter topic in particular acquired renewed relevance, as debates around globalisation began to impact energy politics. For example, Colitti and Simeoni examined growing networks of interdependence between oil producing and consuming states and international oil companies, and possibilities of cooperation between these actors (1996).

The rationalist research programme was typically highly responsive to developments in real world, as events impacted on the global oil industry and new trends emerged. This was the decade that witnessed relative decline of OPEC and the opening up of Russia and the oil-producing regions of the former Soviet Union, heralding a new "Great Game" (see Croissant and Aras, 1999; Lane, 1999, Adams, 2002).

The 1990s saw a massive expansion of financial markets in oil and some of the most volatile prices in the industry's history, as well as other shocks such as the 1997 Asian financial crisis, violent conflict in the Niger Delta and the emergence of Hugo Chavez in Venezuela. It was also an era of some of the biggest corporate mergers in the history of the industry, including that of Exxon and Mobil, two of the largest oil companies tracing their lineage back to the break-up of Standard Oil in 1911 (the percentage split in the newly amalgamated company ExxonMobil (eighty percent – Exxon and twenty percent - Mobil) corresponded quite closely to the proportions these companies were allocated in the original 1911 settlement (Yergin, 2012, p. 98)).

These real world developments shaped the currents of scholarship and research agendas in international politics of oil, without having much of an impact on their ontological and epistemological commitments. Eventually environmental issues were also gradually subsumed into the analytical framework of the rationalist paradigm, with climate change in particular being added to the wider energy and global security dilemma. This bracketing of environmental debates about energy production and consumption took form of an expanding empirical trend towards securitisation of climate change and wider environmental risks and threats.

This included development of systematic environmental impact assessments of state policies, especially armed conflict – see, for example, El-Baz (1994) for an in-depth study of the extensive environmental damage inflicted upon the fragile desert and shore environments of Kuwait and parts of Saudi Arabia in the Gulf War (when some eight million barrels of crude oil were spilt).

By late 2000s such environmental assessments were standard scholarship in the field, employing increasingly complex combinational mix of comparative historicism and heavy quantitative standards of measurement and assessment (for an impressive example of this, see *War and the Environment: Military Destruction in the Modern Age*, edited by Charles Closmann (2009) and in particular David Painter's contribution "The Global Environmental Footprint of the U.S. Military, 1789–2003" in that volume (pp. 20-24)).

This special focus on the relationship between environmental degradation, climate change and armed conflict is recurrent feature of rationalist thinking on the issue, not only in academia but in wider public debates (see, for example, Brown et al, 2007; Raleigh and Urdal, 2007; Broder, 2009). Another empirical direction involved study of actors' behavior in relation to climate change risk perception (Leiserowitz, 2004). This environmental security agenda was being picked up by international institutions, such as the World Bank (Mearns and Norton (eds.), 2010) and increasingly by governments (Schwartz and Randall, 2003).

The Schwartz and Randall study, known unofficially as the *Pentagon Report on Abrupt Climate Change*, is particularly interesting. Peter Schwartz is a former head of planning at Shell Oil and Doug Randall – a senior analyst at the Global Business Network, a U.S. think tank. The study was commissioned by a highly respected Defense Department official Andrew Marshall and its findings raised the possibility that a rapid onset of climate change (namely, the warming of global temperatures) could represent potentially catastrophic security threat – from draughts to famines, resource wars and global conflict. The U.S. Department of Defense initially suppressed the report but conclusions are telling: "This report suggests that, because of the potentially dire consequences, the risk of abrupt climate change, although uncertain and quite possibly small, should be elevated beyond a scientific debate to a U.S. national security concern" (Schwartz and Randall, 2003, p.3).

Elevation of environmental concerns from empirical fringes to mainstream scholarship and their integration into the rationalist paradigm of international oil politics took place in the context of evolving public debates, in politics and media. Climate change and global warming were increasingly being taken seriously by policy-makers and formed an arena for growing international cooperation as well as competition. Evolution of the IPCC process and the UN Framework Convention on Climate Change centered the issue at the heart of global political agenda.

The signing of the Kyoto Protocol in 1997 served to underline this shift. Kyoto also introduced markets in emissions trading and established several other foundational principles in the process, which eventually led to the Paris Agreement of 2015, when nearly two hundred countries adopted the first-ever universal, legally binding global climate deal to limit global warming to well below 2°C. (UNFCC, 12.12.15; see also Yergin, 2012, pp.487-492).

It is important to reiterate that such factors as the international environmental movement and growing intergovernmental cooperation against the threat of climate change were gradually included in the rationalist analytical model of international oil politics in the 1990s and 2000s strictly within the limits of its broad positivist framework. Global warming is bracketed as a material problem (a security threat, a policy challenge) to be solved or dealt with, rather than a normative dilemma, requiring introspective reflection, critique or questioning of the underlying assumptions of modernity (for example, the normative commitment to unlimited economic growth, scientific progress and capitalist consumerism). As such it is one of many units of analysis requiring attention in the study of global energy and its attendant politics.

To illustrate this point, it is worth considering Daniel Yergin's *The Quest: Energy, Security and the Remaking of the Modern World* (2011) – his follow up to *The Prize* (1991). If environment and climate change were barely mentioned in the latter publication, in *The Quest* Yergin accords them a central place in the narrative. Again, Yergin combines sweeping, expansive historical overview of key themes and subjects of the study with an exhaustively detailed analysis of the material base of his arguments (data-intensive and technical approach to issues of energy supply and demand, technological innovations, risks and costs of environmental degradation and the quest for alternative energy sources).

Yergin opens *The Quest* with three key questions about energy, which in sum constitute the ontology of the contemporary positivist research programme and, at the same time, reflect the changes and transformations in rationalist thinking about energy over the past twenty years and especially, the role of oil: "Will enough energy be available to meet the needs of a growing world and at what cost and with what technologies? How can security of the energy system on which the world depends be protected? What will be the impact of environmental concerns, especially climate change, on the future of energy?" (2012 [2011], p.3).

The idea that there will always be energy to fuel global industrial growth is an *a priori* assumption, from which other questions follow. There is an explicit normative commitment here to a particular positivist understanding of the problem-field. For example, in a rationalist research programme the central important question on climate change is not about its direct impacts on human lives but on how it might affect the global energy regime. This is not because rationalists do not care about the human cost of climate change, but simply because such considerations do not fall within the ontological sphere of the rationalist model of oil politics.

Or, for another example, the reason why the Fukushima nuclear plant disaster of 2011 mattered was not because it was a major nuclear emergency - the worst since Chernobyl, or one that might raise fundamental questions about sustainability of modern energy consumption, but because the incident, "compounded by damage to other electric generating plants in the area, led to power shortages, forcing rolling blackouts that demonstrated vulnerability of modern society to a sudden shortage of energy supply" (Yergin, 2012 [2011], pp. 1-2). The story is no longer just about oil but its underlying ontological, epistemological and normative foundations remain unchanged, connecting various intellectual strands of *The Prize* (1991) and *The Quest* (2011).

Supply of energy, security of this supply and how the environment (climate change) might affect it in the long run, are the three overarching themes of the contemporary rationalist model of international oil and wider energy politics The first decade of the twenty first century saw yet another round of systemic shocks, shifts and crises that affected the world of oil – 9/11 terrorist attacks and subsequent war in Afghanistan, U.S.-led invasion and occupation of Iraq in 2003, violence in the Niger Delta, devastation caused by hurricanes Katrina and Rita in 2005, record high oil prices and then the financial crisis of 2008 in the United States that sent the world into a tailspin of recession. These cataclysmic events, wars and natural disasters served only to amplify the three general themes of the rationalist paradigm, in what Yergin termed as "aggregate disruption" of the global energy regime in 2000s (2012 [2011], see pages: 108-160).

Empirically oil continued to occupy its traditional position in the neo-realist/neoliberal IR analysis – in relation to its role as an economic and strategic resource of critical importance. For example, in John Mearsheimer's *The Tragedy of Great Power Politics* (2001) – his emphatic reaffirmation of realism – oil is mentioned only in conjunction with war, e.g.: "It is also possible for conquerors to gain power by confiscating natural resources such as oil and foodstuffs. For example, any great power that conquers Saudi Arabia would surely reap significant economic benefits from controlling Saudi oil" (p. 150).

Within the subfield of international oil and energy politics global events and trends discussed above manifested themselves in waves of scholarship focusing on one or more of the three key themes. For example, the "peak oil" agenda had a considerable impact on debates, in academia and in the wider public realm, reflecting growing fears of resource depletion. This refers to a complex (largely quantitative or mathematical) argument put forward by some analysts who claimed that the world is rapidly running out of oil (and other resources, for that matter), with potentially devastating results (see Roberts, 2005 [2004]).

By the end of the decade these fears were somewhat assuaged, for as Yergin argued the world is not running out of oil – *Far from it. The estimates for the world's total stock of oil keep growing* (2012 [2011], p. 242). Nevertheless, it is clear that the era of easy oil was over and that new sources would be found in remote, difficult to develop regions, such as the Arctic. The scramble for these last frontiers in the battle for control of natural resources is the current focus of empirical attention (see, for example, Klare, 2012).

Another subject in oil politics that rose to prominence in the past decade and a half is the so-called "resource (oil) curse" (see Ross, 2012) – an argument first put forward by Jeffrey Sachs and Andrew Warner (1995), who argued that economies with a high ratio of natural resource exports to GDP tended to have lower growth rates in the medium to long-term. The wider argument went further - dependence on oil exports and other natural resources and commodities skews economic performance of the producer-country (the petro-state), fuelling stagnation, corruption and political authoritarianism.

For example, in *The Paradox of Plenty: Oil Booms and Petro-States (Studies in International Political Economy)* Terry Lynn Karl (1997) explores why countries such as Venezuela, Iran, Indonesia and others have all experienced disappointing social and economic outcomes despite successive decades of high oil prices, and concludes that there is something specific to oil producing and exporting political economies – a set of common socio-institutional factors and patterns – which account for poor performance.

This scholarship is rationalist analysis par excellence, as Karl uses a combination of structural and choice-based approaches to systematically demonstrate how decisions of policymakers are embedded in the state institutional framework as the latter interacts with domestic and international markets. Such use of quantitative methods and Large-N data in systematic comparative cross-country analysis characterizes much of the empirical work on this subject field. For example, see Gylfason (2001) – on correlation between natural wealth endowment, education policies and poor economic growth; Norman (2008) - on relationship between extractive industries and the rule of law.

Ahmadov (2014) uses meta-regression analysis to examine the integrated results of already existing data-sets to identify the effects of oil on democratic development; Bell and Wolford (2015) apply game-theoretical models to test hypotheses on correlation between oil and civil conflict (see also *Petro-Aggression. When Oil Causes War* by Jeff Colgan (2013)). Developing strategies for mitigating the effects of the "oil curse" and avoiding it altogether provided an empirical agenda for neo-liberal theorizing of the problem (see, for example, Tsalik, 2003; Humphreys et al, 2007).

These largely quantitative research sub-programmes were focused primarily on the economics of international oil politics. Nevertheless, they contributed in important ways to the development and evolution of rationalist thinking on the subject, not least by generating considerable empirical output. Meanwhile, in the wider subfield of international oil politics in 2000s there was a renewed interest in the history of the oil industry. This came, as if in response to foundational challenges facing the global petroleum order as industry observers, scholars and practitioners sought to take stock of the situation.

By 2008, despite slowing demand, oil prices were at record highs, leading to major shifts of wealth and power in world affairs – members of OPEC as well as Russia and other smaller producer-states enjoyed an unprecedented revenue boom. Authors, such as Francisco Parra, former Secretary General of OPEC, sought explanations for growing price volatility – the runaway market – in the structural changes in the world energy order over the past thirty years, as power shifted from oil companies to producer nations and then to free markets (2013 [2004]).

Others, such as Dilip Hiro, sought to bring various strands of analysis up to date by including the "peak oil" thesis and other contemporary energy security issues in his historical study *Blood of the Earth* (2007). Other historians working in area studies and political geography similarly engaged in retrospective analysis of major international oil stories of the preceding decades (see, for example, Steve LeVine's *The Oil and the Glory. The Pursuit of Empire and Fortune on the Caspian Sea* (2007) and Rafael Kandiyoti's *Pipelines. Flowing Oil and Crude Politics*, 2012 [2008])).

The scope of this chapter does not allow for a full expansive study of the rationalist model. But it would be fair to say that by many measures, not least by volume and breadth of empirical output, the latter constitutes the study of international energy today (see Appendix 3). Rationalist thinking about oil and energy politics is in many ways a default mode of analysis which extends its ubiquitous influence across public discourse, not least in the media.

Scholarship surveyed in this chapter is diverse and multi-disciplinary, which further attests to the extent of the rationalist consensus on oil across social sciences – from economics to international law. Yet for all the empirical and disciplinary diversity a rationalist model set out above is formed upon a common ontological and epistemological base; its theoretical foundations are grounded in International Relations synthesis between neo-realism and neoliberal institutionalism.

Over the past few years oil remained at the top of the global agenda. The Arab Spring, a series of popular uprisings against authoritarian regimes, which began in Tunisia in 2011 and quickly spread across North Africa and the Middle East, turned into a long winter as civil wars ripped Syria and Libya apart and brought a wave of instability across the world. The rise and fall of the terror state of Daesh (or "IS") and its invasion of Iraq in 2014 rose the prospect of a terrorist organization with its own oil industry (Solomon et al, 2015).

Meanwhile global economic recession, slowing demand in China and overproduction resulted in a glut in the oil market, pushing prices down, at first gradually, then in 2015 – in a crash, to below $30 per barrel for the first time in over a decade. Covid-19 pandemic and global lockdown of economic activity saw oil prices plunge to as low as $20 a barrel. This degree of price volatility is likely to persist for years if not decades to come.

Yet oil remains the primary fuel of the global energy order. And oil geopolitics – "that high, thin stratum where the business and politics of energy merge into a single, swiftly moving current" (Roberts, 2005 [2004], p. 93) – remain at the heart of the rationalist paradigm of international oil politics. Continued conflicts and new wars, market disruptions and price volatility, and rising threat of global warming remain the dominant issues facing rationalist research programme this decade.

Pipelines Through the Great Debates

The three debates establish key themes and issues in mainstream studies of international politics of oil – the role of states and companies, the institutional, financial and technological processes that shape its dynamics; strategic value of oil in peace and war; security of supplies, issues of financing, relations between oil-producing and consuming states, importers and exports.

It also suggests that contemporary projects, such as BTC and SGC pipelines do not operate in a temporal vacuum; companies, such as BP, oil-rich states such as Azerbaijan or financial institutions such as EBRD, are not historically arbitrary events that become relevant when SGC and BTC come under analysis – they have historical antecedents and foundations. Importantly, these pipelines are set within the structural timeline of international oil politics – a prevailing historical social order determined by the material, strategic value of hydrocarbon petroleum.

The region of present day Republic of Azerbaijan has been renowned for its hydrocarbon reserves since antiquity (Yergin, 1991, p.57; Adams, 2002, p.5; Sebag Montefiore, 2008, p.195; Gŏkay, 1999, pp. 2-20). The Arab conquest marked the beginnings of Caspian oil exploration and its rise as a commercial resource. In the eighth century Caliph Al-Mansur (AD 757-775) imposed a "naphtha tax" on Baku oil, proceeds of which went towards the construction of the Caliphate capital at Baghdad and to fund Arab expeditionary campaigns and garrisons in the North Caucasus (Ashurbeili, 1992, p. 64). This was arguably the first historical record of taxation in transnational oil trade (Adams, 2002, p. 5). In the tenth century the Arab geographer Al-Masoudi wrote of Baku as "a naphtha fountain" with. "burning wells whereby fire emerges from the ground." (Bilkadi, 1996 in Adams, 2002, p. 5)

By mid-nineteenth century all of present-day Azerbaijan and the whole South Caucasus had been annexed by the Russian Empire. A new contractual system was introduced by Tsarist authorities in 1870s replacing state monopoly on oil and the lease back system (LeVine, 2007, p. 7). Instead a new legal regime of publicly tendered long-term oil concessions was introduced, establishing clear legal relationship between oil producers and the state and ensuring multitude of incentives for investment and technological innovation. The age of small-holder was nearing an end. The scene was set for rapid industrialisation of Azerbaijan, with Baku emerging as one of the birthplaces of modern oil industry (Adams, 2002, pp. 8-9; Muttitt and Marriott, 2002, p. 20; LeVine, 2007, pp. 4-27; Yergin, 1991, pp. 57-63).

It was in Baku that the first drilled (as opposed to hand-dug) oil well was constructed in 1844, ten years prior to the method being used in Pennsylvania. By 1878 there were 301 such drilled wells (Adams, 2002, p. 8). First refineries and industrial storage facilities were pioneered in Azerbaijan as was the novel idea of transporting oil in standard-sized barrels. New uses for oil were also being developed with dozens of kerosene refineries opening in Baku by 1870s.

This was the as yet underdeveloped but pregnant with possibilities environment that greeted the Swedish Nobel family upon their arrival in Baku in 1873 (Sebag Montefiore, 2008, p.195). The story of the first Baku Oil Boom is to a large extent the story of the Nobels (see Asbrink, 2002; Tolf, 1976). In 1875 the Robert Nobel Refinery was established in the city's industrial Black Town district. Having pioneered new refining techniques Nobels dominated the Russian kerosene market (Adams, 2002, p.12).

They developed a local pipeline network to connect their wells to transport infrastructure and in 1876 Ludwig Nobel began work on a cistern ship, essentially the world's first oil tanker (Yergin, 19991, p.59). In 1878 the tanker *Zoroaster* and in 1880 the *Moses* were launched from Baku, delivering kerosene and fuel oil to Russia through Caspian Sea and by river Volga. By 1885 the Nobels had eleven tankers in the Caspian and two in the Baltic (Adams, 2002, p.15; Yergin, 1991, p. 59).

Similarly, the Nobels' involvement in Baku oil opened "a further universal theme in global oil - the competitive search for international capital to finance oil development" (Adams, 2002, p. 19). Concerned with overexpansion of their operations in the Caspian, the Nobels sought to mitigate their risks by forming a publicly owned Nobel Brothers Petroleum Company, in order to attract additional private capital.

Eventually this resulted in cooperation between the Nobels and another legendary nineteenth century business – the French arm of the Rothschild family (see Lottman, 1995; Fursenko & Freeze, 1990). As

Yergin contends, Nobels' borrowing arrangements with the Rothschilds' Crédit Lyonnais "set a significant precedent in that it may have been the first loan for which future petroleum production was used as collateral" (1991, p. 60).

One of the end products of this cooperation was a railway between Baku and the Georgian port of Batumi on the Black Sea – a strategic alternative route for Caspian oil to the world markets; its launch in 1883, "opened a door to the West for Russian oil, it also initiated a fierce, thirty-year struggle for the oil markets of the world" (Yergin, 1991, p. 61).

The rail-line was complimented by a 900km pipeline that traversed Azerbaijan and Georgia parallel to the rail line. It was not completed until 1906 when it was the world's longest oil pipeline (Yergin, 1991, p.69; LeVine, p.24). Terry Adams, one of the architects of what came to be the BTC pipeline, points out: "Ninety-two years later the pipeline route again became the preferred strategic option for evacuating South Caspian oil from Baku to the Black Sea" (Adams, 2002, p.22).

The Rothschilds capitalized on their investment in the Baku-Batumi railway and pipelines, setting up the Caspian and Black Sea Oil Company in 1886, with headquarters and refineries in Batumi (Yergin, 1991, p.60). By 1900 Baku was supplying 50% of the world's oil (Ibid. p. 24; Shaffer, 2002, p. 27; LeVine, p. 26). In the United States the industry was dominated by J.D. Rockefeller's Standard Oil cartel; but in Russian Azerbaijan a new level of complexity emerged –Nobels and Rothschilds, as well as local small-holders, all operated in an intricate web of financial and technological relations heralding the advent of modern oil industry - capital and technology were all brought to bear upon the task of bringing Caspian petroleum reserves from Baku to world markets.

Later, to protect oil supplies in the aftermath of World War I, the Bolshevik Revolution and the establishment of independent Azerbaijan Democratic Republic in 1918, the British Oil Administration was set up in Baku under the command of General W. M. Thompson, at the head of 2000 troops (Altstadt, 1992, p.92; Adams, 2002, p.45). Its task was "to supply the British with Baku oil and hold the eastern terminus of the Transcaucasus Railway (Baku-Batumi -ed.)" (Altstad, 1992, p.93).

And from the realist perspective, the abandonment of Baku oil and the Caucasus to the Red Army in 1920 was again down to recalibration of strategic interests by great powers, especially Britain – discovery of oil in Iran and acquisition of concession rights by Anglo-Persian significantly reduced strategic value of Baku reserves (Adams, 2002, pp.56-58).

Despite Wilson's "14 Points" it was clear that neither Britain, nor anyone else will come to the aid of Azerbaijan or Georgia: "Churchill, reflecting the imperial school of thought, argued that it was all right to support self-determination in the abstract but that no vital interests were at stake in the Caucasus; owing to their weakness, these states would be reabsorbed into Russia eventually" (Altstadt, 1992, p.106).

Azerbaijan's incorporation into the Soviet Union in 1920 put an end to international involvement in Baku oil until the collapse of USSR and restoration of Azerbaijan's and Georgia's independence in 1991 (Le-Vine, 2007, pp.144-173; Adams, 2009). Soviet collapse heralded what some described as "the new great game" and others, more sensibly, "pipeline politics:" "…the fact that the decisive clash was not that of weapons but of the routes by which oil and natural gas from the landlocked Caspian would get to the world's markets" (Yergin, 2012, p.4-46).

The newly-independent Azerbaijan did not possess technology necessary to develop its off-shore oil wealth independently and needed foreign companies' expertise and capital (Omarova,1998, p.187). Russia, Britain, the United States, Turkey, Iran, the European Union and major multinational energy companies were all to become players in what Yergin described as the "Caspian Derby" (2012, pp.46-50).

For Georgia and, in particular, Azerbaijan, newly independent but weak, unstable and riven by conflicts, this was seen as an opportunity to avoid the repetition of 1918-1920 and to secure independence through "oil diplomacy" (Adams, 2009, p.229). In the wake of the Gulf War, the U.S. and Europe were seeking ways of diversifying their energy supplies away from Middle East and OPEC-controlled resources, and were particularly enthusiastic about the potential of the region's hydrocarbon future (Carroll, 2010, p.4). Turkey's attempt to position the country as a major transit route for Middle Eastern oil and gas was stumped – a specially constructed deep-water Ceyhan port facility was designed primarily to process Iraqi oil being exported to Europe. But the sanctions against Saddam Hussein's regime effectively shut down the Kirkuk-Yumurtalik (Ceyhan) pipeline, resulting in serious underuse and additional commercial costs for Ceyhan (Baran, 2005, p.104).

The United States government immediately recognized independence of all Caspian states and became actively engaged with them in a policy that effectively remains in place to this day, to lesser or greater extent. As one of its architects, former U.S. Ambassador to the European Union, Richard Morningstar argued (2006): "The principal component of U.S. policy was to help these new states develop as stable independent countries that would ultimately become market democracies in an uncertain part of the World... In addition, the United States believed and still believes that the development of natural resources in the region should provide an alternative source of oil and gas at a time when South Asia and the Middle East are becoming increasingly unstable and demand is soaring from India and China."

Yet it was the British who were first to return to Baku, some seventy years after they were expelled by the Bolsheviks (LeVine, 2007, p. 144). And it was BP, of Anglo-Persian fame, that was to win the prize when on 20 September 1994 the "Contract of the Century" was signed in a ceremony in Baku. This was a comprehensive agreement between Azerbaijan and Azerbaijan International Oil Consortium (AIOC) comprising ten oil majors, led by BP but including the U.S. giant Amoco, Norwegian Statoil, as well as Russian Lukoil and Turkish TPAO. Azerbaijan International Operating Company (AIOC) was formed to explore the Azeri-Chirag-Guneshli offshore oilfield and Shah Deniz offshore gas field (Adams, 2009, p.228).

A "continuous alignment of common interests between the host government and foreign investors" was required to ensure the success of the Contract of the Century (Adams, 2009, p.233). Azerbaijan required participation of oil majors with necessary technology and expertise in development of its oil reserves, representing a broad range of international sovereign interests (especially U.S., UK and Turkey) and who, most importantly, would be prepared to self-finance the early part of the development project. Political and economic considerations went hand in hand in the Azeri government's considerations (Ibid; Yergin, 2012, p.55; LeVine, 2007, pp.174-200).

The Contract was signed, yet the perennial question of how to transport Baku oil to global markets remained (DeLay, 1999, p.47). The idea behind the Contract of the Century was ambitious from the start – in the long-term it envisaged creation of a main export pipeline (MEP) to carry some one million barrels per year. In 1994, however, such ambition must have seemed extremely premature (Yergin, 2012, p.56). A pilot project was needed that would demonstrate credibility of the Contract and of the parties involved, and instil confidence to attract additional investment. It was necessary to show that export of land-locked Baku oil to the energy markets was possible (Adams, 2009, p. 235).

The Early Oil Project (EOP), which emerged as the solution to the problem, involved production of relatively small quantities of oil for export via existing or new pipeline infrastructure (DeLay, 1999, p.51-54; Yergin, 2012, pp-57-59). Two potential pipeline routes emerged– Northern Export Route (NER) from Baku to the Russian Black Sea port of Novorossiysk and Western Export Route (WER) from Baku to the Georgian port of Supsa. The first option would involve re-activation of the existing Baku-Novorossiysk Pipeline, while WER would require considerable construction work in Georgia (see LeVine, 2007, pp.217-235; Yergin, 2012, p.59).

The issue of routing became immediately highly politicized. The United States and Turkey were both initially strongly opposed to NER, while some investors in AIOC were quite happy to proceed without WER. In the end, both routes were chosen (Adams, 2009, p. 239). In Russia two policies seemed to have emerged in the Yeltsin period – one, embracing a zero-sum approach, aimed at frustrating any Azerbaijani attempt to develop its oil with Western help and the other one followed a more realistic aim of improving Russian position in relative terms (Fincher, 2005).

Given that no agreement on sub-division of the Caspian Sea (the seabed and the territorial waters) existed at the time between the newly independent Caspian states (Azerbaijan, Kazakhstan and Turkmenistan) and Russia and Iran, it was claimed by the latter two that Azerbaijan's negotiations with oil companies were in fact illegal and any contract for off-shore exploration unenforceable (Adams, 2009, p.234). This was a major challenge to Azerbaijani sovereignty and one that the Azerbaijani government dealt with by placing Russian interests at the top of the agenda in the Early Oil Project and mobilising major international political pressure on Moscow – Yergin described this policy as "offend no one" (2012, p.56).

Thus, from early on, NER became the main option for transportation of Baku oil. In addition, Lukoil, the Russian energy giant, was given a 10% share in the Contract, becoming a shareholder-member of AIOC. By 1999 (the outbreak of the Second Chechen War which temporarily shut down Baku-Novorossiysk pipeline) WER was also commissioned – a new pipeline from Baku through Tbilisi to the Black Sea port of Supsa, built at a cost of $640 million (Adams, 2009, p. 251). By 1998 scores of additional production sharing agreements were signed with companies representing commercial interests of the United States, Iran, Saudi Arabia, Belgium, France and Italy. EOP was a resounding success, paving the way for wholesale exploration of Baku's off-shore reserves.

For Azerbaijan this meant diversification of its political interests, binding the country closer to the West, while placing it once again at a center of the global energy industry in the early twenty-first century. As Adams concludes in his discussion of the Contract of the Century (Ibid. p.252): "Regional powers [Moscow, Ankara, and Tehran] were well served as well as Washington and London. Most of the capitals in Europe together with Tehran, Tokyo and Riyadh had embassies in Baku. As President Aliyev had predicted from the first, 'Flag would follow Trade.' This was a simplistic but effective definition of what Baku oil diplomacy was all about."

Yet the question of the main export pipeline (MEP) remained unanswered (Carroll, 2010, p.5). While successful, NER and WER were relatively small projects, with limited operational capacity, and beset by technical and operational difficulties. A major new pipeline, capable of carrying up to and above a million barrels of oil per year was needed –

Baku-Tbilisi-Ceyhan was to become that main export pipeline and to reshape politics of energy transportation in the Caspian region.

The beginnings - BTC pipeline

The issue of MEP and its routing has been a subject of much debate and speculation amongst journalists, industry experts and political commentators right from the start – "good media fodder," as Hill describes it (2004, p. 20). Yet it is clear now that BTC was always going to emerge as the primary choice in the selection of export routes for Caspian oil – "the question for BTC as an MEP had always been 'when' and 'how,' not 'if' or 'where'" (Adams, 2009, p. 246; Yergin, 2012, p. 60).

There were several proposals for potential route of the MEP:
- Expansion of the existing Baku-Novorossiysk pipeline (NER);
- Developing WER pipeline and a new port facility in Georgia;
- A new route through Iran to Turkey (Ceyhan) or an Iranian port;
- A route to Ceyhan through Armenia;
- A route to Ceyhan through Georgia.

Adams argues: "Any Russian option for an MEP was to be destroyed by security problems in Chechnya. Likewise, an MEP export from Georgia would have required Black Sea constricted and competitive oil transits through the Bosporus that created an unacceptable long term environmental risk for AIOC investors. The American investors in AIOC, constrained by the U.S. Iran and Libya Sanctions Act, could never accept Iranian transit to Turkey. A similar transit through Armenia was equally unacceptable for Baku, with its unsettled war in Nagorno-Karabakh" (2009, pp.245-246).

This brief examination requires further discussion. It is true that any Russian option would be constantly threatened by security challenges in the North Caucasus. The outbreak of the Second Chechen War in 1999 briefly shut down Baku-Novorossiysk pipeline and necessitated a by-pass through Dagestan in 2000 to avoid areas where fighting was taking place (Carroll, 2010, p. 5). Yet, there is a more important explanation why the Russian option was unacceptable and it is to do with the U.S. policy objectives, which are not confined to commercial interests of American companies.

As Svante Cornell et al argue, BTC represents "the most important pillar" of a major transportation network known as the New Silk Route or the Eurasian Transport Corridor – a planned, fully integrated infrastructure network of pipelines, highways, telecommunication facilities to connect Central Asia/Caspian region to Europe and the Far East, thus facilitating global trade and commerce (2005, p.21).

BTC should therefore be seen in the context of a wider pipeline system in the region (planned and operational), which includes oil and gas pipelines from Kazakhstan to Russia and China; from Turkmenistan to Russia and across the Caspian to Azerbaijan; from central Asian states through Afghanistan to Pakistan and India (TAPI briefly discussed above), and so on (see Map 2).

The United States, chief architect of this vision, pursued a double aim of diversifying energy supplies through support for multiple pipelines system and ensuring that the dynamics of global trade and energy transportation flowed East to West, rather than North to South (Joseph, 1999, p.12). Preventing monopolisation of pipeline routes (by Russia) was thus seen as a fundamental facet of American policy in the region and Washington's intense support and promotion of BTC fits neatly into this paradigm (LeVine, 2007, p. 347). It is "the biggest project anywhere in the former Soviet Union that the United States has backed, promoted and carried out strategically over three differing administrations." (Svante Cornell et al, 2005, p. 30)

U.S. sanctions against Tehran, introduced in 1986 Iran Libya Sanctions Act by the U.S. Congress, imposed severe penalties on businesses investing in the Iranian energy sector, thus precluding possibility of MEP being routed through Iran, despite this being the most economically attractive option (Hill, 2004, p. 19; Carroll, 2010, p. 5; Yergin, 2012, p. 60).

Turkey represents another major facet of the BTC story. With the collapse of Soviet Union, this NATO member found itself at a strategic location – crossroads of Europe, Russia, the Caucasus and Middle East. With significant mineral resources, vibrant young population and growing economy Turkey was an attractive option for newly independent Turkic states of the Caspian, particularly Azerbaijan (Yergin, 2012, p. 49). Yet the Turkish Republic was severely energy dependent with some 75% of all energy expected to be imported by 2025 (Baran, 2005, p.103).

Realising the full potential of the Caspian oil and gas reserves, Turkey immediately saw an opportunity in land-based pipeline connecting Baku oilfields to Ceyhan export terminals on the Mediterranean Sea. This pipeline would help bind the former Soviet states in the Caspian region to Turkey and strengthened Turkey's importance for Europe and the U.S. (Ibid, p.104).

As Adams points out: "Guaranteed access to Turkish military infrastructure was fundamental to the U.S. political policy and practical containment of Iran and Iraq. This would be directly linked to U.S. reciprocal support for BTC. At the same time increased American influence in the Russian near abroad was seen to correspondingly decrease Russian political influence in the same areas, bringing with it direct access to considerable non-OPEC oil and gas reserves in which BTC would play a lead function." (2009, p.246-247)

In addition, there was the issue of the Bosphorus Straits in Istanbul (Yergin, 2012, p. 60). Extensively used for tanker shipment from the states of the Black Sea region, the Straits experienced a massive increase in use in the 1990s due to the additional oil traffic from the Caspian, leading to congestion and a high environmental risk (Baran, 2005, p.106). Turkey argued vociferously against any additional shipments through the Bosporus and sought to restrict these (Carroll, 2010, p.6). Ankara's position was supported even by oil companies who faced "an unacceptable long term environmental risk" (Adams, 2009, p. 246; Hill, 2004, p. 22).

BTC option would avoid the Bosporus by delivering crude oil directly to southern Mediterranean and generating higher revenues in tariffs for the Turkish state (Elkind, 2005, p.5). The Bosporus dilemma severely undermined the case for any MEP routing through Russia and Georgia. Turkey, therefore, pursued BTC from the outset (Carroll, 2010, p.6). Turkish state oil company TPAO was a minor shareholder but nevertheless a founding investor of AIOC. Ankara also offered to provide public-funds as guarantee to meet any construction cost overruns for BTC

(Carroll, 2010, p. 6; Baran, 2005, p.107). This strengthened the Ceyhan option for the MEP.

Any suggestion of the pipeline being built to Turkey through Armenia was unacceptable to Azerbaijan. Azerbaijani strategy was to use oil development in general and pipeline routing in particular to strengthen its position in the ongoing conflict with Armenia over Nagorno Karabakh (Cornell and Ismailzade, 2005, pp.81-83).

The route from Sangachal oil terminal in Baku through Tbilisi, capital of Georgia, and onto the export terminals at the Yumurtalik deep-water Turkish Mediterranean Sea port of Ceyhan, was the only acceptable option for the main export pipeline (Yergin, 2012, p.61). The U.S. government made it clear by 1999 that the AIOC consortium "could build any pipeline they desired, so long as it ran from Baku to Ceyhan without touching either Iran or Russia" (LeVine, 2007, p. 351).

As oil prices began to rise (to $30 per barrel by 2000) and with U.S. and Turkish governments indicating public funding potential for BTC, opposition from investors in AIOC began to wane (Adams, 2009, p. 247). With existing pipelines (NER and WER) hampered by limited capacity and other challenges, BP and other companies were keen to take the project to its logical conclusion (Ibid). BP/AMOCO merger in 1998 had a significant impact on the BTC process – BP, now a super-giant, emerged by 2002 with a massive joint 31% stake in AIOC – western Caspian now constituting a major part of the company's global oil portfolio (Hill, 2004, p. 24; LeVine, 2007, p. 352).

Ten years of negotiations, debates, conflicts and disputes ended on 18 November 1999, when, during an OSCE summit, the leaders of U.S., Turkey, Azerbaijan, Georgia and Kazakhstan signed the Istanbul Declaration on main export pipeline from Baku to Ceyhan – the Intergovernmental Agreement, obliging all parties to provide all possible assistance in financing and building BTC pipeline (LeVine, 2007, p.356).

At the same time, an agreement was made to fully explore large Azerbaijani Shah Deniz gas fields and build a pipeline parallel to BTC but only up to the Turkish city of Erzurum (Baku-Tbilisi-Erzurum or South Caucasus Pipeline (SCP)) – Azerbaijani gas was to supply Georgian and Turkish consumers, greatly alleviating those countries' energy shortages

(Hill, 2004, p.23) (see Map 1). The gas pipeline amplified BTC's regional impact and laid the foundation for future expansion in the twenty-first century – what came to be the Southern Gas Corridor (SGC).

Financing and construction were now the focus of international effort behind BTC (LeVine, 2007, p. 356; Yergin, 2012, p. 62). The issue of funding, which faced the Nobels over a century before, was again of critical importance. Any project of such size would require support from public financial institutions, such as the World Bank (International Finance Corporation (IFC)) and the European Bank for Reconstruction and Development (EBRD), as well as private capital. Over the years that followed BP and its partners embarked upon a long drawn research consultation and development process.

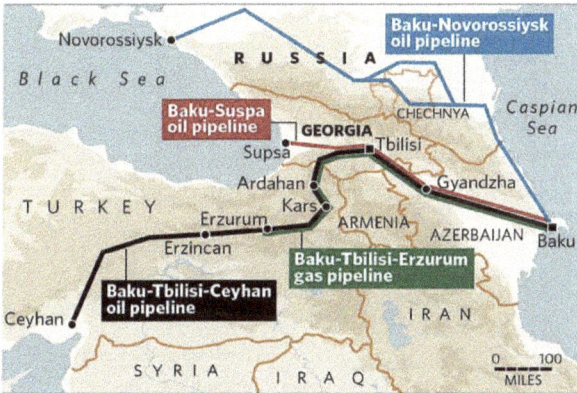

Map 1. Caspian/Black Sea pipeline network *(Source: http://eurodialogue.org/Caspian-Pipelines-Map)*

On top of comprehensive technical, feasibility research, due diligence and planning, topographic and seismic studies, BP (embracing its new motto of corporate social responsibility) carried out major environmental and social impact assessments, publishing all findings and making all documents publicly available (BP, BTC ESIAs, 2017). A massive consultation process, involving NGOs, interviews with members of affected communities, compensation schemes and other remedial actions were undertaken (Carroll, 2010, pp. 9, 11; Blatchford, 2005, pp.121-122).

BP also publicly committed itself to the UK government's Extractive Industries Transparency Initiative (EITI) requiring the company to "publish what it pays" to host (Azerbaijani) government in revenues and bonuses under both the Early Oil and BTC project – major act of information disclosure (Carroll, 2010, p.9).

In the end, it was U.S. government backing and political support that ensured public funding of BTC and SCP pipelines: "Washington's was the most influential voice with the banks that counted – with its own Export-Import Bank and Overseas Private Investment Corporation as well as with the World Bank and EBRD. All could be relied on to put up money and make it safe for commercial banks to participate" (LeVine, 2007, p. 357).

With public financing from EBRD and IFC approved in 2002-2003, BP and its partners in the Baku-Tbilisi-Ceyhan Pipeline Company (BTC Co) – an eleven-member joint venture led by BP – acquired powerful backers for their investment in BTC, which in turn attracted additional private capital from Citibank, ABN Amro and other institutions (Carroll, 2010, pp. 7-11). In total, the project cost in excess of $3.9 billion with some 70% of the cost met by loans from public financial institutions (Upstream Online, 2006; Carroll, 2010, p.9).

It took two years to complete construction of the 1760 km pipeline and it was officially launched on 24 May 2005, at a ceremony at Sangachal, Baku (Yergin, 2012, p. 63). Some ten million barrels of oil was needed to fill the pipeline and it took over a year to arrive at Ceyhan and by 2017 "it carried a total of about 2.8 billion barrels (more than 374 million tonnes) of crude oil loaded on 3,674 tankers and sent to world markets" (BTC co., 2017). In a characteristic style Daniel Yergin gave the following assessment of BTC's completion:

> After all the battles of the Great Game, all the clash and clamor of the Caspian Derby, all the manoeuvring and diplomacy, all the negotiating and trading and deal making, it all comes down to science and engineering, and construction – underground steel tubular highway that has reconnected Baku to the global market. As it carries oil, that pipeline also seems to be carrying the cargo of history, connecting not only Baku and Ceyhan but also beginning of the twenty-first century back to the beginning of the twentieth (2012, p. 64).

BTC – a rationalist model

Yergin's quote is an emblematic articulation of the rationalist model of the BTC pipeline, envisaged first and foremost as a symbol of power. As Wheeler and Whited put it in their seminal account of the oil industry: "The name of the game is power" (1971, p.1). Morgenthau is even more emphatic about "the power of oil" (1985, p.133). He too recognized historical relationship between raw materials, economic power and military strength (ibid, p.131). For Morgenthau competition for oil has important implications in terms of distribution of power – as states seek to control energy reserves they do not merely aim to add to their own resources but to deprive their competitors proportionately (Ibid, p. 133).

Morgenthau goes on to argue that since oil. "...has become the lifeblood of industrially advanced nations...," it represents a revolutionary value in international politics (1985, p.134). States which do not necessarily possess all or any elements of national power (large territory, population etc.) suddenly become very powerful factors in international politics if they have the strategic asset of oil.

Historically low oil prices in the late nineteenth and early twentieth centuries were product of colonial and semi-colonial relations which existed between powerful imperial consumer states and weaker producer-colonies. Possession of oil in the twentieth century reinforced independence of these former colonies and enabled them to raise prices by controlling production (e.g. through formation of OPEC).

At the same time demand for energy grew exponentially and many industrial societies are totally or in considerable measure dependent on supplies from abroad (Ibid, p.134). This helps explain why Azerbaijan failed to secure independence in 1918-1920. Having extracted itself from a colonial relationship with imperial Russia, Baku was plunged into a semi-colonial relationship with the British, before being recolonized by Bolshevik Russia. With Britain acquiring sovereign control over the Anglo-Iranian Oil Company and thus Iran's oil reserves, prices for oil plunged to record lows. Under such conditions Azerbaijani "oil diplomacy" was bound to fail.

By contrast, BTC in the early twenty-first century represents the success of Azerbaijan and Georgia, their independence underpinned by hydrocarbon reserves and transportation infrastructure, far more valuable now that at the turn of the last century. Operating in this new "sellers' market," two small Caucasian states, with tiny populations, beset by separatist conflicts and territorial disputes with neighbors were nevertheless able to transform their petroleum wealth into political power (Yergin, 2012, pp. 63-64). Azerbaijan, for instance, was able to use BTC pipeline as an economic weapon against Armenia, ensuring that country's economic isolation and exclusion from regional projects, while simultaneously helping to weaken Russia's hold over the Black Sea/Caspian littoral (Cornell and Ismailzade, 2005, p.80).

Yet E.H. Carr is far less certain about transformative power of economic resources. He clearly identifies pre-existing asymmetries of power as critically material to political outcomes. Economic policy is necessarily a weapon of the powerful (Carr, 1939 (1981), p.119). Carr identifies export of capital and control of foreign markets as two key policy instruments of economic power. Powerful states use political measures to export their capital abroad in support of national objectives.

Governments often use political power to stimulate private investment in furtherance of political objectives – they provide banks and private capital with patronage, diplomatic support and access (Carr, (1939)1981, pp.114-115). The historical record suggests that this was the case with BTC, as the U.S., Turkish and British governments intervened repeatedly in support of the pipeline and companies behind them, and provided political legitimacy and security through funding of the project by international public institutions, such as the World Bank (Adams, 2009, p. 249; Carroll, 2010, p. 10).

Control of overseas markets is another direction of government policy and powerful countries often found their "natural markets" close to where their political interest lay. Purchasing power of rich states is an international asset that allows them "to call the tune" and not, as Morgenthau insists, the producer (Carr, (1931) 1981, pp.116-117).

Carr brings up the example of Britain's Export Credit Guarantee Department, which was established by the Board of Trade (precursor of DTI) in 1939 to provide UK state financial guarantees for British firms investing abroad or engaged in transactions "in connection with which it appears to them (ed. – the Board of Trade) expedient in the national interest that guarantees should be given." (Ibid, p.116). For Carr, ECGD represents a substitution of the military weapon by the economic.

Sixty years later, the same ECGD served as the institutional framework for British public funding of the BTC project. Providing a $150 million of taxpayers' money in credit for the construction of Baku-Tbilisi-Ceyhan pipeline, ECGD argued that the project "contributes to the development of further energy supply routes in accordance with the Government's policy of ensuring a range of secure energy sources to Western markets" (ECGD, 2003, p. 2)

Realist interpretation of BTC is avowedly state-centric, conceptualising the project within the context of political power. It provides a compelling narrative of oil as political value and economic wealth as component of national policy. BTC, therefore, is a purely political project devised by states as an economic instrument in pursuit of power. BTC is simply an outcome of power politics.

Neo-liberal institutionalist vision of BTC, by contrast, views the project as triumph of free trade – "end of history" in action. For Fukuyama Soviet collapse signalled a final victory of world democratic capitalism (Fukuyama, 1992 in Burchill, 1996b, p. 30). Azerbaijan's and Georgia's independence from the USSR and their adoption of western democratic model and free trade, symbolized by the Contract of the Century and BTC, represent a natural culmination of the countries' historical evolution to liberal democracy.

Neo-liberal institutionalists stress the importance of transnational institutions of governance and global economic forces in development of world politics (Keohane and Nye, 1977). In this context, BTC is first and foremost an economic project, devised and implemented by multinational energy corporations, supported by global financial institutions. The single, most repeated statement about BTC is that economics still had to make sense before the project could be implemented (Adams, 2009, p. 247; Carroll, 2010, p. 6; Starr, 2005, p. 9; Yergin, 2012, p. 62). It was primarily a commercial venture that only went ahead when business conditions were right and it was profitable to build the pipeline.

MNCs involved in the development of Caspian oil pursued interests of their global shareholders and not those of individual nation states (Adams, 2009). Despite heavy political pressure from the U.S., UK and Turkey in support of BTC, members of AIOC insisted on the Early Oil pilot project, built two preliminary pipelines to diversify their risks and acquired extensive financial support from the public funders before proceeding with the BTC project. As Adams categorically argues:

> Despite so many later claims to the contrary, when BTC was finally built, it was on the basis of commercial not political decisions. Investment had always been dependent on AIOC first proving bankable oil reserves at ACG, that were required to finance this international mega project. Claims of a geopolitical "win" by Washington and Ankara over Russian regional interests could not have been further from the truth. Commercial reality had prevailed. (2009, p. 247)

In addition to this, liberal institutionalists will point to international legal architecture and formalized ethical and political standards that govern the BTC project. The legal and policy regime of the BTC project is designed to have binding authority on international level and provides not just for commercial and technical issues, but for enforceable social, environmental and human rights standards (Blatchford, 2005). MNCs operate within a regulated global environment, where international standards are set by international financial institutions - provision of funding for BTC was based on normative *and* commercial conditions.

Yet, at the same time, BTC represents diminution of state powers. Host Government Agreements signed by Azerbaijan, Georgia and Turkey with energy corporations can be viewed as challenging state sovereignty, by taking precedence over national legislation. As Blatchford argues, local social, environmental, safety and emergency laws apply only in so far as they do not conflict with provisions of the HGAs (2005, p.120).

There is, in fact, a neo-liberal critique of the BTC project and the underlying logic of strategic competition underpinning the politics of energy development in the South Caucasus. For some neo-liberals BTC is a manifestation of unnecessary geo-political confrontation brought about by state conflict and detrimental to the goals of free trade and individual prosperity (de Waal, 2010, p.4). For mainstream neo-liberals, however, BTC is a transformative project, delivering normative outcomes as well – local economic development, strengthening of domestic liberal-democratic regimes and tying Azerbaijan and Georgia to the West Starr, 2005; Yergin, 2012, p.64).

This argument is strongly opposed by neo-realists. Kenneth Waltz, while recognising the importance of natural resources in making up of national power, dismisses the idea of interdependency and uses example of the oil crisis of 1973 to illustrate his point (1979, p. 152). BTC project should therefore be seen in the context balance of power and of increasing Western dependency on oil and its efforts to diversify energy supplies. According to neo-realists, BTC represents value in terms of its contribution to capabilities of states within the anarchic international political structure. That is the only historical meaning that BTC possesses – it is not a unique phenomenon but a continuation of inter-state economic interaction that began in 1870s but was interrupted by Soviet nationalisation of Baku oil (LeVine, 2007, pp.144-175; Yergin, 2012, pp. 52-53).

BTC is a state-led process, devised and engineered by political architects. As Adams points out it was the leadership of the three countries traversed by the pipeline that made the political decision to make the project a reality (2009, pp.231-232). Frederick-Starr also concedes that the project happened. "...because it made sense from the perspective of public policy in all the participating countries" (2005, p.10). Ismailzade argues that realisation of BTC was contingent on the most significant factor – "... it was the strategic decision of the Azerbaijani government to export its energy assets through a western pipeline" (2005, p. 83). The bulk of the funding for the project came from the public finance, underlining the dependency and subordination of commercial interest to political decision-making. For Frederick-Starr. "...this demonstrates that on this important issue democratic states have proven themselves capable of taking a long-term and strategic view, notwithstanding the ebbs and flows of politics" (2005, p.14).

The role of MNC is also disputed. Adams refers to the corporate membership of AIOC as reflecting national interests in the Baku oil bonanza (Adams, 2009, p.252). Several companies involved in Baku oil development and transportation are in fact state enterprises - SOCAR, TPAO, BOTAS and Transneft. Western oil majors, such as BP and Statoil, also enjoy a special relationship with their respective home states.

Authors writing on BTC stress that regardless of all other discussions, commercial factors in the end determined the choice of BTC as main export pipeline. While this may be true, there seems to be an odd discrepancy between claims of primacy of commercial factors and the reality of BTC as a political project. If economic factors were all that mattered, then the Iranian route option would have been a natural choice.

Yet the political fact of U.S. sanctions precluded that option. Similarly, the most commercially viable route to Ceyhan was through Armenia but was deemed unacceptable from the start by Azerbaijan. These examples suggest that while economic factors are important, political factors are decisive – a project like BTC might not be implemented if economic conditions are not right; but it will definitely not be implemented, regardless of economic factors, if the political environment is not right.

Neo-realists reject the assertion that trans-national economic factors such as oil corporations and global financial institutions undermine state sovereignty. Bull pointed out that states have displayed a considerable ability to challenge the conduct of MNCs and even when engaging with them were able to effective pursue national objectives (1995, pp.261-262). Agreements, such as those for BTC, which states enter with multinational corporations, "... may be viewed as an exercise of their sovereignty and not as an impairment of it" (Ibid, pp. 262-263).

Together, neo-liberal and neo-realist accounts of BTC represent the "neo-neo" synthesis model of the project. In this rationalist model BTC operates as a geo-strategic pipeline fulfilling political objectives of participating states and as a commercial project resulting from operation of global market forces. It is composed of a complex mesh of relations between South Caucasus states and the EU, Russia and Iran; the role of the United States, Turkey and Britain; balance of power in the region, the role of energy multinationals and international financial institutions, issues of public and private corporate funding, risk mitigation and management and technological processes (see, for example, Adams, 2009; Cornell et al, 2005; Chufrin, 2001; Hill, 2004, Elkind, 2005; Hoffman, 1999).

SGC - a rationalist model

A Rationalist model of SGC is epistemologically and ontologically congruent with that of BTC, the two elements forming part of a wider geo-strategic confrontation in international oil politics, marked by the moment in the 1990s, "when the U.S. decided to challenge Russia's domineering hold on Central Asia and the Caucasus by championing the construction of independent oil and natural gas pipelines from these former Soviet hinterlands to the West" (LeVine, 2.12.2014; see also, Yergin, 2012, pp.341-343; Kandiyoti, 2012, pp.163-172).

The launch of the South Caucasus Pipeline (SCP) in 2006 heralded the next round of interstate competition for energy dominance, with Russia seeking to stem growing power of the U.S. and the EU (Yergin, 2012, p.342; BP 4, 2017). The same year Russian-Ukrainian gas dispute brought into sharp relief EU's dependence not only on Russian gas but also on Russian-controlled gas transmission infrastructure in Europe (BBC News, 01.01.2006).

With demand growing exponentially through 2000s, natural gas was increasingly being seen as the "fuel of the future" – a relatively low-carbon resource that could help reduce use of coal and oil in energy generation and transport (Yergin, 2012, p. 343). The EU was seeking to increase and to diversify its gas supplies and supply-routes, while the United States was seeking to expand influence in the post-Soviet sphere and across Central Asia (especially so in the wake of 9/11 attacks) (LeVine, 02.12.2014; Kandiyoti, 2012, pp. 170-171). With BTC fully operational the stage was set for a new gas pipeline to bring "non-Russian gas to Europe by skirting Russia's southern border" (Yergin, 2012, p. 342).

The strategic rationale for what came to be Southern Gas Corridor was first laid out in the proposal for Nabucco gas pipeline (so called in reference to the Verdi opera) (Yergin, 2012, p.342; LeVine, 02.12.2014).

The ambitious project envisaged a single transmission system carrying gas from Erzurum in Turkey all the way to Vienna, Austria (see Map 3).

The project, spearheaded by a consortium of mostly European companies, quickly won the backing of the United States and Europe (Taylor, 22.02.2008; Cendrowicz, 13.07.2009). The EU Commission identified it as a project of strategic significance and a host of intergovernmental agreements were signed in 2009 between Nabucco Co and each of participating transit countries - Turkey, Romania, Bulgaria, Hungary and Austria (Van Aartsen, 2009, pp.2-3; Turkish Press, 13.07.2009). By 2012 a financing framework was established, involving participating states, companies and important international financial institutions, including World Bank and the European Investment Bank (DW staff, 29.01.2009).

**Map 2. The route of the proposed and unrealized Nabucco pipeline
(Source: Deutsche Welle, 26.04.2012)**

However, it soon became clear that Azerbaijan's gas supplies from the Shah Deniz field would not be sufficient to make Nabucco economically viable (Rowley, 2009). Prospects of Iranian gas providing additional sources did not impress Washington (Conor, 5.06.2008; Kandiyoti, 2012, p. 184). Furthermore, a series of competitor-projects emerged to challenge the Nabucco vision.

First, Russia launched its own proposal for an alternative South (or Blue) Stream gas pipeline to run across Black Sea to Turkey and onwards into Europe, and to be operated by Russia's state energy giant Gazprom (Dempsey, 22.06.2006; Rodova,15.11.2012). Second, two other consortium-led projects – Trans-Anatolian Pipeline (TANAP) and Trans-

Adriatic Pipeline (TAP) – offered politically and economically credible alternatives to Nabucco (Demirmen,19.12.2011; Socor, 04.04.2012).

TANAP was launched in 2012 by the governments of Azerbaijan and Turkey, and offered Baku a reliable transit route for its Shah Deniz Gas to the rapidly growing Turkish market. It runs from SCP termination point in Erzurum across Anatolia to Turkish-Greek border. TANAP consortium is dominated by Azerbaijani and Turkish state energy giants SOCAR and BOTAS, with BP holding a 12% minority stake (Agayev, 23.12.2011; Socor, 27.06.2012). TAP, on the other hand, is a corporate-led project and envisages a pipeline running from TANAP's termination point in Turkey across northern Greece, through Albania and along Adriatic seabed to southern Italy (Tungland, 20.01.2013; TAP, 2017; TANAP, 2017).

Nabucco consortium responded to these challenges by proposing a drastically revised and de-scaled version of the project in 2012 – the so-called Nabucco-West (Socor, 24.05.2012). But its fate was already sealed – without secured gas supplies to fill the pipeline and facing completion rival projects championed by Azerbaijan and Turkey, Nabucco had no chance. In the end it was fatal lack of American support that killed the project off, as it "withered on the branch, in the face of opposition to Washington" (Kindiyoti, 2012, p.194).

In March 2013 BP and SOCAR-dominated Shah Deniz consortium announced TAP as their chosen route for the export of Azerbaijani natural gas to southern Europe. Speaking at a press conference after the decision Kjetil Tungland, TAP Managing Director, said: "I am very pleased that the selection to transport Shah Deniz II gas to Europe has been made in favor of the TAP pipeline. This is the first and important step in opening up the Southern Gas Corridor and, as we look ahead, the Southern Gas Corridor will have a major role to play in Europe's energy security and ensuring the diversification of gas supplies to Western and South Eastern European markets." (TAP, 28.06.2013).

Pipeline wars were over, Nabucco was dead and SGC was born. Southern Gas Corridor (SGC), therefore, is not a single pipeline but a network of three interlocking pipelines – South-Caucasus Pipeline (SCP), Trans-Anatolian Pipeline (TANAP) and Trans-Adriatic Pipeline (TAP), running from Azerbaijan to Italy: "The Southern Gas Corridor is one of the most complex gas value chains ever developed in the world. Stretching over 3,500 kilometres, crossing seven countries and involving more than a dozen major energy companies, it is comprised of several separate energy projects representing a total investment of approximately U.S.$40 billion" (TAP 3, 2017) (see Map 4).

It represents a complex system of state, corporate and institutional interests – separate consortiums of private and state energy companies operate separate elements and segments of SGC, with BP and SOCAR present if not dominant across the length of the Corridor (BP Magazine. 12.10.2017). It is a geo-political mega-project project, which excludes Russia and Iran, is backed by the U.S. and the EU, involves a dozen countries and strongly promoted by its chief gas supplier – Azerbaijan (The Jamestown Foundation, Conference Report. 13.09.2013).

It is a commercial mega-project, representing key corporate interests of multinational oil and gas majors, especially BP. It is a financial mega-project requiring some $40 billion worth of investment (TAP 3, 2017) and involving a plethora of international financial institutions (IFIs), including the World Bank, EBRD and the financial arm of the EU – the EIB (EBRD, 18.10.2017; Buckley and Foy, 18.10.2017).

Map 3. Southern Gas Corridor (Source: TAP 1, 2017).

SGC is also an international legal regime, governed by a series of intergovernmental agreements and commercial contracts for each of the value chain pipelines – a complex legal structure representing a fine balancing act of multiple interests (TAP 3, 2017). It was subjected to a set of extensive social and environmental impact assessments to satisfy a plethora of regulatory requirements for major international infrastructure and energy projects.

By end of 2017 SCP segment of the Corridor was near completion– the original Baku-Tbilisi-Erzurum pipeline has been significantly expanded to raise capacity to in excess of 20 billion cubic metres per year (BP 4, 2017). The work on TANAP went underway in 2015, with bulk of its financing secured early (Burroughs, 15.08.2017). The completed pipeline was officially launched in November 2019 (Sezer, Kucukgocmen, 30.11.2019). TAP, meanwhile, is under construction, having secured funding from EBRD and a record €2 billion credit agreement from the European Investment Bank, although it faced a number of delays (Morgan, 13.12.2017).

SGC will deliver six billion cubic metres of Shah Deniz natural gas to Turkey and a further ten to markets in Europe; early deliveries to Turkey began in 2019 (BP 5, 2017; Mammadova, 8/10/2019). SGC represents a piece of critical energy infrastructure that not only connects Caspian gas reserves to Europe, but also provides politically independent, non-Russian East-West gas route analogous in significance to the BTC oil route of a decade earlier.

It serves the EU's goal of diversifying both its gas supplies and gas supply routes, while meeting urgent energy demands in southern member-states. It fulfils U.S. policy aims of strengthening independence of post-Soviet states and supporting EU energy security. For Azerbaijan the Corridor is a flagship national project of strategic significance, both politically and economically.

For Turkey it represents a critical step in establishing the Republic as strategic energy transit hub. SGC reinforces Georgia's role as the cockpit of the entire East-West energy transmission system, the key piece in the strategic chain. For BP and other energy majors SGC is a valuable asset in their portfolio, attractive to private investors, reassured by support from various public IFIs.

In sum, the project is a perfect model of strategic interest alignment between states, oil and gas majors and international institutions, balancing economic viability with geo-political realities and bringing technological and innovation to realize what in the end is a major engineering challenge.

Conclusion

Discussion above demonstrates that BTC and SGC pipelines are underpinned by a materialist paradigm of oil and gas politics – these projects are ultimately about power, state and corporate. This is the core of the rationalist models or rather model, for both projects constitute a single geo-political enterprise, that has its antecedents in past historical power relations. Some of the players have changed, some are the same but the structural properties of the game are the same, and are often referred to as such – the New Great Game (Yergin, 2012, pp.45-46; Cooley, p.3).

Hydrocarbons remain the primary fuel of the global energy order. And oil geopolitics – "that high, thin stratum where the business and politics of energy merge into a single, swiftly moving current" (Roberts, 2005 [2004], p. 93) – remain at the heart of the rationalist paradigm of international oil politics. Continued conflicts and new wars, market disruptions and price volatility, and rising threat of global warming remain the dominant issues facing rationalist research programme this decade.

Yet, as much as neo-realists and neoliberals ignore the reflectivist, critical turn in IR its implications are inescapable and are made ever more pertinent as world events unfold. As debates about BTC and SGC continue to unfold, issues and subject matter long ignored and dismissed by positivist orthodoxy, and groups and interests marginalized and excluded by rationalist scholarship, are increasingly finding their recognition and empirical attention in the Fourth Debate, and is having a political impact. A reflectivist research model of international oil politics is set out in the next chapter.

V
Reflectivist Models

Introduction

This chapter sets out the reflectivist critique of the rationalist paradigm of international oil politics and formulates a reflectivist model of BTC/SGC pipeline projects. The Fourth Debate has had a profound impact on debates around global energy and the environment and while the chapter follows the contours of the debate, particular attention is paid to neo-Marxism, critical theory and to poststructuralist and social constructivist insights, with a special focus on environmentalism.

The chapter opens with a reflectivist critique of the problem-solving paradigm of international oil and gas politics. The task of the anti-positivist critique is not only to unpick and problematize rationalist consensus on fossil fuels but to provide a theoretical alternative to the dominant orthodoxy around the prevailing social energy order, and to offer a praxeological direction to achieving that alternative (Cox, 1986). Differentiating between rationalist treatment of issues in the world of oil and gas and that of anti-positivist approaches enables envisioning of alternative energy realities.

The chapter explores these approaches and possible alternatives by examining BTC and SGC projects through the prism of the Fourth Debate – from classical Marxism to post-structuralism. This is by no means a comprehensive account but is intended to demonstrate the alternative vision of these pipeline projects, establishing these complex infrastructural assemblages as social, ideational, as well as material artefacts.

Critique of the problem-solving theory of oil politics

Who was Hugo Chávez? Was he a great social reformer who championed the rights and interests of marginalized communities and transformed Venezuela from a corrupt petro-oligarchy into a progressive social democracy? Or was he a proto-communist authoritarian who ruined his country's economy and undermined human rights and free press, turning Venezuela from a developing capitalist democracy into a failing petro-state?

Was he an inspirational anti-imperialist who had reenergized the developing world and reawakened South American liberation movement under the banner of the Bolivarian revolution? Or was he simply a populist anti-American firebrand, friend to dictators such as Saddam Hussein and Fidel Castro?

In his assessment of Hugo Chavez's presidency, author Bart Jones argued: "Chávez has retaken control of the oil industry, implemented laws taking a larger share of profits from foreign companies, and instituted a historic shift of the revenues to the majority poor" (2008, p.11).

By contrast, Daniel Yergin argues that oil – "the soul of the Venezuelan state" – became subject of Chavez's growing authoritarianism as he asserted control over PDVSA, Venezuelan national oil company and used it to further consolidate his hold on power: "He could use the money as he wanted, whether social spending and subsidies for favored groups at home or pursuit of his political objectives within the country and abroad. More than ever before, Venezuela was truly a petro-state" (2012, p. 125).

Such divergent perspectives may not be simply a result of some arbitrary biases of these particular scholars. They may reflect deeper underlying conditions borne out of these authors' specific theoretical and normative commitments, which in turn are tied to their specific temporal and spatial political standpoints.

This observation could well serve as the starting point in the discussion of the reflectivist paradigmatic model of international oil politics. What all reflectivist approaches do have in common is a deep scepticism about mainstream definitions of what constitutes proper subject matter in the study of petroleum politics and those traditional methodologies most commonly associated with rationalist IR.

Reflectivists, especially proponents of the Critical Theory, argue that "the way the academy limited the scope of IR has impacted, and continues to impact, drastically on the practice of world politics" (Sutch and Elias, 2007, p.14). From this angle comments on Hugo Chavez's presidency above carry important implications. As Robert Cox put it: "Theory is always for someone and for some purpose. All theories have a perspective. Perspectives derive from a position in time and space, specifically social and political time and space" (Cox, 1986, p. 207).

In addition to being a Pulitzer Prize-winning author, Daniel Yergin is the Vice Chairman of IHS, Inc. and the founder of IHS Cambridge Energy Research Associates, a leading oil and gas industry consultancy. He also serves on the U.S. Secretary of Energy's Advisory Board and is a member of the National Petroleum Council, among other roles (IHS website, 2016). Meanwhile, Bart Jones is a journalist and social commentator, who had spent eight years in Venezuela, having worked as the *Newsday* and the Associated Press correspondent, and also as a Catholic mission worker in the Caracas slums (Milne, 2008).

Of course, Yergin's and Jones' specific professional qualifications and experiences do not necessarily determine their respectively negative and sympathetic assessments of Chavez's presidency. Rather, their perspectives on Venezuelan oil politics are determined by their implicit, unspoken theoretical commitments. And theories are not merely explanatory tools – they inform and arbitrate on the very possibility of human intervention and define "our ethical and practical horizons" (Smith, 1996, p. 13). Thus, theoretical commitments can serve particular purposes in an intellectual enterprise – explicitly or implicitly they reflect political choices, loyalties and identities of those who espouse them.

Robert Cox (1986, pp.207-208) posited that as all theories have a perspective they ultimately serve one of two possible purposes: either help to solve the problems that arise within the framework of their original perspective, or reflect upon how that perspective came to be chosen for theorizing in the first place and whether there may be another valid perspective which, if chosen, could give rise to an alternative world – the dichotomy of the problem-solving vs. critical theory. By such definition all of rationalist scholarship on international oil politics falls within the realm of the problem-solving theory.

This type of theory operates within a given socio-political framework, where power relationships and institutional arrangements are taken as a given reality and not called into question - for example, the pre-Chavez Venezuela. The purpose of such theory is to ensure that "these relationships and institutions work smoothly by dealing effectively with particular sources of trouble" (1986, pp.207-208).

According to Yergin, in the 1980s and the early 1990s Venezuela's sources of trouble were low economic growth, falling incomes, high inflation, rising foreign debt and rapid population growth (2012, p. 114). The solution, therefore, lay in economic reforms – privatisation, inviting back foreign oil companies and fiscal discipline – which failed in part due to opposition from special interests but most importantly because of Chavez-led failed coup of 1992 and his subsequent victory in 1998 presidential election (Ibid. pp. 114-122).

Problem-solving theoretical approaches, exemplified by Daniel Yergin's scholarship (1991; 2012), all start with a general *a priori* acceptance that the reality of the international petroleum order is a given fact – human progress in the Modern Era is driven by consumption of energy, derived largely through combustion of fossil fuels, and the task is to ensure that this process is as smooth and effective as possible. Problems arise because the process may well be driven by global energy markets and international oil companies but ultimately it takes place amongst competitive nation-states, under conditions imposed by an anarchic international system. Energy resources are finite and their use produces externalities, such as pollution.

The task of problem-solving theories is to develop a sound political-economic understanding of structural properties of all these challenges, which may in turn be used to devise comprehensive policy solutions to address them. The task is not to question the prevailing social order of international energy politics or to ask how and why it came about, or who benefits from it (and who does not). If anything, rationalist approaches serve to validate and legitimize the status quo. Daniel Yergin is particularly effusive in his celebration of the advent of the hydrocarbon dominance:

> If it can be said, in the abstract, that the sun energized the planet, it was oil that now powered its human population, both in its familiar forms as fuel and in the proliferation of new petrochemical products. Oil emerged triumphant, the undisputed King, a monarch garbed in the dazzling array of plastics. He was generous to his loyal subjects, sharing his wealth to, and even beyond, the point of waste. His reign was a time of confidence, of growth, of expansion, of astonishing economic performance. His largesse transformed his kingdom, ushering in a new drive-in civilisation. It was the Age of Hydrocarbon Man (Yergin, 1991, p. 523).

Here, the prevailing political-economic order is almost anthropomorphized to the status of royalty – a benevolent patriarchal and paternalistic overlord of the entire civilisation. Rhetorical flourishes aside, what is evident here is a whole range of underlying normative assumptions. For example, growth and expansion are automatically assumed to be the desired outcome. Economic performance is the sort of measure that makes for "astonishing" in the rationalist world-view - one where there is nothing about human activity which does not have a material base and cannot, therefore, be measured and quantified, assessed and evaluated.

This general attitude characterizes much of the rationalist, or problem-solving thinking about global energy. It is, perhaps strikingly exemplified in the following passage from Scott L. Montgomery's aptly named *The Powers That Be*:

> A book, in short, is no static object but a kind of social container, bursting with resources and processes. The same, indeed, can be said for any other object d'art, whether made of stone, canvas, film, or text. We may speak of genius and inspiration, higher pleasures and heavenly beauty, yet it is the things of this Earth – coal, petroleum, gas, water, wind – that give such brilliance a material reality. A simple truth, conveniently (and

understandably) left out of courses on the humanities (2010, p.5).

Within this statement are contained elements of both: a self-legitimising positivist discourse of the rationalist orthodoxy and an epistemological mechanism for disciplining alternative modes of scholarship. Having bracketed (perhaps even reduced) the full complexity and entire intellectual capacity of the human condition to the framework of a purely materialist reality, positivist discourse seeks to delegitimize and exclude those insights and methods of enquiry which deal with the non-material, social and imaginational elements. Determining what counts as proper science, therefore, allows for effective means of policing scholarship and deciding upon what constitutes legitimate questions and correct answers.

For example, when it comes to dealing with a state oil company, the "right" question to ask is how to ensure that it is run professionally and effectively. By contrast, asking who benefits from the operations of that oil company and under what conditions is not the right question. Such judgements are not, however, made in accordance with some immutable universal standard of truth and objectivity, but are in fact reflections of scholars' political and normative choices, forming a rationalist perspective in favor of the existing set of power relations, within the given global energy order.

This specific perspective gives rise to a problem-solving theory of international oil politics, as outlined in previous chapter. Thus in the first decades of the twenty-first century the problem-solving discourse was often focused on the threat of resource depletion (Roberts, 2004; Klare, 2004; 2012). Possibility that the world may be running out of oil, thus heralding the end of the hydrocarbon civilisation prompted a fierce debate, with protagonists warning of impending catastrophe (Dyer, 2009; Leggett, 2005).

Fears of economic and political instability and new threats to Western global dominance informed much of "the end of oil" narrative, exemplified best by Michael Klare's warning that the United States faces four key challenges: "an increasing need for imported oil, a pronounced shift toward unstable and unfriendly suppliers in dangerous parts of the world; a greater risk of anti-American or civil violence, and rising competition for what will likely prove a diminishing supply pool" (2004, p.23).

Sceptics of the so-called "peak oil" thesis differ in the extent to which they reject the central premise of the argument – that geological evidence points to diminishing global stock of oil, as extraction rates across the world reach peak levels (see, for example, Yergin, 2012, pp. 229-265; Mauger, 2006; Mills, 2008). However, they all agree that the problem is grossly overstated and that technological innovation and development of alternative sources of fossil fuels, such as tar sands and shale gas, will ensure long-term dominance of the petroleum order.

Yergin argues: "By 2030 these non-traditional liquids could add up to a third of total liquids capacity. By then, however, most of these unconventional oils will have a new name. They will all be called conventional" (2012, p.265). Similarly, both Maugeri (2006) and Mills (2008) conclude that there is neither a problem of oil scarcity, nor an upcoming geopolitical struggle for oil against forces hostile to the West; and, as is typical of anti-peak oil scholarship, much of their effort is focused on "debunking of myths" surrounding resource depletion debates.

This is, at its core, a technical and highly professionalized debate, centered on differing interpretations of geological and other data differing emphasis on the role of markets, technology, governments and international organizations and (depending on one's paradigmatic standpoint within the neo-neo rationalist synthesis). One reason it has made headlines is the central role petroleum plays in our daily lives.

What this debate really reveals, however, is that all its protagonists on both sides of the apparent divide, share a common rationalist understanding of the energy reality. They all are concerned about preserving prevailing social energy order, even if they disagree about the nature of the problem facing it or how to solve it (even as some of them advocate transition to non-fossil fuels). This problem-solving approach is most unobscured when we turn to these policy-prescriptions (solutions) advanced by various authors.

Whether it is energy conservation, promotion of alternative energy sources, technological innovation etc., all these approaches share a common commitment to the preservation of the modern industrial order

(Klare, 2004). The "peak oil" debate is similar in this way to other thematic discourses in international oil politics, such as energy security; the "resource curse" thesis; the role of the Middle East, the changing function of the oil and gas markets; energy price fluctuations, geopolitics of pipelines, among others. The debates intersect and overlap on many substantive issues but are arced by a common rationalist agenda.

For example, the area where resource depletion and climate change/environment debates intersect provides for a fertile ground for problem-solving approaches. Below is a characteristic take on the issue from Paul Roberts' defining "peak oil" text - *The End of Oil* (2004, p.309):

> In the simplest terms, the energy challenge of the twenty-first century will be to satisfy a dramatically larger demand for energy, while producing dramatically less carbon. Yet the availability of carbon-free energy on a mass scale – whether produced from renewable sources, like solar and wind, of from decarbonized fossil fuels – will not happen without significant technological developments. And such breakthroughs aren't likely until the market regards carbon as a cost to be avoided – not just in "progressive" enclaves like Germany or England, but in the big economies of Russia, China, and, above all, the United States.[16]

The problem is identified – growing demand for energy vs. the costs of carbon emissions. The solution is advanced – market-driven technological innovation, international in nature. Implicit here is a requirement for political action by nation-states. The purpose here, as elsewhere, is not to change the world but to make the existing system work better. This is the antithesis of critical theory of oil politics, which not only seeks to expose underlying power relations within the system but "allows for a normative choice in favor of a social and political order different from the prevailing order" (Cox, 1986, p.210).

---

[16] For a comprehensive example of rationalist problem-solving analysis in the "peak oil" debate, complete with scenario-building, climate change modelling and policy prescriptions, see Roberts, 2004, pp.312-326.

The normative dimension of this reasoning cannot be overstated, for the underlying assumption of the problem-solving approaches is also a normative choice in favor of the status quo. The modern industrial capitalist Western-dominated global energy order is a priori accorded position of the de facto model for human development, more often than not explicitly so:

> Around the world, more than a half billion people – roughly one-quarter of the world – lack access to electricity or fossil fuels and thus have virtually no chance to move from a brutally poor, preindustrial existence to the kind of modern, energy-intensive life many of us in the West take for granted. Energy poverty is in fact emerging as the new killer in the developing nations, the root cause of a vast number of other problems, and perhaps the deepest divide between the haves and have-nots (Roberts, 2004, p.8).

It follows from there that non-Western societies will seek to emulate this modern-industrial model leading to greater demand for energy in the developing world, as countries such as China seek to industrialize and modernize. Whether or not this is the case it is important to recognize that the underlying assumptions of this normative choice in favor of the prevailing energy order is in fact just that - a choice and not some immutable universal law. Critical approaches to oil politics begin by unpicking these assumptions and positing profound, fundamental questions about the nature of the existing social energy order; about its origins and historical processes which shaped it; about underlying power relations between various actors within it; and ultimately questions about its moral legitimacy.

Critical theory views realist-liberal consensus as problematic because it does both – condones the structural injustices of the prevailing global order and helps to perpetuate them by devising problem-solving policy prescriptions, even while, as in the case of the liberal tradition, espousing seemingly benign, universal moral principles and ethos (Monbiot, 2006). Inspired, as it is, by classical and neo-classical Marxist traditions, critical theory is post-Marxist in espousing an explicit normative agenda behind the intellectual enterprise - "...the normative purpose of the inquiry precedes and facilitates the definition of the object of inquiry" (Linklater, 1992, p. 92).

As Robert Cox argues: "When we think now of 'change' in world politics and society we think of what has to be done to ensure the survival of the human race and to moderate conflict among peoples. The primary task of the study of international relations along with the other departments of knowledge about human affairs is to help people to organize so as to achieve this" (2008, p. 87).

Therefore, while the process begins with a substantive critique of the dominant rationalist discourse, it must then necessarily move into the praxeological domain of political and civic action aimed at bringing about substantive change (this is important in the context of international politics of oil).

From classical Marxism to World Systems Theory

E. H. Carr, hardly a Marxist and generally sceptical of socialism did, however, acknowledge that "The Twenty Years' Crisis" was "strongly impregnated with Marxist ways of thinking, applied to international relations" (Carr, *An Autobiography*, pp. xvi-xvii quoted in Cox, 2000). And his work "could loosely be described as being radical and materialistic without ever being properly defined as Marxist itself" (Cox, 2001, p. xix). Yet it is worth considering, that many of Karl Marx's followers were influenced in equal measure by the normative if not the political agenda of liberalism.

For example, classical idealists, such as the economist John A. Hobson, sought to find the causes of war in the relationship between European imperialism and systemic economic failures and inequities of modern capitalist system (1902). Hobson's pacifist normative framework and advocacy of socio-economic reform were hardly radical but his insights did go on to influence Russian revolutionary and Marxist V.I. Lenin, whose own analysis of imperialism borrows extensively from Hobson's as Lenin acknowledged in the preface to his *Imperialism as the Highest Stage of Capitalism* (1961 [1917]), p. 300).

It can, therefore, be said that Marxist thinking and influence in IR predates its establishment as a formal field of study inside the discipline –

a process that in any case was "belated, partial and problematic," bound as it was by the Cold War dynamic (Teschke, 2008, p. 163). Today it can be argued that in International Relations Marxism constitutes "a vibrant and rich subfield that produces some of the most trenchant challenges to mainstream international relations theory and general social science" (Ibid., p. 164).

This is true of critical and other reflectivist approaches influenced by Gramscian political theory, and through which Western Marxism sought to reformulate its materialistic framework and to develop powerful critiques of economic determinism and positivism more generally (Rupert, 2013, p. 167).

Early classical Marxism, however, was influenced in the first instance by liberal cosmopolitanism. Marx and Engels paid little attention to how different political territorially-bound, spatially-defined communities develop and interact with each other over a period of time. This is because Marxism sought a critical understanding of capitalism as a particular historical form of social, economic, political and cultural life which "has never been containable within the boundaries of territorial states" (Ibid., p. 167).

Instead the focus of analysis was on capitalism as a set of universalising, homogenising and trans-nationalising processes. These would ultimately bring forward a unifying model – class-divided society on a global scale, where social antagonisms and polarisation will lead to intensification of class struggle and eventually a global proletarian revolution (Teschke, 2008 p. 164).

Yet revolutionary failures of 1848 led Marx and Engels to correct their early-world historicist thesis (Ibid). Domestic factors, resistance of the bourgeoisie and inter-state war were reconfigured as progressive agents of communism but by the time the *Capital* was published in 1872 there was a growing recognition that proletariats of various nation-states may not necessarily immediately form an International: "Though not in substance, yet in form, the struggle of the proletariat with the bourgeoisie is at first a national struggle. The proletariat of each country must, of course, first of all settle matters with its own bourgeoisie" (Marx and Engels, 1888 in Tucker, 1978, p. 482).

In response to this and wider geopolitical processes and world events - from new imperialism and the Scramble for Africa to the arms race and World War I - classical Marxist theories of imperialism emerged in a sustained attempt to ground these crises in evolving dynamics of capitalism. Marxists observed that capitalism has moved from free competition on to cartelisation, financial oligarchy and dominance of national monopolies, first on domestic but then inevitably also on international level. As Lenin argued: "But the internal market, under capitalism, is inevitably linked to the external one. Capitalism had long created a world market." (1961 [1917], p 366).[17]

In Marxist analysis the quest for raw materials and new markets as well as the export of capital overseas drive competing capitalist alliances (cartels and monopolies) towards securing direct political control over extra-territorial colonies. This leads to empire formation and creation for rival national blocks (Ibid., p. 375). Lenin repeatedly underscored a critical role played by natural resources in stimulating imperialist competition – "…and we have seen the ferocity with which international capitalist unions direct their efforts to remove from their opponents all possibility of competing, to purchase, for example, iron-ore deposits or petroleum sources and so on" (Ibid., p. 382).

The higher the rate of capitalist development, the greater the demand for raw materials, which in turn drives ever greater competition and the race for new sources, requiring ever growing colonial expansion (Ibid.) This dynamic is not limited to already discovered resources – Lenin was accurate in his observation that technological progress and exploration, fuelled by expansion of financial capital, will make potential, yet undiscovered resources subject to future competition (Ibid., p.383).

Classic theories of imperialism played a dominant role in Marxist thinking on international politics and were further reinvigorated by a new historicism, brought about by the emergence of World System Theory (WST) and "core/periphery" and dependency theory analyses, associated with the works of Immanuel Wallerstein (see, for example, 1974; 1983).

An integrated world economy, characterized by specific forms of division of labor is the central unit of analysis in WST approaches.

---

[17] Translations from Russian author's own.

However, geopolitical location of states (core, semi-periphery or periphery) is determined by consolidated and reinforced political hierarchies concerned with ensuring transfer of surplus of economic wealth from periphery to the core e.g. raw materials from the South and East to the West.

Thus, existence of a territorially-defined state system becomes a precondition for reproduction of capitalism and continuing transfer of surplus for core to periphery: "...the function, strength and location of specific states on the world systems' core-semi-periphery-periphery spectrum is determined by their trade-mediated integration into the economic structure of the international division of labor" (Teschke, 2008, pp.169-172; p. 172).

This focus on inequalities between constituent parts of a world economic system provided new opportunities for Marxist analysis of evolving international politics of oil in the post-war period. Successive oil crises of 1960s and 1970s in particular, served as a backdrop to Wallerstein's emphasis on the changing dynamics in the core – semi-periphery – periphery relations.

Noting the cyclical nature of economic crises in the capitalist system, caused by overproduction and falling demand in core countries, Wallerstein located the bargaining power of semi-peripheral states in their capacity to take advantage of changing patterns in the distribution of surplus: "And intermediate elements in the surplus-extraction chain gain at the expense of those at the core of the system. In present-day terms, this means among other things a shift in relative profit advantage to the semi-peripheral nations" (1976, p.464).

Thus, for example, OPEC's ability, on behalf of its semi-peripheral membership, to extract higher share of profit of oil production from consuming (core) nations and international oil companies, represented "the most spectacular example" of just such a shift in bargaining power (Ibid.). When oversupply of high-cost, high-profit goods produced in the core countries leads to more intense competition in a relatively contracting world-market, then "semi-peripheral countries can, up to a point, pick and choose among core producers not only in terms of the sale of their commodities (viz., OPEC oil) but also in terms both of welcoming their investment in manufactures and of purchasing their producer's goods" (Ibid.).

World Systems Theory remains an influential force in Marxist thinking in IR (see, for example, Hurst, 2009). Meanwhile, Robert Cox's (1983) introduction of Gramscian concepts, such as hegemonic power as an irreducible transfiguration of dominant ideas, institutions and world orders, heralded the anti-positivist challenge of the Critical Theory. This (coupled with the positivist backlash in the 1980s and 1990s), in turn, stimulated a later revival in classical, political Marxism (see, for example, Halliday 1994), which can be said to represent a re-foundation of Marxist IR as an international historical sociology (Teschke, 2008, p.177).

This sociological framework extended into Marxist critique of mainstream globalisation theory, prompting a renewed interest in imperialism and neo-imperialism (see, for example, Robinson, 2002; Hardt and Negri, 2000). It is clear that what lies at the heart of Marxist analysis of international oil politics is its normative commitment to an emancipatory international intellectual and political project (see Appendix 4).

On Marxism and the First IR Debate

Looking at issues, themes and topics in oil politics that cut across theoretical boundaries it is possible to formulate multidimensional models of specific empirical questions using analytical toolkits of individual paradigms synergetically to harness their epistemological and ontological knowledge-value.

For example, the development of the concessionary system in the 1900s-1910s features prominently in the Liberal, Marxist and Realist accounts of international oil politics. For Liberals concessions are manifestations of the evolving international commercial legal system which enabled investment of capital, technology and therefore commerce and trade.

For realists they are examples of the political instruments deployed by powerful states against weaker states to secure preferential terms for secure oil supplies. And for Marxists they are the formalized mechanisms through which international capitalist unions (cartels) and their respective national governments exert imperialist control over far-flung corners of the world.

The merits and validity of these accounts should in principle be determined by means of robust empirical contestation. But there are no legitimate grounds for a priori exclusion of any of these accounts from the story of oil politics. To engage with these paradigmatic frameworks synergetically is not the same as to apply some sort of combinational method but to recognize that each theoretical model represents a unique set of epistemological, ontological and normative commitments, which determine the color of the lens through which we see what is in fact a contested social reality.

At the same time, it is essential to recognize that on empirical level the boundaries of this contestation are porous. There has long been an argument that the divisions of the First Debate are overstated and there are clear cross paradigmatic overlaps between Marxist and Liberal, and Marxist and Realist traditions (Williams, 2005). Marxism and Realism, for example, are ostensibly different, even opposed but as Rengger observed, "astute students of both have always seen degrees of commonality lurking just beneath the surface" (2008, p.188).

It can be argued that Marxism and Realism not only have in common elements of a materialist ontology but also share a commitment to normative relativism if not outright scepticism about ethics (see also, Donnelly, 2008). It is therefore a straightforward consequence that such overlaps are manifested on empirical level as convergences around the same subject matter (events, processes).

Table 4. Classical Theoretical Matrix of International Oil Politics

LIBERALISM	REALISM
The business of oil: industry, commerce, finance.	*Oil as component of state power and military strength – a strategic commodity.*
International commercial law and international energy cooperation.	
International oil companies (IOCs) and organizations.	*Pursuit of power as determinant of state preferences and choices in oil politics.*
Oil as determinant of state preferences and choices.	National oil companies and organizations.
Pursuit of technological progress, free trade and modernity.	Territorial competition for oil resources as pursuit of power;

	exercise of political power in pursuit of oil resources. International politics of oil as pursuit of power by states, under conditions of anarchy.

MARXISM

Oil as a raw material with use-value.
Evolution of oil production cycle from feudal system to capitalist system.
Cartels, trusts and monopolies – political economy of oil.
International oil capital and imperialism, anti-imperialism and anti-colonialism.
Oil proletariat and the class struggle and revolution.
National/state oil companies and industries.
Oil and the world economic system.
Critique of capitalism; class struggle and revolution as emancipatory project.

From Marxism to Critical Theory

For neo-Marxists, adherents of the world-systems and structural dependency theory the rationalist consensus serves to legitimize, consolidate and reinforce structural domination of the industrial North over the developing South. For example, Hinnebusch (2003) casts international energy issues in the context of anti-imperialist and Arab nationalist struggles of the 1960s and 1970s, charting what he characterizes as local resistance to Western hegemony and the power of multinational corporations through to the collapse of the Soviet Union and U.S. victory in the struggle for regional dominance (see also, Dannreuther, 2010).

Other Marxist-inspired approaches to international oil politics expand on core-periphery analysis and (re)prioritize Western and specifically U.S. hegemony as a key unit of analysis. Partly prompted by increasing marketization of the oil trade and growing power of producing nations, authors such as Simon Bromley sought to refocus attention on the expansion of U.S. hegemony in the global energy order, arguing that "the structural reach of its power has increased and remains qualitatively and quantitatively more extensive than that of its competitors" (1991, p.2).

In doing so Bromley was implicitly and explicitly responding to neo-realists and neo-liberal institutionalists, such as Stephen Krasner

(1985) and Robert Keohane (1989), who claimed, to greater or lesser extent, that Western oil hegemony was in decline, especially in light of the rise of OPEC and growing relative power of producer-nations (Bromley, 1991, p. 3; see also, Ibid., 1994).

Breaking down prevailing orthodoxies, questioning underlying assumptions, deconstructing various elements of the rationalist discourse are all hallmarks of critical analysis and reflectivist approaches more generally – a sociological project accompanying the normative and praxeological projects (Linklater, 1992; see also Ibid., 1998; 2002).

This persistent challenge to positivism is not limited to mid-level theory but is informed by varying degrees of scepticism about claims of immutability or universality of existing social structures in the global energy order. Not all these approaches are post-modern in terms of their normative commitments but they all hold modern conditions to have been historically constituted by way of complex social processes and that radically alternative social realities are possible and often desirable.

Thus, dissatisfaction with mainstream IR explanations of complex phenomena in the realm of energy politics stimulated growth of theoretically and methodologically diverse, interdisciplinary research agenda (reviewed below). Drawing on Habermasian and Foucauldian analytical traditions, post-structuralism, feminism, post-colonialism and environmentalism, this body of scholarship took on the positivist arguments with renewed radicalism, while decisively moving on from the rigidly bounded neo-Marxist world-systems and dependency approaches. As Bronner (2002) argued, the very complexity of globalized, hyper-technological modernity required a more nuanced and comprehensive critical approach.

Key issues affecting biological survival of the human race should be the first purpose of study in IR (Cox, 2008, p. 87) and critical theory, as if anticipating the coming concerns of the global ecological movement, helped ground this discourse within an explicitly normative domain: "Its willingness to emphasize the human price of progress, the costs of alienation and reification, the implications of scientific reason for moral capacities, and the potential 'revenge of nature' were all major contributions" (Bronner, 2002, p. 252).

The critique should not, therefore, be limited to specific processes, institutions or subsystems of the prevailing social order because: "Commodities like oil link them together: they affect planetary society from the foreign relations undertaken by its most industrially developed governments, to the ways we breath, to the spills that devastate the environment, to the derivative products produced by economic subsystems" (Bronner, 2002, p. 253).

Recognizing this as a holistic analytical framework is the first step in moving towards a critical theory that is engaged not only with questions of the social character of modernity and modernisation but also with ethical implications of scientific and technological progress. On empirical level in the domain of international oil politics this shift to a deep normative critique of the global energy order produced an expansive body of scholarship, which not only served as a critique of rationalist explanations for various problems, but also as an epistemologically autonomous body of knowledge, which dealt with issues marginalized by mainstream academia and the expert community.

Partly, this was a result of a conscious or perhaps reflexive efforts of radical authors who believed in democratising the debate around issues of technological and scientific progress, and argued that it is "incumbent upon critical theory to prevent the scientific enterprise from remaining identified with the discourse of experts" (Bronner, 2002, p. 254; Feenberg, 1991). Partly, as discussed elsewhere, this was the result of the determined effort by the rationalist mainstream to ignore and exclude radical approaches.

For example, the "resource curse" (or "resource dependency") thesis advanced by rationalists as an explanation for the causes of conflict in the international energy politics dominated mainstream debates about oil politics. It also generated a plethora of critical responses which do not necessarily deny that the "resource dependency" thesis provides a good starting point, but argue that "it critically fails to identify some of larger complexities and inter-connections which link energy and minerals to the shifting dynamics of global capitalism" (Dannreuther, 2010, p.11). Thus, on a general level proponents of critical theory reject the material determinism of oil, so characteristic of the rationalist analysis. On specific, substantive issues they seek to critically explore and investigate a complex, historically and politically constituted social order.

Hence, bold claims such as that "oil hinders democracy" (Ross, 2001) are dismissed as crude oversimplifications. These claims are of course more nuanced than that but they appear to suggest that mere possession of the resource predetermines certain negative socio-political outcomes. Instead, reflectivists turn to assessment of a range of socio-historical, political and economic factors which shape international resource politics, as well as trajectories of domestic developments.

Envisaging global energy order holistically, as an integrated production-consumption network, creates conditions and sets the terms for normative enquiry. In the first instance, the task of identifying the inequities and injustices of the prevailing energy order necessitates focus on the production end of the spectrum.

This is because, contrary to problem-solving assumptions, there is "no reason to believe that the mere recognition of future risks will somehow cause the oil industry or nuclear energy to 'reform' themselves... There is ultimately no way around it: achieving accountability with respect to nature requires achieving accountability in respect to production" (Bronner, 2002, p. 254).

Critical theory is called upon to formulate and articulate that organizational pressure. For example, Mitchell (2009; (2011) focuses on production of energy as the central force shaping global evolution of democratic norms and governance and recasts the history of energy politics, showing how intricately consumption of energy is connected to its production, and what political consequences this in turn has in domestic political systems at both end of the spectrum.

Gavin Bridge and Philippe Le Billon (2013) challenge the conventional "peak oil" and "oil curse" theses and provide a reflective, historicist account of an energy industry rearranged by increasingly international state oil companies, shifting demand patterns, the potentially violently revanchist declining powers, and the challenges of transition to a post-oil energy order.

While authors such as Bridge and Mitchell explore broad themes and issues of global energy, others direct their critique of positivist IR to the way national, sub-national and local actors have been ignored by mainstream scholarship. Take the issue of oil production and conflict in the Niger Delta. In Daniel Yergin's *The Quest* (2012) the matter is covered briefly, as part of a wider discussion of aggregate disruption of the global energy order in the first decade of the twenty first century. It is listed as one of its causes, along with Chavez in Venezuela, natural disaster and 11 September 2001 terrorist attacks (pp. 127-142).

According to Yergin conflict in Nigeria and specifically in the Delta region is a problem for the oil industry, not of it. The "gangs," ethnic divisions, Islamist terrorism and straightforward criminality are to blame for the problem of falling production: "Without physical security, the oil could not flow... And it was certainly a loss for the United States, for which Nigeria had just moved up to become its third-largest source of imported oil" (2012, p. 140).

Critical theorists offer a radical counter-narrative to Yergin's rationalist discourse. Geographer Michael Watts' studies of oil production in the Niger Delta focus on the complex social and political realities of oil-producing "enclaves" in the region and the web of inter-linked interests and actors, from international and national oil companies, national states, foreign states, sub-national regions to non-governmental organizations, social movements and local communities, which envelop the functioning and general operation of the oil industry (Watts, 2009; see also Watts 2001 and 2004; see de Oliveira, 2007 for analogous analysis of oil industry in Angola).

Critical feminist authors focus on the role of women and patterns of feminist organization in the Niger Delta which provided particular saliency to local community demands and opposition to central government and multinationals. Turnera & O. O'Hare (1993) explored the 1984 Ogharefe and the 1986 Ekpan women's revolts, which involved attacks on oil installations and pipelines in the Delta, demonstrating how legal and political regulations imposed by government and oil companies disrupted traditional farming practices to a particular disadvantage of women, prompting violent protests. Ecofeminism is a vibrant empirical theoretical subfield deserving of a more thorough examination than is possible here (see, for example, King, 1989; Gaard, 2011).

Popular resistance, indigenous struggles and grass-root, local communities' opposition against corporate and state interests is an important empirical strand in critical engagement with international energy and mineral politics. Dunning and Wirpsa, for example, critically examined the entry of U.S. oil companies into Columbia in the 1980s and the consequent civil conflict, which in turn brought the United States' military support for the Colombian government counterinsurgency effort (2004).

Protests at Standing Rock against the Dakota Access pipeline in 2016 and 2017 helped reprioritize indigenous local opposition to the energy industry and served to recast the issue in terms of resistance to colonial oppression (Hayes, 2016). A clear connection is maintained here between local/subnational, national and international factors, along with a normative assessment of the causes and consequences of resource-linked conflict.

The aftermath of 9/11 and wars in Afghanistan and Iraq also provided an additional impetus for counter-hegemonic, normative critical scholarship. Some authors, like Phyllis Bennis (2006), seek to offer a systematic critique of U.S. unilateralism and identify global public opinion and growing willingness of non-Western governments to challenge U.S. power as key elements in reclaiming institutions and powers of global governance for the purpose of the global peace movement.

Such radical critiques of American oil hegemony contend that the United States exploits the developing world's natural resources, compelling the rest of the advanced industrial countries to remain dependent on American domination of the global economy. The central concern here is "to untangle the global structure and in particular the world economic system through which the United States has been exercising control in the fast-changing environment of the post-Cold War world" (Fouskas and Gökay, 2005, p. 6).

Elsewhere, a more direct link is made between U.S. dominance, capitalism, oil trade and wars, and it is often made in almost exclusively normative terms – actively locating the causes of oppressive, anti-emancipatory dynamics in the ethical failure of the prevailing capitalist order. This polemical quote is from *America in Islamistan: Trade, Oil and*

Blood (2011) by Abdulhay Zalloum: "The culture of mafia is indeed the culture of capitalism. Both are based on extortion, lies and wars, one among the gangs, the other among nations. Both have no moral codes to discipline them" (p. 5).

There is another critical tradition in the study of oil politics – that of *the exposé,* and it has been taken up with renewed vigor by post-structuralist researchers and social investigators. This tradition harks back to Ida Tarbell's (1904) devastating take-down of the Rockefeller empire and the Standard Oil monopoly in the1900s, which eventually led to the breakup of the company and the passing of anti-trust legislation in the U.S.

Works such as Ken Silverstein's *The Secret World Oil* (2014) is a recent example of such deconstructive, investigative approach. It follows the pattern of establishing complex connections in the oil production-consumption cycle, looking at the role of various actors – financiers, fixers, politicians, lobbyists and so on – in ensuring the smooth functioning of a system, which at its core is invariably corrupt and unjust.

In less conventional and non-academic discourses, critical interest is often directed at exploring production-consumption nexuses with a particular focus on the relationship between the material and ideational quality of energy, and of oil in particular. In *Oil on the Brain* (2007), journalist Lisa Margonelli charts "petroleum's long, strange trip to your tank," as the sub-title states.

The book begins with the story how Margonelli became obsessed with oil, having witnessed an experiment involving burning of crude: "Oil the abstraction died and was reborn as a mythic molecule – powerful, violent, and charismatic – capable of running the world" (p.1). She even mentions the time and date the moment occurred, such its significance.

Then follows an account of the global flow of oil that quite literally follows it down the pipelines backwards, from the gas station to drilling rigs scattered around the world, from trading floors of the NYMEX to the energy-hungry middle class communities in China – a whirlwind journey that seeks to expose the hidden and reified world of oil, while simultaneously seeking to emphasize the cultural, social quality of energy consumption, and ultimately the future of the energy order: "Ideas, even more than oil, are fuel" (p. 282).

Poststructuralism and Environmentalism

Poststructuralist thinking on oil and wider issues of energy politics requires a separate examination, not least because of the impact it had had on the wider environmental movement and the growth of global awareness of ecological issues. As Arran Gare put it: "Reflection on the postmodern condition and reflection on environmental crisis have much in common. They both involve efforts to understand the culture of modern civilisation and how it has come to its present state" (1995, p.1).

For Gare the task is to reconfigure the environmentalist and postmodernist discourses, to relate them to each other in critical and politically significant ways in order to produce a postmodernist theory – "a grand narrative" – capable of reconciling science and culture. The purpose is to show how "a new ethics, political philosophy and economics can be, and are being built upon this grand narrative, and how they are able to provide the foundations for an effective environmental movement" (1995, p. 2).

Yet, considerable force of critical postmodernist environmentalism was at least in part generated by the tension between anti-foundational postmodernist ethos and the humanist ethos of the environmental movement – question of the relationship between nature and culture. And it was also driven by a growing dissatisfaction with the way environmental reasoning evolved from its radical political origins in the social movements and revolutionary protests of the 1960s to fit in with the conventional structuralist thinking and new positivist orthodoxy in the late twentieth and early twenty first century.

Thus, Verena Andermatt Conley drawing on contemporary French critical theory and feminism, and eco-feminism specifically, seeks to re-locate environmentalism and wider eco-politics back to the realm of humanist ethos of the emancipatory project, arguing that in the decades since the 1968 revolts, "some of the most precocious reflections on philosophy and ecology have become, like the world itself, irrevocably polluted" (1997, p.2). Conley draws on the works of radical theorists, such as Jean-François Lyotard (1993 [1989]) and Jacques Derrida (1993), to argue for a comprehensive reappraisal of poststructuralist eco-political theory.

These French philosophers were united in their dismissal of the emerging post-Cold War consensus on a whole range of issues, not least the relationship between technological and economic progress and the environment. Lyotard cast the post- World War II period in post-modern terms, identifying conflicts between humans and nature, and the developed world and the global South as prevailing dynamics in the postmodern world.

Derrida, in turn, proffered withering critiques of the "end of history" and "triumph of neo-liberalism" accounts, saying of Francis Fukuyama's 1992 book: "If such works have a certain fascination, their very incoherence and often pathetic primitivity, play a role of a symptomatic sign that surely needs to be accounted for" (1993). This is because positivist narratives actively de-historicize concepts such as democracy and progress, thus naturalising and legitimising particular social forms and ideological claims, existing within a given specific cultural market, elevating them to a status of universal law.

What is characteristically reflectivist of postmodernism is the way in which the normative and the political, the intellectual and the praxeological are enmeshed within a single practical and analytical framework. Consider, for example, the way in which Conley charts the environmentalist agenda from Claude Lévi-Strauss's critique (1962) of Jean Paul Sartre, to contemporary struggle for the preservation of nature:

"By arguing against Sartre, in favor of decentering of human subjects, for the inseparability of nature and culture, Lévi-Strauss opens the way in contemporary French theory to ecological thinking. The endpoint of this project is, of course, in the here-and-now, in the collective labors that need to be expended so safeguard the future of the planet" (Conley, 1997, p. 9).

Conley is therefore explicit in recognising that the roots of postmodernist ecological theory (and critical theoretical tradition in general) must be in the socio-political (Hegelian, Neo-Marxist) thinking on the issue back in the 1960s and 1970s (1997, p.4). And while she does propose a reassessment of poststructuralism as part of an explicitly environmentalist ethos, she sees this effort as complementary to the tradition espoused by earlier scholars. This is not a view shared by all.

As Vassos Argyrou argues in *The Logic of Environmentalism: Anthropology, Ecology and Postcoloniality* the fact environmentalism emerged from certain underlying modernist assumptions ensured that "at a more fundamental level than phenomenological, environmentalism reflects a return of the same, the reproduction of the same sort of global power relations and the same sort of logic that mark the modernist paradigm at its core" (2005, x).

Attempting to rehabilitate the widespread assumption that environmentalism reflects a radical departure from modernity, carries with it significant political implications. As Argyrou contends reproduction of "the same" also concerns power – power of groups and societies to shape and determine world order – and here environmentalism "repeats the historical gesture that marked the colonial enterprise and its civilising mission" (2005, xi). In other words, environmentalism's implicit modernist project serves to reconfirm the position of the West as the source of all legitimacy, including legitimacy of culture and meaning.

The charge is that environmentalism is "problem solving approach" writ large – a quest to sustain the status quo, while removing ecological and other environmental threats to its survival (Argyro, 2005, xi). This tension between environmentalism and poststructuralism is a manifestation of an underlying tension between radical eco-centrism of some environmentalist discourses and no less radical anti-foundationalism of postmodernist critiques of "nature," exemplified by the social theory of Jean Baudrillard (Biro, 2002). The notion that we can save modernity by responding to material ecological threats, e.g. by switching to renewable sources of energy, is questioned and problematized by the postmodernist critique - should we be seeking to replace fossil fuels at all?

Taken further (and perhaps, simplified) this argument informed the view that our civilisation is ultimately so dangerous to the global system of nature that it cannot possibly be sustained. Over the past three decades it was steadily reinforced by progressive accumulation of scientific evidence of potentially catastrophic, human-made climate change (le Page, 2016). But it was also this eco-centrist foundationalism of the environmentalist discourses that prompted accusations of antihumanism (e.g. Ferry, 1992) and stimulated poststructuralism's growing scepticism towards eco-political discourses.

Some poststructuralists attempt to bridge these differences by identifying how postmodernist normative critique does nevertheless rely on material, naturalist claims; meanwhile, many eco-centrist assumptions ultimately depend on socially constructed understandings of nature (Biro, 2002). Others seek to ground this debate within a broader empirical framework, employing methodologically eclectic approaches and engaging with other theoretical traditions, such as post-colonialism and Global South perspectives.

For example, N. Patrick Peritore's comparative case study of elite decision-making in several developing countries seeks to show how a general post-modernist cultural shift contributed to growing environmental awareness with profound political implications: "The new environmental politics is truly international. Global environmentalism overrides differences among the widely varying cultures and economies" (1999, p.1).

Yet such arguments are unlikely to settle the debate. First, it is important to distinguish "post-modernity" as "the cultural, economic, social, and political formation within modernity that results from changes in time-space relations," and poststructuralism as a reflectivist analytics that "critically engages with the production and implication of these transformations" (Campbell, 2013, p. 231).

For poststructuralism the ethical prerogative (of saving the world from environmental catastrophe) raises the intellectual stakes; it predicates and prioritizes a normative engagement with the issue. It can be argued that this by itself constitutes a foundational paradigm which, in turn accounts for the tension between poststructuralism's imperative to critique and the eco-political imperative to act "to change the world."

What poststructuralism does not do is attempt to "resolve or transcend the sometimes violent tensions between many forms of human identity" (Ibid., p. 385). To do so would be to engage in universalising accounts of ultimately subjective notions and narratives, such as environmentalism or human rights. Instead, poststructuralism asks how these differences are constructed, developed and maintained in the prevailing social order. Hence, cosmopolitan projects like eco-politics are treated with suspicion in poststructuralist thought, precisely because it holds them as imposing a particular order: they identify ethical problems and then seek to develop universalising solutions.

While poststructuralists have clearly engaged empirically with environmentalism, oil politics and other substantive issues, they do not follow a linear approach of identifying the ethical issues and then proceeding to delivering institutional or strategic responses: "For poststructuralists, the impossibility of tidy, final, ethical responses to the violence of international politics is something we cannot escape but have to live with and in" (Lawler, 2008, p. 387).

It is important to note here that poststructuralist debates and tensions are essentially ontological. Questions posed have little if anything to do with day-to-day management of oil production or the wider operations of the energy industry. Instead the discourse is centered on fundamental relationship between the material and the ideational, and how it determines normative and political outcomes.

International politics of oil (and energy more generally) cannot be separated from this discourse, just as they cannot be compartmentalized within it. In fact, by and of itself the subject is not particularly interesting – a set of historically-contingent, socially and linguistically constituted structures and processes which belie the true but mystified and hitherto obscured essence of oil-fuelled modernity.

Poststructuralist analysis of international energy politics is set within a wider critical inquiry which asks existential questions about relationship between humans and nature; about the status of nature as material reality and as a social, imagined kind; about science and progress as social forces and how they account for distribution of power; and about possibility of change in the prevailing energy order. Critical theory and poststructuralism represent a radical anti-positivist challenge to the rationalist mainstream – an epistemological and ontological reordering of social-scientific enterprise.

Constructivism

By contrast, social-constructivist critique of rationalism has not involved wholesale rejection of positivist scientific method. Constructivism does emphasize immaterial, ideational and social dimensions of international relations and challenges instrumentalist materialism that underpins neo-realist and neo-liberal assumptions. For example, when Mearsheimer (1995) states: "the distribution of material capabilities among states is the key factor for understanding world politics" (p. 91), he is articulating the rationalist argument that material objects such as oil, determine political outcomes, regardless of any ideas that actors – people – might attach to them (Hurd, 2008, p. 300).

Constructivists reject such instrumentalist logic and shift focus instead on the ideational properties in IR – the central role of beliefs, expectations and interpretations in shaping international affairs; the social, rather than the material, content that makes up state interests and identities; the effects of various interactions between structures and agents, and that these are mutually constituted (Ibid., p. 304). What this may suggest is that the constructivist debate with rationalist approaches is primarily ontological, rather than epistemological (Fierke, 2013, p. 193).

One result of marrying a social ontology to an epistemology indebted to positivism was a thriving research tradition, and consistent and rigorous empirical defence of constructivist arguments (Price, 2008, pp. 317-318). However, the key question is whether this combining of a constructivist ontology with an empiricist method of knowledge generation is consistent? For example, constructivism is not specific about what constitutes primary unit of analysis in IR – inquiry proceeds at different and all levels, often treating actors and processes as "a given." However, does taking oil companies, for example, as a given imply that previous social construction of these oil companies as institutions is somehow to be set aside?

Underlying these questions is an assumption that rationalism and constructivism are two irreconcilable ontological commitments. Hurd (2008) suggests an alternative position, which holds that "the two are relevant to the same subject matter, but their different emphases allow, when combined, for greater insight into a problem than is provided by each alone" (p. 312).

Whatever the case, this internal ontological tension does nonetheless go some way to account for both – the breadth and volume of constructivist empirical input on substantive issues in international energy politics, and the often contentious dynamics in social constructivists' debates with fellow reflectivists and rationalists alike. While the literature reviewed below does not, by any measure, offer a comprehensive account of all this, it is intended to illustrate some key elements of constructivist arguments on international energy issues, and to assess their impact on the wider political debates on the subject.

Turning again to the discussion of environmentalism, it is interesting to contrast post-positivist IR social-constructivism with the anti-positivist radicalism of critical theory and poststructuralist approaches. Here, constructivism has had significant impact, especially in the field of environmental sociology, where some have argued it acquired "prime paradigmatic status" (Hannigan [1995], 2006, p. 29; see also Freudenburg, 2000, p. 103). Lockie similarly suggests that the idea that the environment is socially constructed may well be the key foundational concept in environmental theory (2004, p.29).

Social constructivism moves beyond positivist materialism and rejects oversimplifications of nature-centric ecological approaches. It focuses attention on how environmental issues and related subjects are framed and presented in public discourses; on the norms and belief systems which inform various political and social processes that, in turn, shape public understanding and decision-making on environmental matters; and on how these norms and values came to be in the first place (Savigny and Marsden, 2011, pp. 237-238).

Steven Yearley's *The Social Construction of Environmental Problems* (2002) is a good example of such scholarship as it explores precisely the kind of ways in which specific environmental problems are "constructed" and how this "construction" of environmental discourses serves as "an arena for social action or policy interventions," leading to some topics to rise to the top of political agenda and the center of public attention, and others not.

The outcome, he argues, depends not so much on whether the issue is the most salient or the best documented but on whether "the agents that propel issues into the public consciousness have worked most effectively" (Ibid., p. 275; p.276). Such modes of constructivist thinking involve system and unit-level analysis – Yearley explores the role of states and NGOs, examining how social processes involved in unit-level interactions affect system-level political outcomes. Yet a degree of epistemological and ontological uncertainly, if not ambiguity, is evident here; for example, if the environment is socially constructed, does it follow that environmental crisis is also socially constructed, and hence "un-real?"

This opens up charges of relativism, with critics painting social constructivism, as Hannigan ([1995], 2006, p. 29) put it, as "a sort of Darth Vader, perverting the force of sociological understanding and ignoring the 'reality' of environmental crisis." But this is a misreading of constructivist claims. Just because something is interpreted as having been socially constructed does not mean it is not real: "Pollution does cause illness, species do become extinct, ecosystems cannot absorb stress indefinitely, tropical forests are disappearing. But people can make very different things of these phenomena and – especially – their interconnections, providing grist for political dispute" (Dryzek, 2005, p.12, cited in Hannigan, [1995] 2006, p. 31).

Thus, for example, the debate around air pollution in London includes amongst other issues, such matters as the performance of the elected Labour Mayor Sadiq Khan (Hill, 2016) and the impact of Brexit (Shankleman, 2016). Social constructivism is not denying the power of nature but holds that its material impact is open to human interpretation and therefore construction.

> As Hannigan notes: While not denying the validity of concern over pollution, energy shortages and runaway technology, social constructionists nonetheless insist that the central task ahead for environmental sociologists is not to document these problems but to demonstrate that they are the products of a dynamic social process of definition, negotiation and legitimation ([1995] 2006, p. 31).

To say that environmental crisis is a product of a dynamic social process of definition, negotiation and legitimation, while not denying its very real implications might suggest some sort of ontological mishmash; but only if one is to ignore constructivism's implicit epistemological pluralism. As Hannigan argues, there are in fact standards of evidence when it comes to evaluating truth claims and agnosticism "does not mean that we must automatically accord all claims equal weight" (ibid., p. 32).

In the same vein, to claim that social constructivism is merely a methodological approach, an ontology devoid of normative commitments, is to misread ethical humility for cynicism. Social constructivism is in fact a normative stance, which holds that "moral progress... comes at the price of creating new moral dilemmas" (Price, 2008, p.235).

Turning to other substantive issues in the study of energy, social constructivist scholarship is characterized by this combination of epistemological pluralism, normative humility and the "deep ontology" of its social theory. Oil politics, for example, provide fertile ground for empirical constructivism. Starting with rejection of crude materialism of rationalist approaches, constructivists proceed to develop complex socio-historical modes analyses of various substantive issues.

This is because, as Ross Coen notes, "an oil strike requires more than simply oil in the ground, men with a daring spirit, and state-of-the-art machines at their disposal" (2012, p.6). Social constructivism offers a more useful paradigmatic lens to the study of oil politics because it helps reveal how different stages of energy exploration, discovery, production and transportation "always occur within particular set of political, social, economic, and historical circumstances whose cumulative influence equals if not exceeds the mere physical nature of the operation" (Ibid.).

As is with environmentalism, the social construction of oil politics is simultaneously the act of imaginational construction and an arena for social and political behavior of various actors; and when it comes to political outcomes what is "counted in" matters as much as what is "counted out."

Ross's study *Breaking Ice for Arctic Oil* (2012), is the story of the oil-tanker *SS Manhattan*, the first commercial vessel to successfully complete the transit of the Northwest Passage. It was hoped that the ship's epic journey would herald the advent of a new transit route for recently discovered Alaskan oil. But the plans failed to materialize and the story came to be largely forgotten, a non-event. However, as Ross argues: "Non-events such as Manhattan provide an important perspective... the history of development schemes that did not pan out may prove as instructive as those that did" (2012, p.6).

Constructivist study of oil politics offers a compelling alternative to the deterministic materialism of rationalist approaches. By examining co-constitution of identities and interests in the interplay and interactions of the material and the ideational, constructivist analysis de-centers the physical commodity of oil and focuses instead on its social and imaginative properties.

A good example is Robert Thomsen's (2001) argument that while discovery of oil served as a catalyst for the renewal of Scottish nationalism in the last three decades of the twentieth century, its actual material (economic) impact was limited. Cultural factors proved far more important in sustaining and increasing support for the Scottish National Party. Events since then seem to bare this fact out e.g. global oil price fluctuations in 2014-2019 seem to have had no impact on the outcome of the Scottish independence referendum or the SNP's electoral advance to become the largest party in Scotland.

Another example is Robert Y. Shum's *Where Constructivism Meets Resource Constraints: The Politics of Oil, Renewables, and a U.S. Energy Transition* (2015) - historical study of domestic and international energy policy-making in the United States. Shum argues that while socially constructed deliberation takes place over the purposes of energy policy, various material, physical constraints in natural resources are also considered and incorporated into reassessed considerations of what is relatively feasible and which policy is not. This assessment of feasibility varies over time and is determined by a range of economic, social, cultural factors, which also change over time, and are themselves determined by market dynamics and technological change.

Constructivism holds that identities and postures are constructed as much by perceptions (including perceptions of threats) as by any meaningful material measures. Andrew Campion (2016) undertakes the task of examining how China's image as an antagonist to the West, especially in the area of energy competition, arose and how "perceptions of Chinese growth have crystalized into a palpable China Threat Discourse, and how this has become the defining image of China in U.S. geopolitical approaches" (p. 3).

Whether or not China is a threat or not is a question "shrouded in so much ambiguity and conjecture" that answering it is not worthwhile without recognising the implicit social constructionism of the question itself (Ibid). Instead Campion devotes his book "to decoding China threat conventions and uncovering its discursive construction so as to illustrate how this particular discourse has affected, and continues to affect, U.S. foreign policy" (Ibid., p.4).

Mutual constitution of structures and agents in international energy politics is of great empirical importance to constructivists, who consistently focus on co-constitutive processes shaping behavior of states and other actors and impacting on energy issues on a systemic level. In this task, social constructivist scholarship tends to be eclectic, multidisciplinary and truly reflective.

Anthony Bebbington's edited anthology *Social Conflict, Economic Development and the Extractive Industry: Evidence from South America* (2011) is an expansive case-study survey, which draws contributions from anthropologists, political scientists, geographers, economists, development experts and practitioners. It provides a comprehensive, multi-dimensional assessment of the impact of extractive industries on development of several South American states. What makes it a striking example of constructivist paradigmatic approach is the consistent focus on the co-constitutive relationship between domestic regimes, the extractive industries, and global actors.

The authors examine these relationships, each from their own disciplinary perspective, to demonstrate the ways in which these interactions transform economies, societies, regimes and social environments. The potential for social conflict is associated closely with the extractive industries. But it is the possibility of political and institutional change that could lead to a more productive relationship between extraction and development, that appears to be the main normative priority of this ambitious project.

Constructivists often turn attention to the role of markets and international corporations in shaping energy politics but here again the empirical interest is centered on the role of identities (those of directors, shareholders, regulators and so on) and the social relations which inform the energy and environmental trajectory of capitalism in a long-term historical context (see, for example, Prasad and Mir, 2007; Pulver, 2007).

Nonetheless, it can be argued that constructivist model of international energy politics is overall state-centric. This is not to suggest constructivists neglect other actors or system-level analysis but simply to highlight the consistent overlap between social constructivist and more traditional, positivist approaches, notwithstanding their different ontological focus – different lenses through which to examine the same phenomena.

For example, Jeff Colgan's *Petro-Aggression: When Oil Causes War* (2013) provides a constructivist critique of the rationalist premise that oil states are more prone to military adventurism, aggression and international conflict. Colgan argues that what makes oil-exporting states more or less prone to military conflict is determined primarily by the nature of their domestic politics, not the mere fact of possession of oil. Wealth generated by oil revenues creates some incentives that increase aggressive tendencies and other incentives that decrease them. The overall outcome depends critically upon the preferences and calculations of local leadership and elite groups; and how these are perceived internationally by other actors.

This is a particularly significant and politically relevant constructivist insight. Consider Henry Kissinger's argument that there are "few nations in the world with which the United States has less reason to quarrel or more compatible interests than Iran" and that the cause of the U.S.-Iranian conflict is the nature of the post-1979 government in Tehran, rather than some immutable structural geopolitical antagonism (2002, pp.196-197). Or take Tony Blair's insistence that the nature of domestic regimes determines assessments of risk posed by their pursuit of WMDs: "In a very profound sense it was in the nature of the Saddam regime that

the ambitions for WMD were to be found and the risks to be judged"
(2011, p.385).

In part such assessments suggest that normative considerations,
ideas and identities have always featured prominently in the calculations
of leaders and decision-makers. Perhaps, Kissinger and Blair are in fact
personifications of Stephen Walt's "complete diplomat" (1998, p. 44).
Furthermore, to suggest that rationalist approaches, such as realism, have
ignored ideational factors or social forces is to misinterpret and
oversimplify their nuanced ontological commitments (Williams, 2005).

Consider Daniel Yergin's prioritization of what he terms "the
anthropological argument," as a third key theme in the study of oil (along
with the global politics and economics of the petroleum order) (1991,
p.14). Oil is important, in Yergin's assessment not only because of its
critical place in the industrial order but because it is central to the "the
nature of civilisation" (Ibid, p.13). Identity, consumer culture, sex and
gender, notions about "the way of life" and other imaginational forces all
feature prominently in Yergin's analysis. They are considered to be critical
in explaining the politics and economics of the oil industry (Ibid., p. 541).
This passage is very illuminating:

> Obtaining a learner's permit and then driver's licence
> became the major rites of passage for teenagers, their own
> "wheels" the most important symbol of their maturity and
> independence. The automobile was also absolutely
> central to dating, going steady, the acquisition of carnal
> knowledge, and the ritual of courtship. One survey in the
> late 1960s found that almost 40 percent of all marriages
> in America were proposed in a car (Ibid., p. 552).

Yergin is explicit in arguing that the emergence of oil as the primary
energy source is intrinsically bounded with notions of modernity and he
deploys (perhaps unconsciously) socially-constructivist modes of analysis
and concepts to examine how these modern norms and values came about.
Oil, Yergin argues, gave rise to a new civilisation – the "Hydrocarbon
Society," transforming modern living and heralding the advent of the
"Hydrocarbon Man."

This transformation was a cultural, social process, as well as a
physical one. Yergin goes to great lengths to chart its development from

the post-World War II Baby Boom and the growth of the suburbs to the rise of the automobile culture and its attendant urban infrastructure - the malls, the motels, drive-in restaurants. The physical environment and the social system are seen as mutually co-constitutive – petrol-driven car "reshaping landscape," turning America into "a drive-in society" (Ibid., p. 551-552).

Positivists, such as Yergin (1991; 2012), have undoubtedly paid considerable attention to the ideas which inform and shape international politics of energy, and fossil fuels in particular. Strands of constructivist thinking, various combinatorial logics and often explicit responses to postmodernist critiques can be found across rationalist scholarship on oil reviewed in chapter IV.

> This should not be surprising; as Scott L. Montgomery argues: It is because energy issues evoke some of the most fundamental questions about the nature of society. Name any related subject – the place of nuclear power, a plan for a carbon tax, the need for public transport – and in the timbre of discussion you will hear, close by, ideas about whether our civilization has been progressive or regressive, whether it is a bringer of treasures or tragedies, and whether it now requires revision or revolution (2010, pp.11-12).

This would suggest that rationalist approaches to energy issues require a more nuanced reading, which in turn would enable a more reflective engagement with various normative critiques juxtaposed against them. It could be that positivists such as Montgomery and Yergin, are in fact making a normative claim – that modern life is good, certainly better than the harsh and brutish pre-industrial existence.

Their scepticism about postmodern claims stems not from some sort of dogmatic materialism and reactionary opposition to emancipatory change but out of genuine concern for the future of humanity and appreciation for the complexity of the global energy order. They acknowledge that "perhaps more than ever before, a stance on energy implies a philosophical, even an ethical, outlook" (Montgomery, 2010, p. 12). It is precisely because Yergin considers growth of the environmental concerns to be extremely important that he characterizes them as challenging "the basic tenets of the industrial society" (1991, p. 14).

It certainly does not mean he opposes them. Much of *The Quest* (2012), Yergin's follow-up to *The Prize* (1991), is devoted to exploring the possibility of a non-fossil fuel energy order, with the notion of Hydrocarbon Man gradually replaced with that of the Carbohydrate Man, as bio-fuels replace petrol and sustainable energy sources become more technically feasible and economical (2012, p. 670).

Yergin caveats this post-oil vision of the future with warnings about technology, price, scale and the environment but nevertheless describes that vision as "breathtaking" (Ibid.). Energy is a problem field that requires a problem-solving approach, and that in itself is a normative commitment: A famous geologist once said, "Oil is found in the minds of men. We can amend that to say that the energy solutions for the twenty-first century will be found in the minds of people around the world. And that resource base is growing" (Ibid., p. 724).

There is a danger, therefore, in binary readings of energy debates or employing single-paradigmatic analytical frameworks, which bracket these debates and often turn them into polemical discourses. As Montgomery charges, "It is not all about eco-vegans, who think Western society qualifies as an unmitigated disaster, battling cigar-smoking capitalists who prefer Hummers to hybrids... Complexities are endemic to positions on energy" (2010, p. 12).

Prominence of these complexities accounts at least in part for the internal tensions in critical and poststructuralist debates around issues such as environmentalism. The pragmatic imperative to do something about existential threats facing humanity comes up against anti-positivist impetus for a normative critique that views these threats as embedded in and constituted by the prevailing social order, with its inequitable distribution of power and marginalisation of oppressed groups.

But those who wield power rarely engage with these issues in such binary terms. This is how Tony Blair assessed the rationale for the capture of Iraqi oil fields by British special forces in the early stages of the Iraq invasion in 2003:

> Had we not done so – and we discovered that the oilfields
> were indeed mined and ready to be fired – the effect
> would have been to pollute the entire area of south of Iraq,
> its marshes, its biology and wildlife and the surrounding
> sea. Saddam had driven the Marsh Arabs – over 100,000
> of them – from the marshlands that they had helped to
> preserve, and so already there were signs that the marshes
> were deteriorating. But an oil slick would have been
> horrific in its consequences (2011, p. 442).

Here, multiple logics are operating simultaneously – military considerations and assessments of risks and threats are framed by ecological policy objectives and concerns for an oppressed minority population. It is easy to take a cynical view and dismiss this as simply a self-legitimising discourse. It may well be but two important observations should be made – first, that the effort to legitimize is explicitly normative; as Blair argues elsewhere, his task is "not to persuade the reader of the rightness of the cause, but merely to persuade that such a cause can be made out" (Ibid., p.374).

And second, that decision-makers and political leaders enmesh normative judgments within a broad spectrum of considerations - strategic, economic, financial and so on - and deploy these in a combinatorial, holistic, dare one say synergetic, fashion. In a telling comment about the role of oil in the Iraq conflict, Blair observes, "In truth, if oil had been our concern, we could have cut a deal with Saddam in a heartbeat" (Ibid., p.383). So it must be that considerations other than material resources and power clearly play central role in decision making.

Eclecticism

This is where a discussion of analytic eclecticism, as proposed by Rudra Sil and Peter Katzenstein (2008; 2010), seems most appropriate. The complexity and messiness of everyday social life encourages political leaders and policy makers to seek out complex, pluralist, multi-level explanations of the problems facing them (Sil and Katzenstein, 2010, p.12).

The pragmatic imperative to develop immediate responses or to deal with crises drives a search for what is effective, rather than for some idealized, abstract, parsimonious paradigm. In fact, practitioners barely pause to reflect on the finer points of theoretical debates in IR and broader social sciences. Again, consider Tony Blair's characterisation of realism vs. idealism dichotomy as "simply two different analyses of what is effective." (2011, p. 368).

What is effective is what matters in the end. Sil and Katzenstein's advocacy of analytic eclecticism is in part driven by a concern that preoccupation with purely academic debates risks marginalising scholarship from public policy debates (2010, p.13). Theoretical knowledge claims must address socially important normative and policy issues. Excessively abstract ontologies, self-imposed analytical brackets and foundational principles of single-framework paradigmatic approaches impede production of practically relevant knowledge – a task that "cannot wait for the emergence of a definitive consensus on methodological procedures or axiomatic principles that may reveal final truths" (Sil and Katzenstein, 2008, p. 113).

Examples of eclectic theorizing about international politics of energy characteristically focus on middle-range theory, multi-causal explanations of specific empirical problems or themes. Falola and Genova's *The Politics of the Global Oil Industry: An Introduction* (2005) provide an eclectic historical study of the global oil industry - a traditional empirical domain of rationalist scholarship on the subject.

What makes it eclectic is that the authors apply different modes of analysis (neo-realism, institutionalism and constructivism), which would normally be developed within separate paradigmatic frameworks, and consistently connect them around substantive issues relating to the development of the oil industry. Building on these empirical convergences facilitates an enhanced historicity – not simply a timeline but a thematic, practice-driven discourse set across history.

Analytic eclecticism proceeds from identifying important substantive questions to integrating empirical observations and causal stories set out in separate paradigms, in order to posit less simplified, more interactive and comprehensive assessment, aiming not only for scholarly but also practical relevance.

For example, the prospect of transition to a post-fossil fuel energy order is the substantive subject of Denis Jacobs and Karen Branden's book *From McEnergy to EcoEnergy: America's Transition to Sustainable Energy* (2008) and Ernst Frankel's "Oil and Security: A World Beyond Petroleum" (2007), which envisages the effect of a post-oil future on the states and societies of the Middle East.

Reading eclectic scholarship such as this encourages greater appreciation for the way in which material, structural factors interact with social and economic forces, cultural currents and historical processes to produce political outcomes. One conclusion to be drawn here is that how much oil there remains in states such as Saudi Arabia matters as much as the changing cultural identity of an average American energy-consumer.

Moreover, the two are interconnected and can have mutually-impacting effects of profound consequences, affecting how states, oil companies, energy-consuming societies adapt to the decline of the petroleum order. What is not clear is whether analytic eclecticism with its pragmatic combinatorial logic, epistemological pluralism and praxeology-orientated ontology, constitutes a normative agenda or if it is simply a framework for problem-driven research. In its eschewal of foundationalism eclecticism risks attracting the charges of conceptual haziness and theoretical inconsistency.

Proponents of analytical eclecticism respond to these criticisms by stressing that decisions to prioritize normatively important problems in social science should be made not because of foundational principles of a given paradigm but because, in the words of Robert Keohane, "we care about improving human behavior... and we should not apologize for making value-laden choices even as we seek to search unflinchingly for the truth" (2009, p. 363). And surely the ability to effectively communicate across paradigmatic boundaries is essential in the task of engaging seriously with normative and policy issues (Sil and Katzenstein, 2010, p. 218).

Various reflectivist approaches to international energy politics outlined above in broad terms suggest an epistemologically and ontologically distinct and complex problem-field, created by the Fourth Debate It is one that encompasses extensive multi-disciplinary engagement across the breadth of the subject-matter and considerably expands its ontology beyond the narrow framework of power-politics and economics of the rationalist model of oil politics. Reflectivist critical model of BTC/SGC pipeline systems is set within this framework.

Reflectivist critique of BTC/SGC projects

Reflectivist model of BTC and SGC pipeline projects makes for a consistent challenge to the rationalist consensus around the projects and is animated by a single overarching paradigm – that there are historical alternatives to the social order represented by these fossil fuel enterprises. BTC and SGC are not products of some immutable "natural" laws of energy politics but are outcomes of historically-constituted, politically significant, normative choices – choices that are different to those made by societies in the past or might be made in the future:

> For centuries the Absheron Peninsula was a place of pilgrimage, a shrine of fire. Burning gas leaked from the ground since the last Ice Age. This was the most sacred site of Zoroastrianism which, prior to Islam, was the dominant faith in the region. The oil-bearing rocks drew people to this place, not to extract petroleum and carry it off to some other site of burning, but to worship it here in the sheets of flame, among the rock (Marriott and Minio-Paluello, 2013, p.23).

Hence, reflectivist assessments of BTC/SGC projects proceed from treating the subject as a unique historical event, unprecedented in the region's history and one with profound normative implications (Muttitt & Marriott, 2002, p.9-14; Thomas, 2004). This is a rejection of positivist view of history as unchanging, structurally-determined and ethically-neutral. Regularities and repetitions in human behavior in different historical periods are not evidence of any universal quality to balance of power processes (Cox, 1986, p.244).

As Marriott and Minio-Paluello forcefully argue, completely different historical structures existed in the region in the past and the materialist conception of hydrocarbons, as opposed to an alternative, rarefied, ideational, is itself constructed by prevailing social orders and dominant ideologies: "As other faiths arrived – Sunni and Shia Islam,

Russian Orthodoxy, Marxism and Capitalism – the holy fire of this peninsula was transformed into a material to be extracted and exported" (Ibid.). Reflectivist paradigm seeks to problematize, question and unpick the very idea of BTC/SGC project, arguing that political and environmental costs, especially the impact on global climate change amongst other factors, are unacceptably high (Muttitt and Marriott, 2002, p. 162).

The aim here is not to solve problems with these projects or alleviate or compensate for their negative repercussions but to question the prevailing order underpinning them in favor of an alternative action, e.g. a non-fossil fuelled vision of the future. In the process, the critique of BTC develops a comprehensive historical account of the project and oil development in the Caspian region, seeking to demonstrate how the existing social order came about and how it serves global power interests and not the people it affects (Ibid).

It is not surprising therefore that the critique and opposition to BTC and SGC are generated by the kind of active, campaigning global civil society that critical theorists believe will generate transformational change in world political order (Cox, 1986). Environmental and human rights groups, such as Friends of the Earth and PLATFORM, carried out extensive research into BTC in the early 2000s and sought to mobilize international public and political opinion against the pipeline (Muttitt and Marriott, 2002).

This normative critique of BTC is set within a wider post-structuralist inquiry, where oil is envisaged as a historical social force: "The presence of crude in the body of society since 1870s has fuelled a kaleidoscope of visions for future social orders... Above all, as planes and cars burst into our consciousness, it has fuelled 'modernity' – the imagination of the machine age" (Marriott and Minio-Paluello, 2012, p. 334). Thus, social construction of modernity is located in the material potential of oil at a particular historical juncture.

For rationalists, however, materialism does underpin the entire historical structure. Whatever ideational or imaginational quality oil might possess, its status as an energy-generating natural kind precedes that and defines its relationship to humanity; as such it is perennial:

Here's a humbling truth: despite all our advances and wealth, the fundamental forms of energy today echo those at the dawn of society... Above all, we remain a world lit, built, and moved by fire... It is fire that brings electricity and modern civilisation into most of our lives, that powers our technology and our modes of transport. Indeed, discovering new forms of fire making defines a hallmark – perhaps the hallmark – of the modern energy era (Montgomery, 2010, p.14).

This is a positivist view of history as unchanging, structurally-determined, shaped by material reality of human condition. Reflectivist approaches reject this view outright. Burning fossil fuels is not a value-free act of energy production: "All of this cornucopia has been powered by a liquid distilled from fossilised ecosystems, from plants and animals that lived from the Jurassic to the Tertiary era. These visions of the future have been dependent upon the ceaseless combustion of ancient rocks, just as Victor Frankenstein constructed his dream from the organs and limbs of the dead" (Marriott and Minio-Paluello, 2013, p.334). There is the implicit scepticism about claims for material foundations of modern social orders but also a clear recognition of the constitutive role the natural, physical kinds fulfil in creating, constructing, inventing, imagining the social kinds.

Rationalists engaging in eclectic theorizing might seek to overcome these antagonisms by integrating elements of social-constructivist analysis into a broadly positivist framework; for example, by engaging with BTC/SGC as both material and ideational constructs: "The challenge is how to understand the role of materials in political life in a period when existence of materials is becoming progressively more bound up with both the production and the circulation of information" (Barry, 2013, p.5).

Material artefacts, including major infrastructural assemblages such as oil and gas pipelines increasingly play a highly visible part in political life, and are therefore becoming increasingly determined by ideational and normative factors underpinning the projects (Ibid.). This in turn necessitates complex regulatory, legal and administrative systems to create normative and material regimes to acquire legitimacy and to ensure effective management and operation of the physical pipelines (Carroll, 2010).

Carroll demonstrates how deployment of corporate social responsibility techniques by corporations and the formalized process through which funding for BTC was procured make up a socially constructed and procedural legitimisation and risk mitigation structure for global capital and political interests (p. 17). There is an on-going interplay between international and domestic law on the one hand, and various intergovernmental environmental, social and developmental standards adopted by global financial institutions, on the other.

At the same time energy corporations have also undergone a shift in their projected identity in response to normative shifts in wider society (e.g. rebranding of BP into Beyond Petroleum in early 2000s). In aggregate, these processes constitute a new social neo-liberalism (Ibid, p. 8). However, for critical theorists and poststructuralists in particular, once the logic of alternative possibilities is established, the entire political timeline of Baku oil can be problematized.

Thus, for Marxists the period of the first Baku oil boom at the turn of the twentieth century is that of social radicalism, providing fertile ground for various competing political and religious ideologies and social movements (Suny, 1972). Rising Bolshevik party and various other socialist and Marxist organizations thrived in the industrial underbelly of Baku, Batumi and other oil towns of the Caucasus. Joseph Stalin established himself as key Bolshevik operative by organising strikes, robberies and kidnappings of oil barons and managers all over Azerbaijan and Georgia in the 1900s (Sebag Montefiore, 2008, p. 195-198). It was in Baku that Stalin established printing press facilities for the Bolshevik flagship publication *Iskra* and other propaganda materials (Marriott and Minio-Paluello, 2013, p.44).

Marxists are interested in charting how "the real control of the oil industry steadily drifted from the city to foreign investors with their headquarters in St. Petersburg or abroad" and how monopolisation of Baku oil stimulated class and nationalist antagonisms and struggles (Suny, 1972, p.5). The rise of Bolshevism and establishment of the Baku Commune in 1918 signalled popular resistance to capitalist hegemony and a possibility of a radically different social vision: "Amid the chaos of the oil rush and the gushers of Balakhani grew a vision of a new order, the Promised Land that is called a Socialist World" (Marriott and Minio-Paluello, 2013, p.46).

According to Muttitt and Marriott, the Baku Commune set a model "for 20th century resistance to capital" (2002, p.20). It captured attention of a generation of Marxist scholars and historians, who often drew analytical parallels with the experience of the French Revolution of 1871 and the Paris Commune (Suny, 1972, pp.353-362). The Soviet period of Baku oil, especially during World War II, often completely overlooked and ignored in mainstream scholarship, is accorded particular attention in Marxist and neo-Marxist analyses (Muttitt and Marriott, 2002, p.21; Werth, 1964; Omarova, 1998).

Critics of BTC and SGC pipeline often point out that the projects had their origins in the discoveries and technological innovations of Soviet planners, who pioneered off-shore drilling in the Caspian oil and gas fields off Baku half a century ago (Hoffman, 1999). The fact that off-shore fields, Azer-Chiraq-Guneshli (ACG), were not explored by the Soviet authorities, however, made BTC and SGC possible (Muttitt and Marriott, 2002, p.24).

It was these reserves that Western energy companies returned to develop, once Azerbaijan regained its independence with collapse of USSR in 1991 (Adams, 2002, pp. 75-77). It is perhaps emblematic of changing social reality of Baku oil that the ACG off-shore oil field (and its Shah Deniz gas sibling) were once named after the twenty-six Baku commissars – commanders of the Baku Commune (Marriott and Minio-Paluello, 2013, p.50).

Similarly, the "return" of the West - governments and companies – to Baku oil after Soviet collapse is another point of contention in critical appraisals. Some have alleged that BP and the American oil giant Amoco (which later merged) played a role in the removal of the democratically-elected Azerbaijani government in 1993, paving the way for the rise of authoritarian regime of President Heydar Aliyev (see Leppard et al, 2000).

Others point to the outcome of post-coup negotiations and highlight differences in the final composition of companies taking part in the project and allocation of shares. Thus Muttitt and Marriott contend that Azerbaijani state oil company SOCAR lost out considerably in the final negotiations with Western companies, with Azeri state share was eventually cut to just 20 per cent ([PLATFORM] 2002, p.23):

> The grandiose title given to the deal, the "Contract of the Century," suited all the signatories. It is still used today, yet few ask for whom it was the contract of the century – for the Azeri people, for the Aliyev clan, or for the oil corporations who had signed an immensely profitable deal and gained control over a major new resource base? (Marriott and Minio-Paluello, 2013, p. 60).

As suggested above critical theorists are concerned with the politics of knowledge. Knowledge is not power-neutral but reflects perspectives and vested interests of those who produce it. Cox's differentiation between problem-solving and critical theory has important implications for the study of BTC/SGC projects, as knowledge produced about them can be tested on that criteria (1986, pp.207-209). Rationalist approaches fail because they are "oblivious to the way power and interest precede and shape knowledge claims" (Devetak, 1996, p. 160). It is clear that most enthusiastic support for the BTC project and its backers is found in the literature within the "neo-neo" model of the project.

Thus, for example, one of the few major contemporary studies produced on BTC and highly supportive of the project - *BTC – Pipeline: The Oil Window to the West* by Frederick-Starr and Cornell et. al. (2005) - was published by the Central Asia-Caucasus Institute at John Hopkins University– an international think-tank with headquarters in Washington and funded by U.S. government grants and corporate donations.

Knowledge claims are not produced in a political vacuum but reflect the agendas of those producing them. It does not automatically invalidate them, but whether acknowledged or not, the purpose of these "problem solving" approaches to BTC or SGC is, having accepted the prevailing framework of the project with its implicit power relationships, institutions and processes, "... to make these relationships and institutions work smoothly by dealing effectively with particular sources of trouble" (Cox, 1986, p. 208).

It is taken for granted that oil and gas had to be extracted from its land-locked location in the Caspian and the problem is how to do it with minimum cost and maximum benefit. Critical theory seeks from the start to question the prevailing order and asks how it came about. This requires a historicist approach and an ever-present concern with "a continuing process of historical change" (ibid, p. 209).

Furthermore, the knowledge critical theory produces is not neutral either – "it is politically and ethically charged by an interest in social and political transformation" (Devetak, 1996, p.161). This interest is amplified by a praxeological enterprise aimed at achieving political goals. From the outset BTC and attendant gas projects were met with fierce opposition from organized civil society.

In the case of BTC this took form of the Baku-Ceyhan Campaign (Baku-Ceyhan Campaign website, 2017). Launched in 2002 it brought together local and international NGOs, human rights and environmental groups and activists to oppose the pipeline, not least by raising "public awareness of the social problems, human rights abuses and environmental damage that are being caused by the Baku-Tbilisi-Ceyhan oil pipeline" (Baku-Ceyhan Campaign website, 2017).

The Campaign aimed to show how international treaties between the AIOC consortium and governments of the countries traversed by BTC have largely exempted BP and its partners from any laws in those countries – present or future – which conflict with the company's project plans: "The agreements allow BP to demand compensation from the governments should any law (including environmental, social or human rights law) make the pipeline less profitable. The agreements have for these reasons been described by non-governmental organizations (NGOS) as 'colonialist'" (Baku-Ceyhan Campaign website, Colonialism, 2017).

Considerable research was also carried out to demonstrate how BTC contributes to conflict, human rights abuses and militarisation of the Caspian region (KHRH et al, 2004) and how it hampers social development and promotes corruption in Azerbaijan, Georgia and Turkey (Baku-Ceyhan Campaign website, Social Impacts of BTC pipeline, 2017).

On climate change the Campaign argued: "The climate impact of this project will dwarf the combined impacts of all UK initiatives to combat climate change. The emissions from the oil and gas coming through the pipelines would be more than twice the emissions saved through the UK's 12.5% reduction under the Kyoto Protocol (73,000 tonnes CO2) and ten times more than the emissions saved through the UK's target of meeting 10% of electricity demand from renewables (wind, sun, water power) by 2010" (Baku-Ceyhan Campaign website, Climate Impact of BTC, 2017).

The central focus of anti-BTC opposition was directed at international financial institutions, such as the World Bank and EBRD, and export-credit agencies, such as the UK's Export Credit Guarantee Department (ECGD) (Baku-Ceyhan Pipeline website, Financial Institutions, 2017). The Campaign criticized the lack of due diligence efforts of these international funding institutions, pointing out the compromising extent to which IFIs have relied on information and factual verification provided solely by BP (Baku-Ceyhan Campaign, 06.09.2004).

Critics charged that BTC was "the most controversial oil pipeline in the world," due to its "damaging geo-political, environmental and social impacts, its role in augmenting the power of corporate interests over national governments… as well as allegations of corruption, incompetence and malpractice" (Lustgarten, 2005). When in 2003 ECGD agreed to underwrite £150 million credit line for BTC project with public funds Human rights groups dismissed the decision as politically motivated, arguing that ECGD should not be using taxpayers' money to support projects "that will further fuel climate change. We're bitterly disappointed that despite its so-called commitments to the environment, ECGD is still supporting unsustainable projects" (Hannah Griffiths of Friends of the Earth quoted in Baku-Ceyhan Campaign press release, 13.12.2003).

Opposition to the BTC project, both political and academic persisted even after the project was completed and operational – see for example, Marriott and Minio-Paluello's seminal "The Oil Road" (2013). More importantly, the same coalitions of global civil society groups, environmental NGOs and human rights campaigners came together to organize against the next phase of pipeline projects – specifically the Southern Gas Corridor (CounterBalance, 28.01.2016; CEE Bankwatch Network, 2017).

The thrust of the campaigning is again directed at international financial institutions and public credit funds with the aim at preventing public funds from being used to enable fossil fuel projects (Bill McKibben, Naomi Klein et al, CounterBalance, 30.06. 2017; Marriott and Minio-Paluello, 2013, p.348; Gotev, 29.03.2017; Stone, 30.11.2017; Bacheva-McGrath, 2015).

Regardless of specific demands of individual campaigning NGOs, the key argument of critical theoretical and poststructuralist challenges to BTC and SGC projects is that opposition to these projects is part of a wider rejection of the prevailing energy order; that the latter is determined and shaped by political and normative choices, and that possibility of alternative choices is therefore credible:

> A society fuelled by community-controlled renewable energy systems might look very different from one dependent on gas controlled by private and state organizations. So this is also a struggle between different social structures. Our current dependency on fossil fuels may frighten us away from experiments and freeze imaginations. Yet when we break out of the internal logic of the Oil Road, we begin to envision other futures (Marriott and Minio-Paluello, 2013, p. 355).

As BTC pipeline goes on transporting oil and the SGC saga continues to unfold, the future of Caspian and European energy future is still undecided. Ultimately, BTC and SGC – the "oil road" and the "gas road" – are representative of a particular political and social order that can be changed - "…this headlong rush to lock our societies into further fossil fuel dependence can be prevented" (Ibid., p. 354). To achieve this, it will not suffice to simply critique these specific projects, not least because those "who benefit from the current system are opposed to changing it, so stepping off the Oil Road and preventing the Gas Road from being locked in will require a struggle" (Ibid., p. 355).

Conclusion

This chapter outlined various reflectivist approaches to oil and gas politics and proposed a reflectivist model – an analytic critique of BTC/SGC pipeline systems and the social orders these projects represent. Different theoretical strands of the Fourth Debate offer different diagnostic prisms, enabling specific angles of normative reflection on energy politics, the environment and the existential threat of climate change. Cumulative effect of looking through these post- and anti-positivist paradigmatic lenses – from their classical Marxist foundations to robust postmodernist take-downs of underlying power structures – is to discern an overarching tapestry of discontent with the material reality of fossil fuels' production, transmission and consumption in modern society.

This discontent manifests itself as two mutually-reinforcing elements: 1) systematic critique of BTC and SGC super-structures and 2) as a praxeological programme aimed at thwarting these projects and changing the wider global energy reality. The first aims to expose environmental, social and human rights costs of the projects and informs the second - a political imperative to act to prevent these. Anti-positivist critiques of international oil politics and anti-BTC/SGC campaigns constitute a common theoretical and praxeological framework – a foundational, not simply paradigmatic, challenge to the prevailing social order represented by these grand infrastructure projects.

VI
Synergetic Model

Introduction

In "International Relations Theories: Energy, Minerals and Conflict," a working paper for Polinares, an EU special project on main global challenges relating to competition for access to resources such as oil, Roland Dannreuther argues for "a synthetic inter-theoretical approach" for the project (2010, p.14).

He identifies potential for complementary readings of different theoretical approaches to oil and mineral resource competition but first points out that there is little explicitly IR-theoretical work on energy politics - *International Security,* one of the discipline's principal journals, has published only eight articles on energy in thirty years (Shaffer, 2009, p. 18 in Dannreuther, 2010, p.1).

Meanwhile policy-focused editions and specialist journals do regularly publish oil and energy-related articles. The world of IR Theory might care not for oil politics, but it is evident from the literature reviewed in the preceding chapters that much of such policy-relevant research and the bulk of empirical output on issues of energy politics tends to be at least implicitly IR-theoretical.

It can and should be analysed, characterized and classified as such, and then placed in its appropriate paradigmatic location on the IR "periodic table." The latter then serves as a "road map" for the vast empirical field that is politics of oil and energy in general. The fact that it is a complex empirical field is another important observation – different paradigmatic analyses are telling different strands of the same story occurring in real time.

Theory-synergetic approach (TSA) is intended to develop a more dynamic, real-time and less parsimonious reading of this deep ontology of oil politics. Synergetic analysis of any given problem or puzzle in international relations begins with a systematic application and modelling of individual IR paradigms. In the preceding chapters Rationalist and Reflectivist models of international oil politics and the case-studies of BTC and SGC pipeline projects were set out.

The chapter opens with exploration of synergetic readings of single-paradigm theoretical claims about wider issues in oil and gas politics before taking the Carter Doctrine as an example of a synergetic problem-field to illustrate TSA operation in greater detail. The aim here is to demonstrate the breadth and depth of synergetic potential of oil politics as an empirical problem field in IR, as well as to explore important themes and milestones in the history of global oil.

These discussions provide the framework for next steps in the TSA process – having set out single-paradigm models of BTC and SGC pipelines in previous chapters, here specific conceptual overlaps and thematic commonalities between them are identified and analysed. First, the BTC project is subjected to synergetic modelling with environment emerging as key cross-theoretical ontological overlap and the progression in developing inter-paradigmatic pivots is set out. In the final part of the chapter, operationalisation and sequencing of inter-paradigmatic pivot is demonstrated upon the substantive issue of SGC pipeline financing.

Synergetic theoretical readings of energy politics

Turning first to the classical models of international politics it is worth reiterating again that arguments for multi-theoretical engagement with Classical Liberalism, Realism and Marxism are not new (Williams, 2005; Rengger, 2008). There are clear cross-paradigmatic conceptual overlaps and thematic commonalities that cut across the three traditions and this often manifests on empirical level.

What characterizes a synergetic quality of analysis is the systematic identification and examination of such empirical intersections – the inter-paradigmatic pivots (see below). *A priori* assumptions regarding, for example structure/agency, do not inform decisions about what constitutes proper units of synergetic analysis. This is determined by substantive issues in a given research.

Liberal research programme begins with the examination of the birth of the modern oil industry and its evolution in the nineteenth and early twentieth centuries. Key areas of interest here is the establishment and growth of the industry, financialization of the oil business, technological innovation in production and transportation, and the increasingly global nature of oil trade. The normative mission of the liberal research programme is concerned with identifying the right regulatory framework for managing the emerging oil industry and prioritizing issues of free trade and competitive markets, good practice and rule of law.

Classical Marxist research programme examines the emergence of oil as "use-value" commodity and charts its entry into the capitalist production cycle. Marxist tradition is concerned with the nature of historical change whereby oil production transforms from a cottage industry into an increasingly global trade, a fundamental part of the international capitalist system.

Whereas, for classical realists the importance of oil stems from its strategic value in the European power politics in the run up to World War I and the inter-war period. Oil as a key commodity in determining preparedness for armed conflict and the political struggle over its control amongst states are the principal directions of the classical Realist research programme.

Empirically these research strands can be synergized in a common research programme built around a number of inter-paradigmatic pivots, for example, the rise, growth and expansion of the original oil majors. The stories of Standard Oil, Royal Dutch Shell, Nobel Petroleum, Anglo-Persian/BP and other industry pioneers are examined by all of the three schools and upon this congruence a synergetic model pivots.

For classical Liberals the oil companies, exemplified by Standard Oil, represented the key agents of the growing oil business and their behavior determined the contours of the emerging market. As such, questions about their regulation and challenges they represent to the liberal order, especially the idea of free competitive trade are to the fore.

It is no surprise therefore, that Iva Tarbell's expose of Rockefeller's Standard Oil (1904), described by Yergin as arguably "the single most influential book on business ever published in the United

States" (1991, p. 105), remains a stand out text of liberal (idealist) critique of cartelisation and monopolisation in the increasingly powerful oil industry.

This led Lisa Margonelli to conclude: "As much as Rockefeller built the oil industry, Tarbell created the way we understand and regulate it" (2008, p.293). The dissolution of Standard Oil in 1911, emergence of strong anti-trust legal regimes in the United States, formalized and institutionalized at state and federal levels and having international jurisdictions, all serve to underline the saliency of classical Liberal insights.

For classical Realists, however, dissolution of Standard Oil is of interest only in the context of the primacy of powerful states in determining the nature and direction of the oil industry. Realist analysis focuses on inter-state competition for the control of oil sources, as the strategic commodity became critical to the war effort in World War I – as Lord Curzon quipped, "The Allied cause had floated to victory upon a wave of oil" (quoted in Yergin, 1991, p.183).

Oil companies are viewed as instruments of state policy, rather than truly independent agents in their own right. Realists view developments such as the British government acquisition of controlling stake in the Anglo-Persian Oil Company or the establishment of the Export Credit Guarantee Department to publicly finance private overseas enterprise, especially in the realm of oil exploration, as examples of the subordinate role oil companies play in view of the dominance of state policy in the evolution of the oil industry.

Classical Marxist analysis charts the growth of oil companies from their early, pre-capitalist origins to consolidation and eventual cartelisation, and is centered on the relationship between European and U.S. imperialism and corporate monopolism: "If it was needed to give imperialism a most succinct definition it would be that imperialism is the monopolistic stage of capitalism" (Lenin, 1961 [1917], p. 88). Competition between oil cartels, such as Standard Oil, Anglo Persian and Bnito is set in the context of global imperial conflicts, with dominant powers facing off challengers (Suny, 1972). There are clear echoes here of Realism's emphasis on the interests of powerful states.

Synergetic approach begins by casting off epistemological determinism altogether and recognising that all these three perspectives are exploring different aspects and dimensions of the same social phenomena. A question "which theory gets it right about early oil companies?," for example, is arbitrary. The real question is what theory uncovers which part of the deeper ontology of the subject matter and how these parts relate to each other within the historical timeline? And such question can only be addressed on empirical level, on substantive matters.

Thus, for example, it is true as Liberals would contend, that the opening of the Suez Canal to oil tanker traffic in 1892 was a major coup for Royal Dutch Shell, giving the company a competitive edge over Standard Oil and others, opening up access to Russian petroleum to enter global markets, and providing a major boost to global oil and maritime trade in general.

At the same time Realists would be correct to point out that opening of the Suez Canal to tankers in 1892 was a strategic decision of the British government, which owned the controlling shares in the canal and was eager to secure its own oil supplies and to protect colonial possessions in the Middle East and Asia. This view would be echoed by Marxists, who view the event in the context of the European imperial struggle (especially between Britain, France and Germany) and growing competition between European and American oil cartels.

Similarly, the story of the Anglo-Persian Oil Company (later Anglo-Iranian, later still – BP) was for Liberals an example of commercial interests driving political considerations and market forces dictating state policy. When just before the outbreak of World War I in 1914 the British government acquired controlling stake in the company and signed a long-term contract with the Royal Navy for exclusive petroleum supply, choosing Anglo-Persian over the larger and better placed Royal Dutch Shell, the decision was driven primarily by commercial considerations and normative opposition to monopolistic tendencies.

As Winston Churchill put it in the Commons debate on the issue, it was essential to protect all consumers, not only the Admiralty, from "a long steady squeeze by the oil trusts all over the world" (quoted in Yergin, 1991, p. 145). Churchill argued (somewhat sarcastically) while the Royal

Dutch Shell has been a reliable partner for the British Empire that partnership was costly – "The only difficulty has been price" (Ibid).

Yet in the very same speech Churchill argued for the Commons' ascent to the purchase of Anglo-Persian shares on the grounds that it has long been a principle of British foreign policy "to preserve the independent British oil interests of the Persian oil-field" and to ensure that that field does not get "swallowed up by the Shell or by any foreign or cosmopolitan companies" (Ibid).

Direct state ownership of the Anglo-Persian, two directors on the board and a twenty years' contract to supply the Royal Navy with fuel oil at highly preferential terms suggest a policy aimed at maximising national power, military strength and physical control of strategic resources. The story of Anglo-Persian is a story of British imperialism in the Gulf region and the 1914 decision had continued to shape Iranian and regional politics in the decades that followed.

Note Churchill's interesting use of the term "cosmopolitan" in the quote above, by which he means inter- or multi-national company – this remark was directed as an attack against Royal Dutch Shell, a consortium of Dutch and British shareholders. And now consider the response to it from Samuel Samuel MP (for Wandsworth), the brother of Marcus Samuel, the founder of Royal Dutch Shell: "I do protest most strongly on behalf of one of the greatest British commercial industrial companies, that the attacks that have been made are wholly unjustified" (Ibid, p.146).

Indeed, the Royal Dutch Shell had been the main kerosene and petroleum supplier to private consumers in Britain as well as the Royal Navy, and it was Shell that gained Britain access to Russian oil from Baku, ensuring commercial viability of tanker traffic through Suez. Britain's decision to go with Anglo-Persian was dictated by a whole range of strategic and commercial factors, not one single one. It is clear that the actors, protagonists and decision-makers involved in the early oil themselves had a complex and multi-layered understanding of the measures they took. This complexity as a whole becomes evident as soon as one engages with substantive issues on empirical level.

Prioritizing empirical engagement ahead of theory selection allows for a more nuanced understanding of this complexity. Synergetic approach does not mean abandonment of normative inquiry but it does involve eschewal of partisanship in the conduct of the inquiry. Paradigmatic dynamism of the synergetic approach requires systematic application of specific theoretical models upon substantive questions and issues, with the aim of generating a synergetic outcome that would be greater than the sum of its constituent parts.

Therefore, judgements about which theoretical perspective offers better causal explanations or responds better to the normative agenda of a particular research project and so on, should be made upon assessment of the empirical output, and not on *a priori* assumptions or partisan standpoints. Thus a synergetic research programme would entail a multidimensional model of classical theories of oil politics, building upon multiple empirical convergences, thematic commonalities and conceptual overlaps.

Just as Liberal, Marxist and Realist accounts converge around the role of oil companies, the nature of various legal regimes which shaped the evolution of the global oil industry provide another field for synergetic theorizing. From "As-Is" Agreement to the Anglo-Soviet Trade deal, from the San Remo Accord to the Red Line Agreement, establishment and growth of the oil industry was marked by seminal international deals, contracts and covenants.

Development of the international concessionary system was one such landmark; it formed and then influenced the dynamics of global oil politics for decades. Just as was demonstrated with the example of the early oil companies, it is possible to view these legal regimes through particular theoretical lenses simultaneously, as in real time, in a synergetic fashion. For example, the Red Line Agreement can be viewed synergetically as an imperialist carve up of the Middle East; an early rules-based format for international cooperation in oil exploration and production; a reflection of the balance of power with strong states maximising their access to strategic oil resources at the expense of weaker states.

The same approach is applied wherever individual paradigmatic accounts converge around the same empirical phenomena. The impact of the Bolshevik Revolution of 1917 in Russia on oil production in Baku and the North Caucasus; the effect of nationalizations of oil industries in USSR and Mexico on the global oil industry; the Wall Street crash and the impact of the Great Depression all provide ample ground for synergetic theorizing.

World War II and its aftermath provide another particularly fertile field. World War II marks a watershed moment in the history of oil, marking the point at which the commodity acquired existential strategic value for states, societies and economies alike. This is recognized implicitly by liberal and radical accounts and explicitly by Realists: "Yet oil is no longer one of many raw materials important in the measurement of a national power. It is now a material factor whose very possession threaten to overturn centuries-old patterns of international politics" (Morgenthau, 1985 [1946], p. 133).

This would lead, as Yergin argues, to a wholesale redefinition of the importance of the Middle East, especially in the United States where oil was now viewed "as the critical strategic commodity for the war and was essential for national power and international predominance" (Yergin, 1991, p. 395). For realists the establishment of the U.S. Petroleum Reserves, the Soviet industrial advances and the Soviet oil boom of the 1940s, the Anglo-American Agreement of 1944, the setting up of the International Petroleum Commission to manage supply and demand and other events and processes all point to the ascendant power of states in the development and massive expansion of the oil industry in the 1940s and 1950s.

Hence the U.S. entry into the politics of the Middle East oil in 1945 and the subsequent establishment of the Arabian American Oil Company (ARAMCO) signify a shifting balance of power – decline of British imperial control and influence and its replacement by the U.S. as the preeminent oil superpower was symbolized by the Suez Crisis. Yet for U.S. policy-makers the process of American involvement in oil politics was driven primarily by the imperative to secure abundant oil supplies, chiefly for military purposes: "America's crown, symbolizing supremacy as the oil empire of the world, is sliding down over one eye" (Ickes, 1943b in Yergin, 1991, p.396).

Meanwhile, radical Marxist critique of imperialism takes on an added impetus after World War II in the context of the emerging Cold

War dynamics. Here the new focus on ascendant power of the American oil empire is balanced by growing attention to other factors shaping post-war oil politics. The triumph of the Soviet oil industry in the 1930s and 1940s, the rise of national state oil companies in Middle East and South America, growing tide of resource nationalism exemplified in the movement for renegotiation of concessions towards more equitable settlement for oil producing states – all feature in an expanding Marxist framework.

Therefore, while both Realist and Marxist accounts differ in their implicit or explicit normative prescriptions, they converge with shared emphasis on the structural quality of international oil politics in World War II and its aftermath e.g. the key role played by states and the essential nature of power in determining outcomes. Critical questions about processes taking place and the events of the period, such as the 1946 Iranian crisis and the 1953 CIA-backed overthrow of Iran's nationalist Prime Minister Mosaddegh; the 1956 Suez Crisis; the emergence of powerful national oil companies (NOCs) in the 1950s, can all serve as substantive research agendas, bringing both Marxist and Realist insights to bear synergetically upon them.

The Realist ascendancy and the effects of the nascent behavioralist turn in the Second Debate, as well as the magnitude of the events of the 1930s and 1940s had had all combined to diminish the impact of the Liberal (idealist) school of thought and to do away with the inter-war Liberal consensus. Behavioralism changed the way that business and politics of oil were being understood and Cold War tensions brought an added political impetus to debates about petroleum and energy. Above all it was the influence of economics in the 1960s that helped transform the study of oil.

Proceeding on with synergetic modelling of the empirical field brings the rationalist and neo-Marxist paradigmatic traditions into the timeline of international oil politics, just as they were being fundamentally transformed. The price wars and crises of the 1950s left the oil industry reeling in the face growing competition from the Soviet Union; its oil policy was increasingly seen in the West as "a political assault, the purpose of which was to create dependence in Western Europe, weaken the unity of NATO, and subvert the Western oil position in the Middle East" (Yergin, 1991, p. 519). The seminal moment was the establishment of OPEC in 1960 to unify and coordinate the petroleum policies of oil producing states.

Synergetic theorizing about OPEC would have the added value of avoiding some of the excessive partisanship that characterizes much of mainstream literature on the subject. This is one of the most contentious phenomena in oil politics and subject of many implicitly and explicitly normative claims. A synergetic approach would enable a common analytical framework, combining rationalist debates around OPEC with neo-Marxian insights on cartelisation of oil producing semi-peripheral states. Identifying linkages between the approaches as they are manifested on empirical level would allow for a deeper analysis of OPEC's role in global oil politics.

For example, the Six Day War of 1967 marked the first deployment of the "oil weapon" – the OPEC embargo. In the context of the theory-synergetic analytical framework insights from both rationalist and neo-Marxist/world-systems theory offer valuable prisms through which to analyse the effects on global oil politics. Examined from either perspective the 1967 embargo symbolically marked beginning of the relative decline in the power of consuming states, the U.S. and Britain in particular, although it may not have seemed so to some observers at the time (Sampson, 1975, p.188).

Several key events that followed the Six Day War suggest a rebalancing of the global petroleum order, with oil importing countries gradually losing their dominant positions, their power weakening. Britain's military withdrawal from the Gulf in 1971, nationalisation of the Libyan oil industry in 1972, international contract renegotiations and the emergent legal framework of the Tehran and Tripoli agreements (both signed in 1971) attest to this weakening.

The Tehran Agreement is particularly important as it established for the first time the benchmark of 55% government share in oil contracts – oil producing countries were now in the ascendancy. For contemporaries at the time the period seemed one of fundamental change: "The extent of dependence of western industrial countries upon oil as a source of energy has been exposed..." (Placke, J. 1970 in Yergin, 1991, p. 587).

Exporting countries were no longer prepared to be rent or tax-collectors – "For the exporters, the greater question was sovereignty over their own natural resources" (Yergin, 1991, p. 583). When the "oil weapon" was deployed effectively in the wake of the 1973 Yom Kippur War it was with a devastating effect, causing "the first oil shock."

This is how Daniel Yergin characterized the cumulative effect of the events of the period: "The post-war petroleum order in the Middle East had been developed and sustained under American-British ascendancy. By the latter half of the 1960s, the power of both nations was in political recession, and that meant the political basis for the petroleum order was also weakening" (1991, p. 565).

And this is how Immanuel Wallerstein assessed the events at the time: "The heyday of U.S. world hegemony is over. This means that at no level - economic performance and productivity, political cohesiveness and influence, cultural self-assurance, military strength will the U.S. ever again match its unquestioned primacy of the period 1945-67" (1976, p. 461).

It is not so much a case of creating synergy as of identifying it. Both approaches emphasize structural properties of the international energy system - rationalists by focusing on changes in the balance of power between states, while the world-systems theory applies core-periphery analysis to relations between oil -consuming/importing and oil-producing/exporting countries.

Both paradigms converge on the same empirical matter, dealing with the same substantive issues, events and puzzles. Importantly both schools of thoughts in this instance are concerned with the nature of change in the realm of international oil politics specifically and global politics generally.

The two quotes above appear to suggest some degree of paradigmatic consensus on the assessment of political outcomes of the late 1960s and early 1970s. Yet this is despite the two approaches having widely different normative agendas. One of the main reasons neo-Marxists were so interested in the activities of semi-peripheral states, such as OPEC members, is precisely because they considered these states to be critically important in promotion of the emancipatory, counter-hegemonic interest and having the potential to determine "the modalities and the speed of the ongoing transition to a socialist world-government" (Wallerstein, 1976, p.482). Distinction between socialist and non-socialist semi-peripheral states emerged in response to the events of 1973-1974.

This contrasts starkly with the "problem-solving agenda" of the rationalist approach. Mainstream literature on oil embargos brings considerable attention to various ways petroleum-importing countries sought to counter OPEC's actions; for example, through policies aimed at coordinating distribution of available stocks, "so that the constriction of supplies was fairly evenly allocated, rather than targeted specifically against the United States and the Netherlands" (U.S. Congressional MNC Report, 1975, pp. 147-8, quoted in Parra, 2013 [2010], p. 188). Thus, for Kenneth Waltz the question posed by events of 1973-1974 was simply whether they "show that the unequal capabilities of states continue to explain their fates and to shape international-political outcomes?" (Waltz, 1979, p. 153).

Neo-Realists, therefore, might emphasize the significance of the new U.S. Strategic Petroleum Reserve, set up in 1975. Or perhaps the establishment the year earlier of the International Energy Agency – an organization of oil-importing countries brought together to coordinate collective response to oil supply disruptions i.e. embargoes or blockades – might be interesting to Neo-Liberal Institutionalists, not least because it involved "the use of a treaty to establish an intergovernmental organization designed to meet the particular problems of the industrial countries" (Scott, 1994, p.20).

Theory-synergetic approach does not require glossing over these real epistemological differences and divergences in normative agendas between different paradigmatic traditions. How and why particular theoretical research strand arrives at a specific empirical observation and what conclusions are drawn, matters as much as their substance. It makes it all the more interesting when such observations of the same social phenomena (for example, oil embargoes of 1967-1974) carried out within different single-theoretical frameworks e.g. Neo-Realism, Neo-

Liberalism, Neo-Marxism, arrive at the same empirical finding (e.g. decline of the West and the ascendancy of oil producers), albeit with different normative assessments of it.

Attenuated empiricism of the theory-synergetic approach enables clear identification of these multidimensional linkages between various paradigmatic standpoints and allows for more nuanced assessments of their normative implications. Regardless of epistemological and ontological divergences, IR empirical project proceeds under its own dynamics. Events took place, processes occurred and so on - facts are facts, although interpretations of them differ.

Hence, for example, there may be a theoretical consensus on the material outcomes of the 1967-1974 period in international oil politics but not on what these outcomes mean and represent. Such convergences often occur across the empirical timeline of oil politics and often they do not. It can be that analysis of the same empirical phenomena within different single-paradigmatic frameworks will produce widely different interpretations and conclusions.

To take the example of the "second oil shock," which came in the wake of the Islamic Revolution in Iran in 1979. It fuelled even greater fears for many in the West that at stake here was not simply the price or availability of petrol, "but perhaps even the international order and word society as they knew it" (Yergin, 1991, p. 698; see also Levy, 1980).

Rationalist consensus laid the responsibility for the crisis upon OPEC and oil-producing states, which having acted as a cartel and pushed up oil prices, were causing inflation and economic stagnation, thus contributing to global aggregate instability. Consider Morgenthau's assessment of the implications of the oil shocks from the later editions of *Politics Amongst Nations*:

> As long as the oil-producing nations cooperate against the consuming nations as long as there is no competition among them for markets or for economic or political advantages, they will be able to impose virtually any conditions on the oil-consuming nations, just as they did in the wake of the 1973 war (1985, p. 135).

Proponents of structural dependency and world-systems theory rejected such, as they saw it, simplistic explanations:

> No doubt the OPEC producers have raised their prices; whether this is outrageous depends on one's perspective. However, not only does the onset of many of the world's current difficulties predate the price rise, but the crucial question is how it was possible for OPEC to raise world oil prices substantially in 1973 and not in 1963 or 1953. The answer lies outside the realms of the political decisions of the OPEC states (Amin et al., 1982, p. 7).

For neo-Marxists, to reduce systemic complexity of the world capitalist system to policies of a few oil-producing states is to underestimate historical contingency of political change – OPEC states could act the way they did only in 1974, due to specific historical conditions present then and not before. Other factors and events - from the legacy of the war in Vietnam to decolonisation and nationalist movements in the developing world - are equally, if not more important.

Differing theoretical assessments of the same events and processes provide synergetic potential of equal, if not greater, value to when different paradigmatic forms of analysis converge on the same substantive arguments. Different epistemologies, varying conceptions of ontology, competing normative agendas is what makes for the kaleidoscopic quality of IR theoretical matrix.

A choice of this or that theoretical research agenda will produce empirical results informed by epistemological, ontological and normative properties of the chosen paradigmatic model. From the TSA standpoint the question is not which theory "gets it right" but how different theoretical models of the problem-field fit together in the grand synergetic tapestry - the expanded and the *deep(er)* ontology of the empirical puzzle.

Synergetic theorizing – the Carter Doctrine

A hypothetical TSA research agenda examining politics of the Carter Doctrine (1980) is set out below as an illustration of the mechanics of the synergetic thought-process. It would begin by setting out a rationalist model in juxtaposition to neo-Marxian and Critical Theory approaches.

The Doctrine, established by President Jimmy Carter in his State of the Union Address on 23 January 1980, was a formal declaration of U.S. strategic interests in the Middle East. Carter was explicit in singling out the Middle East oil as a key strategic aim of the Doctrine, coming as it did in the wake of the Soviet invasion of Afghanistan a month earlier: "The region which is now threatened by Soviet troops in Afghanistan is of great strategic importance: it contains more than two-thirds of the world's exportable oil" (Carter, 1980).

Therefore, theoretical and normative debates in rationalist analyses of the Carter Doctrine center on the latter's efficacy in relation to its stated aim – to prevent, by force if necessary, an outside takeover of the Gulf region. While countries of the Middle East were not taken over by outside powers hostile to the U.S., the Carter Doctrine's overall aim of "a secure and stable Persian Gulf, free from any outside control but our own" had not materialized (Cambanis, 14.10.2012).

Moreover, some neo-realists today argue that "while Middle Eastern oil remains a U.S. interest, it is no longer a vital national interest" and the Carter Doctrine should be abandoned, for it is no longer adequate to meet strategic challenges facing the United States in the region (Davis, 03.02.17). Yergin too suggests that this process of decline in the strategic value of oil began with the emergence of commodity trading in the mid-1980s (1991, p. 747).

Rationalists, therefore, treat the Carter Doctrine in the context of structural power relations and competition amongst states, the Cold War dynamics and the American superpower, the military-strategic value of oil and the emerging influence of energy markets in the early-to-mid 1980s.

World-systems and structural-dependency theorists place the Doctrine within the framework of core/semi-periphery/periphery analysis of the global energy cycle and a critique of U.S./Western hegemony in the global energy order. For neo-Marxists the announcement of the Carter Doctrine was "a blatant assertion of imperialist sphere of influence over other sovereign nations" and marked yet another escalation in the Cold War between the superpowers, which threatened world peace (Saba (Ed.), 1980).

Critical theory builds on Gramscian insights to expand the scope of analysis to include historically-contingent social forces and processes in shaping international oil and energy politics. Robert Cox called for proper attention to these social forces and processes and warned against both - reifying a world system and underrating state power (1986, p.206). Illumination of the emancipatory interest demands a holistic approach.

Hence, for critical theorists understanding the Carter Doctrine requires contextualising and critiquing historical structures of global capitalism in general, because "it was the economic, political and cultural aspects of those structures – including the culture of Fordist mass consumption – which generated American interest in the Middle East and animated the geopolitical project which has led us to where we are today" (Rupert, 2010, p.103).

The empirical field of the Carter Doctrine can then be expanded further by incorporating post-structuralist analysis and wider postmodern critique. In calling for repudiation of the Carter Doctrine, Michael T. Klare, for example, emphasizes the political destructiveness of American reliance on Middle East oil: "So long as the United States adheres to a policy that legitimates the use of military force to protect the flow of oil, we run the risk of involvement in one war after another in the ever-volatile Persian Gulf region" (23.01.2009).

He charts the evolution of U.S. military engagement in the region from 1980 through to the invasion of Iraq in 2003 in the context of "globalisation of the Carter Doctrine," whereby the principles underlying the Doctrine are applied beyond the Gulf - the objective of securing the United States' access to oil resources is accorded the status of "strategic value and vital interest" across the globe, wherever oil is found, which in turn justifies use of military force (Klare, 2011, p.94).

The solution, however, is not in identifying the inequities and the problems of the Carter Doctrine or devising better ways to sustain the global energy order – it is in doing away with the petroleum order altogether and transitioning away from reliance on oil (Klare, 23.01.2009). If critical theory "limits the range of choice to alternative orders which are feasible transformations of the existing world" (Cox, 1986, p. 210), then post-structuralism envisages no such limitations and sets out alternatives that are radically, fundamentally different to existing conditions.

Meanwhile, for social constructivists the Carter Doctrine, like any security measure or policy, constitutes a regime - a socially produced structure of shared meanings (Onuf 1989; Kratochwil, 1989; Wendt 1999). Such a regime requires a volume of common background knowledge comprehensible to all actors - a shared framework of understanding for all participants (Kratochwil, 1978). This framework is determined by language, which not only reflects the social reality but itself comprises shared understandings that produce the social world.

The language of the Carter Doctrine is revealing of the meaning of the political force animating it and represents a set of socially-constructed, linguistically-constituted rules which are intended to be understood by all participants – at the time, principally the Soviet Union:

> Let our position be absolutely clear: an attempt by any outside force to gain control of the Persian Gulf region will be regarded as an assault on the vital interests of the United States of America, and such an assault will be repelled by any means necessary, including military force. (Carter, 1980).

Compare it now to the Foreign Secretary Lord Lansdowne's statement to the House of Lords in 1903 in response to rising naval tensions with Germany, setting out that the British government would "regard the establishment of a naval base or of a fortified port in the Persian Gulf by any other power as a very grave menace to British interests, and we should certainly resist it with all the means at our disposal" (quoted in Yergin, 1991, p.124).

Striking linguistic similarities between the two "doctrines" eighty years apart are not incidental – these are linguistically-constituted power claims which reflect the socially-constructed nature of security regimes in the Gulf and underlie a continuity in the Anglo-American oil ascendancy over the course of the century.

Constructivism enables systemic and unit-level analysis, engaging with agents and structure as co-constitutive parts of the same whole – agents make structure and structure makes agents, linked as they are through the process of practice (Wendt, 1999). Social constructivist inquiry is focused on establishing the historical condition of this process, so as to identify how practices produce and reproduce the rules of social structure over time, while at the same time being shaped and formed by those structures.

Such epistemic flexibility makes social constructivist scholarship particularly suitable for multi-theoretical experimentation. Thus, an eclectic model of the Carter Doctrine would combine the materialist base of Rationalist mainstream approaches with these social-constructivist insights within the same analytical framework. Arguably, this is what many scholars working on oil and wider energy issues today already do in their empirical work, regardless of whether such eclecticism is acknowledged explicitly.

It can be argued, for example, that Daniel Yergin's encyclopaedic *The Prize* (1991) is implicitly an eclectic work with its theoretical center grounded in the dominant triad of Neo-Realism, Neo-Liberalism and Social Constructivism ("Neo-Neo/Con"). These reflect Yergin's "three themes" – the business of the oil industry, the politics of oil and what he termed as the "anthropological argument" – the rise of the "hydrocarbon society" (Ibid., pp.13-15).

In fact, paradigm-dynamic reading of *The Prize* reveals elements of multiple theoretical traditions and sub-fields embedded in its analytical framework – from classical realism and liberalism to security studies, foreign policy analysis (FPA), game theory and historical sociology. For examples of eclectic scholarship on energy see Mitchel, 2011; Noreng, 2002; Wenger et al (Eds.), 2009; Moran, 2010; Steven et al (Eds.), 2014.

As noted previously theory-synergetic approach departs from analytic eclecticism on issues of extent and the degree of epistemological and ontological limits to theoretical pluralism and there are good reasons for that. From the TSA standpoint, a decision to limit the ontological framework of the Carter Doctrine to, for example, a) capabilities of states, b) the role of institutions and norms and c) linguistic discourse of socially-constructed rules, appears at best arbitrary.

Paradigmatic dynamism of theory-synergetic approach involves systematic application of different theoretical properties upon the same broad empirical puzzle. Theoretical overview of the Carter Doctrine sketched out briefly above proceeds from this very starting point of prioritization of the empirical puzzle, while theories are used as methods for knowledge creation about substantive elements of that puzzle. There is no suggestion of *a priori* bracketing of theoretical scope of the study.

From such an open-ended dynamic engagement with the subject-matter TSA proceeds to establish what conceptual overlaps and thematic commonalities exist between different theoretical accounts. This is not an attempt to construct epistemically-integral, convergent narrative structures. Rather it is an effort to establish which sections of the empirical problem-field are being addressed by more than one paradigmatic models – in other words, when and where on the historical timeline of a particular study do single-paradigm models converge and how? Whether such overlaps and commonalities occur on structure or agent-level is less important than how they contribute to understanding the process as a whole.

For example, the theme of Western imperialism is common to classical Marxist, classical Realist, neo-Marxist and Critical Theory single-paradigm accounts of the Carter Doctrine. Each theoretical model brings its own epistemic properties to bear upon the thematic commonality, be it balance of power calculation or core-periphery analysis. Taken together these different treatments of imperialism as a thematic commonality in discussions about the Carter Doctrine, contribute not only to substantive understanding of the problem-field but also towards normative assessments of it – the resultant picture is greater than the sum of its parts.

To take the argument further, a social-constructivist analytical framework can be applied to develop this common theme of imperialism in a historical context of evolution of linguistically-constituted sets of rules governing security regimes in the Gulf region, in turn revealing socially-constructed systemic continuity of the Anglo-American regional ascendancy.

Yet, the rationalist model of the Carter Doctrine is built up from its material foundation in the strategic value of oil. The *raison d'etre* of British and American policy in the Gulf in the 1900s and 1980s respectively is oil, specifically the vital interest it represents in determining material distribution of capabilities amongst states. The object is to secure access to oil and to prevent competitors from gaining access to it.

Neo-Liberal Institutionalists might also emphasize significance of non-state actors and market forces, or the role of Anglo-Persian and the Royal Dutch Shell in encouraging British military commitment in the Gulf comparatively to the role of Exxon and other American oil companies in shaping the U.S. policy in the 1970s and 1980s, and so on. However, the broad rationalist argument is grounded in a conception of oil as a natural kind.

Social-constructivist analysis may build on these materialist assumptions to develop a social theory of the Carter Doctrine, where it is enmeshed in a wider, socially-constituted world of oil. Here oil is conceived as a social kind and its significance is evaluated in terms of its social-constructionist potential. If the Carter Doctrine and its British historical precursors are socially-constructed sets of rules-based normative political regimes, then a conception of oil as a purely material, natural kind risks overlooking its ideational potential, such notions as Yergin's "hydrocarbon society." If oil represents interests which are linguistically constituted as "vital," both in the language of Lord Lansdowne and Jimmy Carter, so vital that the use of force is deemed necessary, then a broader ontological conception of it is required.

Such conceptual overlaps and thematic commonalities between various accounts told within different theoretical traditions serve as inter-paradigmatic pivots of the synergetic model of the Carter Doctrine. For example, a conceptual overlap between social and natural kinds allows for exploration of the problem-field that moves beyond structure/agent problem and involves both system and unit-level analysis. How states formulate their specific foreign policies matters as much as the material structural conditions which are claimed to necessitate them. Importantly, inter-paradigmatic pivots unlock the potential for wider normative reflection.

An inter-paradigmatic pivot operates upon dynamic interplay of different, often competing epistemic and ontological assumptions embedded in its constituent theoretical models. As such it can be utilized in a reflexive normative engagement on substantive issues in a way that would not be possible in a single-paradigm analytical framework or a comparative one. For example, as already argued mainstream rationalist normative debates about the Carter Doctrine are centered on the efficacy of the policy in meeting its strategic aims, specifically secure access for the United States to the Middle East.

For realist and liberal critics of the Carter Doctrine, it should be assessed on its own terms. As Nick Danforth argued in *Foreign Policy* (12.01.2016): "Neither the Soviet Union nor any other 'outside force' ever seized control of Iran. But this seems like odd grounds on which to claim success for an administration that presided over the transformation of Iran itself into a hostile power."

Neo-classical Realists assert that the Doctrine was justified and successful in the context of growing Soviet threat and the need to rebalance power capabilities in the Middle East (Auten, 2008). Some liberals engage in revisionist reassessments of Carter's presidency, focusing on the normative legitimacy of a liberal hegemonic order he championed in order to challenge Soviet totalitarianism and Islamic theocracy in Iran (Dumbrell, 1995).

Other neo-realists call for an even stronger reaffirmation of U.S. strategic objectives and the need to persevere with the Doctrine: "Much is at stake with the Iran issue: U.S. national security, nuclear proliferation, Arab-Israel peace, moderation of the Islamic world, security of Israel and Arab allies, the U.S. global position, and the secure supply of crude oil from the Persian Gulf that is so integral to our economy. It is vital, therefore, for the United States to continue to enforce the Carter Doctrine" (Makovsky and Goldstein, 13.08.2010).

These debates are grounded in a materialist conception of oil which is limited in its normative reach. That Carter Doctrine was called upon to ensure secure access to oil is taken as a given social reality and is not questioned. A normative inter-paradigmatic critique of the Carter Doctrine pivots on a rationalist/reflectivist conceptual overlap, where oil is both a social and a natural kind and where the Carter Doctrine is embedded in a wider socio-political matrix of global oil politics and is not reduced to merely a technicality - a foreign policy instrument.

By contrast, critical theoretical engagement begins by problematizing such notions as "strategic resource" and seeking to debunk the very notion that U.S. military protection is required for oil imports and security (Eland, 2011). Post-structuralist approaches might draw on complex connections between the culture of oil consumption and militarism it gives rise to, exemplified by the Carter Doctrine (Price-Smith, 2015). As Bacevich argues: "The American public's ready acceptance of a prospect of war without foreseeable end and of a policy that abandons even a pretence of the United States fighting defensively or viewing war as a last resort, shows clearly how far the process of militarization has advanced" (2013, p. 35).

This, in turn ties in with vibrant Feminist debates about the implications of the Carter Doctrine, which extended the military draft to women alongside men for the first time in American history (for a contemporary overview see Candarow, 1980). On the one hand, the Doctrine was seen as an advance in gender equality but on the other - as a sign of creeping militarisation. Heated discussions that took place over the issue in the National Organization for Women (NOW) and the National Women's Political Caucus (NWPC) illuminate real tensions between various strands of American feminism; between the aims of the wider anti-war movement and the specific goals of women's liberation movement (Candarow, 1980).

Synergetic modelling of the Carter Doctrine, as suggested above, invites a question – on what grounds would it be legitimate to exclude any of the analytical strands explored so far from scholarship on this substantive question? From the TSA standpoint there are none. Paradigmatic dynamism of the theory-synergetic approach is, at its core, a commitment to hyper-empiricism. The focus is the Carter Doctrine, not *how* we study it.

Synergetic modelling of the BTC project

Even in a course of this brief paradigm-dynamic reading of the problem-field, a deeper ontology of the Carter Doctrine has been revealed – from its place as a foreign policy instrument in the Cold War structure of international oil politics to its impact on gender-relations in the U.S. military, its role in shaping politics and societies of the Middle East, its place in wider culture, and most importantly its place in general history – how it fits in the grand ontology of IR. The implicit historicism of the theory-synergetic approach suggests that *time* be a key unit of measure in International Relations.

Consider these two extracts from literature on Baku-Tbilisi-Ceyhan (BTC) oil pipeline, launched in 2005 as the main export route for Azerbaijan's hydrocarbons:

1. "After all the battles of the Great Game, all the clash and clamor of the Caspian Derby, all the manoeuvring and diplomacy, all the negotiating and trading and deal making, it all comes down to science and engineering and construction – the platforms and oil complexes in the Caspian Sea, and the $4 billion underground steel tubular highway that has reconnected Baku to the global market. As it carries oil, that pipeline also seems to be carrying the cargo of history, connecting not only Baku and Ceyhan but also the beginning of the twenty-first century back to the beginning of the twentieth" (Yergin, 2012, *The Quest*, p. 64).

2. "For centuries the Absheron Peninsula was a place of pilgrimage, a shrine of fire. Burning gas had leaked from the ground since the last Ice Age. This was the most sacred site of Zoroastrianism which, prior to Islam, was the dominant faith in the region. The oil-bearing rocks drew people to this place, not to extract petroleum and carry it off to some other site of burning, but to worship it here in the sheets of flame among the rocks. As other faiths arrived – Sunni and Shia Islam, Russian Orthodoxy, Marxism and Capitalism – the holy fire of this peninsula was transformed into a material to be extracted and exported" (Marriott and Minio-Paluello, 2013, *The Oil Road*, p. 23).

These quotes contain elements of distinct epistemological properties of separate paradigmatic accounts of the story of the BTC pipeline – Yergin's solid rationalism is juxtaposed with reflective postmodernism of Marriott and Minio-Paluello. The first celebrates the industry of oil, the second questions it.

What binds these narratives together in a paradigm-dynamic framework is a common and explicit recognition of the historical condition of oil, both as a natural and social kind. How this condition is interpreted, how normative judgements are attached to these interpretations and how intersubjective meanings are formed about them are the questions animating the synergetic approach.

As argued before, taking the route of analytic eclecticism in attempting to reconcile the materialist and social elements of the pipeline project remains an epistemologically-bound, ontologically-circumscribed analytical format that cannot move beyond the scope of the existing social order, cannot imagine an alternative reality radically different to the one in existence. Because to know what is this particular pipeline is to ask what it is not, or what it could be, and whether it should be at all.

Therefore, synergetic theorizing about BTC moves beyond the "neo-neo-con" boundaries and employs conceptual overlaps and thematic commonalities as platforms for hyper-empirical engagement with the full expanse of the problem-field, without reducing or bracketing of its ontological sphere. Such an approach enables construction of specific inter-paradigmatic pivots upon which these conceptual overlaps and thematic commonalities rotate in a real-time synergetic analysis of the Baku-Ceyhan pipeline.

In summary TSA logic proceeds from 1. paradigm-dynamic reading of a problem-field to 2. identification of thematic commonalities and conceptual overlaps between empirical accounts set out in separate single-paradigm models, to 3) construction of inter-paradigmatic pivots upon which synergetic analytical model can be devised.

Having set out the rationalist and reflectivist models of BTC in previous chapters it is now possible to identify environmental issues as a major common theme addressed at length by cross-paradigmatic scholarship on BTC. Competing conceptualisations of the same substantive questions about BTC and environment overlap across different single-paradigm accounts of the problem field. Several key narratives emerge in empirical treatments of environmental issues and BTC:

- tanker-traffic through the Bosphorus Straits in Istanbul;
- global climate change and local impact on the environment;
- the role of oil companies and corporate social responsibility;
- international environmental regulatory framework.

Contemporary mainstream studies and commentary on BTC emphasize the ecological dimension of the BTC project and point to the final routing of the pipeline as serving an environmental objective of reducing tanker-traffic through the highly-congested the Bosphorus Straits in Istanbul (Blatchford, 2005, p.119).

Nearly two million barrels of oil in addition to other goods was being transported through the Straits by 2005 (Elkind, 2005, p.39). Practically all the new oil from the Caspian region and Russia went to global markets from Black Sea onto Mediterranean via Bosporus. Frequent leaks and accidents added to increasing costs for the companies involved in trade and shipment, as congestion, administrative tariffs and insurance fees rose (Ibid).

A neo-liberal focus on the issue conceives the environmental factor as an economic one. BTC route was chosen because environmental costs precluded additional tanker traffic through Istanbul. Risk assessments and technical studies identified BTC as the optimal method of transportation in terms of managing environmental risks and costs (Ibid).

Similarly, the idea of Corporate Social Responsibility as expressed in extensive Environmental and Social Impact Assessments (ESIA), consultation and local environmental risk assessments, as well as systematic engagement with NGOs carried out by BP is seen in the context of business needs, corporate policy and international institutional regulatory framework (Ibid, p.59).

Neo-realists, however stress the strategic dimension of the environmental factor. Increased tanker traffic through the Bosporus represented a physical security threat to the city of Istanbul. Baran argues that while oil companies measured Bosporus in terms of its commercial value as a transportation route, the Turkish government considered it to be "...a highly sensitive lifeline of Istanbul and the Black sea region" (2005, p. 105; see also Yergin, 2012, p.60).

Neo-realists are interested in showing how environmental factors are in fact political and are deployed as such in the sphere of international relations in the form of state-enacted regulation, standards, tariffs and fees, with which non-state actors must comply. States measure the environmental factor in terms of its material impact on their security (and how to mitigate it) and as a political asset to be utilized through national policy (see Kandiyoti, 2012, pp.29-48).

Critics of BTC echo this concern with state power and its utilisation of environmental security logic to serve political goals. Muttitt and Marriott, for example, point out that Turkey's intentions over the Bosporus issue were far from "green" ([Platform], 2002, p. 30). Since the Straits are classified as "international waters" Turkey would be neither able to collect commercial tariff fees from additional oil passing through them nor control an energy route, whereas pipeline met both those objectives (Ibid.).

Critical engagement challenges knowledge claims about environment and BTC. It identifies "problem-solving" nature of mainstream approaches and seeks instead to provide an alternative understanding of the problem (Thomas, M. 2004; Platform et al. 2006; Platform et al. 2008; Memorandum from Concerned Non-Governmental Organizations, 2002).

Critics do agree with the need to reduce oil transport through the Bosporus, but place it within a wider context of climate change and the need to stop the use of fossil fuels altogether and not add to it by opening up new reserves such as the ones in the Caspian. They demonstrate a direct link between current modes of production and the oil industry in particular, while warning against local, regional and global impact of BTC. The argued for example, that once burnt the one million barrels of oil transported daily through BTC (working at full capacity) would contribute 160 million tonnes of CO_2 emissions per year, while contributing to BP's profits (Muttitt and Marriott [Platform], 2002, p. 159).

Operationalising environmental problem-field as an inter-paradigmatic pivot in a synergetic analysis of BTC reveals full ontological depth. The historical timeline of the pipeline is no longer limited to its physical existence – it is set in a global temporal space, where it occupies its place in relation to the very notion of modernity. Inter-paradigmatic pivots upon which elements of this grand empirical timeline of Baku oil rotate can be constructed upon myriad of conceptual overlaps and thematic commonalities occurring at multiple junctures along the way.

Broadly, the mainstream rationalist account of Baku oil is centered on two great "Oil Booms" – the First in 1870s-1920 and the Second in 1994-2010s. It is a story of how Tsarist reforms in the late nineteenth century first "opened the area to competitive private enterprise," resulting in "an explosion of entrepreneurship" (Yergin, 1991, p.42; see also LeVine, 2007, p.7).

The first Oil Boom came to an end with the Soviet conquest of Azerbaijan in 1920 and nationalisation of Baku oil fields. The second Boom did not come until the collapse of the USSR and restoration of Azerbaijan's independence when the oil industry was opened up to Western investment and modern technology, eventually resulting in the BTC pipeline and heralding the contemporary Boom: "Petroleum had consolidated Azerbaijan as a nation and established its importance on the world stage" (Yergin, 2012, p. 63).

Bringing in reflectivist, critical and post-structuralist insights into the empirical "time-space continuum" of the problem-field allows us to problematize this sequential, ordered narrative, laden as it is with underlying normative assumptions. Each of these so-called "booms" at critical junctures represents social, not only material revolution. As Marriott and Minio-Paluello forcefully contend: "Calling these periods of concentrated change 'oil booms' focuses attention on the geology, technology and capital, as though the changes were almost inevitable and inherently positive" (2013, p.96).

Thus the first "oil boom" "was a social upheaval, guided largely from St Petersburg, Paris and London. It gave birth not only to the oil barons, but also the ecological and social hell of the oil fields and the pogroms of 1905 and 1918" (Ibid.). And so on to the Soviet "oil boom," "accompanied by the Stalinist incarcerations at Bayil (Ed. – infamous Baku prison)" (Ibid.).

And the present day "boom," directed "from offices in London, Washington and Brussels," is also a social transformation that carries with it human rights abuses, inequality and poverty: "The constant drilling of holes in the desert and the seabed was celebrated by those who directed it, both capitalist and state-socialist. And all... have sung of these wells as agents of human advancement, and wrapped the gigantic enterprise in a heavy cloak of positivity, with no space for doubt" (Ibid).

Comparing these accounts of history, it becomes clear that the same common themes are being explored, the same concepts are overlapping but substantive arguments and normative judgements about them differ in accordance to epistemic and ontological properties of single-paradigm modes of analysis. To reiterate, TSA does not ascribe truth-status to these and holds that such assessments should be made on the basis of empirical substance behind competing claims. Inter-paradigmatic pivots that can be constructed along the myriad of these overlaps and commonalities are called to help in this assessment by providing a common analytical framework for testing paradigmatic propositions.

The objective is not simply to tell these stories eclectically in parallel with each other but to set these contesting narratives and competing claims off against each other and to clash them upon a common empirical field. The resulting picture is bound to be larger than the sum of its constituent parts. In summary, theory-synergetic approach is envisaged as a grand IR research programme, a hyper-empiricist endeavor grounded in the ethos of the Critical Realist philosophy of science. It is an expression of an open-ended commitment to knowledge-production in International Relations.

SGC financing as inter-paradigmatic pivot

International financing of Southern Gas Corridor (SGC) was identified in Chapter II as constituting a cross-theoretical conceptual overlap. The question of who pays for the pipelines is central to all single-paradigm models of the SGC project and features heavily in public debates around it (see chapters IV and V). The issue of public funding of projects such as SGC and BTC before it, constitutes a thematic commonality – it is at the core of all single-paradigm treatments of the conceptual overlap. The role of international multilateral public finance institutions, such as EBRD and EIB, in making SGC possible can be operationalized as an inter-paradigmatic pivot through which theory-synergetic analytical model is animated.

Rationalist consensus on the issue proceeds from a starting premise that "securing financing is of primary importance for this strategic energy transit corridor's timely implementation" (Gurbanov, 2017). This is a problem-solving approach, characterized by attempt to identify obstacles to successful realisation of the SGC project and ways to overcome them (Cox, 1986, p.208).

How states, international financial institutions, multilateral agencies, multinational energy corporations and other actors approach questions of oil and gas project financing in general is determined by the interplay of strategic and economic factors, set within the structure of international energy politics (see, for example, Economou et al, 2017, for a structural model of world oil market).

Political developments outside the realm of oil and gas markets and regulatory frameworks (e.g. wider geopolitical events or processes) are treated as exogenous factors. Meanwhile, issues such as investment dynamics within the oil/gas sector are treated as endogenous factors, and outcomes are determined by the interplay between the two.

For example, volatile oil and gas prices, domestic supply squeezes or fluctuations in global supply chains may affect financial viability of a complex regional infrastructure project such as the SGC (Pirani, 2016; Rzayeva, 2018). Yet such endogenous factors are mitigated and mediated by the strategic pull of extrageneous forces – interests of gas-producing states such as Azerbaijan (Jafarova, 2017), actions of transit states such as Turkey (Tagliapietra and Bruegel, 02.07.2015), or gas-consuming EU member-states such as Greece and Italy (Geropoulos, 3.3.2016), as well as EU institutions, such as the Commission and financial bodies under its jurisdiction.

The latter are particularly important. The European Commission has been exploring possibility of a natural gas infrastructure link to Caspian gas reserves for over ten years, having identified early proposals as a strategic priority in the 2007 "energy package" policy framework (Van Aartsen, 2009, p.11). Since then, as the project evolved into SGC the European Commission continued to provide robust support because of underlying strategic priorities of its member states:

> A key part of ensuring secure and affordable supplies of energy to Europeans involves diversifying supply routes. This includes identifying and building new routes that decrease the dependence of EU countries on a single supplier of natural gas and other energy resources. Many countries in Central and South East Europe are dependent on a single supplier for most or all of their natural gas. To help these countries diversify their supplies, the Southern Gas Corridor aims to expand infrastructure that can bring gas to the EU from the Caspian Basin, Central Asia, the Middle East, and the Eastern Mediterranean Basin (EU Commission, 2017).

To achieve this EU policy, the Commission included component pipeline infrastructure projects needed for the Corridor on the EU's list of Projects of Common Interest. This means they can benefit from streamlined permitting process, receive preferential regulatory treatment, and be eligible to apply for EU funding. EU is also committed to cooperating closely with gas suppliers in the region including Azerbaijan, Iraq and Turkmenistan, with transit countries including Azerbaijan, Georgia and Turkey and to a long-term goal of negotiating with Azerbaijan and Turkmenistan on a Trans-Caspian pipeline to transport gas across the Caspian Sea, thus securing more supplies (EU Commission, 2017).

These strategic priorities are then translated into financial policies of multilateral lending organizations such as the European Bank for Reconstruction and Development (EBRD) and European Investment Bank (EIB), functioning under EU and other inter-governmental jurisdictions. Thus, EBRD policy statement on Southern Gas Corridor reads:

> Stretching across five countries of operations of the EBRD, the Southern Gas Corridor is an important

strategic gas infrastructure project aimed at improving the security and diversity of the energy supply to Europe and Turkey. It will expand gas supply options and provide new energy transportation routes enabling Europe to access gas from the Caspian region and, in the longer term, beyond it, including the Eastern Mediterranean, Central Asia and the Middle East (EBRD Policy Statement Document, 18.10.2017).

In justifying its decision to allocate five hundred million dollars' worth of public funds to finance a key component of SGC, the Bank argued that the project will "support the diversification of gas supply sources in Europe and Turkey... The enhancement of energy security and diversification of energy supplies are important elements of well-functioning economies" (Ibid). Securitisation of financial planning in relation to SGC is, another important feature of rationalist modelling of the issue (Jafarova, 2017; Verda, 2016; Karagöl and Kaya, 2014; D'Agostini, 2014; Manolis, 2014).

Neo-liberal institutionalists might emphasize interdependent role of funding institutions, public lenders, oil companies and global financial markets in determining outcomes. Strategic priorities will be served and political risks ameliorated, provided market conditions are right: "Despite the political risks involved in all the Southern Gas Corridor projects, reducing EU dependence on Russian oil and gas is not proving as expensive as initially predicted in terms of borrowing costs" (Burroughs, 15.08.2017).

Neo-realists, however, emphasize pivotal role of states and their strategic interests. Economic factors, such as price volatility, are not seen as determining the decisions of individual states and multilateral lenders, because in the end strategic interests prevail: "The difficult economic environment notwithstanding, the timely implementation of the SGC is unlikely to be affected given the potent commitment of the international financial institutions and Azerbaijan's government, which underlines the strong political will to deliver the project" (Gurbanov, 2017).

If SGC financing process can be explained in a parsimonious structural model populated by interest-maximising states, multilateral lender-organizations and markets, then what explains certain persistent anomalies? For example, why has it taken Italy nearly two years to authorize construction of the Trans-Adriatic Pipeline, the final leg and a key component of SGC (Gotev, 29.03.2017)?

The matter was finally resolved through a complex legal process, subject to challenges in local and national courts and submission of extensive environmental and social impact assessments for each country traversed by the proposed pipeline – Albania, Greece and Italy (Jamestown Foundation, 30.04.2017: TAP-AG, 2017). Delays in the implementation of the project proved a constant irritant for SGC planners and those backing the project. Speaking in 2015 a senior executive of SOCAR, Azerbaijan's state energy giant and key shareholder in all SGC pipeline consortia, said:

> Even though the project is important for Italy, it is important for Europe. We are speaking of gas from an alternative source for Italy, for South-Eastern Europe. So I think common sense will once again prevail. I would like to stress that environmental impact is minimal and all damage on the environment will be repaired. All losses for agricultural producers will be compensated. Social budgets in the regions will get a boost, as I explained. And once again, the projects are implemented under the most modern and I would say strictest standards. I think that nobody can stop progress. (Vitaly Baylarbayov in Gotev, 4.10.2016).

At this stage, infusion of social-constructivist element into the theoretical mix, following Sil and Katzenstein's analytic-eclecticism approach (2010), could provide additional insights into the problem. The quote above suggests that notions such as environment, social development and progress are inter-subjective beliefs – socially constructed ideas widely held to be true by actors.

This gives rise to a plethora of questions – how do actors translate these normative standpoints into regulatory benchmarks governing SGC financing? How do various conditionality principles attached to funding approvals evolve and how these come to be codified and incorporated into institutional identities of actors participating in the process e.g. international benchmark performance requirements attached to EBRD and other bodies' funding criteria requirements?

This suggests that the rationalist conception of the structure of international gas politics is at least incomplete. Social forces, shaped by normative identities of various actors engaged in the project, have significant consequences on political outcomes. For example, strategic priorities do inform EU energy policy, as set out in the European Union Energy Security Strategy (EU Commission, 2018; EU Commission Working Document SWD (2014)330, 02.07.2014).

But so do environmental, climate change and social concerns and these are reflected in the EU's 2030 Framework for Climate and Energy (EU Commission, 2018; EU Commission Working Document SWD (2014)255, 23.7.2014). Together the two regulatory frameworks form the core of the Energy Union – EU's overall energy strategy that "…will lead to a sustainable, low carbon and environmentally friendly economy, putting Europe at the forefront of renewable energy production, clean energy technologies, and the fight against global warming" (EU Commission, 2018).

A situation, therefore, exists where support for SGC and other natural gas projects is coupled with a commitment to reduce carbon emissions and transition to renewable sources of energy. Apparent contradictions of this position give rise to normative reflection and social constructivists seek to raise possibility of alternative courses of action by asking, for example, whether SGC is the only viable method of supply diversification and Europe's energy security (Siddi, 2017)?

The argument here is not only that EU can acquire sufficient and affordable energy resources by other, already existing means but that the goal of the EU's climate agenda implementation is at odds with the EU's financial and political support for long-term, fossil fuels import project, such as the SGC (Ibid. p.19).

Eclectic theorizing enables expansion of structural conception of energy politics to allow for ideational as well as material elements. For example, when it comes to multilateral financing of complex international infrastructure systems, such as the SGC, political decision-making process does not occur in a normative vacuum but is mediated through a continuously evolving complex web of politically relevant inter-subjective beliefs. These are constituted through clearly defined and codified normative frameworks e.g. permissibility standards, compensatory mechanisms, environmental and social impact assessment criteria, policy goals derived from international treaty obligations, and so on.

Thus, each segment of the SGC pipeline (SCP, TANAP, TAP) had to meet certain material standards in delivering the project in order to qualify for funding. These assessments are legal documents, part of regulatory architecture of the SGC project. Their significance demonstrates the extent to which norms are politically actualized – as a) the material articulation of socio-normative aspirations of participating actors and b) standard setting-mechanisms necessary for successful implementation of a project (TAP ESIAs 2012-2014; SCP ESIAs 2013; TANAP ESIAs 2014-2015).

Complimentary application of social-constructivist insights to the structuralist model of SGC financing helps understand how strategic and normative priorities of states and institutions are mediated, formalized through procedural, standard-setting and administrative mechanisms, and internalized by actors in the discourses about the issue. For example, in the quote above, a senior SOCAR executive, Vitaly Baylarbayov (Gotev, 4.10.2016) lists environmental and social benefits of the pipeline in an almost exact match to key parameters set out in the various EISAs for the project, (TAP ESIAs 2012-2014). And from post-structuralist and critical standpoints this is a major problem.

Critical and post-structuralist opposition to SGC project, comprising praxeological project and empirical programme, is motivated by a normative commitment to stopping the project. Preventing public funding of SGC is the center-piece of the political campaign by coalitions of NGOs, local community and civil society groups, human rights campaigners and environmentalists, involving political lobbying and grassroots activism (CounterBalance, 28.01.2016; CEE Bankwatch Network, 2017).

The entire campaign is a direct political appeal to multilateral financial institutions, such as the EBRD and EIB, as well as the European Commission not to fund any of the SGC pipelines (McKibben, Klein et al, CounterBalance, 30.06. 2017). Signatories of another letter to the EIB President argued that "…the Southern Gas Corridor is one of the biggest and most controversial infrastructure projects that have ever seen the light in Europe. This massive financial investment entails serious environmental and geopolitical risks and is likely to become the European equivalent of the Keystone XL pipeline. Therefore, we call for no public money to go to the Southern Gas Corridor" (ACT Alliance EU, Les Amis de la Terre (France) and Others, CounterBalance, 28.01.2016).

Another group of NGOs challenged EIB over human rights impact of SGC, especially in Azerbaijan and Turkey, arguing that: "…the development of the Southern Gas Corridor will only strengthen oppression in these countries where civil liberties and the security of individuals are currently being drastically impaired. This runs contrary to the EU Charter of Fundamental Rights which binds the EIB to not finance projects that would encourage or support human rights violations. Therefore, we call on the EIB to adhere to the principles of fundamental rights and withdraw its offer to finance the project in light of such prevailing conditions" (Article 19, Banktrack and others, 12.09.2017).

Each segment of the SGC project (SCP, TANAP, TAP), requiring multilateral funding has been subjected to the same consistent opposition, aimed at preventing institutional financing of the project (NHC, 19.12.2016). The very same structural mechanisms of standard-setting, environmental and social impact assessment criteria, reporting-compliance and procedural-administrative architecture of SGC financing are utilized with the aim of precluding any potential financing agreements.

Meanwhile, marginalized groups and counterhegemonic forces seek to use the normative framework of financing decisions to challenge human rights abuses and prevailing power relations causing them. For example, former presidential candidate in Azerbaijan, widely believed to be unjustly imprisoned by the government of President Ilham Aliyev, declared himself to be an "inmate of Southern Gas Corridor," arguing that: "International investment in fossil fuel extraction is making me and other Azerbaijani political prisoners hostages to the Aliyev regime" (Mammadov, 20.01.2017; CoE Committee of Ministers, 25.10.2017).

Political praxeological project is informed and energized by a critical research programme which aims to expose the true extent of negative social and environmental consequences of SGC

(CounterBalance, Platform and Re: Common, 08.03.2016). Its empirical output comprises a plethora of methodologies e.g. in-depth environmental and social impact assessments, which challenge results of corporate and institutional ESIAs produced to support SGC projects (Banktrack and Counterbalance, 20.02.2017). These efforts aim to show that SGC fails on its own terms e.g. economic viability or to meet energy diversification targets and on human rights, environmental, climate change and other criteria (Sol, 24.09.2017; Bacheva-McGrath et al, 2015; CEE Bankwatch EBRD Brief, May 2017).

Critique of and opposition to SGC financing can be viewed as a post-structuralist/neo-Gramscian intellectual/praxeological synthesis of a kind that seeks to unbalance prevailing narratives about the issue and to empower marginalized voices, previously excluded and silenced. Whether it is through producing documentaries telling the stories of Azerbaijani prisoners of conscience or community organizers in Melendugno in southern Italy protesting against the Trans-Adriatic Pipeline (CounterBalance, Platform and Re:Common, 08.03.2016) or carrying out research showing how alternatives to SGC are not only possible but credible, the cumulative aim is to make a sustained argument against public funding of the project:

> Preventing the use of public money for massive fossil fuel projects such as the Southern Gas Corridor can open space for more serious efforts on energy efficiency and sustainable forms of renewable energy (Bacheva-McGrath et al, 2015).

Post-structuralist and critical standpoints on SGC financing would not be included in theoretical eclectic mix of the kind advocated by Sil and Katzenstein (2010). Their analytic eclecticism is rooted in theoretically-bound realist/liberal/constructivist matrix on the grounds that these theories are "the most established and most viable contenders for paradigmatic dominance" in IR (Ibid., p.25). Rationale for locating analytic-eclecticism in the dominant theoretical Triad is dictated by the results of recent TRIP surveys, showing that most IR scholars work within these three traditions (Jordan et al, 2009, p.18). It might be a rhetorical question but does the real world really work in accordance with TRIP survey results?

If post-structural forms of knowledge and critical claims about SGC are not valid and are to be excluded from analytical mix, then why do they appear to have effects in real world? From a critical realist philosophical standpoint – why do they meet the correspondence theory of truth test if they are assumed not to be true? Specifically, for example, why the European Investment Bank (EIB), the financial arm of the EU, decided at first not to approve record €1.4bn investment package for the crucial western segment of SGC – the Trans Adriatic Pipeline and postponed the decision to 2018 (Nuttall, 13.12.2017)?

There was widespread expectation that financing will be approved; all the strategic conditions for support of the project were in place, including direct lobbying of EIB by the European Commission itself - vice president Maroš Šefčovič and climate and energy commissioner Miguel Arias Cañete wrote to the bank's president Werner Hoyer to make clear the importance of the project, arguing that the Southern Gas Corridor "is a strategic project for the EU, directly contributing to the diversification of gas sources and security of supply objectives of the European Energy Union strategy" (13.07.2017 in Mathiesen, 27.11.2017).

All the environmental and social impact assessments have been logged and formally processed; EBRD has already approved €500mln worth of funding for SGC (EBRD Project 48376, 18.10.2017). Nevertheless, in December 2017 EIB delayed financing SGC, a spokesperson citing "a number of due diligence issues that merits proper discussion" as the reason (Nuttall, 13.12.2017). This might have been in reference to hundreds officially logged representations and formal complaints raised with EIB compliance and accountability mechanisms against SGC (EIB Accountability, 2018).

EIB decision came out of the blue, leaving the project in limbo and it is just one anomaly that mainstream scholarship and commentary on the issue of SGC financing - single-paradigm, synthetic and eclectic - failed to explain, let alone predict. Structuralist/constructivist framework alone simply cannot account for this real-world outcome – all the strategic interest boxes were "ticked," all insufficiencies, problems were "solved" and yet the empirical outcome did not correspond to theoretical claims about it. This is because analytic-eclecticism remains a theoretically-parsimonious analytical framework and its empirical reach is circumscribed by its foundational theoretical commitments.

It is true that most IR scholarship does fall within the paradigmatic Triad of realism, liberalism and constructivism (Jordan, et al 2009, p 18). The field of international energy politics is no exception and much of its empirical research comes from within this dominant paradigmatic matrix (see chapter 4).

For example, the Oxford Institute for Energy Studies (OIES, 2017) carries out its research programmes within clearly defined ontological boundaries – oil, natural gas and electricity – and sets them out across clear epistemological parameters, described as "the disciplines of the Institute: economics, politics and sociology, international relations of gas-producing, consuming and transit countries;" issues of environment are explicitly bracketed in terms of their relevance to primary ontological focus areas – fossil fuels and generation of electrical power (OIES, Natural Gas Research Programme, 2017).

There is logic to arguing that since the Triad is closest to achieving paradigmatic dominance it makes it convenient to locate multi-theoretical efforts here. Sil and Katzenstein justify this choice for this reason precisely: "Thus, it is in the context of debates between realists, liberals and constructivists that we find it most useful to elaborate on the significance of analytical eclecticism for the study of world politics" (2010, p.25).

But useful for whom? Analytic-eclecticism is ostensibly posited as a problem-orientated research programme, concerned with producing knowledge of relevance "for real-world dilemmas facing political and social actors" (Ibid., p.9). Single-paradigm analytical frameworks are viewed as deficient precisely because in pursuit of parsimony they lead us to overlook complexity of social life, thus inhibiting policy-relevant research (Ibid, p.12).

Yet, there does not appear to be a causal connection between this pragmatic normative motivation for analytic-eclecticism (i.e. policy-relevant, real-world orientated scholarship) and its internal criteria for theory selection (i.e. the means by which such scholarship is to be generated). The latter is in fact determined and justified chiefly by implications drawn from TRIP survey results, not by any would-be empirical needs/demands of political and social actors, nor by any substantive standards for assessing scholarly or practical significance of a given problem. And as the example of EIB decision anomaly demonstrates, there are real-world, practice-level implications and costs in such arbitrary exclusion of certain types of knowledge and means of attaining it – empirical results can end up contradicting theoretical assumptions underpinning research models.

If post-structuralist knowledge forms and critical claims about SGC are not valid, they should not be having any real effects in real-world situations. If they are found to be having such effects, as determined so on empirical grounds, then they should be included in synergetic analytic framework.

Their validity is not absolute – theoretical claims remain open to empirical challenge but the focus always remains on the ontological pivot around which these contested claims are being made. And it is not enough simply to extricate theoretical concepts, logics, mechanisms from single-paradigm or synthesis models of SGC and then attempt to translate and selectively integrate them into a new holistic analytic framework.

Synergetic theorizing must go further and requires looking at causal dynamics and reactive relationships between these analytic elements in real time and identifying how these are manifested in real world situations and in political outcomes, for example, the EIB decision on SGC funding.

Post-structuralist challenge to SGC funding is clearly a normative standpoint grown out of concern over environmental, social and economic consequences of the project. Yet it is not simply a case of opposition to a specific modernist enterprise, but a statement against the prevailing social order that the project represents and the EIB decision, therefore, is assessed in these contexts.

For example, interests of marginalized groups affected by the pipeline are set within a wider counter-hegemonic narrative of a post-fossil fuel energy future:

Communities in Italy, like the people of Melendugno, have been bravely resisting this pipeline in the face of fascist-era laws. Now, everyone that has been demanding the European Investment Bank defund the Trans Adriatic Pipeline just got the decision on a €1.5bn delayed until next year. This is a massive blow to this dangerous new pipeline – we're turning the tide on new fossil fuel projects. TAP will not go ahead (Ratcliffe, in CEE Bankwatch, 12.12.2017).

The climate paradox at the heart of the project, together with the human rights abuses, impacts on local communities and corruption links associated with it have made it harder and harder for the EU's bank to endorse. (Sol in CEE Bankwatch, 12.12.2017).

From a neo-Gramscian critical perspective the focus of counter-hegemonic efforts is not the state but institutions such as the EIB and EU – transnational networks underpinning global capitalist hegemony (Cox, 1981; 1983). The thrust of the anti-SGC campaign, led by international coalition of counter-hegemonic forces, is directed at these networks, with the aim of redirecting their function towards advancement of emancipatory interest.

In fact, these forces are often purposefully formed to target specific elements of these transitional networks – anti-SGC NGOs such as CounterBalanace operate on a normative mission "to make European public finance a key driver of the transition towards socially and environmentally sustainable and equitable societies" (CounterBalance, 2017).

Rationalists underestimated pertinence of post-positivist insights and normative concerns, just as proponents and sponsors of SGC underestimated potency of civic forces opposing them. The extent of these mistakes is underscored by the wider turn taking place – EIB decision is a reflection of changes transforming global energy order, as it moves away from fossil fuels towards renewable, sustainable future: "Clearly it was too much even for the EIB to fund this fossil fuel mega project on the anniversary of the Paris Agreement – now they should make sure that 2018 sees them end support for fossil fuels entirely" (CEE Bankwatch, 12.12.2017)

The EIB's decision on SGC not only coincided with the second anniversary of the Paris Climate Accord but occurred on the same day as the One Planet Summit – gathering of global financial organizations to develop strategies for implementing the Paris climate accord and "to strengthen the financial sector's involvement in combating climate change, financing the energy transition and the adaptation to global warming" (Climate Finance Day. 11.12.2017, No 252, 11.12.2017; Harvey, 12.12.2017).

On the same day, 12 December 2017, the World Bank, one of SGC funders, announced its divestment from fossil fuel projects: "As a global multilateral development institution, the World Bank Group is continuing to transform its own operations in recognition of a rapidly changing world. To align its support to countries to meet their Paris goals: The World Bank Group will no longer finance upstream oil and gas, after 2019." (World Bank, 12.12.2017).

As important and symbolic as these developments undoubtedly are, it is worth considering that the World Bank, EBRD and other financial institutions, as well as individual states, have already agreed and approved funding for various sections of SGC project. Furthermore, EIB merely postponed its decision and did in the end approve the €1.5bln record-breaking credit to the TAP segment of Southern Gas Corridor:

> As part of the Southern Gas Corridor, the project will create a new European gas transmission corridor. This diversification of gas supply routes and sources will increase security of gas supply and reduce energy dependence. It is also classified as a Project of Common Interest (EIB, 06.02.2018).

For all their claims, post-positivist empirical programme and its associated normative-political project cannot account for persistence of power relations between states and the extent to which material factors determine state identities and interests. This leads to persistent overemphasising of ideational factors, even in the face of obvious empirical facts.

For example, Azerbaijan's withdrawal from the Extractive Industries Transparency Initiative (EITI) in 2017 was widely heralded as the death knell for prospects of international financing of SGC: "The withdrawal throws into doubt current and future financing for Azerbaijan's contribution to the $46bn Southern Gas Corridor pipeline to connect its Caspian Sea gas fields to European markets" (Foy, 10.03.2017).

EITI is an international organization, comprised of governments, NGOs and energy companies that sets "the global standard for the good governance of oil, gas and mineral resources" (EITI Standard, 2017). The Standard is meant to ensure transparency and accountability in energy politics across a broad spectrum of criteria, from how exploration rights are issued, to how the resources are monetized and how this advances public interest in resource-rich countries (Rogan (Ed.), 2016).

The European Investment Bank, EBRD, World Bank, European Commission and other multilateral institutions are official partners of EITI and employ its country assessments and compliance reports as regulatory frameworks in assessing funding applications; therefore, Azerbaijan's withdrawal raised questions over SGC: "Azerbaijan's EITI status has taken on greater significance amid discussions with international lenders such as the World Bank and the European Bank for Reconstruction and Development for billions of dollars in loans to fund its share of the Southern Gas Corridor project" (Farchy, 26.10.2016).

In early 2017 Azerbaijan was suspended for non-compliance on human rights grounds, after EITI International Board found that the country "did not fully meet the corrective actions related to civil society space" (EITI Board paper 36-5-A, 09.03.2017). The very next day Azerbaijan unilaterally withdrew from the organization (EITI, 20.03.2017).

Human rights NGOs have sought to use EITI Standard to hold Azerbaijani government accountable over human rights abuses and persecution of civil society, and argued that the country's suspension and withdrawal from the body should "...raise red flags for international financial institutions... which have publicly endorsed the EITI and committed to participation, transparency, and accountability" (Gogia, 10.03.2017).

Funding SGC and other Azerbaijan-led energy projects would lead to erosion of public scrutiny and international normative standards (Mammadov, 20.01.2017). Revoking EITI membership was widely assessed as having major detrimental impact on SGC financial viability: "Azerbaijan's membership in the EITI is considered a key asset to the country's oil and natural gas economy. As a result of leaving the EITI, Azerbaijan might be regarded as ineligible for future loans by the World Bank and other international institutions for projects, such as the Southern Gas Corridor Project (TAP&TANAP)" (Allili and Bitner, 2017, p.3; pp.6-7).

In reality, however, SGC continued to receive financial support from multilateral organizations, with EBRD and World Bank (EITI partners) proceeding to approve new funds despite Azerbaijan's withdrawal and civil society protests. EIB's statement in February 2018, issued after approving TAP funding, simply read: "During the EIB appraisal of TAP, the European External Action Service has confirmed that despite its withdrawal from the Extractive Industries Transparency Initiative (EITI), Azerbaijan is developing, in line with EITI requirements, standards of transparent extractive revenue management" (EIB, 06.02.2018).

In November 2017 the Trump administration took the United States out of EITI compliance mechanisms and the organization dropped out of SGC debates (Simon, 02.11.2017). There are, therefore, limits to how far post-positivist claims can be taken. Post-structuralist single-paradigm models on their own fail to sufficiently account for persistence of state power and strategic-materialist interests underpinning it. The author of this book can confidently predict that no Western-led international financial institution, such as World Bank, EIB, EBRD will be funding fossil fuel projects anywhere in the world by 2030. But China will and so will others.

In summary, neo-realist analysis sets developments around SGC funding in the context of state action - environmental and energy politics as platforms for exercising state power and advancing strategic interests.

Neo-liberal argument explains state action in terms of ideas, such as climate change, and institutions, such as the EIB.

Social-constructivism, in turn, examines how state power, actions and interests are constituted by ideational forces – "the meaning of power and the content of interests are largely a function of ideas" (Wendt, 1999, p. 96; p.134; see chapter V). Anti-positivist, post-structuralist critiques challenge dominant ideational orthodoxies and set out alternative normative and political agendas for changing the prevailing social order, and these are now beginning to have political effects.

These single-paradigm models as well as their synthetic and eclectic configurations, provide useful analytical frameworks that shed light on specific elements of a puzzle and explain certain aspects of a phenomena, as they spin on a single ontological pivot, in this case the issue of SGC financing. The resulting synergetic picture is larger than the sum of its constituent parts.

There are clearly multiple causal explanations for why the European Investment Bank had not agreed funding for the Trans-Adriatic Pipeline segment of Southern Gas Corridor in 2017; then approved it in 2018.

States have multiple, evolving identities and interests, which come about through continuous interplay of both social and material forces – they are not necessarily in alignment. The European Commission, representing collective interests of EU member states, is committed to implementing Paris Climate Accord commitments and to building new gas transmission pipelines: "By 2020, the EU aims to reduce its greenhouse gas emissions by at least 20%, increase the share of renewable energy to at least 20% of consumption, and achieve energy savings of 20% or more" (EU Commission, 2020 Energy Strategy, 2018).

"A key part of ensuring secure and affordable supplies of energy to Europeans involves diversifying supply routes. This includes identifying and building new routes that decrease the dependence of EU countries on a single supplier of natural gas and other energy resources" (EU Commission, Gas and Oil Supply Routes, 2018).

EIB's prolonged indecision on SGC funding arises out of this maelstrom of competing identities and contradictory interests as they are manifested in state actions and institutional dynamics. Ideas about the environment, climate change and energy are undergoing a major shift, not least due to growing democratic pressure, global environmental movements and coordinated actions of international civil society. Climate change agenda dominates political thinking in Europe and this is unlikely to change in the long-run, despite the economic impact of Covid 19 pandemic.

Changing norms cascade through institutional architecture of energy politics as states and other actors adapt to this new normative environment – from standard-setting international quangos, such as EITI to integration of environmental, social and human rights standards into decision-making processes around fossil-fuel projects. It is symbolic, perhaps, that research critical of SGC project, an EU-supported initiative, is often funded directly by agencies of the European Union (CEE Bankwatch, May 2017; Bacheva-McGrath et al, January 2015).

However, this change is running against a prevailing energy order, made up of powerful material and ideational forces – economic, technological, social and cultural forces borne out of over two centuries of fossil fuel consumption (see Yergin, 1991). EIB decision on SGC funding is mediated by material realities of European energy order and reflects European Union's key energy priorities.

The European Commission identifies dependence on energy imports as "…a particularly pressing issue, with the EU currently importing over half its energy at a cost of €350 billion per year. Other important challenges include rising global demand and the scarcity of fuels like crude oil, which contribute to higher prices. In addition, the continued use of fossil fuels in Europe is a cause of global warming and pollution" (EU Commission, Energy Strategy and Energy Union, 2017).

EU states' structural dependence on fossil fuels and dependence on Russia as chief supplier of natural gas, delivered through Russian-controlled pipelines is one factor determining EU energy strategy:

> About one quarter of all the energy used in the EU is natural gas, and many EU countries import nearly all their supplies. Some of these countries are also heavily reliant on a single source or a single transport route for the

majority of their gas. Disruptions along this route caused by infrastructure failure or political disputes can endanger supplies. For instance, the gas dispute between Russia and Ukraine in 2009 disrupted supplies to some EU countries (EU Commission, Secure Gas Supplies, 2017).

Conclusion

Operationalising tanker traffic through the Bosphorus or the EIB decision anomaly as inter-paradigmatic pivots in synergetic analytical framework shows that these substantive issues emerge out of a deeper ontology of global energy, comprising a complex multi-layered socio-political dynamic that cannot be reduced to or explained by reference to any single element or factor. Any theoretical claims about it can only be assessed or verified on the extent to which they correspond to the reality of political outcomes - it is only possible to make relatively more accurate judgements on balance of empirical evidence. By not excluding certain paradigmatic approaches in favor of others, TSA maximizes intellectual opportunity of a given research enterprise and expands the breadth and depth of the empirical pool.

Synergetic modelling of BTC and SGC projects enables greater elucidation of the co-constitutive function of socio-normative and physical-material elements that make up these complex, international structures. Perhaps the clearest empirical implication of synergetic theorizing about these pipelines is discovering the extent to which postmodernist, environmentalist, critical counter-narratives have impacted on political outcomes over the past twenty years.

By ignoring or underplaying transformative effect of structural normative change, rationalist paradigms consistently failed to account for real political changes it brings, not least implications of growing inter-state cooperation against the threat of climate change e.g. the Paris Agreement. By ignoring or underplaying strategic and geo-political factors, post-positivist approaches failed to account for persistence of power-relations and growing resource competition between states and historically consistent role played by national and international oil and gas companies, and multilateral financial institutions.

In November 2017 the European Commission included the Trans-Caspian Pipeline (TCP) proposal into its list of Projects of Common Interest, opening up possibility that the BTC/SGC system might be expanded East, opening up Turkmenistan's vast hydrocarbon reserves to European markets (EU Commission, 23.11.2017; Caspian Policy Center Editorial, 13.12.2017).

Caspian energy politics will continue to evolve and will continue to be shaped by competing dynamics of strategic and normative interests characterising them. How TCP is to be funded will again be at the heart of these tensions and antagonisms. Synergetic readings of Baku-Tbilisi-Ceyhan and Southern Gas Corridor pipelines can help better understand the course these future debates might take.

Conclusion

This book opened with Buzan and Little's question, "Has IR failed as an intellectual project?" (2001). This book proposes that the theory-synergetic approach (TSA) is animated by a belief that international relations has not merely escaped decline, but that it is a thriving intellectual project, which has the potential to serve as a meta-disciplinary enterprise, bringing together different strands of social science to bear upon issues of existential importance of global significance. Buzan and Little's ambition for IR as a holistic theoretical framework with a cross-disciplinary reach is realistic and credible (Ibid., p. 22).

TSA is an explicitly historicist, IR analytical technique that absorbs and integrates intellectual heritage of the Great Debates, viewing them as essential elements in the genealogy of the discipline (Smith, 1995, pp.1-37; Schmidt, 2013, pp. 3-28; Waever, 2011, p.98). TSA is grounded in historiography of IR – the structure of the discipline, shaped in the Great Debates, is viewed not as an impediment to scholarship in IR, but as its road-map - the intellectual prism through which to analyse substantive problems in world politics. Theories of international relations are the tools of our trade, the elements of our periodic table, the equipment of our laboratories, kaleidoscopic lenses through which we view the world.

As full implications of the Fourth Debate become clear, the field of IR is recast and reconstituted with a significantly expanded ontology and widened epistemological reach far beyond the narrow confines of positivism. Rather than view this as a challenge to IR disciplinary identity, TSA instead is designed to take advantage of new empirical opportunities.

TSA is an argument in favor of ontological primacy in IR – the purpose of the discipline is to get at the deeper ontology of world human affairs. Critical Realism provides TSA with its philosophical foundations and imbues it with a commitment to an open-ended social-scientific project, aimed at getting at the reality of international relations, without excluding or bracketing various forms of knowledge.

Taking theoretical pluralism in International Relations seriously requires moving away from attempts to place epistemological brackets on knowledge-production. We have seen that mid-range theorizing and eclectic approaches are limited in their pluralist applications by their restricted ontologies and metatheoretical assumptions. One of the key conclusions of this book is that excluding knowledge claims based on *a priori* foundational assumptions carries significant empirical costs – any advantages brought to research by enhanced parsimony are offset by considerable loss of explanatory and predictive analytical power.

TSA does seek to produce scholarship relevant to practice of world politics – the choice of international oil and gas politics as the empirical field and BTC/SGC projects as case-studies was not arbitrary. TSA, however, is not a proposal for a practice-orientated research programme; at its core, it is a proposal for applied critical realist philosophy of science in IR – an argument that echoes Pearson's remark: "The unity of science consists alone in its method, not its material" (1892, p.15).

A normative challenge for TSA, therefore, is that there are no in-built ethical commitments inherent to what is essentially a method or a technique for approaching substantive issues in international relations; in other words, anyone can use it. Providing that normative commitments are set out throughout intellectual process involved in any given research project, TSA could be used with equal success by adherents of any paradigmatic school of thought in IR or sponsors of any political cause.

This book is primarily a conceptual work - its treatment of the case-study of international oil politics is used here as a problem-field for testing synergetic techniques. However, it has been shown how applying different theoretical models synergetically increases the empirical yield of the study and enhances its analytical impact by pooling different bodies of scholarship, knowledge claims and normative arguments in a maelstrom of ontological and epistemological contestation. It is hoped that the case-study of oil politics in this book served to underline its key argument that theoretical disagreements in IR can be used as tools to advance knowledge about substantive issues in international relations.

To harness the inherent power of IR theoretical pluralism TSA is advanced as a common methodological culture – a language, an analytical toolkit - by means of which scholars can utilize and apply different theories to the limitless substantive field of the science of international relations. A metaphor for IR theories as lenses through which to see different aspects of the same material reality has sometimes been employed (Smith, 2014). The objective is both – to find out about things that occur in stories and about their effect in any given story (Tolkien, 1983, p.121).

Oil is a fascinating topic in its own right; it has a primordial and perennial quality to it and yet is pervasive and persistent in its presence in everyday life. Questions about oil and energy go to the very heart of foundational and normative debates in IR and at the same time have immediate, urgent relevance to real-world political practice. It is arguably an existential global phenomenon, which is perhaps why it generates such partisan academic coverage and public debate.

Yet, it was shown in this book that a deeper, truer reality of international oil politics is to be found in the empirical overlaps and commonalities between competing claims and bodies of knowledge. Synergetic analysis pivots upon these inter-paradigmatic connections, constructing more holistic, multidimensional representations of the reality of oil politics than would be possible with single-paradigm or even eclectic approaches.

Rationalist discourses around BTC and SGC pipelines are underpinned by a materialist paradigm of oil and gas politics – these projects are ultimately about power, state and corporate. This is the core of the rationalist models or rather model, for both projects constitute a single geo-political enterprise that has its antecedents in past historical power relations.

Reflectivist critiques, meanwhile, pose a foundational challenge to the dominant materialist-rationalist conception of the role BTC, SGC and Caspian hydrocarbons play in international energy order. They fundamentally question the prevailing fossil-fuelled social order, expose its costs and existential risks it may pose, and sets out a politically and normatively charged praxeological programme aimed at preventing the pipelines from being built in the first place.

Modelling these competing paradigmatic accounts within a common empirical historical timeline offers new theoretical-comparative perspectives, establishing clear conceptual overlaps and thematic commonalities across theoretical spectrum. Operationalising these overlaps and commonalities (e.g. BTC environmental factors or the SGC funding) as inter-paradigmatic pivots in synergetic analytical framework shows that theoretical claims about substantive issues can only be assessed or falsified upon the extent to which they correspond to the reality of political outcomes (to empirical truth).

For example, the persistence of empirical anomalies in single-paradigm mono-causal explanations of issues around international public funding of corporate energy projects, reflects both - the extent to which the anti-positivist intellectual agenda has been ignored and excluded by mainstream scholarship, and the extent to which post-positivist approaches overlook strategic factors and overemphasize prescriptive normative politics.

Applying synergetic reasoning illuminates these shortcomings in single-paradigm (and eclectic) theorizing and reveals underlying cross-theoretical causal mechanisms determining outcomes in pipeline politics and wider oil and gas developments. Applying TSA systematically across the entire political expanse of the Caspian hydrocarbons helps identify evolving trends in global energy politics and draw conclusions about other pipeline projects elsewhere in the world.

Rather than viewing these mono-theoretical sing-paradigm accounts in opposition to each other, TSA generates greater empirical clarity and insights by engaging with them simultaneously in real time. A history of international oil politics is necessarily made up of different *stories* about international oil politics. Theoretical synergy holds that these stories weave into a grand Tolkienesque picture, each a particular thread but together they make for a tapestry greater than the sum of the individual threads that make it up.

Appendices

1. International politics of oil:
a classical liberal research programme

A brush-stroke chronological overview of the ontological map of the classical liberal theoretical model of international oil politics.

- **1860s**
  - The rise of *Standard Oil Company* (see, for example, Fursenko, 1972; Montague, 2001 [1903]; Tarbell, 2003 [1904].
  - The birth of the modern oil industry driven by private enterprise and capital.
- **1870s**
  - The establishment of the *Nobels'* oil business in Baku, Russia (see, for example, Asbrink, 2002; Tolf, 1976).
  - Invention of oil tankers and the rise of intercontinental kerosene trade: emergence of international competitive commerce.
- **1880s - 1890s**
  - The growing role of banking, finance and credit in the oil industry;
  - The establishment of the Rothschilds' oil enterprise in Russia (see, for example, Lottman, 1995; Fursenko & Freeze, 1990).
  - The launch in 1883 of the Rothschilds-financed Baku-Batum railroad which, "opened a door to the West for Russian oil, it also initiated a fierce, thirty-year struggle for the oil markets of the world" (Yergin, 1991, p. 61).
  - The establishment of *Shell Transport and Trading Company* and the Royal Dutch oil business in East Indies (see, for example, Howarth, 1997; Luiten van Zanden et al, 2007).
  - The opening of the Suez Canal to oil tanker traffic (see Woodman, 1998).
- **1900s**
  - The invention of internal combustion engine and the birth of the automotive industry, fuelled by gasoline; mass conversion of industry from coal to oil.

- Rise of new oil companies, such as Texaco, and the growth of independent producers in the United States and beyond.
- Emergence of a competitive global market in petroleum with U.S. and Russia as key areas of production.
- The growth of domestic and international regulation and anti-trust measures; Ida Tarbell's expose of J. D. Rockefeller and Standard Oil published (2003 [1904]).

- **1910s**
  - Dissolution of *Standard Oil* (in 1911) and the emergence of successor-companies: *Standard Oil of New Jersey* (later *Exxon*), *Standard Oil of New York* (later *Mobil*), *Standard Oil of California* (later *Chevron*), *Standard Oil of Ohio* (later part of *BP*), *Standard oil of Indiana* (later *Amoco* – later part of *BP*) and others (Yergin, 1991, p. 110).
  - The "Oil Wars:" period of intense competition between oil companies and independent producers around the world.
  - The establishment and growth of *Anglo-Persian Oil Company* (*APOC*, later *Anglo-Iranian Oil Company* (*AIOC*), later *BP*) and the first Iranian concession.
  - Evolution of international commercial law, contract law and international legal agreements: the use of "Concessions," agreements granting companies "exclusive right to exploration, development and hydrocarbon production operations in a defined area for a limited period of time" (Parra, 2013, p.9) See, for example, Cattan, 1967b).
  - World War I 1914-1918: APOC contract with the Royal Navy in 1914 and the role of private cpital in military politics of oil; motorisation of oil and invention of the tank; 1916 Inter-Allied Petroleum Conference and international cooperation in distribution of oil supplies among Allied powers.

- **1920s**
  - Soviet capture of Baku and expropriation of oil businesses in Russia.
  - Post- World War I normative framework; Wilson's "Fourteen Points" (especially in relation to the Iraq Concession and the Red Line Agreement.
  - The Iraq Concession and the Red Line Agreement: opening up of the oil industry and establishment of multilateral corporate consortiums.
  - Growth of the global petroleum industry and rising supplies in the age of automobile.

- Anglo-Soviet Trade Agreement and opening up of Soviet oil to foreign involvement (see, for example, Ebel, 1978; McBeth, 1985).
- Achnacarry "As-Is" Agreement to control production (see Bamberg, 1994, pp. 528-34; Yergin, 1991, pp. 243-248).
- Wall Street Crash of 1929 and its impact on the oil industry.
- **1930s**
  - The Great Depression and the crisis in the oil industry.
  - The New Deal in the United States and a new regulatory framework for the oil industry.
  - Evolution of the "As-Is" agreements to control production (supply) of oil on the market.
  - Disruptive effects of growing nationalism, protectionism, autarkic tendencies and militarisation of oil economies.
  - Withdrawal of Soviet oil from global markets; cancellation of concessions in Iran (in 1932) and nationalisation of oil fields in Mexico (in 1938).
  - First Arabian concessions in Kuwait, Bahrain and Saudi Arabia; competition between British and American international oil companies.
  - The oil industries of Japan, Germany and Italy.

2. International politics of oil: a classical realist research programme

A brush-stroke chronological overview of the ontological map of the classical realist theoretical model of international oil politics.

- **1900-1920**
  - European naval race and motorisation of war;
  - British government acquisition of controlling stake in Anglo-Persian Oil Company; the Royal Navy contract and switch from coal to oil fuel (see, for example, Jack, 1968, pp.139-168)
  - Inter-state competition for control of oil sources between dominant national powers such as Britain and the U.S., and new challengers, such as imperial Germany and Ottoman empire (see, for example, McBeth, 1985).
  - World War I: oil as the fuel of military effort; use of oil blockades against Central Powers by the Allies;
  - Growth of state economic power and direct government intervention in the oil market (Yergin, 1991 p. 178), e.g. creation of the British Export Credit Guarantee Department (ECGD) (see, for example, Carr, 1981 (1939), p. 116).

- emergence of "Concessions" as means of state policy for both producing and consuming nations (see, for example, Cattan, 1967a).
- Production and transportation of petroleum as a strategic element of state power and instrument of state policy -oil and balance of power.

- **1920s**
  - Russian Revolution and the Soviet capture of Baku (April 1920); expropriation of oil businesses; Lenin's New Economic Policy and the rise of Soviet oil industry (Yergin, 1991, pp.237-243).
  - Oil and imperialism: San Remo Agreement of 1919 and the carve up of the Ottoman Empire; Franco-British competition in Iraq and U.S. entry into oil politics in the Middle East (see, for example, Jones, 1977).
  - Oil and imperialism: The Red Line Agreement of 1928 and the assertion of American power in the Middle East; the Great Powers and oil companies (see, for example, Blair, 1976; Davenport & Cooke, 1923).
  - Emergence of Mexico and Venezuela as major petroleum producers; U.S. involvement in South American oil industry (see, for example, Lieuwen, 1954).

- **1930s**
  - The Great Depression and its impact on the oil industry; growth of state interventionism, regulation and nationalisation (see, for example, Ely, 1938; Nash, 1968; Nordhauser, 1979; Painter, 1986; Ikenberry, 1988; Libecap, 1989): "As a result of the Depression, autarchy and bilateralism were the order of the day in the 1930s, with consequent pressure to circumscribe the major oil companies" (Yergin, 1991, p. 269);
  - Soviet oil industry and the balance of power;
  - Rise of nationalism: expropriation of the Mexican oil industry and U.S.-Mexican relations (see, for example, Gordon, 1975).
  - "As-Is" Agreement Draft Memorandum (1934) and the national oil carters; politicisation of the oil industry;
  - Oil producing countries and the shifting balance of power: USSR, renegotiation of the Iranian concession, expropriation in Mexico;
  - The first Arab concessions: Saudi Arabia, Kuwait, Bahrain; decline of Britain and the rise of U.S. power in the Middle East: "The Sheikh believed that the entry of an American oil company into Kuwait would bring American politician

interest, which he could use to bolster his position against Britain, as well as against regional rivals" (Yergin, 1991, p.294).
- Japanese, Italian, German oil industries.
- **1940s**
  - The Allied and Axis oil strategies in World War II (see, for example, Ickes, 1943a); Soviet war oil effort (see, for example, Agayev et al, 1995);
  - Oil as a critical strategic resource;
  - Middle East as the new oil center of global political gravity;
  - Growing direct state involvement in international oil politics e.g. establishment of U.S. Petroleum Reserves Corporation, Anglo-American Petroleum Agreement of 1944, setting up of International Petroleum Commission and other measures to control supply/demand;
  - February 1945 meeting between President Roosevelt and Ibn Saud and the start of U.S.-Saudi oil alliance; *Arabian American Oil Company (ARAMCO)* as instrument of national policy.
  - The post-war political economy of oil;
  - The Iranian Crisis of 1946 and American entry into Iranian oil.
  - Establishment of the State of Israel.
  - Truman Doctrine, Marshall Plan and growth of American power in the Middle East and the end of the Red Line Agreement.
- **1950s**
  - Oil producing vs oil-consuming countries and the shifting balance of power: "In other words, a state which has nothing to go on by way of power, which is lacking in all the elements which traditionally have gone into making of national power, suddenly have become a powerful factor in world politics because it has one important asset – oil. This is indeed an event which is of revolutionary importance in world politics" (Morgenthau, p. 134).
  - Nationalism, decolonisation, anti-imperialism, and the struggle for control of oil resources: renegotiation of concessions and the 50/50% principle from Venezuela to Saudi Arabia.
  - The Iranian Crisis of 1953 (overthrow of Prime Minister Mossadegh); The Suez Crisis.
  - U.S. anti-trust action against oil majors and international concession consortiums in Middle East: "...one of the first of many instances when the United States was to pursue

simultaneously two diametrically opposed policies in the idle East" (Parra, 2010; see also Sampson, 1975); National oil companies vs. the Seven Sisters (see Sampson, 1975).
- Arab Oil Congress of April 1959 and the beginnings of the Organization of Petroleum Exporting Countries (OPEC).

3. International politics of oil: a rationalist research programme

A brush-stroke chronological overview of the ontological map of the rationalist model of international oil politics.

- • **1950s – 1970s**
  - Cold War and oil politics in the 1950s/early 1960s: Western-controlled production vs. Soviet-controlled production; oil companies and price wars (see, for example, Hartshorn, 1962; Nash, 1968; Painter, S.D., 1984; 1986; 2009a; 2010; Williamson, 1963);
  - Establishment of *Organization of Petroleum Exporting Countries* (OPEC) in 1960;
  - dynamics in relations between and among petroleum producing countries: case studies Iran/Saudi Arabia, Libya; (see, for example, Sampson, 1976, pp. 179-197; Shwardan, 1974; Mikdashi, 1972).
  - The Six Day War of 1967, the first embargo (OPEC and the emergence of the "oil weapon"); (see, Sampson, 1976, pp. 187-190; Parra, 2013, pp. 89-113).
  - British military withdrawal from the Gulf 197.1
  - The *Texas Railroad Commission* and the regulated oil market in the U.S.A (see, for example, Nash, 1968; Libecap, 1989; Prindle, 1981).
  - Tehran and Tripoli Agreements of 1971, establishing 55 percent as the minimum government stake for producing countries' (OPEC): "The Tehran Agreement marked a watershed; initiative had passed for the companies to the exporting countries" (Ibid., p. 582); "The companies had revealed at Teheran and Tripoli their fundamental weakness, that they could not collaborate either with each other, or with their government" (Sampson, 1976, p. 240); OPEC and oil-importing countries: participation vs. nationalisation: "For various reasons – historical, international, political and economic – the process of the gains of the producing countries was slow and the achievements were very limited. However, the more the producers proceeded with their efforts

the more determined and persistent they became" (Shwardan, 1977, p. 3).

- Yom Kippur War, October 1973 and the first oil shock: embargo; USSR and the OPEC embargo; the tactics and strategy of the embargo: The overall plan was very shrewd; the prospect of monthly cutbacks, plus the differentiation among the consuming countries, would maximise uncertainty, tension, and rivalry within and among the importing countries. One clear objective of the plan was to split the industrial countries right from the start (Yergin, 1991, p. 608); (re)balancing of power redux and the implications of the 1973-74 embargo: "After two decades of talk and several failed attempts, the oil weapon had finally been successfully used... and it had remade the international economy. Now it could be re-sheathed. But the threat would remain" (Ibid., p. 632); "These sovereign states, with their own precious resources had taken a long time to awaken to the need to safeguard their wealth, and to combine to confront the companies" (Sampson, 1976, p.370).

- OPEC after the embargo: from rent redistribution to. "a wholesale redistribution of both economic and political power" (Yergin, 1991, p. 634); intra-OPEC dynamics: Iran, and Saudi Arabia, Venezuela (see, for example, Parra, 2013 [2010], pp. 189-214).

- Establishment of the *International Energy Agency* in 1974 to help importing countries co-ordinate a collective response to major disruptions in the supply of oil;

- oil companies and new production (North Sea, Alaska and Mexico); the United States and energy conservation move; ban on U.S. oil exports (1975) (see Parra, 2013, pp. 257-275); U.S. Energy Policy and Conservation Act and the establishment of the Strategic Petroleum Reserve (in 1975).

- The Iranian Revolution of 1979 and the second oil shock: "another victory for oil power" (Yergin, 1991, p. 698).

- Jimmy Carter administration and the "the moral equivalent of war:" "The energy crisis is real. It is worldwide. It is a clear and present danger to our Nation. These are facts and we simply must face them" (Carter, 1979).

- Soviet invasion of Afghanistan in Dec 1979.

- **1980s**
  - The Carter Doctrine (1980) and the establishment of the U.S. Rapid Deployment Force (the Central Command).
  - Iraq's invasion of Iran in Sep. 1980.
  - "State power or market power?:" restructuring of the oil market and decline of OPEC; rapid growth of spot markets;

introduction of futures markets in oil at the *New York Mercantile Exchange* (NYMEX) (1983);

- deregulation of the oil industry e.g. abolition of *British National Oil Company* (BNOC) in 1985 and the sale of UK government shares in BP.
- decline of integrated corporate systems in the oil industry and the emergence of international oil trading companies; mergers and acquisitions: "Once it had been Standard Oil that had set the price. Then it had been the Texas Railroad Commission system in the United States and the majors in the rest of the world. Then it was OPEC. Now the price was being established, every day, instantaneously, on the open market, in the interaction of the floor traders on the Nymex with buyers and sellers glued to computer screens all over the world" (Yergin, 1991, pp.725-726).
- The battle for the market-share and the price collapse of 1986: Saudi Arabia as "balancing" producer in the early 1980s "explicitly charged with the responsibility of raising and lowering its output to balance the market and maintain the price" (Yergin, 1991, p. 721); for example, OPEC Vienna Conference agreement of 1982: "It should be added that Saudi Arabia was one of the few OPEC member countries, if not the only one, to fulfil its obligations, however couched under the production program adopted" (Parra, 2013 [2010], p. 278).
- The impact of the third oil shock and the scramble for the market share.
- The United States, Reagan and the third oil shock; OPEC Geneva meeting (Dec 1986); OPEC, non-OPEC and Soviet cooperation and competition on quotas/production cuts.
- Iraq-Iran war and U.S./Soviet rivalry (ceasefire 1987) (see, for example, Smolansky and Smolansky, 1991).
- Establishment of the *Intergovernmental Panel on Climate Change* (IPCC) 1988: "a self-regulating, self-governing organism, a coordinated network of research scientists who worked across borders, facilitated by cheaper and better communications" (Yergin, 2012, p. 465): "By endorsing the IPCC reports, governments acknowledge the authority of their scientific content. The work of the organization is therefore policy-relevant and yet policy-neutral, never policy-prescriptive" (IPCC website, 2016).
- *Exxon Valdez* disaster 1989: environmental threats/ securitisation of climate debates: "the almost incomprehensible costs and disruption... that could result if there is a major climate change;" two competing themes:

"energy and security, and energy and the environment" (Yergin, 1991, p. 779).

- **1990s**
  - Iraq's invasion of Kuwait (Aug 1990): "Iraq was a closed police state, but Saddam Hussein's objectives seemed clear: to dominate the Arab world, to gain hegemony over the Persian Gulf, to make Iraq into the predominant oil power – and ultimately to turn Greater Iraq into a global military power" (Ibid., p. 771); U.S. deployment of troops to Saudi Arabia and Saddam Hussein's miscalculation, which showed "that Saddam had failed to comprehend fully the central role of oil in global geopolitics:" "Under no circumstances was an American president going to let an Iraqi leader bolster his oil reserves to the extent of challenging the Saudi monopoly as OPEC's swing producer" (Hiro, 2007, 0.128).
  - OPEC and the first Gulf War: OPEC increased production "further isolating Iraq and, in effect, underlining their commitment to a new alignment with their customers" (Yergin, 1991, p. 772); the war aims: "...first, the elimination of potential Iraqi control over Saudi Arabia's and the UAE's oil; and, second, retention of Iraq as a single political unit strong enough (eventually) to act as a counterweight to Iran" (Parra, 2013 [2010], p. 302).
  - The collapse of USSR (1991): the collapse of the Soviet oil industry and oil politics of the post-Soviet Russia; oligarchs and the Russian oil majors: "These companies – Lukoil, Surgut and Yukos – were the three majors. They were not alone by any means. There remained the state company, Rosneft; six 'mini-majors;' and a number of other companies, including those owned or sponsored by oil-rich regional governments" (Yergin, 2012, p. 31); TNK/BP deal and the return of international oil companies; Kremlin vs oil companies (see, for example, LeVine, 2007; Bower, 2009).
  - The new "Great Game:" the struggle for Caspian oil and gas reserves: Azerbaijan, Kazakhstan, Russia, Iran and Turkmenistan; issues of production and transportation; pipeline geopolitics; Russia, the U.S., Europe, Caspian states and international oil companies: "With as many as 200 billion barrels of oil and trillions of cubic meters of natural gas at stake, the new 'Great Game' on the shores of the Caspian will have an impact not only on the world's energy supply, but also on the very geopolitical map of Eurasia in the next century" (Croissant and Aras, 1999, xv); (see also, for example, Yergin, 2012, pp. 44-83; Kandiyoti, 2012, pp. 154-202; Tsalik, 2003; Hiro, 2007, pp.149-172; LeVine, 2007).

- The Asian financial crisis of 1997 and the collapse in oil prices: "the largest and most significant remaking of the structure of the international oil industry since 1911" (Yergin, 2012, p. 88; p.106);
- the super-mergers and "integration:" BP and Amoco (1998) and Arco (1999); Exxon and Mobil (1999), Total and Elf (1999), Conoco and Phillips (2001) (see, for example, Ibid., pp. 174 – 237).
- Oil and security: Nigeria and the Delta, and Venezuela and Chavez: "The complex conflict involved broad militant alliances like MEND… which combined lethal attacks and sabotage of oil installations with the effective use of global media to publicize its campaign of 'fighting for the control of oil revenues by indigenes of the Niger Delta'" (Obi and Rastad, 2011, p..20); "Chavez made a decisive policy change that would reverberate throughout the world. Venezuela would no longer pursue a strategy of increasing revenues by increasing outputs" (Yergin, 2012, p.125); "With prices solidifying, Chavez set his sights on his other goal: unifying the nearly collapsed Organization of Petroleum Exporting Countries. He had a grand vision. He wanted to organize the second summit in the group's history. And he wanted to hold it in Caracas" (Jones, 2008, p. 279).
- Oil, energy, climate and security: Rio Earth Summit 1992 and the U.N. Framework Convention on Climate Change, aimed to achieve "stabilization of greenhouse gas concentrations in the atmosphere at a level that would prevent dangerous anthropogenic interference with the climate system" (UNFCCC, Article 2, 1992); the contentions around Kyoto agreement (1997) between Europe, U.S., Russia and the developing countries; emergence of carbon emissions trading: Emissions trading, as set out in Article 17 of the Kyoto Protocol, allows countries that have emission units to spare - emissions permitted them but not "used" - to sell this excess capacity to countries that are over their targets. Thus, a new commodity was created in the form of emission reductions or removals. Since carbon dioxide is the principal greenhouse gas, people speak simply of trading in carbon. Carbon is now tracked and traded like any other commodity. This is known as the "carbon market." (UNFCCC, 2014b).

- **2000s**
  - 11 September 2001 and the new international politics of oil: "Petroleum had, since the beginning of the twentieth century, been entwined with security and the power and position of nations. But 9/11 led to a new emphasis on oil's risks,

including the fact that the world's biggest oil region, the Middle East, was also the region from which Al Qaeda had emerged" (Yergin, 2012, p. 129).

- war on terrorism and oil; U.S.- led invasion of Afghanistan. Iran and the sanctions regime.
- U.S.- led invasion of Iraq (2003) and the second Gulf War.
- hurricane Catrina and the impact on the oil industry and markets: "While it will always be unhelpful to view climate as 'the enemy,' it makes eminent sense to realize that its impacts, whether in the form of natural disasters or slow build-up of stress, can affect security in an insecure world" (Montgomery, 2010, p. 275)
- The "financialization of oil," electronic trading in oil derivatives, emergence of speculative oil markets: "Oil was no longer just a physical commodity, required to fuel cars and airplanes. It really had become something new – and much more abstract. Now these paper barrels were also, in the form of futures and derivatives, a financial instrument, a financial asset." (Yergin, 2012, p. 173).
- The rise of China and implications for international oil politics: growing demand, consumption and the emergence of international "national" oil companies (INOCs); U.S./China rivalry and oil supplies (see, for example, Andrews-Speed et all, 2014).
- Russian oil and gas industry and policy: Europe and *Gazprom*, the fall of *Yukos* and the fate of international oil companies; gas pipeline contest in Eastern Europe, Caspian and Mediterranean; Russian action against Georgia (2008) and Ukraine (2014) and Western responses (see, for example, Sim, 2008; Gustafson, 2012; Henderson and Ferguson, 2014; Cornell and Frederick Starr, 2015; Grant, 2015).
- European (energy) Union and energy security of Europe: diversification of supplies, policy coordination/contestation and political cooperation/competition; European pipeline politics (see Buchan and Beay, 2016).
- Peaking prices and the Peak Oil movement; the oil bubble, rising demand and the $148 barrel (July 2008); another rebalancing, consuming countries vs. OPEC, Russia, other non-OPEC producers (see, Roberts, 2005 [2004]).
- Oil markets and the Lehman Brothers collapse, the financial crash of 2008 and the resulting global recession.
- The race for alternative and renewable fuels – new race for the Arctic (see Klare, 2012).

- **2010s**
  - The Arab Spring and energy security: "The turmoil that swept over much of North Africa and part of the Middle East in 2011 and 2012 disrupted supplies and added a fear premium to the oil price" (Yergin, 2012, p. 267); civil war in Syria and the emergence of an Islamic State oil industry; (re)securitization of oil (cyber threats, piracy, terrorism).
  - Middle Eastern oil politics: lifting of sanctions on Iranian oil exports (2016); resurgent Iran vs. Saudi Arabia and Gulf states; Russia and non-OPEC producers; the oil glut and the collapse in price 2013-2016 ($30 per barrel).
  - The road to a comprehensive agreement on carbon emissions cut: an international climate regime: The United States, the European Union, China, India, and Brazil; Copenhagen Summit (2009); Cancun and Durban (2010/2011); Paris Agreement under the United Nations Framework Convention on Climate Change (Dec 2015).
  - U.S. Congressional lifting of the ban on U.S. oil exports (Dec 2015): "In places like Albuquerque, Youngstown, Detroit, and Kansas City, nearly all post-recession growth has been driven by exports." (Penny Pritzker, U.S. Secretary of Commerce, quoted in American Petroleum Institute, 2015, p. 2), (see, also Harder and Lynn, 16.02.16)

4. International politics of oil:
a classical Marxist research programme

- **PRE-INDUSTRIAL PERIOD**
  - Oil production and trade in the Middle Ages; oil under the Feudal system (see, for example, Latham (Marco Polo), 1958, p.48).
  - Development of early kerosene-industry (1800s) (see, for example, Bell, 1930; Owen, 1975, Loris, 2003).
- **1850s-1900s**
  - The birth of the capitalist oil industry in Pennsylvania, U.S.A in 1859: commerce + finance + engineering (Rock Oil and Seneca Oil companies) (see, for example, AMIW, 1901); oil, as raw material, first enters the production cycle and acquires "use-value," as capitalists seek "a new source for the raw material that went into an existing established process" (Yergin, 1991, p.25); beginnings of kerosene trade (on natural resources and "use-value/surplus value" see Marx, 1978 [1867], pp. 344-361); division of labor in the

early oil industry and the emergence of the oil proletariat in the United States.
- U.S. Civil War and the beginnings of international kerosene trade between U.S. and Europe and trans-nationalisation of capital; growth of internal U.S. kerosene/petroleum market; development of key characteristics of its commercial and financial systems.
- Establishment and growth of *Standard Oil Company* in the U.S. and *Nobel Petroleum Company* in Russian Azerbaijan; the First Baku Oil Boom; Rothschilds and the role of finance in the Baku oil industry; establishment of the Caspian and Black Sea Petroleum Company (*Bnito*) (see, for example, Henry, 1905).
- The rise and organization of the oil proletariat, revolutionary activity and the beginnings of class struggle in the U.S. and Russian oil industry in the late nineteenth century (see, for example, Suny, 1972).
- Monopolies and trusts: cartelisation of the oil industry (see, for example, Lenin, 1961 [1917], pp. 369-371).
- Inter-cartel competition: Standard Oil vs. the Rothschilds vs. the Nobels vs. other Russian producers vs. The Royal Dutch.
- **1900s-1910s**
  - The Oil Wars between international oil cartels and the relationship between oil monopolies and European and American imperialism;
  - Dissolution of Standard Oil Company (1911) and reorganization of the U.S. oil cartel system.
  - Baku oil and the Russian revolution of 1905; Social Democrats and the radical revolutionary movements; the oil strikes of 1903, 1904 and 1907; socialism, religion and nationalism (see, for example, Henry, 1905; Suny, 1972; Montefiore, 2008); "Nationality tended to accentuate differences of status within the working class. National animosities were thus coupled with social and economic antagonisms which led to tension and disunity in the working class rather than cohesion the Social Democrats tried to promote" (Suny, 1978, pp.13-14); "In the Caucasus, it was race and ethnic conflict, and not socialism that drove events" (Yergin, 1991, p. 131); "The news from Baku had a profound effect on the outside world. Here, for the first time, a violent upheaval had interrupted the flow of oil, threatening to make a vast investment worthless" (Ibid.).

- British Imperialism in Persia; the *Anglo-Persian Oil Company* and the Constitutional Revolution in Iran (1906) (see, for example, Abrahamian, 1982; Keddie, 2006);
- Oil and Mexican revolution of 1911 (see, for example, Brenner, 1985; Hart, 1987).
- Oil and the European arms race; oil proletariat in World War I.
- World War I and the carve-up of the Middle East: from San Remo Agreement to the Red Line Agreement; international oil cartels and the imperialist battle for control of oil production; concessionary system as instruments of colonisation (see, for example, O'Connor, 1955; 1962; Rachkov, 1967).
- The Russian Revolution of 1917 and Baku oil; Baku Commune 1918; oil and the Russian Civil War (see Suny, 1978; Gasanli, 2011).

- **1920s-1930s**
- Red Army capture of Baku April 1920; expropriation of foreign capital and the fall of *Bnito* and the rise of *Front Uni* (Standard of Jersey, Royal Dutch/Shell and the Nobels vs. Soviet authorities: "Private companies… would not easily be able to defend their rights against confiscation and nationalisation" (Yergin, 1991, p. 241).
- The New Economic Policy and the Anglo-Soviet Trade Agreement.
- U.S. and European imperialism in South America; class struggle in Mexico and Venezuela oil industries.
- Wall Street Crash of 1929 and the impact on oil cartels.
- The crisis of capitalism: Great Depression and the world oil industry; cartels vs. independent producers in the U.S. oil market.
- Protectionism, rise of national capitalist monopolies and the impact of the New Deal in the U.S.
- From competition to cartelisation: international capitalist union consolidation and the "As-Is" Agreement 1928-1939.
- Anti-colonialism and oil: renegotiation of the Iranian concession and Mexican oil nationalisation: "For Mexico, what had occurred was a great symbolic and passionate act of resistance to foreign control, which would be central to the spirit of nationalism that tied the country together" (Yergin, 1991, p. 276).
- National oil industries in the USSR and Mexico (see, for example, Igolkin, 2006).
- Imperialist struggle for oil/raw materials and the build-up to World War II

- **1940s-1950s**
  - World War II and the problem of petroleum overproduction and market control: Anglo-American Petroleum Agreement of 1944: "… the Anglo-American Petroleum Agreement was, in fact, a direct link to the market management of the late 1920s and the early 1930s" (Yergin, 1991, p. 402).
  - The Soviet oil industry and the war effort: the Second Baku Oil Boom.
  - The beginnings of the Cold War: Tudeh Party, Iranian communism and the Iran Crisis of 1946 (see, for example, Abrahamian, 1970; 1982; Zabih, 1966).
  - World War II and the rise of U.S. oil empire in the Middle East; the Group Agreement of 1948; the reconstitution of the *Iraq Petroleum Company* and the rise of new cartels; the new political geography of oil;
  - Western imperialism in the Middle East and South America: resistance, nationalism, labor movements and socialist organizations e.g. renegotiation of concessions and introduction of the 50/50 principle in Venezuela and Iraq, Kuwait and Saudi Arabia (see, for example. Meyer, 2014).
  - Imperialism in the Middle East: overthrow of M. Mosaddegh in Iran and the Crisis of 1953; the Suez Crisis of 1956; the road to national oil cartel – OPEC.
- **1960s-1970s**
  - September 1960 Baghdad Congress and the establishment of OPEC; cartelisation of oil producing semi-peripheral countries (Saudi Arabia, Venezuela, Iraq, Iraq, Kuwait).
  - Six Days War and the oil crisis of 1967; first unsuccessful embargo (semi-periphery vs core countries).
  - 1971 Tehran Agreement and the benchmark 55% government share mark; contract renegotiations (1969-1970); Libyan oil nationalisation of 1972: "The Tehran Agreement marked a watershed; initiative had passed from the companies to the exporting countries" (Yergin, 1991, p. 582).
  - Yom Kippur War, October 1973; the first Oil Crisis and the OPEC embargo: "The embargo and the shortage it caused were an abrupt break with America's past and the experience would severely undermine Americans' confidence in the future" (Ibid, p. 617).
  - The decline of the Middle East and South American concessionary systems (mid-1970s); establishment of PDVSA, Venezuela's national state oil company;

nationalisation of ARAMCO (Saudi Arabia) and Kuwait's oil holdings.
-    Iranian Revolution of 1979 and "the second oil shock;"

5. From Classical Marxism to Eclecticism: Reflectivist Research Approaches to International Energy Politics

CLASSICAL MARXISM
• *Oil as a raw material with use-value/ evolution of oil production cycle from feudal system to capitalist system.*
• *Cartels, trusts and monopolies – political economy of oil.*
• *International oil capital and imperialism, anti-imperialism and anti-colonialism.*
• *Oil proletariat and the class struggle and revolution.*
• *National/state oil companies and industries.*
• *Oil and the world economic system.*
• *Critique of capitalism; class struggle and revolution as emancipatory project.*
NEO-MARXIST STRUCTURAL DEPENDENCY THEORY
• *Core-periphery analysis (the West/Middle East).*
• *Structural dependency in international oil/energy politics.*
• *Global North vs Global South with a critical focus on the production end of the global energy cycle.*
• *U.S./Western hegemony of the global energy order.*
• *Critique of rationalist approaches (neo-neo synthesis) to oil politics and wider international energy realm.*
CRITICAL THEORY
• *Critique of the prevailing capitalist industrial global energy order as a sociological, normative and praxeological project.*
• *Revealing historical political constitution of the existing social reality of oil and identifying the interests of previously excluded and marginalized groups.*
• *Holistic understanding of production-consumption cycle in the shaping of the global energy order and pursuit of ethical alternatives to it.*
• *Rejection of materialist determinism of rationalist discourses on oil politics.*
• *Identifying and amplifying various forms of resistance against hegemonic and dominating forces in global energy politics (indigenous groups, local communities, global civil society, violent opposition).*

POSTSRUCTURALISM
• *Antifoundational meta-theoretical critique of oil-driven modernity and deconstruction of universalising discourses.* • *Prioritization of ideational over material claims and rejection of anthropocentric determinism.* • *Critique of environmentalism and eco-politics.* • *Eco-feminism, poststructuralism and postmodern environmentalism.* • *Radical anti-positivist critique of rationalist approaches to oil and energy issues.*
SOCIAL CONSTRUCTIVISM
• *An intersubjective ontology of energy politics, emphasising norms, social agents and systems, and the mutual constitution of agents and structures.* • *An epistemologically pluralist approach to the study of international energy politics, indebted to positivism.* • *The material of oil and the social construction of energy systems, ecology and conceptions of nature.* • *Environmental sociology.* • *Social construction of energy geopolitics and global corporate energy industries.* • *Rationalism and Social Constructivism: analytical convergences in the study of energy issues.*
ANALYTIC ECLECTICISM
• *Middle-range theorizing and multi-causal explanations of specific substantive issues and problems in international energy politics.* • *Eschewal of single-paradigmatic research in favor of combinatorial analytical logic, encompassing insights that would normally be posited in separate paradigmatic frameworks.* • *Combining insights generated by rationalist approaches and social constructivist analytical models within specific research fields centered on substantive issues in international energy politics.* • *Epistemological pluralism and praxeology-orientated ontology*

Bibliography

Abdurasulov, A. *Is Turkmenistan's gas line a pipe dream?* BBC News. 16 July 2015 (Retrieved 20.01.2016 http://www.bbc.co.uk/news/world-asia-329814 69).

Abrahamian, E. Communism and Communalism in Iran: The Tudah and the Firqah-I Dimukrat. *International Journal of Middle East Studies*, Vol. 1, No. 4. (Oct., 1970), pp. 291-316.

Abrahamian, E. 1982. *Iran Between Two Revolutions*. Princeton: Princeton University Press.

Abrahamian, E. 2008. *A History of Modern Iran*. Cambridge: Cambridge University Press.

Adams, T. D. *Baku Oil Diplomacy and "Early Oil" 1994-1998: An External Perspective*. pp. 225 - 252 in Peterson, A. and Ismailzade F. (Eds.). 2009.

Adelman, M.A. 1972. *The World Petroleum Market*. Baltimore: The Johns Hopkins University Press.

Agayev, V., Akhundov, F., Aliyev, F. T. and Agarunov, M. World War II and Azerbaijan. *Azerbaijan International*. Summer 1995 (3.2). Pp. 50-55, 78.

Agayev, Z. .23.12.2011. *Pipeline to Ship Azeri Gas to Central Europe, Balkans, WSJ Says*. Bloomberg. https://www.bloomberg.com/news/articles/2011-12-23/pipeline-to-ship-azeri-gas-to-central-europe-balkans-wsj-says - retrieved 5.10.2017

American Manufacturer and Iron World (AMIW). 1901. *Greater Pittsburgh and Allegheny County, Past, Present, Future*. Pittsburgh, Pa. (original at the New York Public Library).

Amin, S., Arrighi, G., Frank, A. G., Wallerstein, I. 1982. *Dynamics of Global Crisis*. London: New York: Monthly Review Press.

Argyrou, V. 2005. *The Logic of Environmentalism: Anthropology, Ecology and Postcoloniality*. New York: Berghahn Books.

Ahmadov, A.K. Oil, Democracy, and Context: A Meta-Analysis. *Comparative Political Studies*. August 2014. Vol. 47, no. 9. Pp. 1238-1267.

Aitken, D.W. 2003. *Transitioning to a Renewable Energy Future*. White Paper. International Solar Energy Society. (Online: https://ises.org/fileadmin/user_ upload/PDF/ISES-WP-72-English.pdf; first accessed: 16.08.2015).

Alao. A. 2007. *Natural Resources and Conflict in Africa: The Tragedy of Endowment*. New York: University of Rochester Press.

Al-Zoubi, J. 4.12.2017. *New Protests Erupt Against Removal of Olive Trees for TAP Pipeline*. Olive Oil Times (https://www.oliveoiltimes.com/olive-oil-business / new-protests - erupt - removal - olive-trees-tap-pipeline/ 61143 – retrieved 20.12.2017).

Alnasrawi, A. 1991. *Arab Nationalism, Oil, and the Political Economy of Dependency*. Westport, CT: Greenwood Publishing Group.

Andrews-Speed, P. Herberg, M.E, Zhidong, Li and Shobert, B. 2014. *China's Energy Crossroads: Forging a New Energy and Environmental Balance*. NBR Reports. Seattle, U.S.: The National Bureau of Asian Research.

Angell, N. 1913. *The Great Illusion: A Study of the Relation of Military Power in Nations to their Economic and Social Advantage*. New York and London: G. P. Putnam's Sons

Archer, M., Bhaskar, R., Collier, A., Lawson, T., Norrie, A. 2007. Critical Realism: Essential Readings. London and New York: Routledge.

Armaroli, N. and Blazani, V. 2010. Energy for a Sustainable World – From the Oil Age to a Sun-Powered Future. Wiley-VCH

Asbrink, B.   The Nobels in Baku: Swedes' Role in Baku's First Oil Boom. *Azerbaijan International.* Summer 2002 (10.2). Pages 56-59.

Auten, B.J. 2008. *Carter's Conversion: The Hardening of American Defense Policy*. University of Missouri Press.

Ayson, R. 2008. Strategic Studies in Reus-Smit, C. and Snidal, D. (eds.) 2008.

Bacevich, A.J. 2013. *The New American Militarism: How Americans Are Seduced by War*. Oxford: Oxford University Press.

Bamberg, J.H. 1994. *The History of the British Petroleum Company, Volume 2: The Anglo-Iranian Years, 1928-1954*. Cambridge: Cambridge University Press.

Baran, Z. *The Baku-Tbilisi-Ceyhan pipeline: implications for Turkey* in Frederick Starr, S. and Cornell, S. E. (Eds.). 2005.

Barnett, M. and Sikkink, K. *From International Relations to Global Society* in Reus-Smit, C. and Snidal, D. (eds.) 2008.

Barry, A. 2006. "Technological Zones," *European Journal of Social Theory*, vol. 9, no. 2, pp. 239-53.

Barry, A. 2013. *Material Politics: Disputes Along the Pipeline*. Wiley Blackwell.

Bebbington, A. (Ed.) 2011. *Social Conflict, Economic Development and the Extractive Industry: Evidence from South America*. London and New York: Routledge.

Bell, G. C. 1930. *Kentucky Petroleum*. Owensboro, Kentucky: Bell Publishing.

Bell, C., Wolford, S. Oil Discoveries, Shifting Power, and Civil Conflict. *International Studies Quarterly*. Volume 59, Issue 3, pages 517–530, September 2015.

Bennett, A. 2013. The mother of all isms: Causal mechanisms and structured pluralism in International Relations theory. *European Journal of International Relations*. No 19, pp. 459-482.

Bennis, P. 2006. *Challenging Empire: How People, Governments, and the UN Defy U.S. Power*. Northampton, Mass.: Olive Branch Press.

Berenskoetter, B. 18.09.2013. Theories Never Die. Guest post in Nexon, D. (Ed.) "End of IR Theory" companion symposium for the special issue of the European Journal of International Relations. *The Duck of Minerva.* http://duckofminerva.dreamhosters.com/2013/09/19951.html (accessed 27 October 2014).

Betancourt, R., 1978, Venezuela: oil and politics. Houghton Mifflin Company, Boston, MA

Bhaskar, R. 1975, *A Realist Theory of Science*, London: Routledge.

Bhaskar, R. (1979) 1998. *The Possibility of Naturalism A Philosophical Critique of the Contemporary Human Sciences.* Routledge: London and New York.

Biro, A. Towards a Denaturalized Ecological Politics. *Polity.* Vol. 35, No. 2 (Winter, 2002), pp. 195-212

Blair, T. 2011. *A Journey.* London: Arrow Books.

Blair, J.M. 1978. *The control of oil.* Vintage Books.

Blaney, D.L and Inayatullah, N. 2008. International Relations From Below in Reus-Smit, C. and Snidal, D. (eds.) 2008.

Blatchford, D. *Environmental and social aspects of the Baku-Tbilisi-Ceyhan pipeline* in Frederick Starr, S. and Cornell S. E. (Eds.). 2005.

Bohi, D. R., Toman, M.A., Walls, M.A. 1996. *The Economics of Energy Security.* London: Kluver Academic Publishers.

Bronner, S. E. 2002. *Of Critical Theory and Its Theorists.* New York: Routledge

Booth, K. and Smith, S. (Eds.) 1997. *International Relations Theory Today.* Cambridge, UK: Polity Press.

Brenner, A. 1984. *The Wind that Swept Mexico.* Austin: University of Texas Press

Bridge, G. 2008. "Global Production Networks and the Extractive Sector: governing resource-based development," *Journal of Economic Geography* 8 (3) March.

Bridge, G., and Le Billon, P. 2013. *Oil.* Cambridge: Polity.

Broder, J. M. Climate Change Seen as Threat to U.S. Security. *The New York Times.* 9 August 2009.

Bromley, S. 1991. *American Hegemony and World Oil: The Industry, the State System and the World Economy.* The Pennsylvania State University Press.

Simon Bromley, 1994. *Rethinking Middle East Politics.* University of Texas Press.

Brown, C. 2013. The Poverty of Grand Theory. *The European Journal of International Relations* September 2013; 19 (3), pp. 483-497.

Brown, O., Hamill, A. and Macleman, R. Climate change as the "new" security threat: implications for Africa. *International Affairs.* Volume 83, Issue 6, November 2007. Pp.1141–1154.

Buchan, D. and Keay, M. 2016. *Europe's Long Energy Journey: Towards an Energy Union?* Oxford University Press.

Buckley, N. and Foy, H. 18.10.2017. *EBRD to lend $500m for Azerbaijan gas pipeline.* Financial Times. https://www.ft.com/content/533fc822-b3db-11e7-a398-73d59db9e399 - retrieved 29.10.2017.

Bucknell, H. 1981. *Energy and the National Defence.* Lexington: University Press of Kentucky.

Bull, H. 1995. *The Anarchical Society. A Study of Order in World Politics*. London: Macmillan.

Bülow, Bernhard von. 1932. *Memoirs of Prince von Bülow. Vol IV, 1849-1897* (translated from German by Geoffrey Dunlop and F. A. Voight). Boston: Little, Brown and Company.

Burchill, S., Devetak, R., Linklater, A., Patterson, M., Reus-Smit, C., True, J. 1996. *Theories of International Relations*. New York: Palgrave.

Burchill, S. *Introduction* in Burchill, S. et al (eds.) 1996.

Burke, A. 2008. *Postmodernism* in Reus-Smit, C. and Snidal, D. (eds.) 2008.

Burroughs, C. 15.08.2017. Southern Gas Corridor: Pipe dream to pipe reality. TXFNews. https:// www.txfnews.com / News / Article / 6194 / Southern-Gas-Corridor-Pipe-dream-to-pipe-reality - retrieved 19.10.2017.

Buzan, B. and Little, R. 2001. Why International Relations has failed as an intellectual project and what to do about it. *Millennium: Journal of International Studies* 30(1), pp. 19-39.

Byers, M. 2008. *International Law* in Reus-Smit, C. and Snidal, D. (eds.) 2008.

Cambanis, T. The Carter Doctrine: A Middle East strategy past its prime. *The Boston Globe*. 14.10.2012 (Retrieved on 17.12.2015).

Campbell, D. 2013. *Poststructuralism* in Dunne, T. et al. 2013.

Campion, A. S. 2016. *The Geopolitics of Red Oil: Constructing the China threat through energy security*. Routledge.

Cantarow, E. 01.03.1980. Staying Out of the Trenches. *New Republic*. (Accessed on 13.03.2016 https:// newrepublic.com / article / 105023 / staying -out- the-trenches).

Carlsnaes, W., Risse, T., and Simmons B.A. (eds.) 2012. *Handbook of International Relations*. Thousand Oaks, CA: Sage.

Carr, E.H. 2001 (1981). "The Twenty Year Crisis." London: Palgrave Macmillan

Carroll, T. 2010. New Approaches to opening markets: the Baku-Tbilisi-Ceyhan pipeline and the deployment of social and environmental risk mitigation. Political Studies Association Conference Proceedings. Singapore May 2010. (Accessed on 17.11.2014 www.psa.ac.uk/journals/pdf/5/2010/1157_1007. pdf).

Carter, J. *Crisis of Confidence Speech*. 15 July 1979 (retrieved on 18.09.2015 http://www.cartercenter.org/news/editorials_speeches/crisis_of_confidence. html)

Carter, J. *The State of the Union Address Delivered Before a Joint Session of the Congress*. January 23, 1980. 1999-2016 - Gerhard Peters and John T. Woolley - The American Presidency Project (retrieved, 18.09.2015 http://www.presidency.ucsb.edu/ws/index.php?pid=33079).

Cattan, H. 1967a. *The Evolution of Oil Concessions in the Middle East and North Africa*. Dobbs Ferry, New York: Oceania Publications.

Cattan, H. 1967b. *The Law of Oil Concessions in the Middle East and North Africa*. Dobbs Ferry, New York: Oceania Publications.

Celestina Ihayere, C., Ogeleka, D.F. and Ataine, T.I. The effects of the Niger Delta oil crisis on women folks in *Journal of African Studies and Development,* Vol. 6(1), pp. 14-21, January 2014

Cendrowicz, L.13.07.2009. *Europe Tries to Break Its Russian Gas Habit.* Time. http:// content.time.com / time / world / article / 0,8599,1910123,00.html Retrieved 29.12.2017.

Chernoff, F. 2002. Scientific Realism as Meta-Theory of International Relations. *International Studies Quarterly.* 46(2); pp. 189-207.

Chufrin, G. (Ed.). 2001. *The Security of the Caspian Sea Region.* Oxford: Oxford University Press.

Churchill, W. S. 1928. *The World Crisis, vol.1.* Scribner: New York. Pp.130-36 in Yergin, 1991, xiv.

Coen, R. 2012. *Breaking Ice for Arctic Oil: The Epic Voyage of the SS Manhattan through the North West Passage.* Fairbanks: University of Alaska Press.

Colgan, J. D. 2013. *Petro-Aggression. When Oil Causes War.* Cambridge: Cambridge University Press.

Colitti, M. and Simeoni, C. 1996. *Perspectives of Oil and Gas: The Road to Interdependence.* Dordrecht, NL: Kluver Academic Publishers.

Conley, V. A. 1997. *Ecopolitics: The Environment in Poststructuralist Thought.* London: Routledge.

Colley, A. 2012. *Great Games, Local Rules: The New Power Contest in Central Asia.* Oxford: Oxford University Press.

Conor, S. 5.06.2008. *U.S. still opposes Iran as Nabucco gas supplier.* Reuters. https:// uk.reuters.com / article / russia-nabucco-bryza / interview -us-still-opposes -iran-as-nabucco-gas-supplier-idUKL0583264520080605?sp = true Retrieved 13.12.2017.

Cornell, S. E. et al. *Geostrategic implications of the Baku-Tbilisi-Ceyhan pipeline* in Frederick Starr, S. and Cornell, S. E. (Eds.). 2005.

Cornell, S.E. and Frederick Starr, S. 2015. *The Guns of August 2008: Russia's War in Georgia.* London and New York: Routledge.

Cowhey, P. F. 1985. *The Problems of Plenty. Energy Policy and International Politics.* Berkeley: University of California Press

Cox, R. W. Social Forces, States and World Orders: Beyond International Relations Theory, *Millennium,* 10 (1981), 2.

Cox, R. 1983. *Gramsci, hegemony, and international relations: an essay in method.* Pp. 124-143 in Cox, R. and Sinclair, J.J. 1996. *Approaches to World Orders.* Cambridge: Cambridge University Press.

Cox, R. W. 1986. *Social Forces, States and World Orders: Beyond International Relations Theory* in Keohane, R.O. (ed.). 1986. *Neorealism and Its Critics,* New York: Columbia University Press Cox, M. (ed.). 2000. *E.H. Carr: a Critical Appraisal.* Basingstoke: Palgrave.

Cox, R. W. 2008. *The Point is Not Just to Explain the World but to Change It* in Reus-Smit, C. and Snidal, D. (eds.) 2008.

Croissant, P. & Aras, B. 1999. *Oil and geopolitics in the Caspian Sea Region.* Westport, CT: Praeger Publishers

Cruickshank, J. A tale of two ontologies: an immanent critique of critical realism. *The Sociological Review*, Volume 52, Issue 4 November 2004 Pages 567–585.

Damiani, V. and Navach, G. 28.03.2017. *Italian police disrupt protest to prevent olive grove removal*. Reuters (https://www.reuters.com/article/us-italy-tap-protests / italian-police-disrupt-protest-to-prevent-olive-grove-removal-idUS KBN16Z2G7) – retrieved 1.1.2018

Dannreuther, R. International Relations Theories: Energy, Minerals and Conflict. *POLINARES working paper* n. 8, September 2010. (Accessed on 16.5.2015 http://www.polsci.chula.ac.th/pitch/ep15/roland.pdf).

D'Agostini, M. *Protecting Trans-Adriatic Pipeline – TAP as a Case-Study* in Niglia, A. (Ed.). 2015. *The Protection of Critical Infrastructure Against Emerging Security Challenges*. Part V – The Protection of the Trans-Adriatic Pipelines – TAP as a Case Study. Pp. 103-148. Amsterdam, IOS Press.

Darby, P. *A Disabling Discipline?* in Reus-Smit, C. and Snidal, D. (eds.). 2008.

Davenport, E.H. and Cooke S.R. 1923. *The Oil Trusts & Anglo-American Relations*. London MacMillan.

Davis, D. L. Don't Take the Oil: Time to Ditch the Carter Doctrine. *National Interest*. 03.02.2017. (Accessed on 21.03.2017) http://nationalinterest.org/feature/dont-take-the-oil-time-ditch-the-carter-doctrine-19310).

Demirmen, F. 19.12.2011. *BP-SOCAR duo deliver "coup de grace" to Nabucco*. News.az. https://news.az/articles/economy/51212 - retrieved 2011-12-25.

Dempsey, J. 13.07. 2006. *Gazprom's grip on Western Europe tightens with pipelines to Hungary*. The New York Times. http://www.nytimes.com/ 2006/ 06/22/business / worldbusiness /22iht-gas.2031021.html Retrieved - 10.11 2017.

Derrida, J. 1993. *Spectres de Marx: l'état de la dette, le travail du deuil et la nouvelle Internationale*. Éditions Galileé

Donnelly, J. *The Ethics of Realism* in Reus-Smit, C. and Snidal, D. (eds.). 2008.

Downey, M. 2009. *Oil 101*. Wooden Table Press LLC.

Dryzek, J. S. [1997] 2005. *The Politics of the Earth: Environmental Discourses*. Oxford: Oxford University Press.

Dunne, T., Kurki, M., Smith, S. 2013. *International Relations Theories. Discipline and Diversity*. Oxford: Oxford University Press.

Dunne, T., Hansen, L., Wight, C. The end of International Relations theory? in Wight, C., Hansen, L. and Dunne, T. (eds.). Special Issue: The End of International Relations Theory? *The European Journal of International Relations* September 2013; 19 (3); pp. 401-425.

Dunning, T. and Wiprsa, L. 2004. Oil and the Political Economy of Conflict in Columbia and Beyond: A Linkages Approach. *Geopolitics*, vol. 9, no. 1, pp. 81-108.

Dyer, G. 2009. *Climate Wars*. Random House.

DW Staff, 27.01. 2009. *Proposed Nabucco Gas Pipeline Gets European Bank Backing*. Deutsche Welle. http://www.dw.com/en/proposed-nabucco-gas-pipeline-gets-european-bank-backing/a-3980038 - retrieved 22.11.2017.

Ebel, R.E. 1978. *Communist Trade in Oil and Gas: An Evaluation of the Future Export Capability of the Soviet Bloc.* New York: Praeger.

Ebinger, C. K. 1982. *The Critical Link: Energy and National Security in the 1980s.* Cambridge, Mass.: Ballinger Publishing Co.

Eckersley, R. *Green Theory* in Dunne, T. et al. 2013.

Eland, I. 2011. *No War for Oil. U.S. Dependency and the Middle East.* Independent Institute.

El-Baz, F. 1994. *The Gulf War and the Environment.* Switzerland: Gordon and Breach Science Publishers.

Elkind, J. *Economic implications of the Baku-Tbilisi-Ceyhan pipeline* in Frederick Starr, S. and Cornell, S. E. (Eds.). 2005.

Ely, N. 1938. The Conservation of Oil in *Hansard Law Review* 51:7. Pp. 1209-44.

Enloe, C. 2007. *Feminist international relations: how to do it, what we gain* in Griffiths, M. (ed.). 2007. *International Relations Theory for the 21st Century.* NewYork: Routledge.

Epstein, C. Constructivism or the eternal return of universals in International Relations. Why returning to language is vital to prolonging the owl's flight. In: Wight, C., Hansen, L. and Dunne, T. (eds.). Special Issue: The End of International Relations Theory? *The European Journal of International Relations* September 2013; 19 (3); pp. 499-519.

Erskine, T. 2008. Locating responsibility: the problem of moral agency in International Relations. In: Reus-Smit, C. and Snidal, D. (eds.) 2008.

Erskine, T. 2013. *Normative International Relations Theory* in Dunne, T. et al. 2013.

Eulau, H. (ed.). 2011 [1969]. *Behavioralism in Political Science.* New Brunswick, N.J.: Transaction Publishers

Falola, T. and Genova, A. 2005. *The Politics of the Global Oil Industry: An Introduction.* Westport, CT: Praeger.

Farchy, J. 26.10.2016. *Azerbaijan gas loans under threat after NGO ultimatum.* Financial Times (https://www.ft.com/content/dee61e6c-9b5e-11e6-8f9b-70e3cabccfae) – Retrieved 22.11.2017.

Feenberg, A. 1991. *Critical Theory of Technology.* Oxford University Press.

Feng, L., Hu, Y., Hall, C.A.S. and Wang, J. 2012. *The Chinese Oil Industry: History and Future.* New York: Springer.

Ferrier, R. W. 1982. *The History of the British Petroleum Company, Vol 1: The Developing Years, 1901 – 1932.* Cambridge University Press.

Ferry, L. 1992. Le Nouvel Ordre Ecologique. Bernard Grassett.

Ferguson, Y.H. and Mansbach, R.W. 2014.03.20. *Reflections on the "Third Debate"* in Jackson, P.T. (ed). The Third Debate Twenty-Five Years Later Symposium. *International Studies Quarterly Online.* http://www.isanet.org /Publications/ISQ/Posts/ID/312/Reflections-on-the-Third-Debate

Fouskas, V. and Gökay, G. 2005. *The New American Imperialism: Bush's War on Terror and Blood for Oil.* Westport, Connecticut and London: Praeger Security International (Greenwood Publishing Group).

Foy, H. 10.03.2017. *Azerbaijan risks gas pipeline loans by quitting transparency monitor*. Financial Times (https://www.ft.com/content/4fad74e8-056c-11e7-ace0-1ce02ef0def9) – retrieved 22.11.2017.

Frankel, E.G. 2007. *Oil and Security: A World beyond Petroleum*. Dordrecht, NL: Springer.

Freudenburg, W. R. (2000) "Social construction and social constrictions: toward analyzing the social construction of 'the naturalized' as well as 'the natural,'" in G. Spaargaren, A. P. J. Mol and F. H. Buttel (eds) (2000) *Environment and Global Modernity*. London: Sage.

Friedman, Michael. 1999. *Reconsidering Logical Positivism*. New York: Cambridge University Press

Friedman, Milton. 1966. *The Methodology of Positive Economics* in *Essays In Positive Economics*. Chicago: Univ. of Chicago Press, pp. 3-16, 30-43.

Fursenko, A.A. 1972. *Die Dynastie Rockefeller*. Deutscher Verlag d. Wiss., VEB.

Fursenko, A. A. and Freeze, G. L. 1990. *The Battle for Oil: The Economics and Politics of International Corporate Conflict Over Petroleum, 1860-1930*. JAI Press.

Gaard, G. C. 2011. Ecofeminism Revisited: Rejecting Essentialism and Re-Placing Species in a Material Feminist Environmentalism. *Feminist Formations* 23(2): 26-53

Gare, A. 1995. *Postmodernism and the Environmental Crisis*. London: Routledge.

Gaddis, J. L. 2007. *The Cold War*. Penguin Books.

Gasanli, D. 2011. *Russkaja Revolucija i Azerbajdzhan 1917-1920*. Moskva: Flint.

Gilpin, R. 2001. *Global Political Economy*. Princeton and Oxford: Princeton University Press.

Griffiths, M. (ed.). 1997. *International Relations theory for the twenty-first century: an introduction*. London and New York: Routledge.

Gordon, W.C. 1975. *The expropriation of foreign-owned property in Mexico*. Westport, Conn.: Greenwood Press.

Gotev, G. 29.03.2017. Italy approves TAP pipeline, but activists attempt to block. Euractive Network. (https://www.euractiv.com/section/global-europe/news/italy-approves - tap-pipeline - but - activists - attempt-to-block/) – retrieved 22.11.2017.

Gotev, G. 04.10.2016. *SOCAR: The TAP project is at risk*. Euractive Network. (https://www. euractiv.com/ section / energy/interview/socar-the-tap-project-is-at-risk/) – retrieved 09.12.2017.

Gotev, G. 05.10.2015. *Future uncertain for TAP and DESFA, following European Parliament vote*. Euractive Network. (https://www.euractiv.com/ section/ energy/ news/future - uncertain - for -tap-and-desfa-following-european-parliament-vote/) – retrieved 09.12.2017.

Graeber. D.J. *Kazakhstan keen on TAPI gas pipeline*. United Press International 3 December 2014. (Retrieved on 6 January 2016 - http://www.upi.com/ Business_News/ Energy – Industry /2014/12/03/Kazakhstan-keen-on-TAPI-gas-pipeline/1741417604335/).

Grant. T. 2015. *Aggression against Ukraine: Territory, Responsibility, and International Law.* Palgrave Macmillan.

Grovogui, S.N. *Postcolonialism* in Dunne, T. et al. 2013.

Gurbanov, I. 09.03.2017. Southern Gas Corridor Seeks Financial Backing Amidst Volatile Oil Prices. *Eurasia Daily Monitor.* Volume: 14 Issue: 32. The Jamestown Foundation (https:// jamestown.org / program / southern-gas-corridor-seeks-financial – backup – amidst - volatile-oil-prices/) – retrieved 19.11.2017.

Gurt, M. and Auyezov, O. *Turkmenistan starts work on gas link to Afghanistan, Pakistan, India.* Reuters UK. India Top News, 13 December 2015. (Retrieved on 16 January 2016 http://uk.reuters.com/article/turkmenistan-gas-pipeline-idUKKBN0TW05Q20151213)

Gustafson, T. 2012. *Wheel of Fortune: The Battle for Oil and Power in Russia.* Harvard University Press.

Guzzinni, S. 1998. *Realism in International relations and International Political Economy. The continuing story of a death foretold.* London and New York: Routledge.

Guzzinni, S. 2013. The ends of International Relations theory: Stages of reflexivity and modes of theorizing. In: Wight, C., Hansen, L. and Dunne, T. (eds.). Special Issue: The End of International Relations Theory? *The European Journal of International Relations* September 2013; 19 (3). Pp. 521-541.

Gylfason, T. Natural resources, education, and economic development. *European Economic Review.* Volume 45, Issues 4–6, May 2001, Pages 847–859.

Halliday, F. *A Necessary Encounter: Historical Materialism and International Relations,* in Halliday, F. 1994. *Rethinking International Relations.* London: Macmillan.

Hannigan, J. [1995] 2006. *Environmental Sociology.* London and New York: Routledge

Harder, A. and Cook, L. *Congressional Leaders Agree to Lift 40-Year Ban on Oil Exports.* 16.02.2016. The Wall Street Journal. (Retrieved on 15.02.2016: http:// www.wsj.com / articles / congressional-leaders-agree- to -lift-40-year-ban-on-oil-exports-1450242995).

Hardt, M., and Negri, A. 2000. *Empire.* Harvard University Press.

Hart, J. M. 1987. *Revolutionary Mexico: The Coming and Process of the Mexican Revolution.* Berkeley and Los Angeles: University of California Press.

Hartshorn, J. E. 1962. *Oil Companies & Governments. An Account.* Faber & Faber.

Hartshorn, J. E. 1993. *Oil Trade: Politics and Prospects.* Cambridge: Cambridge University Press.

Harvey, F. 12.12.2017. *Calls for greater fossil fuel divestment at anniversary of Paris climate deal.* The Guardian (https://www.theguardian.com/environment/2017/dec/12/calls-for-greater-fossil-fuel-divestment-at-anniversary-of-paris-climate-deal) – retrieved 01.12.2018.

Hasanov. M. 07.12.2016. An analysis of economic benefits of the Southern Gas Corridor. *Energy Sources, Part B: Economics, Planning, and Policy*; Volume 11, 2016 - Issue 11. Pp. 999-1005.

Hay, C. *International Relations Theory and Globalisation* in Dunne, T. et al. 2013.

Henderson, J., Ferguson, A. 2014. *International Partnership in Russia: Conclusions from the Oil and Gas Industry*. Palgrave Macmillan.

Henry, J. D. 1905. *Baku: An Eventful History*. London: Archibold Constable & Co.

Hill, D. 28 July 2016. *How bold will Sadiq Khan's air quality improvement programme be?* The Guardian. (first accessed on 28 July 2016 - https://www.theguardian.com/ uk -news / davehillblog/2016/jul/28/how-bold-will-sadiq-khans-air-quality-improvement-programme-be).

Hill, F. 2004. Pipelines in the Caspian. *Georgetown Journal of International Affairs*. Winter/Spring (25).

Hinnebusch, Ray. 2003. *The International Politics of the Middle East*. Manchester:

Manchester University Press.

Hiro, D. 2007. *Blood of the Earth. The Battle for the World's Vanishing Oil Resources*. New York: Nation Books

Hobson, J. A. 1902. *Imperialism: A Study*. New York: James Pott and Co.

Hoffmann, T. and Johnson, B. 1981. *The World Energy Triangle: A Strategy for Cooperation*. Cambridge, Mass.: Ballinger Publishing Co.

Hoffman, D. 1999. Oil and Development in post-Soviet Azerbaijan. *NBR Analysis*. 10.3 (August, 1999): 6.

Holsti, K.J. 2002. *Interview with Kal Holsti*, A. Jones. Review of International Studies, 28/3: 619-33.

Howarth, S. 1997. *A Century in Oil: The "Shell" Transport and Trading Company, 1897-1997*. Weidenfeld & Nicolson.

Hurd, I. 2008. Constructivism in Reus-Smit, C. and Snidal, D. (eds.) 2008.

Humphreys, M., Sachs, J.D., Stiglitz, J. E. 2007. *Escaping the Resource Curse*. New York: Columbia University Press.

Hurst, S. 2009. *United States and Iraq Since 1979: Hegemony, Oil and War*. Edinburgh: Edinburgh University Press.

Ickes, H.L. 1943a. *Fightin Oil*. Alfred A. Knopf, New York.

Ickes, H. L. We're running out of oil. *American Magazine*. December 1943.

Igolkin. I. I. Sovetskij neftjanoj eksport v gody predvoennyh pjatiletok. *Neftjanoe Hozjajstvo*. 09.2006 (Accessed on 18 December 2015 - http://www.oil-industry.ru/images/upload/Arhiv_Jurnala/2006_09_139-141_Igolkin.pdf).

Igorev, V. A Man-Made Island of Oil Treasures. *Oil of Russia*, No. 3, 2010 (Retrieved, 25 June 2015 http://www.oilru.com/or/44/925/).

Ikenberry, J. G. 1988. *Reasons of State: Oil Policies and the Capacities of American Government*. New York: Ithaca.

Jacobs, D.A. and Branden, K.A. 2008. *From McEnergy to EcoEnergy: America's Transition to Sustainable Energy*. Pittsburgh: Whitmore Publishing Co.

Jack, M. 1968. The Purchase of the British Government's Shares in the British Petroleum Company 1912-1914. Past & Present. No. 39 (Apr., 1968), pp. 139-168

Jackson, P.T. and Nexon, D.H. International theory in a post-paradigmatic era: From substantive wagers to scientific ontologies. In: Wight, C., Hansen, L. and Dunne, T. (eds.). Special Issue: The End of International Relations Theory? *The European Journal of International Relations* September 2013; 19 (3); pp. 543-565.

Jackson, P.T. (ed). 20.03.2014. "The Third Debate" Twenty-Five Years Later Symposium. *International Studies Quarterly Online*. (http://www.isanet.org/Publications/ISQ/Posts/ID/297/LINK-TO-PARENT-ARTICLE) Accessed 01.06.2015.

Jafarova, E. 2017. *The Role of Azerbaijan in Shaping Regional Cooperation for Regional Security*. Pp. 41-45 in Novogrockiene, J. and Siaulyte, E. (Eds.). *Addressing Emerging Security Risks for Energy Networks in South Caucasus*. Amsterdam: IOS Press.

Jones, B. 2008. *Hugo! The Hugo Chavez Story from Mud Hut to Perpetual Revolution*. London: The Bodley Head.

Jones, G. G. The British Government and the Oil Companies 1912–1924: the Search for an Oil Policy. *The Historical Journal*. 20/03. September 1977. pp 647-672. Cambridge University Press.

Jordan, R., Maliniak, D., Oakes, A., Peterson, S., Tierney, M.J. 2009. *One Discipline or Many? TRIP Survey of International Relations Faculty in Ten Countries. Teaching, Research, and International Policy (TRIP) Project.* The Institute for the Theory and Practice of International Relations. The College of William and Mary. Williamsburg, Virginia (Online: http://www.wm.edu/offices/itpir/_documents/trip/final_trip_report_2009.pdf; accessed on 7 April 2014)

Joseph, J. and Wight, C. 2010. *Scientific Realism and International Relations*. London: Palgrave.

Kandiyoti, R. 2012 [2008]. *Pipeline. Flowing oil and crude politics*. London and New York: I.B. Taurus.

Karl, T. L. 1997. *The Paradox of Plenty: Oil Booms and Petro-States (Studies in International Political Economy)*. Berkley and Los Angeles: University of California Press.

Karagöl, October 2014. E. T. and Kaya, S. *Energy Supply Security and the Southern Gas Corridor*. SETA.

Katzenstein P. and Sil, R. 2008. *Eclectic Theorizing in the Study and Practice of International Relations* in Reus-Smit, C. and Snidal, D. (eds.) 2008.

Kelly, P.J. 2011. *Tirpitz and the Imperial German Navy*. Indiana University Press, Bloomington

Kemp, S. Critical Realism and the Limits of Philosophy. *European Journal of Social Theory*. Volume 8, Issue 2, May 2005, pp. 171–191.

Keohane, R. O. Political Science as a Vocation. *Political Science and Politics*, Vol. 42 (2), April 2009, pp. 359-363.

Keohane, R.O. 2008. Big questions in the study of world politics. In: Reus-Smit, C. and Snidal, D. (eds.) 2008.

Keohane, R. O. 1989. *International Institutions and State Power*. Boulder, CO, Westview.

Keohance, R. O. *Theory of World Politics: Structural Realism and Beyond* in Keohane, R.O. (ed.). 1986. *Neorealism and Its Critics*, New York: Columbia University Press. Pp. 158-203.

Keohane, R. O. 1989. *After Hegemony: Cooperation and Discord in the World Political Economy*. Princeton University Press.

Keohane, R.O and Nye, J. (Eds.). 1977. "Power and Interdependence: World Politics in Transition." Boston: Little, Brown.

Keohane, R. O. and Nye, J. S. 1974a. Transgovernmental relations and international organizations. *World Politics* (October) Volume 27, Issue 1, pp. 39-62.

Keohane, R. O. and Nye, J. S. Multinational Corporations in World Politics. *Foreign Affairs* (October, 1974b).

Keohane, R. O. and Nye, J. S. 1973. Power and Interdependence. *Survival: Global Politics and Strategy*. (July) Volume 15, Issue 4, pp. 158-165.

Keohane, R. O. and Nye, J. S. (Eds.). 1972. *Transnational Relations and World Politics*. Cambridge: Harvard University Press.

King, Y. *Healing the Wounds: Feminism, Ecology and Nature/Culture Dualism* in Jaggar, A. M. and Bordo, S. 1989. *Gender/body/knowledge: Feminist Reconstructions of Being and Knowing*. New Brunswick, New Jersey: Rutgers University Press.

Kissinger, H. 2002. *Does America Need a Foreign Policy? Toward a Diplomacy for the 21 Century*. London: Free Press.

Klare, M. T. 2004. *Blood and Oil*. London: Penguin

Klare, M. T. *Repudiate the Carter Doctrine*. 23.01.2009. FPIF. (Accessed on 25.03.2016 http://fpif.org/repudiate_the_carter_doctrine/).

Klare, M. T. 2011. *Protecting Overseas Oil Supplies: The Globalization of the "Carter Doctrine"* in Byrne, J., Toly, N. Glover, L. (Eds.). 2011. *Transforming Power: Energy, Environment, and Society in Conflict*. New Brunswick (U.S.A) and London (UK): Transactions Publishers.

Klare, M. T. 2012. *The Race for What's Left*. New York: Metropolitan.

Krapels, E.N. 1980. *Oil Crisis Management: Strategic Stockpiling for International Security*. Baltimore: The John Hopkins University Press.

Krasner, S. D. 1985. *Structural Conflict: The Third World Against Global Liberalism*. University of California Press.

Kratochwil, F. V. 1989. *Rules, norms, and decisions: on the conditions of practical and legal reasoning in international relations and domestic affairs, Cambridge studies in international relations*. New York: Cambridge University Press.

Kratochwil, F.V. 1978. *International order and foreign policy: a theoretical sketch of post-war international politics*, Westview replica edition. Boulder, CO: Westview Press.

Kuhn, T.S. 1962. *The Structure of Scientific Revolutions.* Chicago and London: The University of Chicago Press.

Kukla, A. 2000. *Social Constructivism and the Philosophy of Science.* London and New York: Routledge.

Kurki, M. 2007. Critical Realism and causal analysis in International Relations: Causes all the way down. *Millennium: Journal of International Studies.* 35 (2); pp. 361-378.

Kurki, M. and Wight, C. 2013. *International Relations and Social Science* in Dunne et al. *International Relations Theories. Discipline and Diversity.* Oxford: Oxford University Press.

Lakatos, I. 1970. Falsification and the methodology of scientific research programmes in Lakatos, I. and Musgrave, A. (eds.) *Criticism and the Growth of Knowledge.* New York: Cambridge University Press. Pp. 91-196.

Lake, D.A. "The State and International Relations" in Reus-Smit, C. and Snidal, D. (eds.) 2008.

Lake, D.A. 2011. Why "isms" Are Evil: Theory, Epistemology, and Academic Sects as Impediments to Understanding and Progress. *International Studies Quarterly* 55, pp. 465–480

Lake, D.A. 2013. *Theory is dead, long live theory: The end of the Great Debates and the rise of eclecticism in International Relations* in Wight, C., Hansen, L. and Dunne, T. (eds.). Special Issue: The End of International Relations Theory? *The European Journal of International Relations* September 2013; 19 (3), pp. 567-587.

Lane, D. S. 1999. *The Political Economy of Russian Oil.* Plymouth, UK: Rowman & Littlefield Publishers, Inc.

Langlois, A. J. *Worldviews and International Political Theory*, in Griffiths, M. (ed.). 1997.

Lapid, Y. 1989. The Third Debate: On the Prospects of International Theory in a Post Positivist-Era. *International Studies Quarterly*, Vol. 33, No 3 (Sep., 1989), pp. 235-254.

Lapid, Y. 20.03.2014. 25 Years after The Third Debate: Two (pianissimo) bravos for IR Theory in Jackson, P.T. (ed). The Third Debate" Twenty-Five Years Later Symposium. *International Studies Quarterly Online.* http://www.isanet.org/Publications/ISQ/Posts/ID/304/25-Years-after-The-Third-Debate-Two-pianissimo-bravos-for-IR-Theory (accessed 1.06.2015).

Latham, R. (ed.) (Marco Polo). 1958. *The Travels of Marco Polo.* London: Penguin.

Laudan, L. 1977. *Progress and Its Problems: Toward a Theory of Scientific Growth.* Berkeley, CA: University of California Press.

Lawler, P. 2008. *The Ethics of Postmodernism* in Reus-Smit, C. and Snidal, D. (eds.) 2008.

Lebow, R.N. *Classical Realism* in Dunne, T. et al. 2013.Leplin, J. (ed.) 1984. *Scientific Realism.* London, Berkeley and Los Angeles: University of California Press.

Leggett, J. 2005. *Half Gone: Oil, Gas, Hot Air and the Global Energy Crisis.* London: Portobello Books.

Leiserowitz, A.A. Day After Tomorrow: Study of Climate Change Risk Perception. *Environment: Science and Policy for Sustainable Development.* Vol. 46, Issue. 9, 2004.

Lenin, V. I. 1967. *Imperializm kak vysshaya stadija kapitalizma.* Polnoe Sobranie Sochinenij. Izd. 5. Tom 27. Str. 299-426. M.: Izdatelstvo Politicheskoj Literaturi (Ленин, В. И. 1967. *Империализм, как высшая стадия капитализма.* Полное собрание сочинений, изд. 5, т. 27, стр. 299–426. М.: Издательство политической литературы).

LeVine, S. 2007. *The Oil and Glory. The pursuit of empire and fortune on the Caspian Sea.* New York: Random House.

Lévi-Strauss, C. 1962. *La Pensée sauvage.* Paris: Librairie Plon.

Levy, W. Oil and the Decline of the West. *Foreign Affairs.* Summer 1980. Pp. 999-1015.

Libecap, G.D. The Political Economy of Crude Oil Cartelization in the United States,1933–1972. *The Journal of Economic History.* 49:04. December 1989, pp 833-855.

Lieuwen, E. 1954. *Petroleum in Venezuela: A History.* Berkeley: University of California Press.

Linklater, A. 1992. The question of the next stage in international relations theory: a critical-theoretical point of view. *Millennium: Journal of International Studies*, 21: 77-98.

Linklater, A. 1998. *The Transformation of Political Community: Ethical Foundations of the Post-Westphalian Era.* Cambridge: Polity.

Linklater, A. 2002. The problem of harm in world politics: implications for the sociology of states systems. *International Affairs,* 78: 318-38.

Little, R. *International Relations Theory From a Former Hegemon* in: Reus-Smit, C. and Snidal, D. (eds.) 2008.

Lockie, S. 2004. Social nature: the environmental challenge to mainstream social theory, in R White (ed), *Controversies in environmental sociology*, Cambridge, UK: Cambridge University Press.

Loris, R. S. 2003. *A Heritage of Light: Lamps and Lighting in the Early Canadian Home.* Toronto: University of Toronto Press.

Lottman, R. H. 1995. *Return of the Rothschilds: The Great Banking Dynasty Through Two Turbulent Centuries.* I.B. Tauris: London and New York.

Luiten van Zanden, J., Jonker, J., Howarth, S., Sluyterman, K. 2007. *A History of Royal Dutch Shell.* Oxford University Press: Oxford.

Lyotard, Jean-François. 1993. *Political Writings.* Minneapolis: University of Minnesota Press.

Magill, K. Against Critical Realism. *Capital and Class.* Issue no.54, Autumn 1994, pp.113-136.

Makovsky, M. and Goldstein, L. 13.08.2010. Iran, Oil, and the Carter Doctrine. Two cheers for the return of the Carter Doctrine. The Weekly Standard.

http://www.weeklystandard.com/iran-oil-and-the-carter-doctrine/article/490691

Malaniak, D, Oakes, A., Peterson, S., and Tierney, M.J. 2007. "The View From the Ivory Tower: TRIP Survey of International Relations Faculty in the United States and Canada," Williamsburg, VA.: Program on the Theory, Research and Practice of International Relations at the College of William and Mary. https://www.wm.edu/offices/itpir/_documents/trip/ivory_tower_view_2007.pdf (Accessed 17 April 2015).

Mammadova, L. 8/10/2019. *TANAP delivers 2.7 bcm of Shah Deniz gas to Turkey.* AzerNews (https://www.azernews.az/oil_and_gas/156978.html - retrieved 2/11/2019)

Mammadov, I. 20.01.2017. *A letter from an inmate of the Southern Gas Corridor.* OpenDemocracy (https://www.opendemocracy. net / od-russia / ilgar-mammadov/open-letter-from-inmate-of-southern-gas-corridor) – retrieved 18.12.2017.

Margonelli, L. *Oil On the Brain.* New York: Broadway Books.

Marx, K. (1867). *Capital, Volume One.* In Tucker, R. C. (ed.). 1978. The Marx-Engels Reader. New York and London: W.W. Norton & Company.

Marx, K. and Engels, F. 1978 [1888]. *Manifesto of the Communist Party* in Tucker, 1978.

Manicas, P. A *Realist Social Science* in Archer, M., Bhaskar, R., Collier, A., Lawson, T.,

Mathiesen, C. 27.11.2017. EU commission urged bank to support Azerbaijan gas pipeline. Climate Home News (http://www.climatechangenews.com/2017/ 11 / 27/ eu-commission - urged-bank-support - azerbaijan-gas-pipeline/) – retrieved 7.12.2017.

Mattern, J.B. "The Concept of Power and the (Un)Discipline of International Relations" in Reus-Smit, C. and Snidal, D. (eds.) 2008.

Maugeri, L. 2006. *The Age of Oil.* London: Praeger

McBeth, B.S. 1985. *British Oil Policy, 1919-1939.* London: Frank Cass

McKibben, B. et al. 30.06.2017. *Why European must turn off the gas TAP: NGOs, academics and artists sign against the pipeline.* CounterBalance (http://www.counter-balance.org/why-europe-must-turn-off-the-gas-tap-ngos-academics-artists-sign-against-the-pipeline/) – retrieved 28.10.2017.

Meadows, D. H., Meadows, D. L., Randers, J., Behrens III, W. W. *The Limits of Growth. A Report for the Club of Rome's Project on the Predicament of Mankind.* New York: Universe Books.

Mearns, R. and Norton, A. (Eds.). *Social Dimensions of Climate Change: Equity and Vulnerability in a Warming World.* Washington, DC: The World Bank.

Mearsheimer, J.J. *Structural Realism* in Dunne, T. et al. 2013.

Mearsheimer, J.J. and Walt, S.M. 2013. Leaving theory behind: Why simplistic hypothesis testing is bad for International Relations. In: Wight, C., Hansen, L. and Dunne, T. (eds.). Special Issue: The End of International Relations Theory? *The European Journal of International Relations* September 2013; 19 (3). Pp. 427-457.

Mearsheimer, J.J. 1995. A realist reply. *International Security*, 20: 82-93

Meyer, L. 2014. *Mexico and the United States in the Oil Controversy, 1917–1942*. Austin: University of Texas Press.

Mikdashi, Z. M. 1972. *The Community of Oil Exporting Countries*. Ithaca: Cornell Univ. Press.

Mikdashi, Z. M. 1966. *A Financial Analysis of Middle Eastern Oil Concessions: 1901-65*. F. A. Prager.

Mills, R. M. 2008. *The Myth of the Oil Crisis*. London: Praeger

Milne, S. 7 June 2008. Review of "Hugo!" *The Guardian*. http://www.theguardian.com/books/2008/jun/07/biography

Mitchell, T. 2009. "Carbon democracy," *Economy and Society*, Volume 38, Number 3, August 2009, pp. 399-432(34).

Mitchell, T. 2011. *Carbon Democracy: Political Power in the Age of Oil*. Verso Books.

Monbiot, G. 2006. *Heat: How to Stop the Planet Burning*. Allen Lane.

Montague, G.H. 2001 [1903]. "The Rise and Progress of the Standard Oil Company." Books for Business: New York and Hong Kong.

Monteiro, N.P. and Ruby, K.G. 2009. IR and the false promise of philosophical foundations. *International Theory* 1.1, 15-48.

Montefiore, S. S. 2008. *Young Stalin*. London: Phoenix.

Montgomery, S.L. 2010. *The Powers That Be. Global Energy for the Twenty-First Century and Beyond*. Chicago and London: The University of Chicago Press.

Moran, D. (Ed.). 2010. *Energy Security and Global Politics* (Routledge Global Security Studies). Routledge.

Morgenthau, H.J. 1985. *Politics Among Nations: The Struggle For Power And Peace*, 6th ed., New York: McGraw-Hill.

Muttitt, G. and Marriott, J. [PLATFORM]. 2002. *Some common Concerns: Imagining BP's Azerbaijan-Georgia-Turkey Pipelines System*. Campagna per la Riforma della Banca Modiale, CEE BankWatch Network, The Corner House, Friends of the Earth International, The Kurdish Human Rights Project, PLATFORM.

Nardin, T. *International Ethics*. In: Reus-Smit, C. and Snidal, D. (eds.) 2008.

Nash, G. 1968. *United States Oil Policy, 1890-1964: Business and Government in Twentieth Century America*. Greenwood Press

Nau, H. R. 2008. Scholarship and Policy Making: Who Speaks to Whom? In Reus-Smit, C. and Snidal, D. (eds.) 2008.

Nelson, A. 1994. How could scientific facts be socially constructed?: Introduction: The dispute between constructivists and rationalists. *Studies in History and Philosophy of Science Part A*. Volume 25, Issue 4, August 1994, pp. 535–547.

Nexon, D. (Ed.) 9.5.2013. "End of IR Theory" companion symposium for the special issue of the European Journal of International Relations. *The Duck of Minerva*. http://duckofminerva.dreamhosters.com/2013/09/special-event-the-end-of-ir-theory-symposium.html (Retrieved 14 June 2013).

Nordhauser, N.E. 1979. *The quest for stability: domestic oil regulation, 1917-1935.* New York: Garland Pub.

Noreng, O. 2002. *Crude Power: Politics and the Oil Market.* I.B.Tauris

Norman, C.S. Rule of Law and the Resource Curse: Abundance Versus Intensity. *Environmental and Resource Economics.* June 2009, 43:183 (first published 27 August 2008).

Norrie, A. 2007. *Critical Realism: Essential Readings.* London and New York: Routledge.

Norton, A. (2004). *Political science as a vocation.* In I. Shapiro, R. Smith, & T. Masoud (Eds.), *Problems and Methods in the Study of Politics* (pp. 67-82). Cambridge: Cambridge University Press.

Nuttall, C. 13.12.2017. *EIB postpones decision on €1.5bn TAP pipeline loan.* BNE Intellinews (http://www.intellinews.com/eib-postpones-decision-on-1-5bn-tap-pipeline-loan-134063/) – retrieved 22.12.2017.

Nye, J. S. Jr. Tripoli Diarist. *The New Republic.* 10 December 2007. http://www.newrepublic.com/article/tripoli-diarist?keepThis=true&TB_iframe=true (Accessed 19.07.2015).

Nye, J.S. Energy Nightmares. *Foreign Policy.* No. 40, Tenth Anniversary (Autumn, 1980), pp. 132-154.

Nye, J. S. 2008. International Relations: the relevance of theory to practice. In: Reus-Smit, C. and Snidal, D. (eds.) 2008.

Nye, J. S. Scholars on the Sidelines. *The Washington Post.* 13 April 2009.- http://www.washingtonpost.com/wp-dyn/content/article/2009/04/12/AR2009041202260.html (Accessed on 7 April 2014).

Nye J.S. Why the Gulf War Served the National Interest. *The Atlantic.* July 1991. http://www.theatlantic.com/past/docs/issues/91jul/nye.htm (Retrieved first on 1 March 2014).

Obi, C. and Rustad, S.A. 2011. *Oil and insurgency in the Niger Delta. Managing the complex politics of petroviolence.* London: Zed Books.

O'Connor, H. 1955. *The Empire of Oil.* New York: Monthly Review Press.

O'Connor, H. 1962. *World Crisis in Oil.* New York: Monthly Review Press.

Onuf, N. G. 1989. *World of our making: rules and rule in social theory and international relations.* Columbia, SC: University of South Carolina Press.

Owen, E. W. 1975. *Trek of the Oil Finders: A History of Exploration for Petroleum.* Tulsa Okla.: American Association of Petroleum Geologists.

le Page, M. *Record warming is terrifying but long-term trend is even worse.* New Scientist. 11 March 2016. (Accessed first on 27 May 2016 - https://www.newscientist.com/ article / 2080312-record-warming-is-terrifying-but-long-term-trend-is-even-worse/).

Painter, S.D. 2012. Oil and the American Century. *The Journal of American History* 99 (1): 24–39.

Painter, S.D. 2010. *Oil, resources, and the Cold War, 1945–62.* In Leffler, M.P. & Westad, O.A. (eds.). *The Cambridge History of the Cold War*, Volume I: Origins (pp. 486–507). Cambridge: Cambridge University Press.

Painter, S.D. 2009a. The Marshall Plan and Oil. *Cold War History* 9 (2). Pp. 159–175.

Painter, S.D. 2009b. *Global Environmental Footprint of the U.S. Military, 1789–200* in Closmann, C. E. (Ed). *War and the Environment: Military Destruction in the Modern Age* College Station, TX: Texas A&M University Press. Pp. 20–24.

Painter, S.D. 1993. Oil and World Power. *Diplomatic History* 17 (1). Pp.159–170.

Painter, S.D. 1991. International Oil and National Security. *Daedalus* 120 (4). Pp. 183–206.

Painter, S.D. 1986. *Oil and the American Century: The Political Economy of U.S. Foreign Oil Policy, 1941–1954.* Baltimore, MD: Johns Hopkins University Press.

Painter, S.D. 1984. Oil and the Marshall Plan. *Business History Review* 58 (3). Pp. 359–383.

Parra, F. 2013 [2004]. Oil Politics. A Modern History of Petroleum. London and New York: I.B. Tauris

Patomaki, H. and Wight, C. 2000. After Postpositivism? The Promises of Critical Realism. *International Studies Quarterly* 44, pp.213-237.

Pearson, K. 1892. "The Grammar of Science." London: Walter Scott. Online: https:// archive.org/ stream/grammarofscience00pearrich#page/n9/mode/2up (Retrieved on 14 July 2015).

Peritore, N. P. 1999. *Third World Environmentalism: Case Studies from the Global South.* Gainsville, FL.: University Press of Florida.

Peterson, A. and Ismailzade F. (eds.). 2009. *Azerbaijan in Global Politics. Crafting Foreign Policy.* Azerbaijan Diplomatic Academy, Baku: Chashioglu Publishers.

Plack, J. Embassy in Tripoli to Washington, 23.11.1970. A-220. State Deartent Papers. In Yergin, 1991, p. 587.

Popper, K. 1959. *The Logic of Scientific Discovery.* Hutchinson & Co.

Prasad, A. and Mir, R. Digging Deep for Meaning: A Critical Hermeneutic Analysis of CEO Letters to Shareholders in the Oil Industry. *International Journal of Business Communication.* January 2002, vol. 39, no. 1, 92-116.

Price, R. *The Ethics of Constructivism* in in Reus-Smit, C. and Snidal, D. (eds.). 2008.

Price-Smith, A. T. 2015. *Oil, Illiberalism, and War: An Analysis of Energy and U.S. Foreign Policy.* MIT Press.

Prindle, D.F. 1981. *Petroleum Politics and the Texas Railroad Commission.* Austin: University of Texas Press.

Pulver, S. Making Sense of Corporate Environmentalism. An Environmental Contestation Approach to Analyzing the Causes and Consequences of the Climate Change Policy Split in the Oil Industry. *Organization Environment.* March 2007, vol. 20, no. 1 44-8.

Putnam, H. 1984. *What is Realism?* in Leplin, J. (ed.) *Scientific Realism.* London, Berkeley and Los Angeles: University of California Press; pp. 140-153.

Rachkov, B. V. 1967. *Oil, Nationalism and Imperialism*. New Delhi: People's Publishing House.

Raleigh, C. and Urdal, H. Climate change, environmental degradation and armed conflict. *Political Geography*. Volume 26, Issue 6, August 2007, Pages 674–694.

Ravenhill, J. 2008. *International Political Economy* in Reus-Smit, C. and Snidal, D. (eds.) 2008.

Rengger, N. *The Ethics of Marxism* in Reus-Smit, C. and Snidal, D. (eds.). 2008.

Reus-Smit, C. *Constructivism* in Burchill, S. et al (Eds.). 1996.

Reus-Smit, C. and Snidal, D. (eds.). 2008. *The Oxford Handbook of International Relations*. Oxford: Oxford University Press.

Reus-Smit, C. and Snidal, D. 2008. "Between utopia and reality: the practical discourses of International Relations" in Reus-Smit, C. and Snidal, D. (eds.) 2008.

Reus-Smit, C. 2013. *Beyond Metatheory?* in Wight, C., Hansen, L. and Dunne, T. (eds.). Special Issue: The End of International Relations Theory? *The European Journal of International Relations* September 2013; 19 (3), pp. 589-606

Roach, S. C. 2013. *Critical Theory* in Dunne, T., Kurki, M., Smith, S. 2013. *International Relations Theories. Discipline and Diversity*. Oxford: Oxford University Press.

Roberts, R. 2004. *The End of Oil*. London: Bloomsbury

Robinson, W. I. 2002. *Capitalist globalisation and the trans-nationalisation of the state*. Pp. 210-229 in Rupert and Smith (eds.). *Historical Materialism and Globalisation*. London: Routledge.

Rodova, N. 15.11.2012. *Russia, Bulgaria sign final investment decision on South Stream gas pipeline*. Platts. https://www.platts.com/latest-news/natural-gas/moscow/russia-bulgaria-sign-final-investment-decision-8916177   - retrieved 17.11.2012.

Rosenberg, A. 2012. *Philosophy of Science. A Contemporary Introduction*. New York and London: Routledge.

Ross, Michael. 2001. Does Oil Hinder Democracy? *World Politics*, Vol. 53, No. 3, pp. 325-361.

Ross, M. 2012. *The Oil Curse: How Petroleum Wealth Shapes the Development of Nations*. Princeton, NJ: Princeton University Press.

Ross, H. M. and Williams, R. H. 1981. *Our Energy: Regaining Control*. New York: McGraw-Hill.

Rowley, M. The Nabucco Pipeline Project: Gas Bridge To Europe? Pipeline and Gas Journal. September 2009 Vol. 236 No. 9. https://pgjonline.com/2009/ 09/ 07/the-nabucco-pipeline-project-gas-bridge-to-europe/-retrieved 1 .11.2017.

Rupert, M. 2010. *Post-Fordist capitalism and imperial power: toward a neo-Gramscian view* in Aievas, A (Ed.) *Marxism and World Politics*. New York and London: Routledge.

Russett, B. *Liberalism* in Dunne, T. et al. 2013.

Saba, P. (Ed.) State of the Union Message: "Carter Doctrine" reflects mounting superpower contention. *Unity,* Vol. 3, No. 3, February 1-14, 1980 (Source: Encyclopedia of Anti-Revisionism On-Line; accessed 11.10.2015: https://www.marxists.org/history/erol/ncm-5/lrs-carter.htm).

Sachs, J. D. and Warner, A. M. 1995. *Natural Resource Abundance and Economic Growth.* NBER Working Papers 5398, National Bureau of Economic Research, Inc.

Sampson, A. 1976. T*he Seven Sister. The Great Oil Companies and the World They Made.* Coronet Book, Hodder and Stoughton, London.

Savigny, H. and Marsden, L. 2011. *Doing Political Science and International Relations: Theories in Action.* Palgrave Macmillan.

Can Sezer and Kucukgocmen, A., 30/11/2019. Turkey and Azerbaijan mark completion of TANAP pipeline to take gas to Europe. Reuters (https://www.reuters.com/article/us-turkey-energy-tanap/turkey-and-azerbaijan-mark-completion-of-tanap-pipeline-to-take-gas-to-europe-idUSKBN1Y40CP- Retrieved 12/12/2019)

Simon, J. 02.11.2017. *U.S. withdraws from extractive industries anti-corruption effort.* Reuters (https://www.reuters.com/article/us-usa-eiti/u-s-withdraws-from- extractive -industries - anti - corruption-effort-idUSKBN1D2290) - retrieved 22.12.2018.

Schmidt, B.C. 2008. International Relations Theory: Hegemony or Pluralism? *Millennium: Journal of International Studies*, 36/2: 295-304.

Schmidt, B. C. 2013. On the history and historiography of International Relations. In: Carlsnaes, W., Risse, T., and Simmons B.A. (eds.) *Handbook of International Relations.* Thousand Oaks, CA: Sage. Pp. 3-28.

Schmidt, B. C. 02.02.2014. *The End of Great Debates?* E-International Relations. http:// www.e-ir.info/ 2014 / 02 / 02 / the-end-of-great-debates / (Accessed 02.06.2015)

Schwartz, P. and Randall, D. 2003. *An Abrupt Climate Change Scenario and Its Implications for United States National Security.* (Retrieved from http://eesc.columbia.edu/courses/v1003/readings/Pentagon.pdf of Columbia University Department of Earth and Environment on 15 January 2016).

Schweller, R. 2014. *Maxwell's Demon and the Golden Apple: Global Discord in the New Millennium.* Johns Hopkins University Press.

Scott, R. 1994. *History of the IEA: Volume I. Origins and Structures.* Paris: OECD/IEA

Shaffer B. 2009. *Energy Politics.* Philadelphia: University of Pennsylvania Press

Shankleman, J. 5 July 2016. London Seeks to Rescue Anti-Smog Plan From Brexit Debate. Bloomberg (First accessed on 28 July 2016 http:// www.bloomberg. com/ news/ articles/2016-07-05 / london-seeks-to-rescue-anti-pollution-plan-from-brexit-debate).

Shapcott, R. 2008, *Critical Theory* in Reus-Smit, C. and Snidal, D. (eds.) 2008.

Sherman, A. Power Slick Oil Companies and Governments. The Spectator. 2 May 1963. P.25. (Retrieved on 5 May 2015 http://archive.spectator.co.uk/article /3rd-may-1963/25/power-slick-oil-companies-and-governments-by-j-e-h).

Shiriyev, Z. 19.07.2017. Oil Price and Russian Pressure Put Azerbaijan's Strategic Gas Project at Risk. The Royal Institute of International Affairs. Chatham House, 2017 (https://www.chathamhouse.org/expert/comment/oil-price-and - russian - pressure- put- azerbaijan-s-strategic-gas-project-risk) – retrieved 27.11.2017.

Shojai, S. 1995. *The New Global Oil Market: Understanding Energy Issues in the World Economy.* Westport, CT: Praeger.

Shum, R. Y. 2015. *Where Constructivism Meets ResourceConstraints: The Politics of Oil, Renewables, and a U.S. Energy Transition. Environmental Politics.* Volume 24, 2015 - Issue 3 (Accessed first in 20 November 2015: http://www.tandfonline.com/doi/abs/10.1080/09644016.2015.1008236).

Shwardon, R. 1977. *Middle East Oil. Issues and Problems.* Cambridge, Mass.: Schenkman Publishing, Co.

Shwardon, B. 1974 [1955]. *The Middle East, Oil, and the Great Powers.* New York: Wiley.

Schwartz, H. 1950. *Russia's Soviet Economy.* New York: Prentice-Hall.

Schwartz, P. and Randall, D. 2003. *An Abrupt Climate Change Scenario and Its Implications for United States National Security.* Washington, DC: Climate Change Institute (2007-2010). (First retrieved 12 October 2013 http://www.climate.org/topics/climate-change/pentagon-study-climate-change.html)

Siddi, M. 27.12.2017. The EU's Botched Geopolitical Approach to External Energy Policy: The Case of the Southern Gas Corridor. Pages 1-21. Taylor & Francis Online. (http://www.tandfonline.com/doi/full/10.1080/14650045.2017.1416606?scroll=top&needAccess=true) – retrieved 3.01.2018.

Sil, R. 2000. The Foundations of Eclecticism The Epistemological Status of Agency, Culture, and Structure in Social Theory. *Journal of Theoretical Politics.* 12 (3), pp.352-358.

Sil, R. and Katzenstein, P.J. 2010. *Beyond Paradigms. Analytic Eclecticism in the Study of World Politics.* New York: Palgrave Macmillan.

Silverstein, K. 2014. *The Secret World of Oil.* New York: Verso.

Sim. L-C. 2008. *The Rise and Fall of Privatization in the Russian Oil Industry.* Palgrave Macmillan.

Slade, E. J. W. The Influence of Oil on International Politics. *Journal of the British Institute of International Affairs.* Vol. 2, No. 6 (Nov., 1923), pp. 251-258

Smith, S. 1995. "The Self-Images of a Discipline: A Genealogy of International Relations Theory," in Ken Booth and Steve Smith (eds.), *International Relations Theory Today.* University Park: Pennsylvania State University Press: pp. 1-37.

Smith, S. 1996. *Positivism and Beyond.* In S. Smith, K. Booth, and M. Zalewski (Eds.). *International Theory: Positivism and Beyond.* Cambridge: Cambridge University Press.

Smith, S. 2008. Debating Schmidt: Theoretical Pluralism in IR. *Millennium: Journal of International Studies,* 36/2: 295-304.

Smith, S. 2008. Six Wishes for a More Relevant Discipline of International Relations in Reus-Smit, C. and Snidal, D. (eds.) 2008.

Smith, S. 2013. Introduction: diversity and disciplinarity in International Relations theory." In: Dunne, T., Kurki, M., Smith, S. 2013. *International Relations Theories. Discipline and Diversity.* Oxford: Oxford University Press.

Smith, S. 2014. Steve Smith on bringing International Relations theory to life. Oxford Academic video intro to Bayliss, J., Smith, S. & Owens, P. (eds). "The Globalization of World Politics. An Introduction to International Relations." Sixth Edition. Oxford University Press. https://www.youtube.com/watch?v=zvKRAd9b0zU (Accessed 25 July 2015).

Smolansky, O. M. and Smolansky, B. M. 1991. *The USSR and Iraq: The Soviet Quest for Influence.* London and Durham: Duke University Press.

Socor, V. 04.04.2012. Interest Growing All-Round in Trans-Anatolia Pipeline Project. *Eurasia Daily Monitor.* 9 (70). Jamestown Foundation. https://jamestown.org/program/interest-growing-all-round-in-trans-anatolia-pipeline-project/ - retrieved 29.12.2017.

Socor, V. 27.06.2012. Aliyev, Erdogan Sign Inter-Governmental Agreement on Trans-Anatolia Gas Pipeline to Europe. *Eurasia Daily Monitor.* 9 (122). Jamestown Foundation. https://jamestown.org/program/aliyev-erdogan-sign-inter-governmental-agreement-on-trans-anatolia-gas-pipeline-to-europe/   - retrieved 2012-06-29.

Socor, V. 23.05.2012. Nabucco-West: Abridged Pipeline Project Officially Submitted to Shah Deniz Consortium. *Eurasia Daily Monitor.* 9 (98). Heritage Foundation. https://jamestown.org / program / nabucco-west-abridged-pipeline-project-officially-submitted-to-shah-deniz-consortium/ Retrieved 24.11.2017.

Sol, X. 24.02.2017. Southern Gas Corridor's dubious contribution to energy security. Euractive (https://www.euractiv.com/section/energy-environment /opinion/southern-gas-corridors-dubious-contribution-to-energy-security/) – retrieved 12.11.2017.

Solomon, E., Chazan G. and Jones, S. Isis Inc: how oil fuels the jihadi terrorists. *The Financial Times.* 14 October, 2015 (Retrieved on 3 January 2016 - http://www.ft.com/cms/s/2/b8234932-719b-11e5-ad6d-f4ed76f0900a.html#axzz4 2Mg5lo8o).

Sondhaus, L. 1997. *Preparing for Weltpolitik: German Sea Power Before the Tirpitz Era.* Maryland: Naval Institute Press

Starr, Frederick S. and Cornell, S. E. (Eds.). 2005. *The Baku-Tbilisi-Ceyhan pipeline: oil window to the West.* Washington DC: John Hopkins University, Central Asia-Caucasus Institute & Silk Road Studies Program.

Starr, Frederick S. *The Baku-Tbilisi-Ceyhan pipeline: school of modernity* in Starr, Frederick S. and Cornell, S. E. (Eds.). 2005.

Stein, A.A. 2008. *Neoliberal Institutionalism* in Reus-Smit, C. and Snidal, D. (eds.) 2008.

Sterling-Folker, J. *Neoliberalism* in Dunne, T. et al. 2013.

Stern, N. 2007. *The Economics of Climate Change. The Stern Review*. Cambridge: Cambridge University Press

Steven, D., O'Brien, E., Jones, B. D. (Eds.). 2014. *The New Politics of Strategic Resources: Energy and Food Security Challenges in the 21st Century*. Washington, DC: Brookings Institution Press.

Stocking, G. W. and Watkins, M. W. 1948. *Cartels or competition: the economics of international controls by business and government*. New-York: Twentieth Century Fund.

Stocking, G. W. 1970. *Middle East oil: a study in political and economic controversy*. Vanderbilt University Press.

Stoff, M. B. 1982. *Oil, War and American Security: The Search for a National Policy on Foreign Oil, 1941-47 (Historical Publications)*. Yale University Press.

Stuart, D.T. 2008. *Foreign Policy Decision Making* in Reus-Smit, C. and Snidal, D. (eds.) 2008.

Suny, R. G. 1972. *The Baku Commune 1917-1918*. Princeton, New Jersey: Princeton University Press.

Sutch, P. and Elias, J. 2007. *International Relations: The Basics*. London and New York: Routledge.

Tagliapietra, S. and Zachmann, G. B. 2.7.2015. *Designing a new EU-Turkey strategic gas partnership*. Financial Times. (https://www.ft.com/content/c59e3419-464e-35c2-ada1-aa64331cca82) – retrieved. 01.10.2017.

Tanchum. M. *A Fillip for the TAPI Pipeline*. The Diplomat. 3 December 2015. (Retrieved on 4 January 2016 - http://thediplomat.com/2015/12/a-fillip-for-the-tapi-pipeline/)

Tarbell, I. M. 1904 (2003). *The History of the Standard Oil Company: Briefer Version*. (Ed. Chalmers, D. M.). New York: Dover Publications, Inc.

Taylor, P. 22.02.2008. *U.S. throws weight behind EU's Nabucco pipeline*. Reuters. (https://uk.reuters.com/article/eu-energy-usa/update-1-u-s-throws-weight-behind-eus-nabucco-pipeline-idUKL2212241120080222) - retrieved 15.12.2017.

Teschke, B, Marxism in Reus-Smit, C. and Snidal, D. (eds.). 2008. *The Oxford Handbook of International Relations*. Oxford: Oxford University Press.

Thomas, M. 2004. Mark Thomas thanks Hilary Benn for his interest. New Statesman, 19 January 2004. http://www.newstatesman.com/node/159005

Thomsen, R. 2001. *Selves and Others of Political Nationalism in Stateless Nations: National Identity-Building Processes in the Modern Histories of Scotland and Newfoundland*. Copenhagen: Aarhus University.

Tickner, A.J. and Sjoberg, L. 2013. *Feminism* in Dunne, T., Kurki, M., Smith, S. 2013. *International Relations Theories. Discipline and Diversity*. Oxford: Oxford University Press.

Tolf, R.W. 1976. *The Russian Rockefellers: The Saga of the Nobel Family and the Russian Oil Industry*. Stanford: Hoover Institution Press.

Tolkien, J.R.R. (1947, 1964) 1983. *On Fairy-Stories* in *The Monsters and the Critics and Other Essays*, edited by Tolkien, C, pp. 109-161. London: George Allen and Unwin.

Totten. George E. 2004. A Timeline of Highlights from the Histories of ASTM Committee D02 and the Petroleum Industry. ASTM International. (Accessed on 11 June 2015 - http://www.astm.org/COMMIT/D02/to1899_index.html)

Townsend, P. and Harris, P. Now the Pentagon tells Bush: climate change will destroy us. *The Guardian.* 22 February 2004. (First retrieved on 12 October 2013 http:// www.theguardian.com/environment/ 2004 / feb / 22 /usnews.the observer).

True, J. 2008. *The Ethics of Feminism* in Reus-Smit, C. and Snidal, D. (eds.) 2008.

Tsalik, S. 2003. *Caspian Oil Windfalls: Who Will Benefit?* New York: Open Society Institute.

Tungland, K. 20.01.2013. Time to Act on Diversifying EU Gas Supplies. New Europe. https:// www.neweurope.eu / article / time-act-diversifying-eu-gas-supplies/ - retrieved 27.10.2017.

Turnera, T. E. & Oshareb,M. O. Women's Uprising against the Nigerian Oil Industry in the 1980s. *Canadian Journal of Development Studies / Revue canadienne d'études du développement.* Volume 14, Issue 3, 1993.

Turkish Press. 13.07.2009. *Nabucco Summits Begins.* http://www.turkish press.com/news.asp?id=346171 Retrieved 13 July 2009

Van Aartsen, J. 04.02.2009. Activity Report September 2007-February 2009. Project of European Interest No NG 3. European Commission. file:///C:/Users/user/Downloads/blg-12831.pdf (retrieved - 01.10.2017).

Van der Linde, C. 1999. *The State and the International Oil Market: Competition and the Changing Ownership of Crude Oil Assets.* New York: Springer Science & Business Media.

Vaughan, A. 10.12.2017. *EIB accused of marring EU climate goals with €1.5bn gas pipeline loan.* The Guardian. (https://www.theguardian.com/business/ 2017/ dec/ 10 / eib-accused-eu-climate-goals-gas-pipeline-loan-european-investment-bank-summit-paris) – retrieved 29.12.2017.

Verda, M. 2016. *The Foreign Dimension of EU Energy Policy: The Case of the Southern Gas Corridor* in Godzimirski, J. M. (Ed.). *EU Leadership in Energy and Environmental Governance. Global and Local Challenges and Responses.* Palgrave Macmillan.

Vietor, R. H. K. Review of "The Prize" *in Business History Review.* Volume 65. Special Issue 04. Winter 1991. Pp. 988 – 989.

de Waal, T. 2010. Call Off the Great Game. *Foreign Policy.* 13.09.2010. http://foreignpolicy.com/2010/09/13/call-off-the-great-game/

Wæver, O. 1996. *The rise and fall of the inter-paradigm debate* in Smith, S., Booth, K. And Zalewski, M. (eds.). *Positivism and Beyond.* Cambridge: Cambridge University Press. PP. 149-185.

Wæver, O. *Still a Discipline After All These Debates?* in Dunne, T. et al. 2013.

Waever, O. 2011. "The Speech Act of Realism: The Move That Made IR," in Guilhot, N. ed., The Invention of International Relations Theory: Realism, the Rockefeller Foundation and the 1954 Conference on Theory. New York: Columbia University Press.

Wallerstein, I. 1974. *The Modern World-System, vol. I: Capitalist Agriculture and the Origins of the European World-Economy in the Sixteenth Century*. New York/London: Academic Press.

Wallerstein, I. 1976. Semi-Peripheral Countries and the Contemporary World Crisis. *Theory and Society,* Vol. 3, No. 4 (Winter, 1976), pp. 461-483

Wallerstein, I. 1983. *Historical Capitalism*. London: Verso

Wallerstein, I. 2004. *World-Systems Analysis: An Introduction*. Durham and London: Duke University Press.

Walt, S.M. 1998. International Relations: One World, Many Theories. *Foreign Policy*. 110: 29-35.

Waltz, K.N. 1959. "Man, the State and War: A Theoretical Analysis." New York: Columbia University Press.

Waltz, K.N. 1979. *Theory of International Politics*. McGraw-Hill, Inc.

Wendt, A. 1999. *Social Theory of International Politics*. Cambridge, UK: Cambridge University Press.

Wenger, A., Orttung, R. W., Perovic, J. (Eds). 2009. *Energy and the Transformation of International Relations: Toward a New Producer-Consumer Framework* (Oxford Institute for Energy Studies). Oxford: Oxford University Press.

Watts, M. 2001. *Petro-Violence: Community, Extraction and Political Ecology of a Mythic Commodity.* In Nancy Lee Peluso and Michael Watts (eds.), *Violent Environments*. Ithaca: Cornell University Press.

Watts, M. 2004. Resource Curse? Governmentality, Oil and Power in the Niger Delta, Nigeria. *Geopolitics*. 9 (1): March, pp. 50–80.

Watts, M. 2009. *Crude Politics: Life and Death on the Nigerian Oil Fields*. Niger Delta Economies of Violence Working Papers. Institute of International Studies, University of California.

Werth, A. 1964. *Russia at war 1941-1945*. London: Barrie and Rockliff.

Wheeler, R.R. and Whited, M. 1971. *Oil – from prospect to pipeline*. Houston: Gulf Publishing Company.

Whitworth, S. 2008. *Feminism* in Reus-Smit, C. and Snidal, D. (eds.) 2008.

Wight, C. 2006. *Agents, Structures, and International Relations: Politics as Ontology*. Cambridge: Cambridge University Press.

Wight, C. 2007. A manifesto for scientific realism in IR: Assuming the can-opener won't work! *Millennium: Journal of International Studies*. 35(2); pp. 379-398.

Wight, C., Hansen, L. and Dunne, T. (eds.). Special Issue: The End of International Relations Theory? *The European Journal of International Relations*. September 2013; 19 (3).

Williams, M.C. 2005. *The Realist tradition and the limits of International Relations*. Cambridge: Cambridge University Press.

Williamson, H. F., Andreano, R.L., Daum, A.R. and Klose, G.C. 1963. *The American Petroleum Industry*. Evanston: Northwestern University Press.

Wilson, W. 8 January 1918. *War Aims and Peace Terms. Address to Congress.* (Retrieved on 19 December 2015 - http://www.ourdocuments.gov/doc.php? doc=62)

Woodman, R. 1998. *The History of the Ship: The Comprehensive Story of Seafaring from the Earliest Times to the Present Day.* New York: Lyons Press.

Yearley, S. 2002. The social construction of environmental problems: a theoretical review and some not-very-Herculean labors, in R. E. Dunlap, F. H. Buttel, P. Dickens and A. Gijswijt (eds). *Sociological Theory and the Environment: Classical Foundations, Contemporary Insights.* Lanham, MD: Rowman & Littlefield.

Yergin, D. 1991. *The Prize. The Epic Quest for Oil, Money and Power.* New York: Simon &Schuster.

Yergin, D. 2012 [2011]. "The Quest. Energy. Security, and the Remaking of the Modern World." London: Penguin Books.

Zabih, S. 1966. *The Communist Movement in Iran.* Berkeley and Los Angeles: California University Press.

Zalloum, A. Y. 2011. *America in Islamistan: Trade, Oil and Blood.* Trafford Publishing.

Zimmer, A. 1918. *The Economic Weapon in the War Against Germany.* London: Allen & Unwin.

OFFICIAL DOCUMENTS AND ONLINE SOURCES

Aberystwyth, University of. "The Legacy of One Man's Vision." http://www.aber.ac.uk/en/interpol/about/ (accessed 25 January 2015).

ACT Alliance EU and others. 28.01.2016. *Object: The EIB should not finance the Southern Gas Corridor.* CounterBalance (http://www.counter-balance.org/ wp-content / uploads/2016/01 / NGO-Open-Letter_EIB-President_Southern-Gas-Corridor_28-01-2016.pdf) – retrieved 28.10.2017.

Alili, A. and Bittner, V. 2017. *The cost of Azerbaijan's leaving the Extractive Industries Transparency Initiative (EITI): Analysis of the impact on the economy and civil society.* Center for Economic and Social Development (CESD) (https://eiti.org/sites/default/files/documents/CESD_EITI_Assess ment_Paper.pdf) – retrieved 12.11.2017

American Petroleum Institute. 2015. Every Major Study Agrees: Crude Oil Exports Would Put Downward Pressure on U.S. Gasoline Prices (Retrieved on 5.1.16 http://www.api.org/~/media/files/policy/exports/economic-studies -crude-oil-exports.pdf).

APA. 9.1.2018. *TAP: Talks with EIB on funding for TAP are ongoing* (http://en.apa.az/azerbaijan_energy_and_industry/tap-talks-with-eib-on-funding-for-tap-are-ongoing.html)- retrieved 9.1.2018.

ARTICLE 19 and Others. 12.09.2017. *Subject: Human rights concerns over EIB loan to TANAP* (http://www.counter-balance.org/wp-content/uploads/ 2017/09/TANAP-EITI-and-HR-letter.pdf) – retrieved 15.12.2017.

Asian Development Bank website, *Regional: Turkmenistan-Afghanistan-Pakistan-India Natural Gas Pipeline, Phase 3*. (Retrieved 12 January 2016 http://www.adb.org/projects/44463-013/main#tabs-0-0).

Bacheva-McGrath, F., Gallop, P., Gerebizza, E. et al. January 2015. *Pipe Dreams: why public subsidies for Lukoil in Azerbaijan will not reduce EU dependency on Russia*. CEE Bankwatch. (https://bankwatch.org/sites/default/files/ PipeDreams-LukOil-21Jan2015.pdf) – retrieved 29.12.2017).

Baku-Ceyhan Campaign, "ECGD's support for the Baku-Tbilisi-Ceyhan pipeline project," Submission to the Trade and Industry Committee,6 September 2004. Baku-Ceyhan Campaign website http:// www.baku. org.uk / about.htm - retrieved 22-24.12.2017.

BankTrack and Counter Balance. 20.02.2017. *Trans-Adriatic Pipeline*. BankTrack and Counter Balance (https://www.banktrack.org/project/trans adriatic_pipeline/pdf) – retrieved 14.12.2017.

BP Azerbaijan. South Caucasus pipeline. South Caucasus Pipeline Expansion project. *Environmental and Social Impact Assessment report for Georgia*. BP p.l.c. 2017 (https://www.bp.com/en_az/caspian/sustainability/environment/ env- and- social-documentation/SCP/SCPX-ESIA-Georgia.html) – retrieved 30.12.2017.

BP Operations and Projects 5. Shah Deniz II. BP plc. 2017. https://www.bp.com/en_az/caspian/operationsprojects/Shahdeniz/SDstage2. html -retrieved 29.10.2017.

BP Magazine. 12.10.2017. *New energy supplies for Turkey and Europe: a visual guide to the Southern Gas Corridor*. BP p.l.c. 1996-2017 (https://www. bp.com/ en/ global/corporate/bp-magazine/locations/visual-guide-to-europe-southern-gas-corridor-tanap-turkey.html) – retrieved 29.12.2017.

BP Operations and Projects 1. Baku-Tbilisi-Ceyhan pipeline. BP p.l.c. 2017 (https://www.bp.com/en_az/caspian/operationsprojects/pipelines/BTC.html) – retrieved 17.11.2017.

BP Operations and Projects 2. The Southern Gas Corridor. BP p.l.c. 2017 (https://www.bp.com/en_az/caspian/operationsprojects/Shahdeniz/Southern Corridor.html) – retrieved 17.11.2017.

BP Operations and Projects 3. Baku-Tbilisi-Ceyhan pipeline. BTC co. Shareholders, 2017 (https://www.bp.com/en_az/caspian/operationsprojects/ pipelines/BTC.html) – retrieved 27.10.2017.

BP Operations and Projects 4. South-Caucasus Pipeline. BP p.l.c. 2017. (https://www.bp.com/en_az/caspian/operationsprojects/pipelines/SCP.html) – retrieved 27.10.2017.

BP Azerbaijan. South Caucasus Pipeline. Environmental and social impact assessment. BP p.l.c.2017 (https:// www. bp.com/ en_ az/ caspian/ sustainability / environment/env – and - social-documentation/SCP.html) - Retrieved 30.12.2017.

CEE Bankwatch Press Release, 12.12.2017. *EUR 1.5 billion public loan for controversial pipeline withheld* (https://bankwatch.org/press_release/eur-1-

5-billion- public - loan-for - controversial - pipeline-withheld) – retrieved 28.12.2017.

CEE Bankwatch, EBRD Project Brief. May 2017. *Why the EBRD should not finance the Southern Gas Corridor* (https://bankwatch.org/wp-content/uploads/2017/05/briefing-EBRD-SGC-04May2017.pdf) – retrieved 20.12.2017.

Caspian Policy Center. Editorial. 13.12. 2017. *Caspian Pact Paves Way for Turkmen Gas Exports to Europe.* http://www.caspianpolicy.org/energy/caspian-pact - paves - way - for-turkmen-gas-exports-to-europe/ - retrieved 29.12.2017

Climate Finance Day. 11.12.2017. 3rd edition of the Climate Finance Day: Acceleration! The financial industry fully committed to fighting climate change. Statement N°252 (http://www.climatefinanceday.com/wp-content/uploads/ 2017/12 / Press-release-The-financial-industry-fully-committed-to-fighting-clima....pdf) – retrieved 22.12.2017.

CoE Committee of Ministers. 25.10.2017. *Ilgar Mammadov case: Council of Europe notifies Azerbaijan of intention to launch a special procedure for the execution of the judgment.* Council of Europe (https://www.coe.int/en/web/portal/news-2017/ - retrieved 29.12.2017).

CounterBalance, 28.01.2016. NGOs urge the European Investment Bank not to finance the Southern Gas Corridor (http://www.counter-balance.org/ngos-urge -the-european-investment - bank-not - to-finance-the-southern-gas-corridor/) – retrieved 28.10.2017.

Duck of Minerva. Online resource. URL: http://duckofminerva.com/about. First accessed: 2013.

IHS, Inc. 2016. *Dan Yergin. IHS Vice Chairman.* https://www.ihs.com/experts/dan-yergin.html

EIB Accountability homepage. TAP complaints search. http://www.eib.org/infocenter/search.htm?q=Trans-Adriatic+Pipeline – retrieved 20.11.2017.

EITI Secretariat. 10.03.2017. *Azerbaijan withdraws from the EITI.* (https://eiti.org/ news/ azerbaijan - withdraws-from -eiti) – retrieved 11.11.2017.

EITI Homepage. 2017. *How we work?* https://eiti.org/about/how-we-work#degrees-of-progress-country-statuses-explained – retrieved 11.11.2017.

EITI Homepage. 2017. The cost of Azerbaijan's leaving the Extractive Industries Transparency Initiative (EITI): Analysis of the impact on the economy and civil society (https://eiti.org/document/cost-of-azerbaijans-leaving-extractive-industries-transparency-initiative-eiti) – retrieved 12.11.2017.

European Commission 1. Policies, Information and Services. *Energy. Gas and oil supply routes.* 2017 (https://ec.europa.eu/energy/en/topics/imports-and-secure-supplies/gas-and-oil-supply-routes) – retrieved 30.10.2017.

European Commission. Policies, Information and Services. *2020 Energy Strategy.* 2017. (https://ec.europa.eu/energy/en/topics/energy-strategy-and-energy-union/2020-energy-strategy) – retrieved 30.10.2017.

European Commission. Policies, Information and Services. Energy. *Secure Gas Supplies*. 2017 (https://ec.europa.eu/energy/en/topics/imports-and-secure-supplies/secure-gas-supplies) – retrieved 30.10.2017.

European Commission. Policies, Information and Services. Energy. Energy Strategy and Energy Union. *Energy Strategy and Energy Union*. 2017. (https:// ec.europa.eu/energy/en / topics/energy-strategy-and-energy-union) – retrieved 30.10.2017.

EU Commission, 23 November 2017.The list of the projects of common interest (PCIs) by country – the (third) Union list of PCIs. https://ec.europa.eu/ energy/sites/ener/files/documents/memberstatespci_list_2017.pdf - retrieved 2.01.2018.

European Bank for Reconstruction and Development (EBRD). 18.10.2017. *EBRD Board approves financing for Trans-Anatolian Natural Gas Pipeline.* http://www.ebrd.com/news / 2017 / ebrd-board - approves - financing-for-transanatolian-natural-gas-pipeline.html - retrieved 29.10.2017.

European Bank for Reconstruction and Development (EBRD). 04.08.2017. *Project Summary Document 48376. Azerbaijan: Southern Gas Corridor.* EBRD 2017 (http://www.ebrd.com/work-with-us/projects/psd/azerbaijan-southern-gas-corridor.html) – retrieved 30.10.2017.

European Investment Bank (EIB). *The Southern Gas Corridor and the Trans Adriatic Pipeline (TAP).* 6 February 2018. https://www.eib.org/en/infocenter /press/ news / topical_briefs/2018-february-01 / southern-gas-corridor-trans-adriatic-pipeline-tap.htm (Retrieved - 03/03/2018).

E-International Relations (E-IR). Online resource. URL: http://www.e-ir.info /about/. Accessed: December 2014; URL: http://www.e-ir.info/about/ what-others-say/. Accessed January 2015.

Gogia, G. 10.03.2017. *Azerbaijan Suspended Over Rights Crackdown.* Human Rights Watch (https:// www.hrw.org/ news / 2017 / 03 / 10 /azerbaijan-suspended-over-rights-crackdown) – retrieved 11.11.2017.

Intergovernmental Panel on Climate Change website, 2015 (Retrieved on 28.1. 2015 http://www.ipcc.ch/organization/organization.shtml)

Institute for Global Energy Research, Alexander's Gas & Oil Connections. *Gas pipeline project Turkmenistan-Afghanistan-Pakistan-India approved.* 21.11. 2006. http://www.gasandoil.com/news/central_asia/c945d096920b47dd8cfa 1c9be30c5389 (Retrieved on 14 January 2016).

The Jamestown Foundation. Conference Report. 13.09.2013. *Azerbaijan and the Southern Gas Corridor to Europe. Implications for U.S. and European Energy Security.* Washington, DC: The Jamestown Foundation. https://jamestown.org / wp-content/uploads/2014/02/Conference_Report_-_Azerbaijan_and_the_Southern_Gas_Corridor_-_FINAL_web_version.pdf

Kurdish Human Rights Project et al. Baku-Tbilisi-Ceyhan Pipeline: Human Rights, Social and Environmental Impacts Turley Section. Final Report of Fourth Fact Finding Mission. 19-24.09.2004. http://www.baku.org.uk/ publications/turkey_ffm_2004.pdf - retrieved 28.10.2017

Lustgarten, A. The Baku-Tbilisi-Ceyhan Pipeline: exporting an "environmental timebomb." European ECA Reform Campaign. Apr 2005. Project Factsheet. Issue 01. http://www.fern.org / sites/ fern.org/files/media/documents/ document_2651_2652.pdf - retrieved on 28.10.2017

Memorandum by the State–War–Navy Coordinating Committee to Major General John H. Hilldring (in his capacity as Department of State member of the State–War–Navy Coordinating Committee); U.S. Joint Chiefs of Staff FOREIGN RELATIONS OF THE UNITED STATES 1946, VOLUME VII, THE NEAR EAST AND AFRICA [DOCUMENT 396] Washington, 12 October 1946. https://history.state.gov/historicaldocuments/frus1946v07/d 396#fn1 (Retrieved 5 January 2015).

Morgan, S. 13.12.2017. EU bank delays decision on mega pipeline loan. Euractive. https://www.euractiv.com/section/energy/news/eu-bank-delays-decision-on-mega-pipeline-loan/

OPEC Statute, 2012, Vienna: OPEC Secretariat (Retrieved 17.03.2015 http://www.opec.org/opec_web/static_files_project/media/downloads/publi cations/OPEC_Statute.pdf).

Oxford Engineering Alumni, May 2008. The Centenary Maurice Lubbock Memorial Lecture, 15 May 2008: *On Being an Engineer*. Lord Browne, President of the Royal Academy of Engineering (http://www.soue.org. uk/souenews/issue7/lubbocklect.html) – retrieved 02.10.2017).

Pulitzer Prize for General Nonfiction. 1992. The Pulitzer Prizes — Columbia University. New York (Accessed 3 January 2013 - http://www.pulitzer.org/ winners/6735).

Rogan, D. (Ed.). 24 May 2017. *The EITI Standard 2016.* EITI International Secretariat (https://eiti.org/sites/default/files/documents/the_eiti_standard_ 2016_-_english_0.pdf) – retrieved 12.11.2017.

Trans-Adriatic Pipeline (TAP) 1. 2017. https://www.tap-ag.com/the-pipeline - retrieved 08.12.2017.

Trans-Adriatic Pipeline (TAP) 2. *Environmental and Social Impact Assessments.* TAP 2017. (https://www.tap-ag.com/our-commitment/to-the-environment) – retrieved 8.12.2017.

Trans-Adriatic Pipeline (TAP) 3. Southern Gas Corridor. 2017. https://www.tap-ag.com/the-pipeline/the-big-picture/southern-gas-corridor   -   Retrieved 08.12.2017.

Trans-Adriatic Pipeline (TAP). 28.06.2013. *Shah Deniz Consortium selects the Trans Adriatic Pipeline (TAP) as European export pipeline.* https://www.tap-ag.com/news-and-events/2013/06/28/shah-deniz-consortium-selects-the-trans-adriatic-pipeline-tap-as-european-export-pipeline

Trans-Anatolian Pipeline (TANAP). 2017. http://www.tanap.com/tanap-project/why-tanap/ Retrieved – 15.12.2017

Trans-Anatolian Pipeline (TANAP). Reference Documents. TANAP 2017 (http://www.tanap.com/reference-documents/) – retrieved 15-20.12.2017).

The Oxford Institute of Energy Studies. About Us. OIES 1982-2016. (https://www.oxfordenergy.org/about/) – retrieved 12.12.2014.

The Oxford Institute of Energy Studies. Natural Gas Research Programme. OIES
    1982-2016. (https://www.oxfordenergy.org/gas-programme/) – retrieved
    12.12.2014.
World Bank. 12.12.2017. *World Bank Group Announcements at One Planet
    Summit*. Press Release No 2018/087/CCG (http://www.worldbank.org/en/
    news / press- release/2017/12/12/world-bank-group-announcements-at-one-
    planet-summit) – retrieved 22.12.2017.
United Nations Framework Convention on Climate Change. United Nations,
    1992. (Retrieved 15 January 2015 - http://unfccc.int/files / essential
    _background/convention/background/application/pdf/convention_text_with
    _annexes_english_for_posting.pdf)
United Nations Framework Convention on Climate Change. *First steps to a safer
    future: Introducing The United Nations Framework Convention on Climate
    Change*. United Nations, 2014a. (Retrieved 15 January 2015 -
    http://unfccc.int/essential_background/convention/items/6036.php).
United Nations Framework Convention on Climate Change. International
    Emissions Trading. United Nations, 2014b. (Retrieved 15 January 2014 -
    http://unfccc.int/kyoto_protocol/mechanisms/emissions_trading/items/2731.
    php).
United Nations Framework Convention on Climate Change. *United Nations
    Durban Platform for Enhanced Action. Paris Agreement under the United
    Nations Framework Convention on Climate Change; 12 December 2015* –
    (Retrieved 10 January 2016 - http://unfccc.int/resource/docs/2015/cop21/
    eng/l09r01.pdf).
United States Congress. Senate. Committee on Foreign Relations. Subcommittee
    on Multinational Corporations, ("Church" Committee) Report and Hearings,
    1973 and 1974. *Multinational Corporations and United States Foreign
    Policy*. Washington 1975. (https://catalog.hathitrust.org/Record/007417517
    – retrieved 14 March 2017)
U.S. Energy Information Administration, *India – International Energy Data and
    Analysis Report*. 26 June 2014. (Retrieved 12 January 2016
    http://199.36.140.204/beta/international/analysis.cfm?iso=IND).
Yergin, D. 2016. *Official Website* (Accessed on 3 January 2013 and 8 February
    2016 - http://danielyergin.com).
350.org and others. 19.12.2016. NGOs Urge the World Bank to Postpone
    Discussion on TANAP. Netherlands Helsinki Committee
    (https://www.nhc.nl/ ngos-urge -world -bank-postpone- discussion-tanap/) –
    retrieved 28. 10.2017.

Index